Bread and the British Economy, *c*1770–1870

For
Becca, Oliver, Rachel, Roslyn, Sophie and Amelia

Bread
and the
British Economy,
*c*1770–1870

CHRISTIAN PETERSEN

edited by Andrew Jenkins

Published by
SCOLAR PRESS
Gower House
Croft Road
Aldershot
Hants GU11 3HR
England.

Ashgate Publishing Company
Old Post Road
Brookfield
Vermont 05036
USA

The publication of this book has been made possible by a grant from the Scouloudi Foundation in association with the Institute of Historical Research.

British Library Cataloguing in Publication Data
Petersen, Christian
  Bread and the British Economy,
  c.1770–1870
  I. Title II. Jenkins, Andrew
  338.4766475230941

Library of Congress Cataloging-in-Publication Data
Petersen, Christian
  Bread and the British economy, c.1770–1870 / Christian Petersen : edited by Andrew Jenkins.
      p. cm.
  Includes bibliographical references and index.
  ISBN 1–85928–117–6
  1. Bread—Prices—Great Britain—History. 2. Wheat trade—Great Britain—History. 3. Great Britain—Economic conditions—19th century. 4. Great Britain—Economic conditions—18th century. I. Jenkins, Andrew. II. Title.
HD9058.B743G76 1995
338.4'76646523'094109034—dc20   94–17868
                                    CIP

ISBN 1 85928 117 6

Typeset in 10/12pt Sabon by Photoprint, Torquay, Devon and printed in Great Britain by Biddles Ltd, Guildford.

Contents

Notes: for economy, when a book or article is cited, only the author's name is given if there is only one work by that author listed in the bibliography (eg: 'Stern' = STERN, Walter M: 'The Bread Crisis in Britain, 1795–6', Economica, 1964). Where more than one work by an author is listed in the bibliography, the book or article concerned is indicated by a brief reference, such as a key word or phrase (eg: 'Burnett: Baking' = BURNETT, John: 'The Baking Industry in the Nineteenth Century', Business History, 1963), or by initial letters (eg: 'Wrigley: CCC' = WRIGLEY, E A: Continuity, Chance and Change, Cambridge, 1988), or by year of publication (eg: 'Fairlie: 1965' = FAIRLIE, Susan: 'The 19th-C Corn Law Reconsidered', Ec H R, 1965).

List of Tables

List of Maps

Foreword

To all who knew him it is a matter of the greatest sadness that this book does not appear during the lifetime of its author, Christian Petersen. He turned to an interest in scholarship in mid-life after a pioneering and highly successful business career. He was co-founder of one of the earliest sales promotion consultancies in Britain and of another that became the first such company to have a London Stock Exchange listing. Before coming to Oxford as an undergraduate in his mid-forties, he had also found the time and energy to write or edit two books designed to advance the understanding of sales promotion as an arm of business.

At Oxford he read history as an undergraduate, took a first, and embarked on a D. Phil. degree. He was in the final stages of completing his thesis when he died suddenly at the age of 50 in January 1993. Before he died he had already begun negotiations designed to secure the publication of this work suitably modified from a thesis form. It is a slight consolation to all those who mourn his loss that it has proved possible to bring his plans to fruition.

A substantial amount of work remained to be done after Chris Petersen's death in order to convert the text to a publishable form. Some parts of the work were in final draft but others were some way short of this point, and there were matters of internal organization, cross-referencing, completion of footnote references, and the like to be attended to. Work of this type is always taxing, and can often prove more difficult in the era of the word processor than in the days of the typewriter because of the existence of alternative versions of sections of the text on floppy disks. Those who were concerned to try to overcome all such problems in order to be able to forward a 'clean' text to the publisher were immensely fortunate that Andrew Jenkins proved willing to undertake the task of collating and integrating the existing chapter drafts, completing the notes, checking the tables, introducing the cross-references, and so on. That the full value of Petersen's work is now available to the world of scholarship is due to his persistence and clear-mindedness.

Many D. Phil. theses, whatever their scholarly and technical merits, are severely restricted in their scope. It was typical of Chris Petersen's breadth of interest and energy of mind that he was determined that this should not be the case with his thesis. It addresses a topic that is central to the economic and social history of Britain in the eighteenth and nineteenth centuries. During the period from 1770 to 1870 the great bulk of the income of the mass of the population was spent on food and much the largest single item in the average family food budget was bread. Moreover this was the period in which wheaten bread slowly replaced its rivals throughout the country. It had long been dominant in the south and east but barley, oats, and rye rather than wheat had been the dominant cereals in parts of the rest of Britain until this period. Chris Petersen set out to give an authoritative description of this process; to provide reliable estimates of trends in the scale of bread consumption throughout the period together with parallel estimates of wheat production, and wheat imports and exports; to demonstrate the pervasive importance of transport improvements in facilitating the triumph of the wheaten loaf; to chronicle the technical changes in milling and baking; to describe the impact of the dismantling of the legislation dealing with the production and sale of bread, once one of the most minutely regulated of all productive activities; to make plain the reasons why the wheaten loaf was the best available solution to the food needs of the population of the day when nutritional qualities and cost were balanced against one another; and to describe the baking and distribution of bread both commercially and domestically (and the changing relative advantage of home and commercial baking).

Readers of this book will have the opportunity to judge for themselves with what remarkable success Chris Petersen succeeded in covering such a wide historical terrain. I am hopeful that it will prove to possess each of two qualities that can set a work of real importance apart from run-of-the-mill publications: first, that it succeeds in advancing our understanding of a topic of importance by bringing together into a single, satisfying whole elements which previously existed only as disparate elements; and, second, that the interest that it arouses induces a new wave of investigation of the topic because it has come to assume a new importance. It would be a singularly appropriate tribute to Chris Petersen's dynamism and personality if the latter proved to be the case.

E.A. Wrigley
Professor of Economic History,
University of Cambridge
Master of Corpus Christi College,
Cambridge

Publisher's Note

Publishing a posthumous book is a difficult process. Credit for the success of this project should be given to Andrew Jenkins, who proved to be a model editor, and to Professor Tony Wrigley, who added the burdens of guidance and supervision to his already heavy workload, and who successfully applied on our behalf to the Scouloudi Foundation. Above all, Alan Toop should be praised, not only for providing the initial impulse for the project but also for taking on the administrative tasks that test the enthusiasm of all authors. He has proved himself a doughty negotiator and friend indeed to Chris Petersen's family.

Introduction

Bread was the chief food of industrializing Britain. It sustained a population that increased threefold between 1770 and 1870. Bread was the fuel that powered the muscle and sinew of labour in 'the workshop of the world'.

A commodity of such importance deserves study in its own right. To examine not only the 'how' of its supply, but also the 'why': why bread was the accepted staple, and why demand for it differed not only in scale, but also in kind, from the demand for other foods and goods.

But the study of bread can expand in many directions. The demand for bread shaped, and in turn was shaped by, the development of agriculture, transport, and commerce, in Britain and around the world.

Also, it was held that the fluctuating price of bread regulated the whole economy, influencing the trade cycle, the cost of credit, and the foreign exchanges; that the importation of wheat for bread either strengthened the country economically, or weakened it strategically; and that the satisfactory supply of bread, above all things, was essential to social stability, especially in the cities. Lines of class and interest were delineated according to who bought and who sold 'the people's food'. The Bread Question animated the recurrent controversy of the age: Protection or Free Trade?

By the latter part of the eighteenth century, Britain had become a net importer of corn. During the Revolutionary and Napoleonic Wars of 1793–1815 grain prices (and hence the cost of bread) were high, but once peace was restored prices slumped. This alarmed agricultural interest groups in Britain and they clamoured for protection. The result was the Corn Law of 1815 which prevented importation until the domestic price reached 80s per quarter. This absolute limit was modified to a sliding scale in the 1820s.

But one of the themes of the 100-year period covered by this book is the eventual triumph of the idea of economic *laissez-faire*, set out most influentially in Adam Smith's *Wealth of Nations*. Various import duties were repealed by Huskisson in the 1820s, and by Peel's government of the 1840s. In particular, due in part to the effective propaganda of the manufacturing interests represented by the Anti-Corn Law League, and by the events of the Irish Potato Famine, repeal of the Corn Laws came in 1846. In the short-term this was mainly of symbolic importance for grain prices only fell significantly after 1870 with the large-scale importation of North American wheat.

1

In the market for bread itself there was also the removal of some government regulation during this period. The assize of bread was of ancient origin, first becoming law in the thirteenth century. It was intended to guarantee bakers a fair profit, and no more, so preventing excessive prices. By the eighteenth century, as will be seen in Chapter 4, there was much variation in how, and indeed whether, local government set the assize. It was finally abolished in 1836.

The study of bread therefore takes the historian to the heart of the economic, social, and political life, of a remarkable age. Yet there are relatively few dedicated histories of bread in the age of industrialization.

Although the predominant importance of food within the consumer economy of the 18th and 19th centuries has been fully recognized, and has informed many debates, not least the 'standard-of-living' controversy, the particular and in some respects unique nature and role of bread (and of white bread especially) needs consideration, apart from general conclusions about diet; while the extant histories of bread give more emphasis to earlier centuries than to the period of continuity, chance, and change.[1] There are particular accounts of regulation,[2] dearth,[3] milling,[4] and of local circumstances[5] during the 18th and 19th centuries, but apart from work by John Burnett,[6] little has been written about commercial baking, though it was one of the principal, albeit backward, industries of the age. Certainly, and inevitably, bread features in professional histories of food (the 'remarkable lack' of which is being remedied[7]), and is frequently mentioned in political and social histories of the 18th and 19th centuries, if only to introduce the Corn Laws and Repeal. But generally the treatment is slight.

However, since bread was a topic of recurrent public, private, and official concern, there is a wealth of contemporary material on which the historian can draw. My main primary sources have been:

1. parliamentary records, especially the reports of successive bread committees;
2. administrative records, especially those concerning prescribed diets, and the operation of the Assize of Bread;
3. contemporary surveys and reports of food, and particularly of bread, consumption;
4. contemporary books, tracts, newspapers and periodicals;
5. official and private documents found in local record offices.

This study is intended as an introductory review, outlining some of the key features, relationships, and dynamics of an extensive topic. I hope it will help to shape questions for further exploration.

Such exploration ought to involve the contributions of specialists in many branches of economic history, and social and political history, in the sciences and technologies of grain husbandry, milling and baking, nutritionists and biochemists, social anthropologists, and many others, as well as local historians. The scope is worldwide, and not confined, as is this study, to the history of bread in Britain.

Against the advice given long ago by Porter,[8] I have attempted to estimate the volume and value of the bread (and particularly, the wheat bread) consumed in Britain between 1770 and 1870. Although quite plentiful information exists to help calculation of some components, other estimates rely heavily on judgement; however, the results can be compared to estimates made by different methods (eg, of domestic grain output), which comparisons may be useful not only when they coincide, but also when differences have to be considered and explanations suggested. I have no doubt that my estimates will be improved upon. However, the process of producing a British Bread Table does give a framework to this study, requiring that not only the principal influences, but their relative importance and interactions be considered.

Notes

1. eg Ashley: The Bread of Our Forefathers; J Ashton: The History of Bread; Sheppard & Newton: The Story of Bread; Storck & Teague: Flour for Man's Bread.
2. eg S & B Webb: The Assize of Bread.
3. eg Stern: The Bread Crisis in Britain 1795–96; Galpin: The Grain Supply of England; Wells: Wretched Faces.
4. eg Bennett & Elton: History of Corn Milling; M D Freeman: A History of Corn Milling c1750–1914; Orbell: The Corn Milling Industry in the Industrial Revolution 1750–1820; Tann: Co-operative Corn Milling.
5. eg Barnsby: The Standard of Living in the Black Country; Gourvish: A Note on Bread Prices in London and Glasgow; Neale: The Standard of Living 1780–1844; Richardson: The Standard of Living Controversy; Thwaites: The Marketing of Agricultural Produce in Eighteenth Century Oxfordshire.
6. Burnett: The Baking Industry in the Nineteenth Century.
7. Burnett: Plenty & Want p 19; Livi-Bacci: Population and Nutrition p 79.
8. Porter: The Progress of the Nation p 538.

CHAPTER 1

The Bread Question

By 1770, wheat bread had become the chief food of a majority (if only just) of the British people. Over the following century the annual volume of wheat bread consumption increased more than fourfold; its value increased more than fivefold.[1] Roughly speaking, about three-quarters of volume growth represented (and permitted) the tripling of the national population during the century, the rest being due to the switch, in certain regions, from other grains and foods to wheat bread. From the 1870s on, thanks to the transformation of worldwide food production and distribution, the mass diet of Britain became more varied; bread gradually lost its singular importance as 'the staff of life', becoming one of, and often the mere accompaniment to, many foods. Whatever other, and less prosaic, labels might be attached to it, the century from 1770 to 1870 can be called 'the age of the wheat loaf'.

Such growth in the bread supply was beyond the imagining of 18th century observers. How it was achieved is discussed in later chapters. But first, the nature and effects of bread dependency will be outlined.

The consumer economy of industrializing Britain was dominated, as it had been in the agrarian past, by food and drink, which accounted for perhaps 75 to 80 per cent of all household expenditure (see Appendix 1). In the UK today, a rough equivalent share would be 26 per cent (though there is difficulty in allocating 'eating out' expenses).[2]

Even among the middle classes, expenditure on food was high in relation to income. If seven estimates offered by contributors to *The Family Oracle of Health* in 1824 are reliable, such families spent between 38 per cent and 60 per cent of all their incomes on food.[3] The proportion may have been higher still had allowance been made for the fuel families used in cooking, and for the servants paid to prepare and serve meals.

Among the masses, bread was overwhelmingly the chief food, generally accounting for 40 to 80 per cent or even more of weekly income, according to family circumstances and the prevailing price of the loaf (see Appendix 2). Thomas Ruggles asserted, in 1792, that 'everybody knows that bread covers at least two-thirds of the expenditure on food'. More than sixty years later, Eliza Acton commented that 'it is no unusual circumstance for the entire earnings of a poor hard-working man to be expended upon bread only, for himself and family (without their being nourished as they ought to be, even then)' and

4

Edward Smith recorded that both for indoor and outdoor workers, bread was undoubtedly the principal part of the food of all poor families.[4]

At national level, the cost of bread was a substantial, and markedly variable, component of GNP. Implicitly, it formed a large part of the costs of agricultural and industrial production, in an economy that was still heavily dependent upon human muscle and dexterity.

Kind

The demand for bread (and for wheat bread particularly) differed from most other demands not only in scale, but in kind. As E P Thompson has observed,[5] 'it is notorious that the demand for corn, or bread, is highly inelastic . . .' And though the consumption of beer was broadly comparable to that of bread, in its scale and normal inelasticity, the price of beer varied little, whereas the price of bread could fluctuate considerably. So that a fluctuating price, combined with high inelasticity, produced sharp swings in the cost of satisfying bread dependency. It was observed that 'when prices rose labourers might eat the same quantity of bread, but cut out other items in their budgets; they might eat more bread to compensate for the loss of other items.[6]' The effect is clearly demonstrated by Dr Richardson's analysis of the household budgets of Kentish labourers' families (see Table 1.1).

Table 1.1 Agricultural labourers: distribution of household expenditure on food and drink in Kent, 1793–1838

	1793 %	1812 %	1814 %	1821 %	1835 %	1837 %	1838 %
Bread/flour	48.0	74.2	55.8	64.2	49.0	46.1	57.1
Meat	26.2	6.0	10.0	9.3	16.2	16.2	15.1
Cheese	10.0	9.0	13.4	10.4	8.5	12.2	5.3
Butter	8.0	6.0	10.2	7.8	11.3	13.5	11.8
Sugar	5.3	2.0	4.7	3.0	5.8	7.0	5.0
Tea	2.5	2.2	4.0	3.4	5.0	5.0	5.7
TOTAL	100.0	99.4	98.1	98.1	95.8	100.0	100.0

Source: Richardson thesis p 134; also in Oddy & Miller (eds) p 105.

Conversely, when grain, flour, and bread prices were low, the mass demand for other foods and manufactured goods could increase.

Qualitative variation in consumption, though given great importance by Professor Labrousse and his followers in their analysis of *ancien regime* France, has been comparatively neglected (as Hoskins and Kindleberger have noted[7]) by historians of the British economy. However, in 1965, A H John argued that low grain prices in England in the first half of the 18th century stimulated the *per capita* consumption of other foods (including imported tea and sugar) and manufactures,[8] thus indicating that consumer expenditure, so far as it can be established, related not so much to a constant 'shopping list', but to an expanding or contracting variety of consumables. Thus the notion of a fixed 'basket of commodities', though often used in the standard-of-living debate, is a counter-factual. The degree to which consumption expanded or contracted is complicated by other variables, chiefly the purchasing power of the agricultural sector, on the assumption that, if wheat prices were low, farm profits and wages were lower too.[9] That variable diminished, however, as the proportion of the population dependent upon agriculture declined. Professor Wrigley's estimates show the rural agricultural population declining from 60.4 per cent of the total population in 1670 to only 36.3 per cent in 1801.[10]

Such short run fluctuations apart, however, it seemed axiomatic that, in a primarily agrarian economy, a substantial rise in bread prices, especially if sustained, would cause widespread starvation and death, a point demonstrated by the 'steeples of mortality' that followed harvest failures and high prices in much of Europe in 1740, and for instance in Bohemia in 1770 and periodically and regionally in France up to 1854–5.[11] That the price of bread (corn) regulated the size, by checking the natural tendency to increase, of a population was central to the scheme of classical economics. Adam Smith acknowledged that the effect on population would be offset if wages rose in step with prices. But given that wages could rise only to a point, beyond which labour would be uneconomic, any sustained increase in bread prices would surely result in the starvation and death of a proportion of the poorest classes. Whereupon the factors of production would return to balance. Malthus' 'positive check' amplified the point, and Ricardo demonstrated that, given the law of diminishing returns, the probability of such a check accelerated as the population grew.[12] The development of international commerce, the exchange of manufactures and minerals for food, might delay but would not avert a 'positive check'; as late as 1848 J S Mill argued that only large-scale emigration would prevent a mortality crisis in Britain.[13]

But the classical economists, by pursuing a universal principle, overlooked the circumstances of their own country, of England at least. There was only a weak, and at times a contradictory correspondence between English mortality levels and wheat prices between 1541 and 1871 (and little if any coincidence of English and continental mortality crises in the 18th century).[14] Professor Chartres has noted the contrary argument that, until the end of the 17th century, mortality did remain strongly sensitive to the harvest;[15] thereafter, however, the effect faded, though national aggregates may conceal regional variations: for instance, Bohstedt notes that after the dearth of 1795–6 there was a sharp increase of burials in Devon; but Stern finds a barely perceptible effect over the country as a whole, and in the next and longer dearth, English mortality was below average in 1799–1800,[16] and only average in 1800–1. If they did not starve, however, people may often have been hungry.[17]

There is a demonstrable short-run, inverse, relationship between wheat prices and nuptiality;[18] but on trend, the English population increased as the price of bread rose, and the rate accelerated when the loaf sold at previously unimagined levels, as is apparent from Table 1.2.

Table 1.2   The price of bread and the increase of population, 1700–1815

Period	Ave. price of bread per lb d*	Price increase over previous period	Population '000**	Annualized population increase in period
1700–49	1.273	–	1700: 5,027	
			1749: 5,703	+0.268%
1750–92	1.504	+18.1%	1750: 5,739	
			1792: 7,937	+0.891%
1793–1800	2.291	+52.3%	1793: 8,025	
			1800: 8,728	+1.100%
1801–15	3.125	+36.4%	1801: 9,061	
			1815: 11,004	+1.427%

* Assized price of bread in London, Mitchell p 770.
** 1700–1800: Wrigley & Schofield estimates for England only; 1801–15: mid-year estimates for England and Wales.

Tooke observed that England's high wheat and bread prices were not generally matched elsewhere in Europe,[19] though meaningful comparison is difficult, given differing local dietaries, the relative ease of substitution, costs of production and marketing, and varying qualities of wheat. However, taking conditions of 'identical scarcity'[20] in 1817, and, for closest comparison, including only those places where *percentage* increases in the price of wheat were greater than in England (see Table 1.3), the English *maxima* were exceeded only at Lisbon and Rotterdam, and the continental mean was 17 per cent lower.

Table 1.3 Highest price per quarter of wheat, 1817

England	94s 0d
Lisbon	117s 6d
Rotterdam	104s 4d
Christiania (Oslo)	81s 10d
Bordeaux	80s 7d
Hamburg	80s 0d
Danzig	75s 8d
Lubeck	68s 9d
Konigsberg	57s 8d
Riga	56s 9d
St Petersburg	56s 8d
CONTINENTAL MEAN	78s 0d

Source: PP XLIV (360) 19, HoC 29.5.1846, p 4.

Prices could reach such high levels in England, according to Tooke, because the poor did not starve: their demand was not removed from the market.[21] Parliament acknowledged the same, with anxiety; during the dearths of 1795-6 and 1799-1801, local authorities were urged (though with mixed success) to provide the dependent poor with food other than wheat (for instance: inferior grains, rice, potatoes, and herrings), so that a rise in the price of the staple might be restrained.[22] But authority did not deny its duty to sustain the poor. And duty also was prudence, in a country with a small standing army and no network of spies. Should the supply of food, and of wheat particularly, be imperilled, government intervened directly or indirectly in the market to correct the deficiency; while at local level, the Poor Law, though applied variously and with differing generosity and efficiency, was the ultimate guarantor of existence.[23]

Also, it might be argued, public policy had indirect as well as direct effects. Since in the last resort government guaranteed survival, landowners and tenants could reasonably anticipate demand, as surety for their investment, effort, and persistence in increasing the domestic output of wheat. Importers, too, could take a sizeable position, whether or not their risk was directly offset by a bounty, or underwritten by the state. British priorities were demonstrated most clearly at those times when Parliament, by opening the ports, consciously over-rode the country's perceived strategic interest. Bullion, the wherewithal to pay for armies and fleets, was allowed to flow out, often to France, Britain's chief global rival.

Larger Effects

Therefore in Britain (or at least in England and Wales, and at least in aggregate) the price of bread did not regulate the population. The premise of classical economics, if not impossible, was confounded in practice. But, since the poor did not starve, the economy was bound to conform to their survival. In principle, other material effects of fluctuating bread prices would be experienced in Britain to a greater degree. Those effects were described, within a comprehensive scheme, by the free-trade economist James Wilson.[24]

Wilson considered the consumer economy of industrializing Britain to be much the same as that of a primarily agrarian society.[25] His starting premise was, that since bread was the 'first necesary of life' it had priority in the nation's order of expenditure. Only after the 'bread account' was paid, so to speak, was there money to spare for other things. The demand for bread being highly inelastic, and the survival of the poor being assured, any rise in its price automatically increased the proportion of national expenditure required, while reducing the proportion available for other goods, services, and investment. Vice versa, when the price of bread fell, so its proportion of national expenditure would fall, allowing 'discretionary' spending to rise.[26]

In sum, the price of bread regulated the whole economy. For example, when the price of bread rose (and especially if that rise was sustained, for two or more years) the market for other goods (especially cheap manufactures) contracted. All those concerned with such output were affected: not only the workers, who might lose their jobs or be underemployed (thus reducing their spending power, and increasing the knock-on effect), but also wholesalers and retailers, and the masters and shareholders, whose profits and dividends fell. Falling demand meant that producers would cut their purchases of raw materials and postpone business investment, while existing capital, in the form of plant, would lie idle. However, as wheat was imported to make good the deficiency, the opportunities for exports increased: but, since it took time for manufacturers to re-gear to overseas demand there was a gap, during which imported wheat was paid for in bullion (causing a drain of reserves) or by credits against future exports (which borrowing drove up interest rates).

Under Protection, the effect of sudden and substantial importations of wheat, by definition at scarcity prices, was well observed: the 'savage fluctuations' of the grain trade, unpredictable both in occurrence and scale until the quantity and quality of the domestic harvest was known, posed the only threat to the gold balance that Rothschild feared.[27] Wilson argued that such a drain of bullion, with concurrent high interest rates, caused further contractions in the home economy (an effect exaggerated after the passing of the Bank Charter Act in 1844, when note circulation was strictly related to the amount of the reserves). Conversely, when the price of bread fell, the market for other goods expanded, there was full employment, and good profit, ordinary trade resumed and exports fell; the bullion reserves were replenished and interest rates tumbled.[28] But even then, it seemed, there was danger if, after a run of cheap-money years, investors were tempted to apparently high-yielding but dubious securities, and if their anticipations then proved foolish, a financial crash could follow, even in years when bread was cheap (its very cheapness being the indirect cause). Also, years of boom made manufacturers over-confident: they over-invested and over-produced.[29]

Moreover, and as Wilson observed at first hand, since businessmen anticipated the consequences of good or bad harvests, their reactions intensified the effect. At the first sign of a deficient harvest the makers of cheap textiles, for instance, cut production; at the first sign of plenty, they raised output. Thus the economy was hurled from extreme to extreme.[30]

In Wilson's view, the interest least served by Protection was agriculture. Despite the Corn Laws, and the demand of an increasing population, from 1815 the price of wheat fell on trend, till in 1835 the loaf was cheaper than it had been for forty years. So abundant and inexpensive was home production that Parliament deemed it safe to radically reform the Poor Law in 1834, and to abolish the last vestiges of the Assize of Bread in 1836. But, as most of the testimony to the successive House of Commons' committees on agriculture showed, producers, especially those farming marginal land, could not make a profit from abundance. Nor, argued Wilson, would they be compensated by future dearth: in the event of harvest failure, their volumes would be too small to gain substantially from high prices; the chief beneficiaries would be foreign suppliers. So that, when bread prices rose in 1837, and fears of scarcity revived, Wilson did not support the contention of the Anti-Corn Law League, that free trade would assure the cheap loaf; rather, he argued that if the artificial impediment of Protection was removed, wheat would find a level (that he put at 52s per quarter) which gave profit both to the home producer and to the foreign supplier (after the costs of transport, insurance, and marketing had been added to continental prices). Under free trade, therefore, the price of bread would be fair to all, but even more, it would be stable.[31] Therefore the cycle of boom and slump could be abolished.

Needless to say, Repeal did not fulfil that, or other, of Wilson's expectations. 'Free' bread did prove to be cheaper, on the whole, than 'taxed', though not by much (by 4 per cent over the 20 years after Repeal, versus the 20 years before). Imports took a far larger share of the British market than he had first thought possible, though as early as 1843, in the first issue of *The Economist*, he had revived Ricardo's argument of comparative advantage, to justify such an effect.[32] Comparative advantage of a kind was also argued by Caird: those districts producing wheat at a disadvantage ought to leave the trade to those better advantaged, and to imports, concentrating instead on meat, dairy, and fresh produce.[33]

If such consequences of Repeal were unanticipated, one desired result was achieved: British agriculture entered on its (albeit brief) 'golden age'. Furthermore, the much increased and permanent demand for foreign wheat was amply reciprocated by increased exports. Between 1854 and 1870 all imports averaged £230.2m annually, of which grain and flour averaged £27.8m or 12.1 per cent, second only to the leading import, cotton (which averaged £44.9m or 19.5 per cent). Allowing the external trade in cotton to be more or less self-liquidating in financial terms (cotton goods exports averaged £51.9m), the UK's imports of grain and flour might be said to have 'paid' for her exports of coal, iron and steel, machinery, and non-ferrous metals and manufactures, which averaged £27.4m annually.[34]

Paradoxically, because free trade did not stabilize bread prices, nor abolish boom and slump, Wilson's influence was extended: his analysis of the dynamics of the UK economy proved to be as plausible after Repeal as before. Caird estimated that, in 1863, £40m was spent on wheat breadstuffs in the UK, but £70m in 1867[35] (my own figures for British bread are £50m and £69m respectively:[36] they are differently derived, but demonstrate the same point). The fundamental principle that bread was the regulator of the whole economy was lucidly summarized by Bagehot in 1873:

> As the amount of absolute necessaries which a people consumes cannot be much diminished, the additional amount which has to be spent on them is so much subtracted from what used to be spent on other things. All the industries ... are somewhat affected by an augmentation in the price of corn, and the most affected are the large ones, which produce the objects in ordinary times most consumed by the working classes. The clothing trades feel the difference at once, and in this country the liquor trade (a great

source of English revenue) feels it almost equally soon. Especially
when for two or three years harvests have been bad, and corn has
long been dear, every industry is impoverished, and almost every
one, by becoming poorer, makes every other poorer too. All trades
are slack from diminished custom, and the consequence is a vast
stagnant capital, much idle labour, and a greatly retarded production.[37]

However, when bread was cheap the reverse applied:

The effect of this cheapness is great in every department of industry.
The working classes, having cheaper food, need to spend so much
less on that food, and have more to spend on other things. In
consequence, there is a gentle augmentation of demand through
almost all departments of trade.[38]

Perception

The argument that the price of bread was the regulator of the British
economy lost force after 1870. Mass dependency on bread lessened, as
ordinary diets became more varied,[39] so that by the beginning of the
20th century no single food could be described as a staple, with the
significance as once attached to the wheat loaf. Also, productive
dependency on human muscle had eased progressively with the greater
use of coal, a smaller component of GNP, with a much more stable
price.

It is beyond the scope of this study to attempt a *post hoc* evaluation
of the liberal thesis. And it should be noted that when the main
principles of the argument were considered at length by Gayer, Rostow,
and Schwartz, and by Rostow alone (in the latter case with reference to
Bagehot, though it would appear none had at hand Wilson's original
works), they concluded that, while harvests and bread price fluctuations
had powerful effects, other underlying forces were at work in the period
of industrialization.[40] It might be argued too that bread had an unusual
significance while the powers were at peace, but less when war, or
preparations for war, affected the world economy. And liberal economics did not displace classical theory: the two co-existed: in some
respects complementary, but generally opposed.

However, liberal principles are interesting, whether or not they
contributed to the development of economic thought, since they
represent economic *belief*. Wilson did not claim originality (as Bagehot
remarked, his ideas were 'in the air of the age'[41]); rather he formalized
views then in common currency among businessmen like himself. He
observed at first hand the general attention to the harvests, and the
consequent cuts or increases of industrial production; the powerful

effect of interest rates, monitored daily, and of bullion drains; beliefs that, whether in the abstract right or wrong, could have decisive effects. Those observations, with numerous illustrations and inferences, were reiterated weekly in *The Economist*, reaching not only Wilson's own subscribers, but also the readers of those many newspapers that cited, or lifted entire, his columns: they were 'a household concept among nineteenth-century economic journalists'.[42] And Wilson did make a direct contribution to policy. While keeping at arm's length from the League, he had powerfully influenced Cobden, and even more import-antly, erstwhile opponents of free trade, and so was instrumental in achieving Repeal.[43] Accepted both by Peelites and Liberals, Wilson, as financial secretary to the Treasury, steered policy through the first and daunting crisis of free trade, the Crimean War.[44] He was both 'an economic mandarin of high standing'[45] and the articulate voice of business orthodoxy.

W S Jevons attempted to put liberal orthodoxy onto a scientific footing, particularly to attract academic interest,[46] but perhaps the greater merit of the Wilsonian scheme lies in its essentially unscientific and inductive nature. It represents a popular contemporary view of the working of the economy, and may capture quite well the pragmatic approach of government policy, especially in the period up to 1815.

Wheat bread, then, was of major significance in the economy of Britain c1770–1870. Contemporaries were much concerned about the effects of fluctuations in bread prices. In subsequent chapters the reasons for the predominance of wheat bread, the means by which production was expanded to feed a growing population, and the intervention of governments attempting to guarantee subsistence, are discussed.

Notes

1. See the estimates in Chapters 7 and 8 below.
2. Annual Abstract of Statistics, HMSO 1992, table 14.9.
3. See Appendix 6, case 7.2.
4. Ruggles cit Salaman p 495; Acton: E B B p 3; Barker, Oddy & Yudkin p 27.
5. E P Thompson: Moral Economy p 91.
6. E P Thompson: Moral Economy p 91; Burnett: P & W p 61.
7. Hoskins in Minchinton (ed): Essays I p 93; Kindleberger: Manias p 13.
8. John in E L Jones (ed) p 174.
9. See Landes: 1950; Daniere: 1958 with reply by Landes, rejoinder by Daniere, and second reply by Landes; O'Brien: 1985.
10. Wrigley: PCW p 170.
11. Mennell pp 25–26; Wrigley & Schofield p 341; Levy Leboyer and Bourgignon p 25; Appleby: 1979 pp 865 et seq.

12. Adam Smith pp 86–8, 395; Barber p 64 et seq; Clapham Vol I pp 312, 335.
13. J S Mill pp 102–3.
14. Wrigley & Schofield pp 320, 325, 341–2; Watkins and van de Walle in Rotberg & Rabb (eds) p 23; Livi-Bacci p 55.
15. Chartres: Introduction p 10, citing Outhwaite, pp 401–2.
16. Appleby: 1979 p 867; Bohstedt p 145; Stern p 172; Wrigley & Schofield p 325.
17. Shammas: Pre-industrial Consumer p 123 et seq.
18. Wrigley & Schofield p 368.
19. Ashton: Changes pp 185–6.
20. PP XLIV (360) 19, HoC 29.5.1846, p 4.
21. Ashton: Changes pp 185–6.
22. eg HoC Sessional Papers vol 131, Cd 5105, 24.11.1800, and succeeding reports of the Committee on the High Price of Provisions.
23. Appleby: 1979 p 886.
24. Wilson ops cit, and *The Economist*.
25. See eg Bowden in Ag H of E & W V–II pp 55–6, 59.
26. Wilson: F pp 11, 17, 22–5, 64, 117; CL pp 27, 29, 33 et seq.
27. Wilson: CC & B pp 23–4; Clapham Vol I pp 281–2; see also Ashton: I R p 117.
28. Wilson: CL pp 28–32, 35; F pp 16–20, 38 et seq, 66–8, 75, 90, 105, 117.
29. Wilson: F pp 11–12, 25, 47, 68.
30. Wilson: F pp 86–8.
31. Wilson: CL pp 33, 47; F pp 22–5, 118–19.
32. *The Economist*, 2.9.1843.
33. Caird: English Agriculture pp 483–6
34. Calculated from the import and export returns given in Mitchell pp 474, 482.
35. Caird: ODF p 13.
36. See Chapter 8.
37. Bagehot: Lombard Street p 123.
38. Bagehot: Lombard Street p 140.
39. Oddy p 318.
40. Gayer, Rostow & Schwartz esp I.4, pp 563–5; Rostow: British Economy.
41. Bagehot: Memoir p 337.
42. John in E L Jones (ed), p 173.
43. Bagehot: Memoir p 334
44. Petersen: Crisis of Free Trade.
45. Marx p 338.
46. W S Jevons: Investigations pp 8, 10, 217.

CHAPTER 2

The Wheat Loaf

Thus, contemporaries perceived that dependency on the wheat loaf involved considerable risk to the nation and its social order, bringing periodic turmoil to the exchanges and money markets, at times requiring the subordination of Britain's strategic interest and the transfer of resources from rich to poor. And according to the liberal economists, wheat dependency also induced the wasteful cycle of boom and slump. Surely a pragmatic society would have lessened such fraught dependency? And surely the poor too, would have benefited from a less vulnerable, more varied, and cheaper diet? Yet, during the century in review, dependency on wheat did not lessen, but intensified. Whereas in the decade 1771–1780 wheat represented approximately 60 per cent by value of Britain's breadstuffs, by 1861–1870 the proportion had risen to 90 per cent of a much increased total.[1]

In this chapter, I shall attempt to explain the country's commitment to wheat.

2.1 PREFERENCE

All the four principal grains could flourish in Britain: rye, barley, and oats in almost any part; wheat was better suited to the southern and eastern seaboards, though hardier strains were raised elsewhere. All four grains were valuable human foods, far more cost efficient when consumed directly, than indirectly as meat, eggs, or butter. Adam Smith observed that a cornfield of moderate fertility would produce much more food than the same land as pasture; Bain thought bread to be ten times more efficient as food than bullock-meat; Bairoch puts the superiority of cereal production over stock-raising at about eight times, Braudel at something from ten to twenty times. The exact relationship depends, of course, on many variables, not least prevailing prices. Thus Braudel, citing the Paris markets c1780, shows grain 'costing' (prices related to calories) an eleventh of meat, a sixth of eggs, and a third of butter (and also, one sixty-fifth of sea fish and a ninth of fresh-water fish). His argument (echoing that of Adam Smith) is that a predominantly cereal diet was the pre- requisite of a growing population and expanding economy.[2]

The grains can be consumed in 'wetter' or 'drier' forms. With a pot, drinkable water or milk, and fire, grain can be made into various 'mushy' foods. Types noted by Eden included *hasty pudding* (oatmeal boiled in salted water, with a little milk or beer, butter or treacle, added); *crowdie* (a northern version of hasty pudding, sometimes with fat from a broth added instead of butter or milk); and *furmenty*, which as eaten in Cumberland consisted of pearl barley, boiled for two hours or so and mixed with skimmed milk, sometimes with sugar added.[3] But furmenty varied as much as its spelling, elsewhere signifying a gelatinized mixture of wheat and water or milk, like a blancmange. A similar dish called *flummery* or *sowens* was made with oaten bran and husks. Boiled cracked wheat produced a gritty sludge similar to couscous. Wheat offal mixed with a little breadflour made into a pudding called *crammings*.[4] The nutritional value of these dishes may have varied considerably, depending on whether the water used was thrown away or eaten as soup (for instance, by today's reckoning, boiled pearl barley has only one-third of the energy and protein value of raw).[5]

Drier forms included 'hard cakes' such as *clap-bread* (made of unleavened barley or oat meal, baked on a griddle), a kind of oaten biscuit called *kitcheners'* bread; thick sour *riddle cakes*, otherwise *bannocks* (made of oat or barley or pease meal, sometimes with milk, butter, or eggs added), and leavened loaves of oat or barley meal called *jannocks*, which survived in parts of Lancashire until late in the 19th century. Such loaves were hard and dry and were made more palatable and digestible by breaking or grinding, the crumbs being mixed with milk or water (like today's *Grape Nuts*, the crumbs of a hard-baked barley loaf).[6] Moister, and more risen leavened loaves, were made from rye, and especially from wheat.

Convenience of preparation and use can be a powerful influence affecting the choice of food form. If a food is to be eaten several times a day, for every day of one's life, prosaic efficiencies become towering benefits. Wetter forms imply practical difficulties, especially if food is to be eaten away from the home, for instance by labourers in the fields: the need to carry pots, bowls, and spoons, to have access to drinkable water or milk, and fire, and time for preparation. Whereas, for all ordinary purposes, once made the loaf is highly efficient. It is readily stacked and carried; 'portion control' can be exact; and a loaf can be eaten anywhere without need of fire, pots and cutlery. A slice of bread is also an efficient 'carrier'; two slices (the sandwich, 'invented' *c*1750) are both container and content; and the loaf could be a meat-safe

> He purchased a sufficiency of ready-dressed ham and a half-quartern loaf . . . the ham being kept clean and preserved from dust,

by the ingenious expedient of making a hole in the loaf by pulling out a portion of the crumb, and stuffing it therein.[7]

The grains differ significantly in their suitability for loaf-making. Wheat and rye have two principal advantages over barley and oats. First, wheat and rye lose their hulls when threshed, whereas barley and oats do not (though the husk of barley can be removed by polishing). Thus a meal made of wheat or rye is relatively free of fibre, which has virtually no nutritive value to man. Second, wheat and rye contain gliadin, a water-insoluble protein that has the property of stretching almost indefinitely. Wheat also contains, but rye does not, the tougher protein glutenin, which combines with gliadin in gluten. Some of the gas released by yeast is trapped by gliadin, causing a rye loaf to rise somewhat; far more is trapped by strong, elastic, gluten, so that wheat loaves rise higher and have the lightest texture.[8]

The fineness of a flour and the propensity of a dough to rise are closely related to absorbency. In the process of bread-making, three things can happen to the water content of the dough: it can evaporate, separate, and/or be fused chemically into the texture. Coarser meals absorb relatively little water, producing a dense and dry bread: if the loaf is underbaked, then separated water produces a slurry, that may be easier to swallow but is difficult to use. The finer the flour, and the more expandable the texture, in principle the greater degree of fusion, which means first that the weight of the bread is significantly greater than the weight of the flour used, and second, that though firm, the texture is slightly moist (until it dries out during the staling process): that adds to the ease of swallowing and digestion. As a rule of thumb, a fine 'soft' wheat flour will produce about 4 lbs of bread to every 3 lbs of flour used. A 'hard' wheat flour will yield more.

Rye, because it contains gliadin, is the closest to wheat in bread-making properties. But rye has two particular disadvantages. First, while all flours can be 'temperamental' during bread-making, especially in warmer weather, rye-flour is especially unpredictable: even skilled bakers have difficulty with it, and batches can easily be ruined.[9] Second, rye is vulnerable to ergot, a blight yielding twenty poisons, including LSD (ironically, though, the best-known case of ergot poisoning in modern England was caused by rotten wheat).[10]

Given the many advantages of the loaf form, barley and rye often were 'improved' to make them better breadstuffs, by mixing-in wheat. Barley mixed with wheat, in any proportion, was known as *muncorn* (monk's corn); rye mixed with wheat was called *maslin* or *mistling* (from the middle-French miscelin, or 'mixture').[11]

The qualities that favour wheat as a breadstuff limit its value as an animal feed. For animals such as cattle and horses, that can digest fibre and gain nutriment from it, barley and oats make a suitable feed: barley for its fattening properties and oats for energy. Wheat and rye are unsuited to such use: they cause digestive upsets. However, the bran and pollards left after extracting white and whitish flours from wheat are a good feed for pigs and hens.[12] And the grains had differing values as raw materials. Barley was the principal drinkstuff. Rye, though a fading crop, was valued for its stalks (the best material for thatching).

The properties of the grains defined their preferential uses, within what might be termed 'the Corn Constitution' of the country. According to Gregory King, by the end of the 17th century in England, preferential use of the grains was strongly, even starkly, established. In his estimates, all wheat and rye appear as human food; 90 per cent of barley is allocated to drink (the other 10 per cent being aggregated to human and animal food); he seems to have treated all oats as animal feed. No specific allowance was made for the use of grains as raw materials. Probably King simplified. Sir Charles Smith gave a more complex account of grain use in England and Wales c1760. Although like King, Smith believed that wheat was almost entirely used as human food (98 per cent of volume as against 2 per cent shared between drink and raw material use), of barley he allocated only 74 per cent rather than 90 per cent to drink, with 23 per cent for human food and 3 per cent for 'other' uses (which probably included animal feed); his calculation for oats was that 58 per cent was fed to animals (horses) or eaten in 'soup, etc', with a further 42 per cent used as a breadstuff. The importance given by Smith to oats as a human food is somewhat surprising, since his calculations concerned only England and Wales; certainly, he contradicted Dr Johnson's dictum that oats were 'a grain which in England is generally given to horses but in Scotland supports the people'.[13] Rye was allocated as: 97 per cent for human food and 3 per cent for 'tanners and hogs'.[14]

Smith cautioned the reader that his guesstimates, though informed, might be wide of the mark; and had Scotland been included, the aggregates would have changed noticeably. But the assumptions are interesting. By the 18th century it was thought odd, or even offensive, to waste wheat fit for humans by feeding it to animals. And it was deemed wrong, or at least of marginal value, to distil wheat, so that in years of scarcity its distilling was banned (and at other times, deprecated),[15] as was the use of wheat-flour for hair powder (perhaps 350,000 people used hair powder c1795), starches, or pastes (though generally only inferior wheat was used for such purposes). In 1801 it was reckoned that just under 6 per cent of all the wheat consumed in Britain went for distilling and starch manufacture.[16]

Contemporaries fully acknowledged the superior loaf-making properties of wheat. But wheat was a markedly more expensive grain than rye,
barley, or oats. In the 1770s, for instance, the average national price per
bushel of wheat, on the open market, was 46 per cent higher than for
the same measure of rye, 90 per cent higher than barley, and 185 per
cent higher than oats.[17]

In past centuries availability, and perhaps price, had limited the
consumption of wheat: the masses in England and Wales, especially the
rural poor, had like their continental counterparts subsisted on rye or
barley bread; the Scots and border English were heavily dependent on
oats. But by 1767, according to Arthur Young, even poor cottagers
looked with horror on rye and barley; they demanded wheat, and
wherever it could be obtained, the finest and whitest wheat bread.[18] By
the mid-18th century, as Hogarth observed, Londoners demanded bread
as 'white as any curd'; by 1784 their preference was shared by the poor
of small country towns such as Wallingford. Londoners continued to
insist on the best wheaten bread even in dearth; so too the poor of
Abingdon and many Oxfordshire towns, where muncorn was refused in
1795 (though barley bread still was used in remoter parts of the
county).[19] As Mountmorres remarked, experience showed 'that
labourers and the lower classes will always purchase and consume the
best and whitest bread, and no other ...', a comment echoed by
contributors to the Annals of Agriculture: 'our labourers reject anything
but wheaten bread'; 'the poor eat as good a flour as gentlemen'; 'they
want the best'.[20] Turton observed: 'people won't eat brown bread'.[21]
Even in County Durham, where rye was the traditional staple, the poor
now refused it 'except under greatest necessity'.[22]

Undoubtedly those commentators over-generalized their first-hand
observations: the other grains and coarser wheat flours still were used,
especially by home bakers, in many parts of the country. Even
commercial bakers in the north and on the Scottish border sold rye,
barley, oaten, and mixed breads, as Young himself noted.[23] And in the
dearths of 1795–6 and 1799–1801, numbers of dedicated wheat eaters
were forced back onto other grains, or mixed breads, if only at
subsidized prices or as a dole (though much was thrown away).[24] By
1807, however, Parliament accepted that a surplus in the barley crop
would not allow any reduction in wheat imports.[25] And by 1813 the
magistrates of York were alone, among all the jurisdictions replying to a
bakers' questionnaire, in continuing to set an assize for maslin, rye, and
'rubble' bread, as well as for wheat loaves.[26]

Thus the appearance of near universal dependence on wheat bread
was plausible enough. And commentators referred with anxiety, disdain,
or in the case of Pitt, with regretful resignation, to the habits of the

poor.[27] It was alleged that by insisting on wheat, and especially white, bread, the indigent indulged in luxury that they could ill afford, when coarser breads (or soups or other substitutes) would nourish them at much less cost.[28] Burke condemned them for aping their betters.[29] They were 'chastised' for being 'too fine-mouthed'; 'dainty' was the word often used to describe such unwonted taste, and it passed into popular historiography.[30]

Even some of those sympathetic to the poor accepted that wheat bread was a luxury, but argued that its use was justified by its sweeter taste and appetizing appearance, if people lived on little else.[31] And historians have justified 'pretension', given that white bread was a symbol of status, of improved living standards, that the working classes understandably defended.[32]

But arguably, for a large and increasing proportion of the population, wheat and especially white bread was not (or not simply) a luxury: it was the most cost-efficient food available. That possibility is discussed next.

2.2 THE COST EFFICIENCY OF BREADS: PHYSICAL FACTORS

Although at market prices wheat was the most expensive grain by far, its relative cost was diminished by several 'physical' factors. First, the bushel measures volume, a poor guide to value, given the markedly different weights of the grains. If the average open market grain costs of the 1770s, for instance, are re-expressed in terms of officially-measured average weights, the price differential narrows considerably as shown in Table 2.1.

Cost relationships were changed further by milling (see Table 2.2).

As can be seen, a relatively low flour yield substantially reduced the apparent cost advantage of oats.

The amount of bread that could be made from the flour of each grain varied substantially, according to the quality of the crop, flour extraction rates, absorbency, the season ('temperamental' variations were most likely in warmer weather), and the baker's skill and methods. A contemporary official estimate of bread yields, re-expressed per Imperial quarter of each grain, is shown in Table 2.3.

If those yields are related to the grain prices of the 1770s, and to an operating cost of milling and baking (allowing for the 'hidden' element of bran and pollard worth), of say 15s per Imperial quarter, the results are as given in Table 2.4.

Table 2.1 Average costs of the grains by officially assessed weights, 1771–80

	OMP* per bushel (shillings)	Weight lbs	Cost per lb (shillings)
Wheat	5.7	60	0.095
Rye	3.9	57	0.068
Barley	3.0	48	0.063
Oats	2.0	40	0.050

* Open Market Price

Sources: Officially-assessed weights of rye, barley, and oats (converted from Winchester to Imperial measure at the rate 31/30) cit Edlin p 98 (nb: the weight of barley varied greatly: Edlin also gives 52.5 lbs per bushel in a recipe (p 104)). The weights for wheat, barley, and oats given also by Collins p 108. Rye is also given as 57 lbs in the Statistical Appendix to the Agrarian History of England & Wales Vol VI, p 1124.

Table 2.2 Calculated costs per lb of flour/meal, 1771–80

	OMP + 0.25s allowed for milling* (shillings)	Flour/meal weight extracted lb	Extraction Rate %	Cost per lb flour/meal (shillings)
Wheat	5.95	45.00**	75%	1.322
Rye	4.15	43.00	75%	0.965
Barley	3.25	38.66	81%	0.841
Oats	2.25	23.31	58%	0.965

* 3d per bushel was a common cash toll before the war.
** Standard Wheaten extraction rate.

Source (for rye, barley, and oats): Edlin p 98.
Farmers Magazine, January 1801, gave extraction rates of 80% for wheat (appropriate for household bread), 78% for barley, and 56% for oats: cit Collins p 108.

The further diseconomies of making bread from oats are demonstrated, and probably understated, at least for England, where millers generally may have charged more to grind oats, either according to opportunity cost or because the hard husks wore out their stones at a faster rate. In Scotland it seems the millers were inured to the risk, or

Table 2.3   Typical bread yields

Wheat*	440 lbs
Rye	398 lbs
Barley	413 lbs
Oats	195 lbs

* averaging statutory Wheaten and Household grades to represent the Standard Wheaten quality.

Source: 31 Geo II c.29, calculated from Table II.

Table 2.4   Cost of processing the grains into bread, 1770s

	OMP plus 15s for processing (shillings)	Bread Yield per Qr lbs	Cost per lb of bread d
Wheat	60.6	440	1.65
Rye	46.2	398	1.39
Barley	39.0	413	1.13
Oats	31.0	195	1.91

used tougher stones: thus in 1800, on average, oatmeal in England was 93 per cent dearer than in Scotland.[33] Also, it was common to add milk or butter (an additional expense) to oatmeal, as binding, lest the bread crumble.[34]

Possibly, the cost of baking coarse breads is understated: barley bread, for instance, needed longer in the oven and greater heat.[35]

In summary, the 'cost gap' between the grains was progressively reduced during processing. Table 2.5 shows the effect proportionate to wheat.

Table 2.5   Costs at 1770s prices, proportionate to wheat

	Grain price per bushel	Grain price per lb	Flour/meal price per lb	Bread price per lb
Wheat	100	100	100	100
Rye	68	72	73	84
Barley	53	66	64	68
Oats	35	53	73	116

Leaving aside oats, an obviously expensive breadstuff, the premium cost of wheat compared to rye diminished from 46 per cent at grain prices to 19 per cent at calculated bread prices; compared to barley it diminished from 90 per cent to 46 per cent. And the differential was further narrowed as the price of wheat fell on trend, relative to the prices of the other grains. Comparing the decadal averages of the 1860s to those of the 1770s, the price of wheat had fallen by 26 per cent relative to barley and by 24 per cent relative to oats;[36] only rye, by then in little demand, became relatively cheaper after 1815. Also, as noted, to obtain palatable loaves it was common to mix an amount of wheat with rye and barley.[37] It may be seen that a relatively small admixture of wheat with rye would substantially eliminate the remaining bread price differential (almost wholly so if a mixture in the ratio of one part rye to three parts wheat, as cited by Dr Edward Smith in the 1860s, was used). The remaining, and apparently large, difference between the prices of wheat and barley breads, might also be substantially reduced: the description 'barley bread' must often have meant muncorn (a blurring common today: the late Mrs David, a confessed barley bread 'addict', used four parts wheat flour to one part barley meal). A recipe reported by the Board of Agriculture, as producing a bread 'esteemed' in Yorkshire, required the meal of four bushels of wheat (from which only the coarser bran had been excluded) mixed with the flour of 3.5 bushels of barley. In the 1860s, Dr Edward Smith cited the ratio of one part wheat to one part barley as a commonplace.[38] Given a half-and-half mixture, using a Standard Wheaten flour, then crudely the end cost of a muncorn loaf, at 1770s prices and according to the calculations used here, would be 84 per cent of that of Standard Wheaten bread, or otherwise stated, the wheat bread would be only 19 per cent more expensive than the muncorn.

Even then, comparisons deceive. The quality of wheat bread assumed for these calculations would in average conditions represent a loaf made entirely of digestible flour without bran or pollards (though a 75 per cent extraction rate from poor quality wheat could include an amount of them): thus ordinarily the entire loaf would give nourishment. But to achieve a similar bran-free loaf of rye, an extraction rate of only 60 per cent or less would be necessary[39] (which was uneconomic): at the 75 per cent extraction rate assumed here, a considerable amount of indigestible and therefore valueless bran would be included in the loaf. Moreover, though of denser texture, rye bread held considerably more water, only part 'fused':[40] hence its clamminess; and such water too was of nil value. Barley flour (especially at the 81 per cent extraction rate taken here) contained a large amount of bran (hence its 'brannish' taste and brown colour[41]), and at any extraction rate included the ground fibre of the hull. Mixing with wheat reduced the proportion, but did not eliminate, those valueless constituents.

Any remaining 'physical' cost gap would have narrowed further when allowance is made for the need to accompany coarser breads with, for example, a fat, whereas bread made from wheat, from the Standard Wheaten grade up to fine white, mingled easily with the saliva and needed no such accompaniment: the amount of fat eaten by wheat-eating labourers was 'very low'.[42] Thus the consumer of wheat bread was spared additional expenses.

Thus, in 'physical' terms, though comparison must be rough and ready, the wheat loaf may usually have cost little more or no more than loaves made from coarser grain flours; so that the market prices of wheat, barley, and rye roughly represented a value-parity as human food, while oats cost more than parity (though oats were more efficiently consumed as porridge).

2.3 THE COST EFFICIENCY OF BREADS: NUTRITIONAL FACTORS

Informed contemporaries were aware that the 'physical' costs of breadstuffs were not the only measure of their relative values. For instance, in the 1790s, Mountmorres called for the chemical analysis of nutriment, and for medical enquiries into its employment by the body, to establish scientifically which of the grains was truly the cheapest.[43] Subsequent analysis suggests that, as the 'physical' costs of breadstuffs converged to a point which, if blurred, may not have been far from value-parity, so their 'nutritional' values converged too. Relative to the employable energy obtained by consumers, possibly the wheat loaf, and the white wheat loaf in particular, were no more expensive than coarser breads. However, even today the point cannot be established with any precision, given the many variables encompassed by nutritional account-ancy.[44] Also, present-day nutritional analyses should be used with caution, when considering the strains of grain, types of flour, and breads, common in the 18th and 19th centuries. For instance, most of the wheat then used in British bread was 'soft' ('hard' wheat being imported only periodically before Repeal), with a different balance of carbohydrate and proteins to the wheats generally used today. And stone-grinding did not break bran into small particles, whereas the roller-grinding technique, adopted from the 1880s, did: that significantly affected the comparative digestibility of all 'brannish' flours and meals.[45]

Also, allowance has to be made for the adaptability of humans to different food regimes, and the environments in which people lived and worked.[46] Some differences may be evident: height, body-weight, health, longevity; others are less easily demonstrated, for instance the adaptation of the digestion to a staple, predominant, food. Professor Shammas notes current views that 'men and women can just about live on bread alone, if there is enough of it', because high consumption levels will provide an adequate amount of protein as well as energy.[47] But a person accustomed to a plentiful and varied diet might suffer catastrophically if suddenly made dependent on bread alone;[48] while others might adjust.[49] And the importance of animal protein to children is another argument, as is the importance of vitamins. Here I shall concentrate on the energy-giving properties of the grains and breads made from them.

Ostensibly, by weight, the flours and meals analysed by Dr Edward Smith were roughly equivalent in potential energy value. The relevant data are listed in Table 2.6.

Table 2.6   Analysis of flours and meals made by Dr Edward Smith, 1864

	Kcals* per lb
Wheat: white bread-making flour roughly equivalent to Standard Wheaten type (approx 75% extraction)	2660
Rye flour	2660
Barley meal	2500
Oatmeal	2800

* Given 4300 grains of carbon = 2800 Kcals (Barker Oddy & Yudkin p 26).

Source: Edward Smith: Practical Dietary pp 37–49.

However, their food values were markedly different, because of the varying rates at which potential energy was 'lost' during the process of digestion and absorption. If a food contains a proportion of indigestible matter, such as fibre and bran, then an amount of the energy provided will be used up by the work of digestion. How much depends not only on the components of the food, but on all the variables that distinguish the system of one individual from another, according to age, gender, and physiological condition. So that assessment is 'complicated' and poses problems to which there is 'no clear-cut answer'.[50]

In general, however, not only is the proportion of fibre and bran of nil 'physical' value, in nutritional terms it is a negative, deducting from the consumable worth of the useful matter. That effect might sometimes be desired.

For instance, the amount of energy consumed in digesting coarse rye or oat meals generates such heat that it warms the body. But otherwise nutritional loss would be ill-afforded by those relying on bread as their chief food.[51]

Also, the energy derived from a food depends on the length of time that it is retained by the body. Fibre and bran irritate the bowel and so the food passes relatively quickly. The laxative effect of rye and barley, coupled with a tendency to produce gas, was well observed by contemporaries.[52] In wealthier households, as in many now, the purgative effect of high-fibre and high-bran breads was desirable. But where bread was the chief or only food of poor people, the longer it was retained in the bowel the greater the nourishment. And, of course, the nutritional value of any other food consumed also would be enhanced, if the bowels were settled. White bread, wholly or virtually free of fibre and bran, was a markedly efficient food. The point is not clear-cut, however, since all breads contain an amount of residual starch, not converted and absorbed as glucose, and residual starch has a similar effect to fibre and bran;[53] but since the bowels must be moved from time to time, some such an aid to motion may be valuable in any circumstance.

Jasny termed the calorie gain, after deducting the costs of digestion and absorption, and allowing for length of retention, the 'net energy value' of a food. His estimates of the average net energy values of the grains are in Table 2.7 below.

Table 2.7   Net energy value of the grains
per 100 lb

	Kcals	Index
Wheat	84,700	100
Rye	72,100	85
Barley	70,500	83
Oats	64,900	77

Source: N Jasny: Competition among Grains,
p 30.

Those estimates relate to the strains (and processing methods) common in the United States in the 1940s, but do reflect the general principle that wheat bread is a more efficient producer of net energy than the other grains. The comparative values for wheat and rye might be compared to 19th century estimates, of 71:64 made by Thaer and 100:75 estimated by Schmoller.[54]

Net energy value is expended in two ways. First, it must contribute to maintaining the vital functions, satisfying the Basal Metabolic Rate (BMR) of the individual. Only after such maintenance is there energy left for employment in activity. The BMR of individuals varies considerably, but today a requirement of 1300 Kcals daily for a woman (higher in pregnancy and lactation[55]), and 1600 for a man, might be representative for adults of median height and weight.[56] Among shorter, slighter, industrial workers in the early 19th century, probably a lower BMR was common.[57] But whatever the level, the same principle applies: a relatively small difference in net energy value produces large differences in employable energy. For instance, suppose an individual has a daily BMR requirement of 1500 Kcals, and obtains 2000 Kcals of net energy: then 500 Kcals will be available for employment. Suppose another individual has the same BMR, but obtains only 1800 Kcals of net energy. Ostensibly, the second diet is inferior to the first by 10 per cent, but in terms of employable energy, it is deficient by 33 per cent. Or roughly speaking, the first individual can perform half as much work again as the second.

Where bread is overwhelmingly the chief food, the best indicator of relative employable energy values ought be the amount of each type eaten by those dependent on it, a principle employed by Sir Charles Smith, who (after 'extensive enquiries', supplemented by a small stock of 'case histories' from various sources, which he interpreted with a sizeable dash of judgement) roughly estimated per capita bread-grain consumption, according to which was the staple. The statistical foundation is slender; but estimates also made by Colquhoun in 1814 are close, except in the case of oats, which McCulloch thought he set at least a quarter too low. Averaging Smith's estimates with those of Colquhoun, as amended by McCulloch, gives the figures shown in Table 2.8.

If those estimates are related to the processed costs used earlier,[58] the results in Table 2.9 are obtained.

Again, the diseconomy of oats as a breadstuff is demonstrated. Considering only the calculations for the three other grains, dependency on wheat bread cost only 10.5 per cent more than dependency on rye bread, and 18.6 per cent more than dependency on barley breads. As in the case of the remaining 'physical' cost gap, such differences would have been bridged, or almost so, if much of rye and barley bread was maslin or muncorn, and by the cost of fat as a necessary accompaniment to coarser breads.

Table 2.8 Annual *per capita* consumption of
bread grains, according to which was the staple,
England and Wales *c* 1765/1814

	Winchester qr	Converted to Imperial qrs @ 31/30
Wheat	1.0000	0.9680
Rye	1.1875	1.1490
Barley	1.3125	1.2700
Oats	2.6875	2.6010

Source: Sir Charles Smith: Three Tracts pp 220–2;
Colquhoun p 89; McCulloch cit Orbell, thesis p 12.

Table 2.9 Estimated cost of bread grain consumption, according to
which was the staple

Grain	Processed cost per Imp qr (shillings)	Grain consumed *per capita* p a (Imp qrs)	Processed Cost of grain consumed (shillings)
Wheat	60.6	0.968	58.7
Rye	46.2	1.149	53.1
Barley	39.0	1.270	49.5
Oats	31.0	2.601	80.6

Also, any remaining differential would have been eroded, and finally
eliminated, as the cost of wheat declined on trend during the 19th
century. By the 1860s, when Dr Edward Smith calculated the potential
energy obtained per penny at prevailing prices, the relationship of the
flours and meals was as given in Table 2.10, with the potential energy
derived per penny from wheat exceeding all but rye flour.

Given the indigestibility of rye flour (such as was then available) he
concluded that, as a breadstuff, wheat was unmatched for efficiency and
economy. McCulloch concurred:

> The superiority of wheat to all other farinaceous plants in the
> manufacturing of bread is so very great, that wherever it is easily
> and successfully cultivated, wheaten bread is used, to the nearly
> total exclusion of most others . . .[59]

Table 2.10 Potential energy per penny, 1864

	Kcals per d
Wheat: white bread-making flour roughly equivalent to Standard Wheaten type (approx 75% extraction)	1773
Rye flour	2128
Barley meal	1250
Oatmeal	1400

Given 4300 grains of carbon = 2800 Kcals.

Source: Edward Smith: Practical Dietary pp 37–49.

The same factors that governed the comparative worth of the grains also governed the relative worth of white and brown wheat bread. The main types of wheat bread were Wheaten (white), Standard Wheaten (whitish), and Household (brown or grey); they are described in Appendix 3. Brown wheat bread contained bran, which reduced the proportion of nutriment, made that nutriment more difficult to digest, and speeded the passage of food material. Bran also reduces the gluten-effect, so that brown wheat loaves, as a rule, rise less and are more densely textured than white wheat loaves (again, making them less easy to digest).[60] Successive bread committees of the House of Commons recognized that the bran content of Household bread reduced its nutritive value, so that such loaves represented no saving (those deliberations are discussed in the next section). In common parlance, Household wheat bread was classed with barley, rye, oat, and mixed breads under the common, and usually pejorative description: 'brown bread'.

And, apparently, brown wheat bread was rejected as heartily as breads made from inferior grains by those accustomed to white loaves, even in dearth. In Oxfordshire in 1795, as Thwaites shows, though brown wheat bread was tried at Woodstock, elsewhere in the county it was refused (even when offered at a discount) by labourers purchasing on their own account: they would have only the finest and best. Nothing short of absolute distress would compel them to use brown bread.[61] Such insistence was notorious in London, where even at the height of dearth, in 1800, it was well observed that the poorer the district the finer the bread sold.[62]

So far, nutritional comparisons have been made on the assumption of an 'average consumer', and as noted there are many differences in the food-converting efficiencies of individuals. One substantial variable is the kind of activity engaged in: in principle, the more active an individual (eg the more the exertion required in work), the greater the energy need, but also the more efficient the body's powers of digestion and absorption. Thus an agricultural labourer, for instance, was likelier to convert more nutriment from coarser breads than a sedentary worker, who finding digestion more difficult, would 'waste' more nutriment in the process, and so would have to eat more of the coarser breads proportionate to net energy requirement. Therefore the cost efficiency of coarser breads would be less in such cases, and of finer breads, more. The potential historical significance of the digestibility of white bread, related to the kind of work performed, was pointed out in 1928 by Sir William Ashley:

> Digestibility becomes an increasing merit as life comes to be carried on less in the open air, and involves less use of the large body muscles owing to the introduction of labour-saving machinery. Hence the problem of the substitution of wheat for rye may be bound up with the degree of urbanization of a country. One strong reason why Germany until recently has continued to eat rye bread is because it has continued so much longer than England to be an agricultural country, and so much larger a proportion of the nation could digest it with comfort.[63]

Ashton accepted the point:

> Rye-bread or barley-bread might satisfy the agricultural labourer or the coal-miner; but sedentary workers, including spinners and weavers, needed something more easy to digest: it was not merely emulation of the rich that made them turn increasingly to wheaten flour.[64]

Two aspects of digestibility might be noted. With a less efficient digestion than the labourer, the sedentary worker, if obliged to eat coarser breads, would have had to eat more proportionate to the amount of white bread that otherwise would satisfy need. This would increase the relative cost to him or her of coarser breads (assuming for example that, given the capacity of the stomach, such a worker could take more meal breaks). But, if the coarser breads induced diarrhoea, or filled the stomach with gases, producing pain, the effect could well be to depress the appetite, limiting what could be eaten as well as wasting much of its value. In the latter case, it might be argued, white bread was not only more cost-effective than coarse, but an absolute need.

The question of digestibility, related to occupation, involves large issues. For example: to what degree was the balance of work in Britain altered between active, exertive, labour, and sedentary employment, during the period of industrialization? And to what extent did that require, and to what extent was it permitted by, the adoption of the white loaf as the staple food of the masses? Those issues are somewhat different in kind to the question recently posed by Dr Beckaert, as to whether the *amount* of food available to workers dictated the different pace of industrialization across Europe:[65] they concern quality as well as quantity. But probably, the extensive research that Beckaert calls for would help to provide answers on both counts, though help only to a degree. Because qualitative analysis will depend on the definition of the terms 'active' and 'sedentary', which are of course relative, and in the case of agricultural work, perhaps seasonally variable; and on the view taken of different kinds of occupation, as to whether they were principally of one sort or another. 'Outdoor' versus 'indoor' might be a useful guideline in some respects, but not in all. Bakers, for example, worked indoors with little remittance, but dough-making especially was heavy work.[66] Latter-day attempts at classification have stumbled on the same obstacle: bus and truck drivers, for instance, have a literally sedentary occupation, but their work involves considerable exertion.[67]

Analysis is further complicated by the absence of reliable, detailed, occupational data for Britain before the 1831 census, and thereafter by the aggregation of different kinds of work under each occupational heading. Consequently, I have made only the crudest attempt to indicate the shifting balance of heavy and sedentary work during the century in review (see Appendix 4), to suggest, with every caveat, that if *c*1800 there were two 'heavy' workers to every one 'sedentary' worker, then by *c*1860 those proportions may have been reversed.

A possible guide to the cost-efficiency of, and absolute need for, white bread as the staple of a sedentarily occupied workforce is its relative importance in towns, over many centuries and in various parts of Europe. Detailed analysis of pre-modern and non-British material is beyond the scope of this book, but some selective observations might be made. Dyer, for instance, notes that 'wheat bread was eaten in towns at all times, even in the thirteenth century'.[68] True, there were 'brown' bakers in London as elsewhere, though their separate guilds largely disappeared in the 16th and 17th centuries; however, such bakers may have engaged partly or chiefly in the making of 'horsebread' – cakes of animal feed.[69] Wheat bread was the staple of the urban poor in 18th century France.[70] Elsewhere, 'whiteness' was somewhat obscured by the practice of mixing wheat flour with the flours of other grains. As Pounds notes, the bread sold at Venice in 1764 was 84.5 per cent wheat; in other Italian cities it was two-thirds wheat; but in the countryside only one-third wheat; in Amsterdam and Rotterdam the bread was 70 to 75 per cent wheat, though that proportion was much less in the smaller Dutch towns.[71] The 'rye bread' of Warsaw, *c*1846, was a maslin with a very high wheat content,[72] perhaps not dissimilar to German *volksbrot*, which is mostly wheat.[73] Of course, even where wheat bread was sold, it may not have been available to working people: in Scandinavian towns in the mid-19th century, for example, white or mixed bread with a large wheat content was a luxury affordable only by the better off.[74] And the need of artisans for a more digestible food may have meant that potatoes were substituted for the coarser grains, if wheat was unavailable or too expensive,[75] thus further complicating enquiry.

Perhaps the best available indicators of the value of and need for white bread are the claims and observations of contemporaries. They are discussed next.

2.4   PERCEIVED VALUE

To argue that, when 'physical costs' and the calories obtained per penny are roughly calculated, the wheat loaf, and the best Wheaten grade especially, was good value compared to other breads, and perhaps the best value for those engaged in sedentary work, does not of course deny other values: of taste and appearance, and of imputed status.

When the poor insisted upon white bread, often it is unclear which of those values, or what combination of them, may have been uppermost in their minds. But arguably, taste, appearance, and status were qualities that at least some proportion of the population would sacrifice for economy, especially in years of dearth, and especially if insistence on white bread brought them into conflict with their employers and authority. Whereas, given bread dependency, the need for adequate nutriment and better value seems a plausible, fundamental and common, justification of the stoutest resistance to substitution. Moreover, had the poor sought to defend, for example, their status above all things, would they not have insisted on a little meat or milk (foods more notably a 'luxury' in many parts) rather than sacrifice them, in hardship, to maintain their consumption of white bread, the food of common folk?[76]

And when the preference of the poor for white bread was explained to the bread committee of the House of Commons, or considered by other parliamentarians, the justification of better nourishment, and therefore value-for-money was most often stressed. Thus, like other contemporaries already cited,[77] Pownall noted the 'reasoned' view of poorer people that brown bread (whether wholemeal wheat or the Household grade specified by the 1757 Act) 'would not feed them'; Egmont recorded the same.[78] In 1767 a London baker testified:

> I have made for 40 years Household Bread and always took out the fine flour first and left the remaining for Household Bread and do

imagine that every pound of the fine flour taken is near half of it the
nourishment and therefore the poor where I live prefer the fine and
say the best is the best cheap.[79]

And he agreed with them: 'fine bread goes furthest and is the cheapest'
(his brown bread was bought only by better off people). He was echoed
by others: the poor understood that coarser bread 'would not go so
far':[80] the London poor were convinced that finer bread supported them
better than coarse.[81] Admittedly, the bakers had a trade interest to
defend, but a Member of Parliament also observed that the poor rejected
brown bread because it was less nutritious (being made from the refuse
of the wheat).[82] And as Arthur Young testified, even Standard Wheaten
bread was rejected by poor husbandmen for its lack of nutriment, and
its diseconomy.[83]

But did the poor, when they justified their preference for white bread,
disguise indulgence, or other motives, by citing economy, if that seemed
more rational or laudable both to the respondent and enquirer? As
Elster has argued, such masking selectivity is normal.[84] Observers, too,
can be selective: economists detect or charitably credit people with
rational motives, whereas sociologists more often invoke tradition,
roles, or norms.[85]. But Elster also argues that beliefs and desires can
hardly be reasons for recurrent action unless they are consistent over
time.[86] And perhaps the most consistent motivations are not 'inten-
tional' but 'functional', that is, biological.[87] This is especially so where
the preferences and actions of a multitude are concerned, since intent
may be highly individualistic, but functions are common.

Basic motivations may not be rational, if that implies an indepen-
dency of judgement; rather they may be better described as, literally,
sensible. Thus Maslow conceived of a 'hierarchy of needs', beginning
with physiological drives (and ascending thereafter, by several stages,
to the ultimate 'self-actualization' of individual personality). In this
system, basic need must first be satisfied before motive-drives can be
switched to the next, higher, need; such switching is instinctive, rather
than a matter of choice. Plausibly enough, hunger concentrates the
mind and must be satisfied before other needs can be entertained.
But Maslow, basing himself on the researches of W G Cannon and
P T Young, argued that not only the fundamental need for food, but the
choice of foods, is physiologically driven: without reasoning, we roughly
conjecture the kind of food that we must have: our choice is a 'fairly
efficient indicator of actual needs or lacks in the body'.[88]

Maslow placed wants, such as preference for quality (for example,
taste and appearance), and the desire for status, high in the hierarchy. If
the basic need for food, and for a kind of food satisfying nutritional
need, is not met, then such superior wants 'may become simply

nonexistent or be pushed into the background', as the mind, involuntarily if not voluntarily, concentrates on first essentials.[89]

So the popular view that white bread was more nutritious and better value may not have masked other motives, but have preceded them, and have represented, more or less accurately, a realization of physiological need. Such physiological sensibility might further be indicated by some plausible, supplementary explanations that contemporaries offered, to justify their demand for white bread. Eden noted that southern labourers insisted on the finest wheat bread because, they said, brown bread disturbed their bowels.[90] And though he himself much doubted it, and condemned improvidence,[91] the association of coarser bread and purging, or diarrhoea, was widely recognized. Hawkesbury reported that labourers used to white bread, if forced by necessity to eat brown, could not work, suffered weakness, and indigestion or nausea.[92] Wickens noted the claim of the poor 'that as they live almost entirely on bread, they cannot perform their tasks without good bread'.[93] Arthur Young had information from several 'hard-working people' that when they were obliged to survive on coarser bread, they had 'not been able to labour with that Force and heartiness which they have found to result from the finer Sorts'.[94] Dumbell acknowledged the decayed capacity for labour, a sinking in health, spirits and temper,[95] results to be expected if a reduction in the quality (as well as the quantity) of bread reduced calorie intake to little more than basal metabolic need. Other poor people (with justification, given the possibility of ergot poisoning) feared that coarser breads were unsafe.

The claims of the poor found further contemporary endorsement. Braudel cites Lemery, in 1702, observing that wheat bread was more nourishing than rye, and considerably more so than barley.[96] The Reverend David Davies argued that, since they depended on it so heavily, labourers ought to have bread of good quality: that barley, oatmeal, and maslin were not so nutritious by weight and therefore were of questionable economy.[97] Fox and Sheridan argued against mixed breads, because they gave less nutriment.[98]

As to the grades of wheat bread, Jonas Hanway accepted that a loaf without bran and pollards was more nutritious, and found that his servants needed to eat less of it than coarser bread.[99] Hanway, who had much influence with the bread committee of the House of Commons, was echoed by its subsequent chairman, Thomas Pownall. However, Pownall,[100] though he accepted that brown bread, including the parliamentary Household grade, was less nutritious and digestible, believed that the poor strayed too far to the other extreme by insisting on the finest white loaves. They could pay somewhat less for a loaf made from flour of 75 per cent rather than 70 per cent extraction, and have all the nutriment, without bran and pollards.[101] Hence his recommendation, accepted by Parliament, that the Standard Wheaten loaf be sold to, and at the discretion of magistrates, be imposed upon, the poor.

Given an option, however, people resisted 'Governor Pownall's bread' as resolutely as they rejected brown. At times, there may have been 'physical' justification in doing so, since Pownall's absolute 75 per cent extraction rate, when applied to poorer grades of wheat, and especially to the inferior qualities generally harvested in years of dearth, admitted an amount of bran and pollards, and had a greater proportion of less digestible 'middlings' or 'sharps'.[102] And in any year, the sallow loaves, with their bluish-grey 'bloom' were suspect. Whiteness was the standard by which the poor, the illiterate (and before wrapping and food-labelling, the literate too) could best judge quality and purity. Often they might be deceived, if perfectly wholesome Standard Wheaten bread was whitened with alum; but it was less easy to disguise a loaf with any bran content: even if whitened successfully, it would be betrayed by its taste.

The nutritional values of the different grades of wheat bread were again examined by the bread committee of the House of Commons, in circumstances of dire emergency (a poor harvest and very high bread prices), in 1800. The bakers, Young, and others mentioned earlier all testified to the popularly perceived merits of white bread, but the enquiry began with a dispute between medical experts. Dr Gilbert Blane emphasized the importance of the gluten in wheat, which he considered to be the chief nutritious constituent (in effect identifying the food value of protein); but believing that much gluten was lost if the outer part of the wheat grain was discarded, he concluded that brown wheat bread was more nutritious than white. Dr Sir Walter Farquhar thought wholemeal bread to be as nutritious as white, but recognized the laxative effect; however, he believed that the public's bowels would settle down in time. But Dr William Mackinen Fraser argued that the laxative effect, and relative indigestibility, of wholemeal bread substantially reduced its food value, and that therefore, white bread was more nutritious. He was supported by Dr John Coakley Lettsom, who further observed that the people would have to eat a greater amount of coarse bread to equal the nutriment obtained from white (though he thought the statutory Household grade would involve no loss).[103]

In its conclusions, the Bread Committee distinguished between those for whom bread was only one of several or many foods (who would suffer no serious nutritional loss from, or perhaps, like the 'better sort of housekeepers' mentioned by one of the bakers, might welcome the purgative effect of, brown bread) as opposed to those 'who have no other Food'. It was firmly of the opinion that those heavily dependent on bread would have to eat more of the coarser sort, and so there would be no saving. On which conclusion, the Bread Committee declined to risk unrest by enforcing the sale of brown bread (even so, in the following year, the Bread Committee bowed to 'informed' opinion and proposed the 'Brown George Act', during the brief and farcical operation of which sales of white bread were forbidden).[104]

The purgative effects of brown bread continued to be valued by the middle classes. At Uxbridge, Mr Swayne sold his browner 'household' bread in the town, charging more for it than for the white bread bought by the country labourers. Eliza Acton strongly recommended breads made from wheat meal and whole meal, which may well have suited her readership.[105]

But so far as the bread-dependent masses were concerned, their unremitting insistence on white bread,[106] witnessed by bakers, acknowledged by the bread committee of the House of Commons, and by a minority of correspondents to the *Annals of Agriculture*,[107] among others, was vindicated by scientific experiment and measurement. Dr Edward Smith concluded his study, noted earlier, by observing that the preference of the poor for finer flour 'was based on sound experience of its nutritive value', so that 'the universal adoption of white flour at the present day' represented sound economy, 'both as regards the cost of food and the nutriment which young and old members of a family can derive from it.'[108]

2.5 DEPENDENCY CONFIRMED

The critics of wheat dependency, especially of mass consumption of white bread, frequently alleged that the poor were the unwilling or unwitting victims of profit-seeking farmers, merchants, millers, and bakers. That mass preference for wheat and particularly white bread was both willing and witting has been discussed in Section 2.4, but undoubtedly that preference was confirmed if not enforced by the operations of the market.

Practical reasons for supplying major markets with white rather than brown flours are given in Section 3.2. Material reasons for buying commercially-baked bread are discussed in Section 3.1. In this section I will concentrate on the larger issue of wheat dependency, to outline the market mechanisms that confirmed such dependency, and to a significant extent, prevented the substitution of other foods for wheat.

Any rise in the demand for rye, barley, and oats for use as food was likely to cause a corresponding rise in price. Parliament attempted to offset this, in years of crisis, by limiting other demands: by banning the distilling of barley, for example, thus freeing large amounts of that grain for consumption as food.[109] Such measures did have effect. Whereas it was the rule of thumb that on average barley should fetch half the price of wheat, and oats a third or so less than barley,[110] during the wartime and dearth years, 1793-1815, the price of other grains did not rise so steeply as the price of wheat. On average, the price of barley 'fell' by 19 per cent proportionate to the price of wheat, the relative price of oats fell by 18 per cent; rye fell too, though gaps in the price data make accurate computation impossible.[111] Prices returned to alignment only after the war, and then, in 'free' conditions, the relative price of wheat began to fall.

Even so, relative prices still represented steep increases in the cost of the other grains, and national averages disguise turbulence in local markets, where exceptional demand for the other grains had intense effects on prices.[112]

A chief obstacle to substitution was the sheer volume of food that would be required to replace wheat bread. Colquhoun estimated that in 1813 British wheat consumption was 9,000,000 quarters,[113] which would amount to roughly 3,960,000,000 lbs of bread. For an idea of scale, if each lb can be represented as a cube of 4.8 inches dimension, then a column made of those cubes would be 300,000 miles high. Of course, the actual challenge posed was not to replace all wheat bread, but perhaps 25 per cent of the demand, to reduce consumption down to what might be produced by a poor domestic harvest. In principle, that challenge might be met by substituting the other grains, which were in constant production (assuming that their harvests were not so badly hit as the wheat harvest), but the difficulty in introducing relatively novel foods was much greater. For instance, one favoured substitute was maize, but that had to be purchased from India, and months elapsed before cargoes could arrive. Rice, where available, might be given in dole to the poor,[114] but supplies came chiefly from the distant Carolinas. To meet sudden deficiencies, it was easier by far to purchase wheat from European suppliers (especially when, given the regularity of that trade, much foreign wheat was available as floating cargo, lying in or not far from British ports).[115]

Domestically-produced supplements, such as vegetables for use in soup, and herrings, presented less difficulty of access, but it was no easy matter to swiftly increase supply by a huge amount. The growers of perishable vegetables, for instance, would hardly risk all in advance of a demand that might, but then again might not, arise. The supply of herrings was governed by the capacity of the fishing fleet (and the difficulty of transporting fresh fish inland). Substitution also was limited in cases by a difference of opinion between authority and its advisers on the one hand, and the people on the other. Soup was strongly recommended by the pioneer nutritionist Count Rumford, as the most economical form of food, and a boon to the poor; but the people rejected these 'windy washes', and wisely so: when later a soup diet was imposed on the inmates of Millbank penitentiary the recipients not surprisingly showed signs of malnutrition, and some died.[116]

To an extent, the supply of potatoes was free from difficulty because, as they fitted well to a wheat-and-livestock regime, they were in constant production. A farm producing its own manure could cheaply fertilize land for potatoes, which in turn would feed both animals and people; also (as some but by no means all farmers believed) potatoes cleaned the soil and prepared it for wheat.[117] By the end of the 18th century the use of potatoes as human food was common in Ireland and in the Highlands. The types raised there were usually of the most prolific and bulky sort, known as 'lumpers'; elsewhere, acceptance of more delicate and flavoursome kinds was limited by the already firm connexion of potatoes with horses and Celts. In most parts of England, the first real spur to potato consumption was the corn dearth of 1795–6, during which Rumford noted with relief that people at large had overcome their prejudice against a useful food. But in the following year, at Clare in Suffolk, the labourers refused potatoes priced at a mere 8d the bushel. Despite the high average price of wheat during the wars, Colquhoun reported that in 1813 potato-eating was still uncommon south of the Trent. Salaman cites eleven contemporary comments to show the resistance to the officially recommended substitute, though he suggested that that resistance slowly dissolved.[118] But, although potatoes could be a more economical crop than wheat, in favourable conditions yielding perhaps twice as much food value per acre, they were an even more fickle crop, with a sixfold price span. At the extreme, as the tragedy of Ireland (and of the Highlands) would show, the potato crop could be all but destroyed by ferocious blight.[119]

Moreover, wheat could be stored indefinitely, whereas potatoes soon withered and lost their nutritional value (even in ideal conditions their maximum storage life was 18 months); also roughly speaking, for the same amount of nutriment, they took up three times the space, whether stored or transported, so that original cheapness soon was eroded; moreover, if sold, wholesale and retail margins further dissipated any economy. Thus, for the potato to be a cheap substitute, normally it had to be eaten near to where it was grown, in the winter, soon after harvest (this can be glimpsed in Eden's case of the Cumberland labourer's family, which spent 8.14 per cent of its budget on potatoes in the winter, but only 3.28 per cent in the late summer/autumn). In years of abundance the potato could be a cheap food for poor urban families, who as Engels noted, ate much potato in 1844; but such abundance eliminated the grower's profit. Nor could the Irish in England be counted as regular potato-eaters – a leading Liverpool merchant stated firmly that they abandoned the habit as soon as they landed: while in Britain the Irish ate wheat bread. Accounts of large quantities of potatoes seen on quays at Manchester and Liverpool may mislead, since much potato was manufactured into starch (releasing the wheat formerly used) for the textile trades.[120]

Thus in most years, commercially-grown potatoes were not a viable substitute for wheat bread, though they might be a useful supplementary, and add some variety to diet. Heavy consumption of the potato was largely restricted to country districts, especially where it displaced rye, barley and oats as a mainstay[121] until the railways brought cheap wheat-flour within the reach of all.[122] Thereafter, British consumption, and English consumption especially, was modest, compared to the level of potato dependency in other countries (see Table 2.11).

Table 2.11   Population related to potato acreage, c1868

	People per acre of potatoes
England	66
Wales	26
Scotland	20
Denmark	20
Belgium	13.5
Holland	13
France	12.5
Sweden	12
Prussia	5.5
Ireland	5.5

Source: Caird: Our Daily Food p 35. Caird noted (p 36) that in Prussia potatoes also were used considerably for distilling, so that the above ratio overstates dependency on them as food.

Paradoxically the potato played some part in the development of the wheat loaf. Although originally proposed as a source of cheap flour (and strongly recommended during the dearth of 1795–6: 12 lbs of potato flour mixed with 20 lbs of wheatflour was said to make 'excellent' bread) the recommendation was sanguine, and even *The Times*, normally optimistic, had to admit that the two flours did not mix. Later, however, it was found that the chief, and excellent, role of the potato as a breadstuff was in the mash that controlled the action of yeast on wheatflour, and its use as such became commonplace from the 1820s.[123]

In sum, dependency on wheat was not only justified, on apparent cost efficiency grounds, but reinforced by the difficulties of substitution in any degree. Whatever the economic difficulties caused by such dependency, for both positive and negative reasons wheat remained the staple of the British people till the transformation of world food markets after 1870.

Notes

1. See below, Chapter 8.
2. Adam Smith pp 68, 86; Bain p 26; Bairoch p 453; Braudel pp 104–5. See also comparative prices at Florence 1610–19 cited by Livi–Bacci pp 85–6; Offer p 25.
3. Eden p 101.
4. Burnett: P & W p 41; Edward Smith: Practical Dietary pp 43–4; idem: Foods p 177; Tannahill p 96; Copley 61.
5. McCance & Widdowson pp 39, 41.
6. Eden pp 103–4; Burnett: P & W p 41; Edward Smith: Practical Dietary pp 43–4; idem: Foods p 177; David p 528; General Foods: Grape Nuts pack.
7. The Artful Dodger in *Oliver Twist*, p 101.
8. Jasny pp 35–49; Edward Smith: Foods p 179.
9. Comments to author by Mr Ian Barrett MBE.
10. Camporesi: Bread of Dreams; Drummond & Wilbraham p 298.
11. Tannahill p 96; Records of Buckinghamshire XI p 142; Wentworth p 305; David pp 296–8.
12. Jasny pp 54–66; Walsh p 276.
13. Tannahill p 96; Johnson cit Longmate p 3; Ashton: Changes p 174.
14. King pp 53, 67; Sir Charles Smith pp 139–40.
15. Silvester pp 10–12.
16. Hodson p 26; Sir Charles Smith p 182; Orbell: thesis p 2; D Davies p 49; Barnes pp 40, 73, 74, 78; Galpin p 23.
17. See Table 2.1.
18. Bennett, Dyer, cit Mennell pp 41–2; Young cit Salaman p 480.
19. Hogarth cit Drummond & Wilbraham p 272; Thwaites: thesis pp 323–4, 327, 332; Eden p 136.
20. Mountmorres p 13; Bevan, Poole, Olney cit Salaman p 505.
21. Turton p 84.
22. Mowbray cit Salaman p 506.
23. eg Young: Six Months Tour, Vol II pp 144, 204, 208, 214, 232.
24. 2nd Report of the House of Lords communicated to the House of Commons, HoC Sessional Papers vol 131, 22.12.1800; G: Pam Fo 3426; S&B Webb: Assize p 210.

25. Galpin pp 57–9.
26. G: Ms 7801 2/2 – letter from York.
27. Stern p 183.
28. Majendie cit Salaman p 505; B Thompson: *Essay on Food*.
29. Burke p 5.
30. D Davies p 31; Lord Sheffield cit Salaman p 505; *The Times* cit Stern p 183; HoC Sessional Papers vol 131 Cd 4983, 10.2.1800, p 35 – Scott; Thomas Butts cit Salaman p 505; G M Trevelyan cit David p 6.
31. Stern pp 183–4.
32. Barnes pp 74–5; E P Thompson: Moral Economy pp 80–2.
33. HoC Sessional Papers vol 131 Cd 5101, 18.11.1800, p 15.
34. Edlin p 122.
35. Edlin p 103; G: Pam Fo 3426.
36. Calculated from Mitchell p 756.
37. Edlin p 103.
38. David pp 296–8; Edward Smith: Practical Dietary p 48; Edlin pp 105–6.
39. Jasny p 41.
40. Jasny pp 45–6.
41. Edward Smith: Practical Dietary pp 46–8.
42. Edward Smith: Practical Dietary pp 37, 49; idem: Foods p 179; HoC Sessional Papers vol 131 Cd 4983, 10.2.1800, p 13 – Loveland; David p 45; Barker, Oddy & Yudkin p 29.
43. Mountmorres p 12.
44. Livi–Bacci p 23.
45. Jago pp 101–2; Blandy p 152.
46. eg Floud, Wachter, & Gregory: Height, Health and History; Beckaert: Calorie Consumption; and Shammas: Pre–Industrial Consumer, op cit.
47. Shammas: Pre–Industrial Consumer p 137 and note 26 on pp 153–4; see also Yudkin in Oddy & Miller (eds) p 198.
48. Drummond & Wilbraham p 286.
49. Offer pp 39–53.
50. Widdowson in McCance & Widdowson p 322.
51. Jasny p 43.
52. eg Edlin pp 109, 122.
53. Comment to author by Mr Ian Barrett MBE.
54. cit Ashley p 164.
55. Shammas: Pre–Industrial Consumer p 135.
56. MAFF Manual of Nutrition p 19.
57. See Beckaert p 647.
58. See Table 2.4.
59. McCulloch p 193.
60. Clarke & Herbert p 228.
61. Thwaites: thesis p 332; Willoughby cit Thwaites: thesis p 324; Curzon cit Thwaites: thesis p 325.
62. HoC Sessional Papers vol 131 Cd 4983, 10.2.1800, pp 13–14 – Loveland, p 15 – Urquhart, p 18 – Crichton; Cd 5080, 1.7.1800, p 28 – Loveland; Stern p 183.
63. Ashley p 165.
64. Ashton: Changes p 173.
65. Beckaert p 639.
66. See Chapter 3 Section 3.

67. Damon & McFarland p 272 et seq.
68. Dyer p 197.
69. R C Anderson: The Assize of Bread Book 1477–1517, Southampton 1923 p v.
70. Grantham pp 64–6.
71. Pounds p 174.
72. PP XLIV (7) 31, HoC 29.1.1846.
73. Comment to author by Mr Ian Barrett MBE.
74. PP XLIV (7) 31, HoC 29.1.1846.
75. See Beckaert pp 635–6; see below, Chapter 2 Section 5.
76. I am grateful to Dr Offer for this observation.
77. See above, Chapter 2 Section 1.
78. Pownall pp 10, 26; [Egmont] p 28.
79. CLRO: MSS 117.4 – testimony of Caleb Jacock.
80. HoC Sessional Papers vol 131 Cd 4983, 10.2.1800, p 17.
81. G: Ms 7801 2/2 – Smith.
82. HoC Sessional Papers vol 131 Cd 4983, 10.2.1800, p 43 – Savile.
83. HoC Sessional Papers vol 131 Cd 4983, 10.2.1800, pp 37–8 – Young.
84. Elster: Ulysses pp 77, 114.
85. Elster: Ulysses pp 137, 154.
86. Elster: Sour Grapes p 4.
87. Elster: Ulysses p 1.
88. Maslow pp 35–6, also cited by Fieldhouse p 25.
89. Maslow pp 37–8.
90. Eden p 208.
91. Eden p 100.
92. cit E P Thompson: Moral Economy p 81.
93. Wickens cit Salaman p 505.
94. HoC Sessional Papers vol 131 Cd 4983, 10.2.1800, p 37.
95. [Dumbell] p 5.
96. Braudel p 110.
97. D Davies p 33.
98. Stern p 183.
99. CLRO: Misc MSS 171.8, 3.2.1768.
100. Pownall p 5.
101. HoC Sessional Papers vol 25 Cd 3144, 21.12.1772.
102. HoC Sessional Papers volume 131 Cd 4983, p 24 – Pratt.
103. HoC Sessional Papers vol 131 Cd 4983, 10.2.1800, pp 11–13; Lettsom also cited by [Turton] p 85.
104. HoC Sessional Papers vol 131 Cd 4983, 10.2.1800, pp 3–10; Orbell: thesis p 2; also E. P. Thompson Moral Economy p 82.
105. Acton: English Bread Book (1857) pp 53, 76, 88.
106. Mayhew cit David p 49.
107. Salaman p 525.
108. PP VI (212) 465, HoC 8.4.1824, p 14 – Huntsman, p 16 – Swayne; Acton p 88; Edward Smith: Foods p 175; idem: P D p 48, but see Wentworth pp 302–5; Adam Smith p 74; Jasny p 43.
109. Barnes p 38.
110. PP 1814–5 V (26) 1035, HoL/HoC 23.11.1814, p 19 – Wakefield, p 59 – Custance.
111. Calculated from price data in Ag H of E & W VI, Table I.1, pp 974–5.

112. Thwaites: thesis p 333; Braudel p 111.
113. Colquhoun p 89.
114. Thwaites: thesis p 338.
115. Fairlie: 1965 p 563.
116. HoC Sessional Papers vol 131 Cd 4989, 6.3.1800; Cd 4990, 6.3.1800; PP I/2 312, HoC 23.2.1801; Girdler p 68; Drummond & Wilbraham pp 261, 306–7, 436–7.
117. PP I part 2 item 12, HoC 23.2.1801 – 2nd Report; VIII/I (79) 1, HoC 4.3.1836, Q 57, 183; Pelto & Pelto in Rotberg & Rabb (eds): H & H p 314; HoC Sessional Papers vol 131 Cd 4989, 6.3.1800; Cd 4990, 6.3.1800.
118. Colquhoun p 11, note; O Grada p 24; Salaman pp 368, 493, 505–6, 613; B. Thompson: *Essay on Food* pp 9, 44.
119. Edward Smith: Practical Dietary p 56; Adam Smith p 73; McCulloch n p 468 in 1853 ed of Adam Smith; PP IX (668) 1, HoC 18.6.1821, p 43 – Wakefield.
120. PP I/2 item 12, HoC 23.2.1801 – 2nd Report; VIII/I (79) 1, HoC 4.3.1836: Q 3079, 6011; XXVIII (3416) 1, HMSO 1864, Appendix VI, p 246; Edward Smith: Practical Dietary p 57; O Grada p 27; Eden p 166.
121. Sinclair p 262, Appendix p 41.
122. Bacon p 263.
123. Salaman p 504; Stern p 184.

CHAPTER 3

Milling and Baking

The benefits of the wheat loaf might have been offset, or imperfectly realized, had it not been for the development of the milling and baking trades. Though the loaf is a highly convenient and efficient form of food, it is inconvenient to make. Commercial millers and bakers eliminated that disadvantage to consumers, producing what was in effect the first mass-produced convenience product.[1]. Also, and for town dwellers especially, bought bread was probably better value than home-baked.

3.1 THE CASE FOR BOUGHT BREAD

There are four main stages in the making of loaves: grinding the grain into meal, dressing the meal into flour, mixing the flour with water, yeast, and salt to make the dough, and then kneading, dividing and baking.

All those functions could be undertaken by the individual (or family or community). Grain might be ground manually either (as anciently) in a hollowed stone, by pounding or squeezing with a hand-held stone or wooden pestle (Bennett and Elton knew of a hollowed stone of this type on Colonsay, that was in use till the mid-19th century), or by using the more sophisticated quern; or else by using a rotary handmill, favoured in some middle-class homes throughout the century in review. The resulting meal could be hand-sieved to give flours of varying qualities, then mixed into a dough and kneaded and baked in a bread oven of the type commonly found in farmhouses and in or outside cottages.[2]

Home sufficiency was strongly advocated by popular writers, among them William Cobbett, Mrs Copley, Mrs Rundell, and Eliza Acton,[3] and often by correspondents to the newspapers. Grinding grain at home was held to be economical; also, the consumer could decide the grain used (its type and quality).[4] Dressing your own flour allowed for individual preference, as to fineness, and was a safeguard against adulteration.

Also, it was claimed that the householder could obtain more bread per measure of flour than that allowed by the baker; and that home-made loaves staled less quickly. Even without such benefits, by saving the profits of miller and baker, home-made loaves were cheaper.[5] Or so it seemed.

44

The case for economical home-baking can hardly be doubted where households obtained their grain or flour free or at a discount, where fuel was plentiful, and obtained at low or nil cost, and where there were ample supplies of clean water. Even so, there might be some difficulty in obtaining salt, and more in finding yeast. The scarcity of the latter, in the countryside, 'might mean that loaves were unleavened or more akin to soda bread.'[6]

But where households had to buy most, or all, of the necessaries, probably the balance of advantage lay with commercially baked bread.

First, because if bought daily, commercial bread was fresh. And being fresh, it was more easily digested and absorbed by the system, and thus had the highest net energy value.[7]

The home baker, using the typical cottage oven (of beehive shape, lined with 2.5 inch thick bricks, or in Scotland, built of foot-thick stones, designed to retain and radiate heat), with a capacity for say 56 lbs of bread, could in one batch satisfy the weekly need of say eight individuals each consuming 7 lbs. To make less was probably an uneconomic use of time and effort, and where it was scarce, of fuel. And though home-baked bread was said to stale less quickly, as the week progressed it would steadily age to a rock-hard density. On the other hand, the commercial baker, with an oven capacity of approximately 600 lbs, could satisfy the same rate of consumption of 600 individuals per fresh daily batch.[8]

Apart from its greater nutritional value, fresh bread might be the only warm food eaten by a poor family (at least, on a weekday), though the frugal (and some of the middle class, on medical advice[9]) denied the benefit to themselves (and their children), on the well-observed grounds that more bread was eaten when warm, for pleasure, than when cold.[10] Eating bread fresh also avoided the hazard of mould.

Second, in many cases, the baker may have used breadstuffs generally of better quality and greater consistency. The householder, receiving free or discounted wheat or flour, or buying in the marketplace, would be limited to the sorts locally available at any time. The baker, dealing with factors and mealmen, had a wider choice; and if buying ready-made flour, could use grades mixed to a relatively constant standard by the commercial miller. Also, by buying in bulk (typically 1500 to 3500 lbs of flour weekly, as against perhaps 28 to 42 lbs used by a home-baker), in principle the baker saved considerably, especially compared to the householder buying small amounts of flour from chandlers, and paying their retail margin.[11]

Similarly, by buying wholesale, the commercial baker could make savings on candles (needed, even in daylight, to inspect the oven), salt, fuel, and yeast, a commodity that it was difficult to get other than by way of trade. The home-baker might try Mrs Rundell's recipe for an ersatz yeast, 'but to the inexperienced the detail was still inadequate'. The first reliable recipe for a home-made yeast was given only in 1845, by Eliza Acton.[12] Another necessary (though officially it was an adulterant) was alum, which the trade could obtain by circumspect means. Alum artificially whitened darker bread (hence its proscription), but another of its uses was as a flocculent, to clarify and cleanse water (which often was muddy or polluted, especially in towns). It also 'dried' damp wheat or flour, to make it fit for use, an inestimable benefit when the harvest was poor and also it shortened the 'settling' time needed before new flour could be used.

Third, a further benefit of volume throughput was fuel economy. Apart from buying wood and coal in bulk, the baker's main saving was that, since his oven never or rarely cooled, and because he was likely to bake a full batch of bread every time, he used fuel economically. The demands of an ordinary household, being satisfied by one batch weekly, meant that if the oven was lit specially, and then allowed to cool, the diseconomy was considerable (it might be offset if the family used the oven for warmth also, but that was unlikely in summer). And, by 1800, commercial oven designs were improved, to incorporate a separate coal burning chamber, from which hot air was carried by a flue around the back of the main oven, heating the bricks to, and then maintaining, the requisite ambient temperature (wood faggots still were used in the main oven, for immediate heat). Special coals (coloquially 'bakers' nuts') that burned quickly and gave off furious heat, were sold for the purpose.[13]

The urban baker's advantage can be seen most clearly where the cost of fuel can be isolated, as in the charge made for cooking the public's dinners. In 1804 a London baker would cook a dinner for 1d or 1.5d when it was estimated that the cost of cooking the same at home was 6d. Even after fuel prices fell, and when the differential between the cost of a dinner cooked at the baker's, or at home, was reduced to 2d or 3d, the ordinary public still patronized the bakehouses, at least in the summer.[14]

Even in well-wooded areas of the south-east, such as Kent, fuel could be scarce, since it was 'harvested' on a commercial basis and sold to hop-farmers, shipbuilders, or to the London wholesalers.[15] Elsewhere, especially in the southern and eastern counties, traditional rights of wood-gathering were circumscribed or suppressed, once land was enclosed. Thus the number of commercial bakers, serving country districts, increased as fuel became scarce.[16]

And in the northern and Scottish cities, where the tradition of home-baking was strong and fuel was likelier to be plentiful, it was common (in Manchester, Sheffield, and Newcastle-upon-Tyne, for instance) for housewives to make their own dough, but take it to a public cookhouse for baking (elsewhere, commercial bakers gave the same service, typically charging 0.5d for baking a quartern loaf).[17] And the high density of commercial bakers in much of Scotland indicates that the buying in of bread was common.

Fourth, although bread-making held few mysteries of principle, success was heavily reliant on experience and skill. The temperamental behaviour of dough (especially in warmer weather), the correct heating of a brick oven, and other vagaries, make the difference between a good and a ruined batch. The experienced commercial baker was less likely to fail. Also, kneading dough is heavy work, but it has to be done thoroughly if flour is to 'take' its proper amount of water (and white flour has to take more water than brown). Since most commercial bakers were men, and most home-bakers were women, the trade had somewhat greater strength in its favour: where a gender comparison could be made in identical circumstances, at 'a large public establishment', men were able to produce approximately 10 per cent more bread from the same amount of flour. There must have been exceptions, but only to prove the rule of the 'superior physical strength and skill of the men'.[18] And the greater the yield, the lighter the texture, and the more digestible the bread (though, probably because commercial bakers could force more water in, their bread staled more quickly; however, that was of no account where loaves were bought daily).

Fifth, if a commercial baker did ruin a batch, or if any loaves in his batch were underbaked, he paid the cost. Bakers were answerable at law for the quality and full weight of their loaves. Although the enforcement of the bread acts varied according to the strength, integrity, and experience of local agencies (particularly the bakers' corporations, which in this respect acted as auxiliaries of the magistrates), all bakers were potentially prey to informers, and penalties for infraction were severe. Nor, wherever bread was assized, did the bakers set their own prices or, for the most part, determine their own profits. The operations of the assize are discussed in Chapter 4, but here it is appropriate to note that magistrates could restrain prices to some extent, and that bakers had to pay the fluctuating costs of fuel, yeast, candles, salt, and other incidentals, from fixed allowances.

In many assized jurisdictions during the Revolutionary and Napoleonic wars, bakers were squeezed severely, to the benefit of their customers. Until relieved by increased allowances (in London in 1797 and 1805, and in the provinces in 1813) assized bakers had to absorb the increased costs of the necessaries of their trade. During the war the price of fuel rose rapidly: a hundred spokes of wood cost 14s 0d in London in 1797, 15s 0d in 1798, 18s 0d in 1802, and £1 in 1804; by

1813 the same amount cost 22s 6d in Bristol and 25s 0d in Oxfordshire; coal also doubled in price, at least, off the coal fields.[19] Yeast rose from 1s 10d a gallon in 1797 to 2s 6d in 1804, then to 3s 4d generally in 1813; salt tripled in price, from 10–13s per cwt to 35–36s (though part of that increase was owed to a wartime tax, and an offset was allowed to the commercial baker). The cost of candles increased from 6s 6d for the cheapest sort, per dozen pounds, to 13s 6d by 1813.[20] Between 1797 and 1804 alone, the London bakers' income from bread fell by about 41 per cent (before rent, which also had increased, was paid); that meant, in effect, that the prices of loaves that year were artificially reduced by more than 3 per cent,[21] which may seem a small fraction, but on average it represented a saving of about 14s 6d over the year to a family of six.[22] If the baker could stay in business with margins so squeezed, he offered a bargain to the public for enough years to surely diminish any surviving preference for home-baking.

However, the advocates of home-baking still claimed an economy. Esther Copley estimated that even when fuel was dear the home-baker could produce a bushel of bread at a net cost (taking a particular year's prices) of 10s 6d as against a current baker's price of 11s 9.75d. The apparent worth of the saving, then, was about 11 per cent. But Mrs Copley did not charge for her labour or incidentals, nor allow for wastage and failure.[23]

The value of convenience was substantial. All the processes of bread-making involved gruelling work, and mess as well as waste (which also attracted rats, mice, and cockroaches). Such disadvantages might not deter the mistress of a middle-class household, who could delegate inconveniences to her staff: bread-making usually was the chore of the second kitchen-maid. However, a poorer housewife, if relieved of the chore, was free for other work, possibly a paying occupation. Her time was too valuable, said Dodd of the London wife, and others could do the work better than she could herself; thus the saved opportunity cost represented a considerable reduction in the price of bought bread.[24]

Over time, it became less easy for a majority of people to make their own bread.

As town populations expanded, many of the working classes were packed into tenements which lacked ovens, or certainly, purpose-built bread ovens. Poorer or small families might use a 'Dutch oven' (an open box lined with reflective metal, set facing the fire), though results were less dependable; in any case, few families would keep a fire in summer, unless they needed one for their work.

Nor were the newer artisans' houses, in their terraced rows, suited to bulky bread ovens of the traditional sort. They, like middle-class houses, were likely to have all-metal ranges; and though the manufacturers included 'bread ovens', those were notably less reliable than the older type, tending to bake the bread too dry, or burn it.[25]

Even in the countryside, as bakers' bread became commonly available, fewer cottage ovens were built; old ones, if rarely used, were torn out to give more space.[26] Thus, both in town and country, the first essential of good home-baked bread, the right oven, steadily disappeared. And as it did so, so disappeared the skilled home-baker.

Edward Smith's surveys show that, because in most places baker's bread was cheaper, by the 1860s a 'surprisingly large' percentage of bread was bought rather than home-baked. The buyers were not only, as he had expected, women who worked the whole day in income-producing trades but farm labourers' families in the country as a whole, where bought bread was predominant in 30 per cent of cases and an adjunct in 50 per cent.[27]

Lack of practice and application affected not only the working class, but the middle class too: Eliza Acton complained that it was near impossible to find servants who knew how to bake bread. Hence 'the heavy, or bitter, or ill-baked masses of dough, which appear at table under the name of *household* or *home-made* bread', which were 'well calculated to create the distaste which they often excite for everything which bears its name . . .'[28]

As home-baking lessened, so the retail market for ingredients declined, to the point that those who might still want to make their own bread found it difficult to obtain necessaries. It was almost impossible, in many places, for the public to buy grain in small amounts.[29] If grain could be obtained, often commercial millers refused to grind it, since small batches disrupted their efficient working.[30] And few brewers would sell yeast at retail; fuel in handfuls might be unobtainable. Thus the trend to commercial milling and baking was to some extent self-propelling, and self-consolidating.

In the institutional sector, the decision to mill and bake in-house, or contract-out, was governed largely by volume. As a rule the armed forces milled their own grain (or bought meal at contract prices from appointed suppliers), and had their own bakers, usually former journeymen who had served their apprenticeships.[31] Prisons, work-houses, and asylums might employ their inmates on gruelling tasks – on the treadmill, grinding grain, for instance – simply to employ, exhaust, or punish them, without much thought for labour efficiency. But since larger institutions had a great demand for bread, often their bakehouses were models of efficiency, employing master bakers and trained journeymen.[32]

However, smaller institutions that could not justify the cost of their own mill or bakehouse bought from commercial millers and bakers, either by frequent competitive tender (as at Abingdon almshouse) or on long-term contract. Those institutions that could not afford the cost of employing bakers might use their own inmates to make bread, but if they were unskilled, the costs (as with home-baking) could be considerably higher than trade prices. Eden noted the case of the Norwich workhouse, where baker's bread proved far superior to, and cheaper than, that previously made in the workhouse oven.[33]

3.2 FLOUR PRODUCTION

Needless to say, for a fourfold increase in wheat bread demand to be satisfied, during the century in review, the supplying trades had to expand in step. Such expansion was greatly helped by qualitative changes in flour production. Commercial mills were among the principal factories of the new age; and corn-milling was at the 'cutting-edge' of technological development, in machinery-design and the application of steam-power. However, since commercial output was directed mainly to the cities and towns, it did not necessarily displace traditional methods and small-scale production in the countryside. Dr Orbell thinks it probable that in 1800 there were more than 20,000 grain mills in Britain (that is, roughly one mill to every 525 inhabitants), though some of those were probably derelict, or used only at certain times of the year; his detailed study of Derbyshire, the East Riding of Yorkshire, Nottinghamshire and Suffolk, suggests a ratio of one mill to every 859 inhabitants. In round terms, an overall distribution of one operating corn mill per thousand people would seem safe.[34]

Up to the 1830s, almost all the flour used in Britain for wheat bread was home-produced: only in exceptional years did imports account for more than 1 per cent of estimated requirements. Taking the period 1771–1814 as a whole, imported flour contributed about 0.5 per cent of the wheat breadstuff total (and in the 1770s and 1780s Britain was a net exporter of milled wheat,[35] perhaps most being low-quality meal for ship's biscuits). After 1831, though the contribution of imports (comparing UK statistics to the estimated British wheat breadstuff requirement) significantly increased, by far the larger part of meal and flour still was home-produced as shown in Table 3.1.

Traditional Flour Production

The traditional miller was not a manufacturing principal but the provider of a local service. He had little or no control over his product, but ground whatever corn was brought to him, charging a toll (in kind,

Table 3.1 UK imports of flour as percentage of estimated British wheat breadstuff requirement, annual averages by decade, 1831–40 – 1861–70

Decade	Flour imports (breadstuff equivalent) Imp qrs*	Volume of wheat used for bread m Imp qrs**	Imports as % of total	Home-produced as % of total
1831–40	176,633	9.8	1.8	98.2
1841–50	719,187	11.5	6.3	93.7
1851–60	1,170,893	13.9	8.4	91.6
1861–70	1,514,665	15.8	9.6	90.4

* Calculated from PP 1878–9 LXV (210) 421, HoC 27.5.1879 p 3, estimating 1 cwt of flour to be the breadstuff equivalent of 0.31 Imperial quarters of wheat, given a 75% extraction rate (Kirkland p 15), thus 112 lbs divided by 480 lbs of wheat per quarter x 133%).
** See Chapter 8.

later in cash). Usually he only turned grain into meal: it was then for his customers (whether private individuals or commercial bakers) to dress that meal into flour, should they choose to do so. But, since dressing was arduous work (the meal had to be shaken through a hand-held sieve or *teme*), the miller might undertake the task for an extra charge (or he kept the bran and pollards for his pigs and hens, or else resold them).[36]

Rarely was he his own master. The typical mill was an integral part of the agrarian economy, a utility necessary to farming, and so normally it was built by the landowner and operated by his servant or by a tenant, often on a part-time basis.[37]

Typically, too, the traditional mill did not compete but supplied a 'closed' service to the estate or parish, its franchise protected either by right of property or by convention (it was generally understood that one rural mill should not trespass upon the territory of another). Such monopoly could still be reinforced by the ancient landowner's right (*soke*) to compel his tenants to bring all their grain to his mill, and to none other, nor to grind their own grain (using handmills or querns). Bizarre as it may seem, in the age of *laissez-faire*, and even after the repeal of the Corn Laws, there were parts of Britain, including some of its chief industrial cities, where such sokes were still enforced.[38]

Few traditional millers set a commercial price for their services. Until 1796, many still charged a toll-in-kind, which might vary with the means of their clients or according to local custom: in England the toll might be from a sixteenth to a twenty-fourth of the meal. In Scotland, tolls distinguished *knaveship* (the miller's own earning) from *thirlage* (the landlord's due), the two together amounting to as much as a ninth or as little as a thirtieth. Also in Scotland, unground grain was subject to *abstracted mulcture*: compensation for what otherwise would have been taken at the mill; that toll generally ran to a seventeenth.[39] In 1796, as part of its continuing reform of the truck system, Parliament abolished such tolls in kind, compelling all millers to take their fees in cash. From the millers' standpoint, this reform was untimely: mill fees seem to have lagged far behind grain prices in the following two decades. Orbell detects a rise from 4d per bushel in Kent in 1775, Westmorland in 1794 and Suffolk in 1808, to 6d in Essex in 1812 and in Kent by 1814[40] – well below the increase in wheat, and modest compared to inflation in general. What is significant about the rise from 4d to 4.5d agreed by fifteen Suffolk millers in 1808 is that they had held to their old charge through so many inflationary years.[41]

In towns and cities, where the great majority of inhabitants were dependent upon the market for their breadstuffs, there was less sense in the consumer being a grain-holding principal and the miller his hireling; both volume-need and freedom of choice favoured the commercial supply of flour and meal from many sources. Also, comparative advantage might determine that those sources be further afield. In larger towns, especially those with a variety of industries (such as textile production), which were also dependent on water-power, the competition for mill sites often was intense.[42] Wind-power might be an option, though as a rule, windmills had roughly half the power and therefore throughput capacity of watermills: and again, there was likely to be fierce competition for the best sites, especially when their number could reduce, as a town grew and tall buildings blocked the wind. Thus scarce urban mill sites might best be employed in manufacturing goods which could then be profitably exchanged for grain ground elsewhere. Otherwise, if grain was milled in or near the city, the probably high rental of sites was a powerful incentive to design and operate mills to the highest standard of efficiency.[43]

Considerable ingenuity was applied to the configuration of mills,[44] and to the development of more efficient machinery: improvements in gearing and other sophistications meant that a 'state-of-the-art' mill in the 1780s could achieve about 2.5 times more output from the same head of water as its old-fashioned counterpart.[45]

The Mechanization of Flour Production

Judged by its impact upon the structure of the trade the most significant innovation of all was a prosaic device, introduced into Britain probably towards the end of the 17th century: the automatic sieve or boulter, agitated by the mill's machinery. The boulter transformed the production of flour:[46] no longer was it necessary to shake meal through a *teme*; a hard task was eliminated, and flour (that otherwise would have been lost in spillage, or blown off as dust) was saved, in the self-enclosed boulter box. The mechanization of flour production was achieved at quite trivial cost: from £15 to £20 to install a boulter, with insignificant additional operating charges.[47]

Automatic flour production need not necessarily have changed the miller's standing: he might have charged an additional fee for boulting, as before he had charged for hand-sieving. But instead, the millers supplying the towns soon evolved into principals, exchanging the lowly status of hireling for that of capitalist-manufacturer. Increasingly, such millers bought wheat on their own account, from whatever sources they chose, and converted it into ready-made flours, which they then marketed, chiefly to the baking trade.

Since he now had control over the quality of his product, the commercial miller could establish his own standards for flour: competition defied uniformity. Effectively, the millers offered their own brands, differently named, albeit the distinctions might be fine, especially to untutored observers. Even the names of the approximate grades differed, not only from place to place and from time to time, but in the same place and at the same time. As late as 1856–7, for instance, while Eliza Acton gave the names of the grades common in London as whites, best households, seconds, wheat-meal, whole-meal, and sharps, George Dodd referred to firsts, seconds, and thirds.[48] Thirds sometimes were called middlings, divisible into fine and coarse qualities.[49] And confusingly, as Lord Egmont complained, 'households' flour made white bread, whereas dark 'Household' bread was made from coarser flours.[50] The following synthesis and simplification is a rough working guide:

Main types of flour

> *whites*: fine extractions from best quality wheat, generally reserved for pastries and bread rolls, but also used to make 'parliamentary' White loaves between 1708 and 1758.

> *firsts* (or best households): fine extractions (70 per cent or less) of good quality wheat, the principal flour for making Wheaten (or colloquially, white) bread.

> *seconds* (or second households or Standard Wheaten): medium extractions (75 per cent roughly) of good quality wheat, which might be mixed with firsts for Wheaten bread, or used as the principal flour of the Standard Wheaten bread specified by the 1772 Act.

thirds (or third households, or fine middlings): coarse extractions (up to 80 per cent) of good quality wheat, or medium extractions of middling qualities, which might be mixed with seconds or some firsts, to make Standard Wheaten bread, or else used entire to make Household bread; also used for ships' biscuits.

fourths, coarse middlings, sharps: usually flinty particles left after the flours proper were extracted, which might be mixed with seconds or thirds to make 'economical' versions of Standard Wheaten or Household bread; but usually used for ships' biscuits.

wheatmeal or millstone: the undressed meal of the whole grain after bran and pollards had been removed (in effect, the unsieved version of seconds' flour).

wholemeal: the undressed meal of the whole grain with bran and pollards ground in. Produced the coarsest brown loaves, otherwise used for biscuits, or cakes of animal feed.

Flour manufacturing was far advanced by the middle of the 18th century.[51] A modern trade emerged, as the rising commercial miller accumulated capital, or acquired the confidence of investors. Capital was deployed in several ways.

First, and obviously, it allowed the miller to compete for prime sites, and to build the most efficiently conceived mills, larger in size and laid out for optimum production flow. Gross investment in corn milling may have quadrupled between 1751 and 1821, from about £3m (taking the average of Orbell's high and low estimates) to about £12m. And though the average investment was small (if there were 20,000 corn mills in Britain in 1800, then the gross investment in each averaged something between £370 and £460), that figure aggregates the many parochial mills with the commercial sort, which more typically would be worth £1000 or more: Abbot's Mill at Canterbury was rebuilt in 1791 for £8000.[52]

Second, capital financed continuing improvements in milling technique, for example the introduction from France, in the 1760s, of the double-grinding technique, whereby wheat first was ground with the stones set quite apart, and then reground finely, with the stones close together. Double-grinding further simplified dressing, by doing much of the preliminary work.[53]

Third, the commercial miller could deploy working capital to build stocks of wheat, buying from far afield. The sourcing, mixing, and supply of wheat and meal, for the supply of London especially, was a sophisticated commerce even in medieval times; therefore the rising commercial miller often subsumed the functions of established specialists, such as corn mongers (or 'badgers') and chandlers, and mealmen.[54] He might deal with principal merchants or factors, or directly with farmers, making bulk purchases either by *contract note* (the purchase of an existing crop for delivery to the mill on a specified day at an agreed price), or else by *time sale* (a form of future-contract, with variable conditions stipulated); or he might buy at *primage* (where the cargo of a ship or barge was sold by the captain, acting as a commission-paid agent for the supplier).[55] Thus the miller could secure stocks at best terms without recourse to the open market; but when he dealt openly (at Bear Quay or Queenhithe, and later Mark Lane, in London, or at the provincial corn markets) he could bring considerable buying power to bear, to his advantage. Also, as the Corn Laws permitted, supplies might be obtained on the international market, either by dealing privately, or as later, openly on the Baltic Exchange.[56] The accumulation of stocks of wheat had a qualitative as well as a quantitative aspect. The commercial miller, like the erstwhile mealman, could build a portfolio of wheats of different qualities, from which to select and mix, so producing flours of reasonably constant quality year after year. Mixing allowed the most efficient use of the country's wheat supply, and evened out quality (as well as quantity) fluctuations from year to year: a benefit of national significance.[57]

Fourth, working capital allowed the commercial miller to sell in distant markets, especially those cities, towns, and industrial districts (and London especially) where mill-sites were so scarce, or at such a premium, as to prevent or discourage local corn-milling on a large scale. Since, customarily, flour cargoes were sent at the miller's risk, with purchase completed and liability for payment arising only when the consignee had accepted them, considerable resources were needed to sustain and increase such trade. Mainly, the flour despatched in the long-distance or 'mercantile' trade was sent by sea, river, or canal,[58] to agents who in turn sold to the bakers. For instance, a firm of Liverpool factors, in which Gladstone's father was a partner, negotiated (though apparently without success) to be local agents for the widely-reputed flours made by Robert Stares at Botley Mill in Hampshire.[59]

The practicalities of long-distance trade significantly influenced the quality of commercial flour. Whereas wheat, if properly stacked and stored, was imperishable, stone-ground flours, after a settling period of up to three months, began to stale, as their high content of germ oil turned rancid. The process was faster in summer;[60] and faster too, if the flour had any bran content. Thus the miller, who was liable for the cargo in transit, risked the vagaries of the transport system: of ships delayed by adverse weather, or barges stranded by impediments to the navigation, or dried rivers and canals. To minimize the hazards of round-the-year trade, he was loth to despatch brown flours, and chary even of the Standard Wheaten grade, which in principle was bran-free.[61] Commercial interest dictated that, wherever possible, he should send only white flour (which if fine enough could survive even an Atlantic crossing[62]).

Thus the preference, of town-dwellers particularly, for white bread coincided with the practical interest of distant commercial millers in supplying fine flours: and originally, that supply may have stimulated, as it surely confirmed, the demand. Of course, such considerations did not necessarily apply where flour was milled for local consumption: then brown flours could be used at the optimum moment by the bakers. Even so, there was a danger of such flour staling in store if the demand was small and slow.

The scale of the intranational trade in flour is glimpsed in accounts of the coastwise supply of London. In the decade 1790–9 inclusive, 1,247,711 quarters of British wheat flour were brought coastways to the capital, compared to 2,322,436 quarters of domestically-produced wheat grain (so that flour was roughly 35 per cent of the total[63]). That, of course, represents only part of the overall supply, which included flour carried on the inland navigations, and some brought by road, as the wheat grain total similarly excludes the amounts moved inland, and also such quantities as were imported. Moreover, much of the wheat grain brought to London was then redirected to other markets, or sent out for milling, which the accounts also reflect: in that decade, 649,740 quarters of wheat left London coastwise (but only 98,336 quarters of flour[64]).

Between 1810 and 1813 inclusively, the equivalent of 1,029,579 quarters of flour were brought coastwise to London, and 1,308,184 quarters of wheat grain, suggesting that that flour trade had roughly doubled since the 1790s, and now represented about 44 per cent of the total. The relatively small importance of foreign and Irish flour in those years is illustrated by the 58,893 quarters-equivalent imported, compared to 1,446,961 quarters of foreign (and Irish) wheat grain.[65]

Fifth, millers and/or their agents used capital to support and finance the expansion of the baking trade. Because the prices and profits of bakers were in most places officially regulated by the assize of bread, the trade was notoriously impecunious. Therefore, as bakers came to rely on commercial millers for their flour, so too most came to depend on credit, formally extended for three months, though in practice often for a longer period. Also, millers often advanced loans to new masters, enabling them to set up in trade, in return for an exclusive contract to supply their flour. Those aspects are discussed further in Section 3.3.

Table 3.2 gives a crude indicative estimate of the proportion of working, to fixed, capital employed by millers in 1771.

Clearly, the indications over-estimate both the fixed and working capital employed in the commercial sector, since both Dr Orbell's

Table 3.2 Crude indication of the proportion of working
to fixed capital, *c*1771

	£'000
Stock of fixed capital*:	4,306
Stock of wheat for bread-making, valued at open market price**:	1,498
Stock of flour on hand (settling) or in transit, at book value of wheat***:	1,498
Amount extended in credit to the baking trade, either by miller or agent, at book value of wheat****:	2,248
Total of fixed and working capital, exclusive of loans to bakers:	9,550

* Mean of the high and low estimates given by Dr Orbell in Feinstein & Pollard p 162.
** Given national requirement of 3.7m quarters of wheat for bread (see Chapter 8.4), and assuming two months' stock carried (though possibly much of that, if held on the farm, was at the growers' expense).
*** Assuming two months' stocks on hand or in transit, at the book value of the wheat used.
**** Assuming three months' credit, at the book value of the wheat used.

estimate, and my indication, include non-commercial (or parochial) mills; and the fixed capital figure might be diluted further, to allow for mills that specialized in grinding grains other than wheat.

With plentiful caveats, therefore, the crude indication is that of the total employed in 1771, 45 per cent of capital was represented by fixed stock, and 55 per cent was working capital. A calculation made on a similar basis for 1801 suggests that, during that dearth year, the proportion represented by working capital would have been 66 per cent.

Profits and Profiteering

The growth of commercial milling caused considerable anxiety, heightened at times of high prices. Commercial milling contradicted the fundamental tenet, represented for instance by the bread acts, that none should profit unduly from the supply of the people's principal food. Millers or their agents buying far afield could disrupt local wheat markets for their own benefit; and forward buying, large shipments to other parts of the country, and speculations, contravened at least the spirit, and probably the letter, of the laws against forestalling, engrossing, and regrating. In the 1750s it was alleged that commercial millers, by virtue of their purchasing power, forced farmers to collude in artificially raising the price of wheat (and thus the prices of flour and bread). For instance, a miller might prevail on the farmer to sell him an 'enlarged' bushel, of perhaps ten per cent more quantity than the lawful Winchester measure, though at an appropriately enhanced price; the market clerk recorded only that a bushel (implicitly of standard amount) had been sold for that sum, and his record determined the assized price of bread. Thus the miller could increase his charge per Sack to the baker, whose own price would be raised by the magistrate, in conformity to the clerk's report.[66] The miller pocketed the 10 per cent, and neither the farmer nor the baker lost: the fraud was wholly at the public's expense.

In part, however, the increase in wheat prices surely represented a changing balance of supply and demand; and in part too, perhaps, a steady improvement in the average quality of marketed wheat. In the latter case, a better quality of wheat, yielding more flour (and bread) per bushel, could explain the sustained fall in the price of flour, relative to the price of wheat, over a thirty-year period. The relative decline in price is shown in Table 3.3.

Table 3.3   Cost of flour proportionate to wheat, by decade, 1760s –1780s

Decade	Open market average price of wheat	Fine flour s per sack	Index of flour/wheat
1760–9	36.9	32.4	88
1770–9	46.5	37.8	81
1780–9	46.2	37.1	80

Calculated from Orbell: thesis, Appendix 2.

Relatively low flour prices may also indicate that some of the benefits of increased milling efficiency were being passed on. In the 1750s it was observed that, thanks to boulting and other mechanical improvements, the average extraction rate of flours of comparable quality had increased by 5 per cent.[67]

Also, if at times the miller profited handsomely, at other times his margin was squeezed.[68] An Essex miller testified in 1814 that little or no profit was made in months when the London flour market was saturated, but 'at the latter part of the year' (by which I think he meant the harvest year, so that he was referring to late summer) great amounts could be made.[69] However, those larger margins were likely to reflect the greater risk of dried-out inland navigations, when flour might be held back or stopped in transit, so that cargoes could stale before sale. Or when, if the mill-race was dry, production stopped altogether. In hot weather, therefore, flour prices could rise out of proportion to wheat, a feature of the long-distance trade that perplexed a Select Committee of 1774 ('we find that the Price of Flour per Sack, has varied from the Price of Wheat per Quarter, through all Proportions, from One to Eleven Shillings Difference'),[70] as it would perplex others. Also, the cash to be made from flour varied from year to year, when millers worked on a roughly standard percentage of a fluctuating wheat price. And periodic gluts, the result of over-production, or at least, of over-supplying particular markets, depressed profits, often for years in a run. Between 1774 and 1799 inclusively, the millers supplying London were calcu-lated to have made, on an average price per Sack of 40s 6d, a trading profit of 5s 3d, or approximately 12.9 per cent. But the highest annual cash profit in that period was 11s 6.25d, and the lowest, 2s 1.5d (representing 18.5 per cent and 6.4 per cent respectively of the then prevailing prices).[71]

In some years, the gain or loss on stocks of wheat and flour (settling or in transit) might substantially affect profits. Suppose that a commercial miller had an annual throughput of 50,000 Winchester quarters of wheat, from which he might manufacture 58,000 Sacks of best bread flour: in 1776, when the average profit per Sack was 4s 0.25d, his operating profit on that volume would have been £11,600. However, had he carried say two months' stock of wheat purchased at average open market prices in 1775, and two months stock of flour booked at the same cost, he would have suffered a loss of £5280 (if that stock was revalued at the average 1776 price), being roughly half of his operating profit. In other years, he might gain from advancing grain prices. Even the most prudent miller was a speculator in some degree.

It was widely believed that to lessen risk and maximize profits, the millers operated cartels.[72] Five, six, or seven leading millers were supposed to orchestrate the supply to, and fix the price of flour in, London,[73] though the charge was hotly denied (if, significantly perhaps, with one voice) by the millers concerned.[74] They argued that monopoly was impossible when there were some 150 mills within 20 miles of London (of which perhaps a quarter engaged in the mercantile trade), and when many further off — some far up the Thames (an Abingdon miller, for instance, regularly supplied the metropolis) and others all along the eastern seaboard — also competed for London's business.[75] The problem, they insisted, was not restraint of trade, but over-production. Burke's verdict on the charge of monopoly was 'not proven',[76] but others were unimpressed. Some demanded that flour, like bread, should be assized, with the commercial miller forcibly returned to the rank of public servant, being allowed a living but not a profit.[77]

Others chose to fight commerce with commerce and capital with capital. In the process, industrial technology was further advanced. Two large 'anti-monopolistic' schemes were attempted in London.

The first, conceived by the entrepreneur Samuel Wyatt, in partnership with Boulton and Watt, was intended to break the alleged millers' stranglehold by siting a large corn mill at the very heart of the capital. Since the venture marked the first use of reciprocal-action steam engines, and all-iron machinery, the history of the Albion Mill is well-documented;[78] but the underlying commercial logic might briefly be sketched. Because the sluggish lower Thames was unsuited to water-mills, and because windmills had been forced out by the expansion of the capital, much of London's flour was brought in by ship or barge; or else wheat entering at the port was then sent out for milling up-river at Marlow, Henley, or Reading, or at mills along the Medway, Wey, and other tributaries, before being returned as flour. In the latter trade therefore, a double transport cost was incurred, and, like all traffic on the inland navigations, the flow of flour could be dislocated, especially in summer.[79]

Wyatt argued that Londoners might enjoy the benefits of uninter-rupted supplies of flour at fair prices if a centrally-sited steam-mill could take wheat directly from the port, process it at a constant rate throughout the year, regardless of the vagaries of wind and water, and then sell the flour directly to bakers or to the public without incurring the cost of transport (or a factor's margin). His first projection was of a throughput of 100,000 quarters of wheat annually (perhaps 15 per cent of the capital's entire consumption), returning a profit of £31,250. Given an investment of £60,000, the enterprise would break even in two years.[80]

Since such a large capital sum was more easily raised if the investors were protected by limited liability, a security available only if the company obtained incorporation by Act of Parliament, and as it was necessary therefore to demonstrate public benefit, the promoters stressed the detrimental effects of the alleged millers' monopoly, and also committed themselves to produce Standard Wheaten flour – an economical grade intended by the Bread Act of 1772 to end the trade's 'imposition' of more expensive white flour. Although the company's petition for incorporation was rejected, an aura of benefaction remained.[81]

In its brief operating life, from October 1786 to March 1791, the Albion Mill rarely achieved unit profitability, because, it might be argued, the supposition of previous monopoly was proved all too well. The price of flour in the London market fell relative to the cost of wheat, and profits fell more, as shown in Table 3.4.

Table 3.4   Effect of the Albion Mill

	Price of wheat per Win qr		Price of flour per 280lb sack		Flour/ wheat ratio	Average profit per sack	
	s	d	s	d		s	d
Average of previous 6 years (1780–5 inc)	43	2	38	4	89	6	9
Average of 6 years when Albion Mill operated (1786–91 inc)	45	1	36	6	81	2	10

Source (and calculated from): Bennett & Elton Vol III p 292.

Assuming an average annual breadflour supply in London of 700,000 Sacks for those years,[82] total metropolitan operating profits fell by about £110,000 annually, or by roughly £600,000 for the whole period of the Albion Mill's operation. The fall in operating profit affected the Albion more than its rivals, since the steam-mill was burdened by the cost of coal (and exceptionally high repair and maintenance costs) while water- and wind-power was free. And because its rivals survived, the principal effect of the Albion's entry was to glut an already well-supplied market. The Standard Wheaten flour that it produced was accepted readily by the less respectable London bakers, since it could be doctored with alum and passed off as white, at an enhanced profit; but a considerable amount had to be sent to markets as far off as Bristol, Falmouth, Plymouth, Newcastle, and Liverpool.[83]

That the Albion survived at all was due chiefly to a rising price trend in the wheat market, that allowed large scope for speculation: the price of a Winchester quarter increased from an average 36s 6d in 1786 to 51s 8.5d in 1789, and stayed at roughly that level in 1790 (51s 3d). However, prices fell in 1791 (to an average 44s 11.25d), devaluing stocks; Boulton, Watt and Wyatt were spared the full consequences by the conflagration of 2 March 1791, that gutted the mill and destroyed the wheat and flour on hand: probably, they recouped all their capital from the insurers.[84]

The crowd that gathered and danced joyfully at the sight of the flames[85] apparently believed (as they had been encouraged by the vested trade to believe) that, rather than having acted against monopoly, the Albion itself exerted a yet more malign influence, by blatantly using its buying power to drive up the price of wheat. And that view had support among the influential: thus, when the question of London's flour supply became critical, during the dearth of 1795–6, the Corporation, which was concerned with the London poor, closely examined the possibility of a municipal venture, combining central-site production with (effectively) price control. Finally, though, rather than risk some £100,000 of public money, the Corporation gave its support to a new private scheme: the London Company for the Manufacture of Flour, Meal, and Bread.[86]

The projectors of the London Company drew several lessons from the Albion debacle; they had the firm support of leading City figures, of certain ministers (Lord Hawkesbury especially), and of members of both Houses of Parliament, whose influence was enough to win them, after a 'herculean' battle, an Act of Incorporation, and so the security of limited liability. Their claim to be public benefactors was justified, as in the case of the Albion, by anti-monopolistic sentiments and by a commitment to manufacture Standard Wheaten flour; and apparent public spirit was confirmed by the presence of Eden (author of *The State of the Poor*) as chairman, and of Coke of Norfolk as a leading shareholder. Acknowledging that steam-powered milling was impractical in London, they planned large tide-mills at Rotherhithe. Even so, the promoters displayed a reckless confidence by capitalizing the company at £120,000 and projecting volumes of flour (and bread) that would surely flood the metropolitan market, unless the vested trade capitulated, which, as it proved, was the wrong assumption. The operations of the London Company never achieved the scale, nor solvency, anticipated, but like the Albion, the venture was kept afloat for some years by the immense speculations of its directors in wheat, which according to their critics, had been, from the first, the chief purpose of the enterprise. It collapsed after ten years: neither the capital nor further loans of £31,885, advanced by the proprietors, were repaid.[87]

Though both the metropolitan behemoths failed, and though both appeared to their opponents as more injurious than the monopolies they claimed to oppose, their influence was widely felt. The Albion was, as Boulton and Watt intended, the technical proving-ground of reciprocal-action steam engines, and so had a seminal influence upon the course of Britain's industrialization; and though steam-power proved to be too costly in London, the accountancy was quite different if factories, including corn-mills, were sited on the coalfields. By Dr Orbell's calculation, 142 corn mills using steam power (though not in every case to drive the stones) were built between 1779 and 1821, most of them close to pits.[88] Also, both the Albion and the London Company opened the prospect of heavily capitalized ventures, devoted to large-scale production, that might break vested monopolies, and lower the cost (and perhaps further improve the quality) of flour and bread.

Such opportunities were pursued outside London by numerous co-operative societies. The first co-operative milling and baking ventures, originating in the 1760s and 1770s, were small-scale, with membership and benefits confined to specific workforces, such as the dockyard workers of Woolwich and Chatham, or to friendly societies.[89] A new phase began in 1796 when, in response to dearth-prices, and alleged local monopolies, the Birmingham Union was formed. The Birmingham Union drew its subscribers from a broad section of the city's population; its founding capital was £20,000, which financed a steam-powered mill (cum bakehouse). Unlike the London ventures, with their wealthy shareholders, the co-operatives represented popular capitalism: the Birmingham enterprise, which became the model of the type, issued £1 shares, and no member could own more than twenty. Moreover, as their principal return, members bought their flour and bread from the co-operative at supposedly cheaper prices: thus, at its establishment, each co-operative had a guaranteed, captive, market for its output.[90]

On the face of it, therefore, the co-operatives were well-founded commercial ventures acting in the public interest. And their existence seemed justified by necessity as, in general, the price of breadstuffs soared, and the cost of flour, relative to wheat, rose. Calculations of the relative prices of flour and wheat are given in Table 3.5.

Table 3.5 Proportionate cost of flour to wheat, by decade, 1790s to 1810s

Decade	Open market average price of wheat	Fine flour s per sack	Index of flour/wheat
1790–9	57.6	46.6	81
1800–9	84.5	71.4	84
1810–9	91.4	80.9	89

Calculated from Orbell: thesis, Appendix 2, taking best flour throughout.

However, the apparent savings offered may not have been so significant as they seemed, an aspect discussed in Section 3.3. And, like the London ventures, the co-operatives, especially those that invested in steam-powered milling, were affected by the problems of over-production. The power generated by a Boulton & Watt (or rival) system dictated that, at a minimum, eight pairs of stones should be driven by each engine; roughly speaking, on the Albion's record, such a unit might have a throughput of about 30,000 quarters of wheat a year, which, by the usual rule of thumb, would represent the consumption of 30,000 people. That kind of volume might be vented in Birmingham (if in 1801, say, the Union had the loyal custom of roughly 40 per cent of that city's population) but it represented considerably more than the probable demand of many towns of the time.[91] Moreover, as private millers responded, by converting to steam themselves, local gluts were almost inevitable.

In such circumstances, the form of co-operative organization became a liability rather than an asset. Flour and bread could be sold only to members: it was contrary both to law and to the particular constitutions of the societies, to sell on the open market: in distant cities, for example. Managements overlooking that constraint were sharply reminded of it, by threats of prosecution both from their competitors and their members (who felt they had purchased a privilege not to be shared with others). So that, whilst the private miller could send his flour to any market, and to London especially, the co-operatives were confined to their carefully delineated territories, with no line of escape from local glut.[92] Nor could they compete for long on price, when the cost of wheat reached unimagined levels. Either they reduced output to uneconomic levels, or else, like many private millers, they came to depend upon large-scale speculations in the wheat market. And so, like the Albion and the London Company, the co-operatives themselves could be cast as monopolies, driving up the cost of the people's food. They may also have been affected by the difficulties of their legal status, and the embezzlements of managers; but their chief weakness was enough to assure their downfall, as soon as the price of wheat began to fall from 1814–15. Few co-operatives survived the shock of peace.[93]

Flour Wars

The demise of most co-operatives apparently did little to check the over-production of flour: private operators, especially those with steam-mills sited on the northern coalfields, flooded the London market with their products from 1815 until well into the 1820s.[94] Perhaps by 1830 supply and demand had reached a better balance, given the rapid increase of urban population and signs of returning stability in the London bread market.

However, the falling price of coal improved the economics of steam-milling off the coalfields, and so offered fresh invitation to large-scale enterprise, even in London. In the late 1840s and early 1850s, large mills and their associated granaries sprang up along the metropolitan Thames: the largest of them was the seven-storey City Flour Mill, built in 1851–2 just below Blackfriars Bridge: its 32 pairs of stones could process 2500 quarters of wheat a week (taking a rough average price of 50s per quarter, therefore, the annual value of wheat processed in that mill alone was about £325,000).[95] The result was a new flour war in the capital, as provincial millers fought to protect their volumes from the output of central-site competitors.

Competition intensified also in northern cities, especially where private sokes were brought to an end. The citizens of Wakefield and district bought out the soke there for a total of £21,500, in two agreements of 1833 and 1858; Leeds was freed for £13,000 in 1839; however, at Bradford, despite successive attempts, the soke remained until 1871.[96] In part, competition was stimulated by a revival of the co-operative movement. The People's Mill at Leeds, and the Halifax Mill, both formed in 1847, were to become pillars of the modern co-operative movement. The sales of the People's Mill increased from £22,058 in its first full year of operation to £71,948 in 1856 to £95,095 in 1871; in the same years profits were £37, £793, and £7,321 respectively, and capital increased from £2,734 to £7,843 to £22,615.[97] The Yorkshire model was copied in Lancashire (where the co-operatives had been small and concerned chiefly with general retailing): in 1850 a separate flour society was established at Rochdale, which by 1860 had a turnover of £133,000 and profits of £10,000.[98]

The movement was greatly boosted by the rise of prices during the Crimean War. Co-operation then revived in the south of England, usually on the lines of c1795–1815. Some past encumbrances were removed by the Industrial and Provident Act of 1852 (widened in 1862 and 1876), which gave societies a legal standing, so that members collectively had the right of action against managers for theft of goods and embezzlement.[99]

However, even in 1870 the co-operative movement was small, compared to what it would become. A more evident and immediate competition was posed by the increasing amounts of imported flour, before and especially after Repeal. American flour, especially, was eagerly sought by bakers, for its exceptional strength.[100]

Despite such competition, however, commercial millers, especially those operating large-scale steam mills sited at ports, still had consider-able scope for expansion. From the 1830s, the railways opened up the country, including parts previously inaccessible by water, to intranational trade, and flour was one of the commodities that benefited especially, since carriage not only was cheap but fast, so that the risk of staling en route was eliminated.[101]

Even so, many traditional mills continued in operation. Nor should the impact of steam power be exaggerated. Kanefsky estimates that even in 1870 two-thirds of the 90,000 horse power available for all grain milling was provided by water power. Freeman calculates that in Hampshire, about 1880, more than 80 per cent of potential capacity still was accounted for by watermills and windmills (though twenty years later their share had dropped to 40 per cent).[102]

The combination of old and new may account for an apparent fall in the labour productivity of British milling between the 1830s and the 1850s, and for only partial recovery in the 1860s (see Table 3.6).

Table 3.6 Labour productivity of British millers c1831–71

Decade	Mid-decade estimate of millers*	Deflated by ave decadal WEEP**	Average decadal wheat need less flour imports*** m qrs	Qrs per miller
1831–40	23,942	17,957	9.6	535
1841–50	31,505	23,629	10.8	457
1851–60	36,753	28,300	12.7	449
1861–70	34,962	26,921	14.3	531

* Number of millers calculated from: PP XXVII (587) 1, HMSO 1844, pp 29, 38; LXXXVIII/I (1691–I) 1, HMSO 1852–3; LXXXVIII/II (1691–II) 1, HMSO 1852–3; LIII/I (3221) 1, 265, HMSO 1863; LIII/II (3221) 1, HMSO 1863; LXXI/I (872) 1, HMSO 1873. A figure for all millers in 1831 has been estimated by assuming the same proportion of males aged 20+ as in 1841. Thus census year figures are – 1831: est 22,142; 1841: 25,742; 1851: 37,268; 1861: 36,237; 1871: 33,687.

** = Wheat-eating equivalent population; a crude deflator, to allow for the grinding of grains other than wheat. Average wheat-eating equivalent populations per decade estimated as: 1831–40: 75 per cent; 1841–50: 75 per cent; 1851–60: 77 per cent; 1861–70: 77 per cent.
*** Calculated from the UK's estimated wheat breadstuff requirement (see Chapter 8) averaged per decade, less UK flour imports, shown in Table 3.1, above.

The calculation is too crude to suggest more than that apparent advances in operation, technology, and marketing in the commercial sector may have been offset by the persistence of traditional methods elsewhere. And in the baking trade, discussed next, traditional methods were overwhelmingly predominant.

3.3 COMMERCIAL BREAD PRODUCTION

The baking trade was almost entirely traditional in its means and methods, in England and Wales at least. As Karl Marx observed in the 1860s:

> No other branch of industry in England has preserved up to the present day a method of production as archaic, as pre-Christian (as we see from the poets of the Roman Empire) as baking has.[103]

Such apparent backwardness was the result of four main, interrelated, influences. First, baking was considered to be a unique trade, of literally vital importance. Its particular character was acknowledged, as Adam Smith observed, by continuing official regulation, long after the rest of the medieval, and early modern, structure of intervention had been dismantled.[104] The assize of bread both reflected and determined the character of the baking trade; and though the last assizes were abolished in 1836, the ethos of public service remained. That aspect is examined in Chapter 4.

The other three chief influences – the nature of the product and service, the role of labour, and the character of mastery – are discussed in this section.

The Product

The nature of the baking trade was determined chiefly by the perishability of bread, and by its role as a warm food.

Whereas wheat, if well stored, can last interminably, and stone-ground white flour had a usable life of three months or so, bakers' bread was best eaten within 24, or at most 48, hours of baking. Perishability set a limit to the extent of the market that a traditional bakery could serve. Moreover, in the cities and towns, much bread was eaten warm. Not only was such bread highly palatable, it was the sole warm weekday food of many families. Further, for those without ovens (or saving on fuel, especially in summer) the bakeries also were cookhouses: many opened on Sunday mornings for the sole purpose of cooking their customers' weekly dinners. Therefore, urban bakeries had to be sited within a few minutes walk, or dash, of customers' homes.

As a result, the typical neighbourhood bakery operated only one oven. For an average demand, the baker might process one 280 lb Sack of flour a day, producing from it about 350 lbs of bread. But often an extra batch was baked for sale on Saturday (to cover Sunday too): thus a typical weekly throughput was seven Sacks, or roughly 2450 lbs of bread. Given an average minimum requirement of 4 lbs per head per week, that output would satisfy up to 600 individuals or so. Should a town expand, in principle the number of bakeries would increase in step. Such growth is seen at Southampton (see Table 3.7).

Table 3.7   Southampton bakers' premises 1783/4–1861*

Year	Number of bakers' premises	Approximate population	1 bakery per:
1783–4	11	7,000?	636
1795–6	19	7,500?	395
1803	21	8,500	405
1811	18	10,000	556
1823–4	22	14,000	636
1834	43	21,000	488
1839	47	26,000	553
1845	50	31,000	620
1851	85	35,000	412
1852	78	36,000	462
1855	71	40,000	563
1859	90	45,000	500
1861	100	47,000	470

* The category excludes specialist confectioners, pastrycooks, and biscuit makers, but the figures may reflect different classifications used by different compilers: for instance, the inclusion or exclusion of bread shops without ovens.

Whatever the uncertainties associated with the data, it will be seen that the baker density remained within a fairly narrow band of from 1:395 to 1:636.

Sources: Directory of Hampshire 1783–4; Directory of Hampshire 1795–6; Southampton Directory 1803; The Southampton Register for 1811; Pigot's Southampton Directory 1823–4; Fletcher's Southampton Directory 1834; Robson's Southampton Directory 1839; The Southampton Post Office Directory 1845; Slater's Royal National and Commercial Directory and Topography of Berks etc 1851; Hunts Directory 1852; Kelly's Post Office Directory of Hampshire 1855; Post Office Directory of Southampton 1859; Post Office Directory of Southampton 1861.

In smaller towns in much of England, and in the countryside, a lower throughput, of perhaps five Sacks weekly, often was supplemented by the making of pastries and confectionery, skilled work that in the cities was the preserve of specialists. And the country baker, or his family, might combine several trades, acting also as millers, corn factors, and general retailers.[105] The country trade appears to have spread rapidly from the middle of the 18th century. Wherever fuel was hard to obtain or unaffordable, the commercial bakery became the mainstay of a community. Apart from selling his own loaves, the baker often baked dough brought in by his customers, and like the London baker, cooked their Sunday dinners.[106] The expansion of the country trade might be described as both lateral and vertical. Lateral, as bakeries were established in those districts where before they had been few or absent (the places that Parliament had in mind, in 1757, when it allowed magistrates the option of not setting an assize[107]); and vertical, as the purchasing of bread, and white bread particularly, extended downwards from the 'respectable' classes to the growing proportion and numbers of commercial, clerical, and manufacturing workers. Dr Thwaites argues convincingly that the expansion of commercial baking is registered, in years of domestic dearth, by the change of popular complaint, from protest at the high price of wheat to protest at the high price of bread, a change that in Oxfordshire took place in the 1760s.[108] In 1774 a Select Committee could speculate that in England and Wales outside London, about half the population relied upon commercial bakers, while half still made their own bread.[109]

There were substantial exceptions to the trend. In Leeds, where, as in other Yorkshire towns, the long survival of soke-right prevented the development of commercial milling, and probably constricted commercial baking too, in 1821 most households made their own bread. At Newcastle-upon-Tyne in 1815, fewer than a tenth of the population were said to buy bread, though many took their dough to public bakehouses.[110] In remoter districts where commercial baking may not have been viable, neighbours took turns at bread-making, supplying each other probably by exchange; but Eden noted a Westmorland wife who cleared 2s 0d a week by selling wheaten bread (perhaps surplus to her own requirements).[111] Local records can give conflicting impressions of trade development: Dr Holmes notes that at Dorchester in 1795, people baked their own bread (except some of the poor, who could not always afford flour and fuel), since there was no properly qualified baker in the town; yet the Dorchester magistrates troubled to set an assize (having been asked to do so by the resolution of a public meeting in 1758) on all the parliamentary grades of wheat bread, and made four price changes in 1796 and twelve in 1800: which suggests there must have been a trade of some substance in the borough and its environs.[112]

In larger villages and towns, in Kent for example, white bread predominated,[113] though under the assize, it was for magistrates to determine whether best Wheaten, or Standard Wheaten, or both, should be made and sold. And while the Bread Act of 1757 may have had the effect, in many parts, of improving the quality of Wheaten bread, the 1772 Act may have reversed the position, not only directly, where the Standard Wheaten grade became the best quality available, but indirectly, where bakers passed off loaves made from Standard Wheaten flour, whitened with alum, as of best quality.[114] Few willingly made Household bread, since there was little profit in it, but bakers supplying small villages and the countryside were obliged to do so, by the nature of demand.[115] In the 1830s, however, when all bread was cheap, the browner grades may have been rare even in the countryside, and quality overall probably had improved.[116]

Whereas in London the supply of bread by contract to large institutions, or of loaves for resale by chandlers, had become the speciality of wholesale bakers,[117] in the provinces such work usually was undertaken by the general baker, and it could be the bedrock of his business. During the severe wartime years, perhaps many country bakeries were saved by their contracts with the Poor Law authorities, especially where the Speenhamland system prevailed.[118] After the reform of the Poor Law, the substantial orders placed by the new amalgamated Unions were vigorously competed for.[119] In addition, contracts to supply bread for charitable distribution could constitute a considerable part of the country bakers' trade, especially in winter months;[120] and through the year he might supply those almshouses, hospitals, schools, and garrisons, that did not make their own bread.

By the nature of the trade, it was difficult to overcome the constriction of baking only one batch per oven per day: economy required that, if there was a second daily baking, it too should be a full batch. Thus volume doubled in a leap, requiring an immediate doubling of custom. However, during the century in review, there was a discernible trend toward (though far from universal adoption of) double-batch baking in London. In the late 18th century, the ratio of metropolitan inhabitants to bakers was only slightly higher than at Southampton; but by the 1860s that proportion had increased significantly. This is shown by the figures in Table 3.8.

The Sackage estimate for 1804, though almost certainly too high as an average, reflects an impression that many metropolitan bakers were by then baking two batches daily; by 1865 that proportion almost certainly had increased substantially.[121]

Given dense concentration, if one outlet increased its throughput from one to two batches, almost certainly it would be at the expense of other bakers. And competition, especially on price, went hard against the trade's traditions, traditions upheld wherever possible by bakers'

Table 3.8   London retail and wholesale bakeries

Year	Number of bakeries	Est pop of area served '000	Inhabitants per bakery	Average weekly sackage
c1768–79				7–8 (f)
1797–8	1466> (a)	1,000 (d)	682	< 9.8 (g)
1804				<12 (g)
1814–15	1706 (b)	1,380 (d)	809	9.3 (h)
1865	1935 (c)	1,610 (e)	832	

Sources and notes:
(a) CLRO: 70B (Register of Bakers' Certificates pursuant to 37 Geo III). No certificates are recorded for certain districts (eg: the environs of the Edgware Road); a round estimate of 1500 assized bakers was given in 1800 (G: Fo Pam 894, p 16).
(b) PP V (186) 1341, HoC 6.6.1815, p 115 – Davis; in 1815 roughly 1850 metropolitan masters subscribed to a trade charity, indicating about 150 'institutional' bakeries in addition to those assized.
(c) PP XLVII (175) 261, HoC 31.3.1865, pp 2–4.
(d) Estimated populations of zone of 10 miles radius around the Royal Exchange: see Appendix 7.
(e) Population of the Weekly Bills of Mortality (a less extensive area than the former 10–mile zone), given in PP XLVII (175) 261, HoC 31.3.1865, pp 2–4.
(f) Estimates by the Worshipful Company of Bakers, of 7 Sacks weekly in 1768 and 8 Sacks weekly in 1779 (G: Ms 7801 2/2).
(g) Calculated from bakers' returns of breadflour purchased annually, amounting to 745,720 Sacks in 1798, and 821,607 in 1814: PP V (186) 1341, HoC 6.6.1815, Appendix 5.
(h) Average assumed by the bread committee of the House of Commons when calculating bakers' incomes: PP IV/I (74) item 43, HoC 27.4.1804, p 11.

societies. In older towns those societies had long been incorporated: the 'white bakers' of London in 1155 or earlier; of Exeter (before 1428), of Southampton (1517), of Oxford (1571), and of several Scottish burghs (before 1556).[122]

The incorporations asserted that unbridled competition would harm the livings of masters, and force down the wages of journeymen; and if as a result few were attracted to the trade, and others left it, then the poor especially would be deprived of their principal food. Also, it was alleged that cut prices could be achieved only at the expense of bread quality.[123]

Resistance to competition was strengthened wherever the assize of bread operated. Although the authorities set only a maximum price, making no stipulation as to *minima*, in practice the bakers' societies were in most places at most times, able to enforce the assized price as the sole price in their jurisdictions. They could do so because of their semi-public role as auxiliaries of the magistrates, in enforcing standards of purity, weight, and correct description. Any slip by an underseller was likely to be pounced upon, with exceptional alacrity, by the trade beadle, with draconian consequences for the offender.

And yet there were legitimate ways by which the 'fair' assized price could be undersold. Since Defoe's time,[124] and generally since the middle of the 18th century, London bakers (and increasingly, those in provincial towns) had delivered bread, and extended credit to, respectable families, the costs of which were included in the assize price. Those costs could be substantial, given that the time taken in delivery might require employment of an extra journeyman, and that credit involved the making up of bills, the chasing of slow payers, and the risk of bad debts. The traditional baker, though he refused delivery and credit to the poor, still charged the same price for loaves bought for cash in the shop. But a baker who put his business on a 'cash only, shop only' footing could pass on genuine savings to customers, selling his quartern loaves at a halfpenny or penny below the 'full-priced' trade.[125] The incidence of underselling fluctuated and it had a new vogue in the 1780s, due largely to the activities of an exceptional entrepreneur, Christopher Potter, whose chain of cut-price bread shops thoroughly alarmed the vested trade.[126]

Potter survived for many years, though most of his imitators were deterred by threats, should inspection fail.[127] By various means, by 1797 the numbers of undersellers in London had been reduced to three.[128]

But a new metropolitan bread act, in that year, opened a loophole that undersellers could exploit. And the effects of dearth, including official encouragement to mix in the flour of coarser grains, allowed bakers to sell (both legitimately and illegitimately) cheaper loaves; Girdler described two sorts sold in 1800: a 2d-under loaf that was so musty, griping and pernicious, as to endanger the constitution of any person eating it, and a 4d-under version that was, if possible, ten times worse.[129] But, emergency loaves apart, the quality of undersellers' bread may have been, as its makers declared, as good as any, justifying their success with the public. By Spring 1815, of the 1706 assized bakers in the metropolitan area, 150 were undersellers;[130] since they were likely to produce two batches of bread daily to meet the demand for cheaper bread, perhaps their share of sales was 15 per cent or so. One such underseller was reported to be making an annual profit of £1400.[131]

The success of the London undersellers in benefiting the poor while making considerable profits seemed a striking demonstration of the merits of free enterprise, and helped to persuade Parliament that the metropolitan assize should be abolished. On one projection, if inefficient bakers no longer were cushioned, the number of metropolitan bakeries would halve and average throughput would double. Some members of the bread committee of the House of Commons had higher expectations still, anticipating that a free market would attract considerable capital, and that large and efficient bread factories would then dominate the trade.[132] Such optimism was questionable, given the record of the London Company (which had failed not only in the flour trade, but in an attempt to supply bread too), and given the demand for warm bread and cooked food which, as the millers well knew, dictated the spatial diffusion of metropolitan bakeries.[133]

The abolition of the London assize in 1815[134] threw the metropolitan market into turmoil. As undersellers expanded their activities, the traditional trade responded in kind: soon, not 15 per cent but perhaps 75 per cent of London's bread was sold cheaply,[135] while the trade of the 'full-priced' bakers shrank to the confines of the West End and similarly wealthy districts. And, though the cost of wheat and therefore of bread declined on trend after 1815, many London bakers now cut the quartern not by a penny or so but by twopence or threepence.[136] Even 'full-priced' bakers set their prices for cash sales in the shop, charging an optional penny per loaf for delivery and credit (which may partly explain why the 'official' bread price series for London, which gives maximum prices, shows the cost of loaves rising in proportion to wheat during the 1820s). By one account, there were 'five hundred' different prices for bread in London,[137] an obvious exaggeration, but indicative of the anarchy then prevailing.

Deep cutting of a falling bread price, by a majority of metropolitan bakers, eliminated the profits that once were to be made from underselling: survival itself was precarious. In consequence, the average quality of London's bread declined. The Worshipful Company, though weakened by the abolition of the assize, continued for some time to operate as the auxiliary of authority in policing the purity, full weight, and correct description of loaves; but a further and well-intentioned reform of the metropolitan bread acts in 1819 made prosecution all but impossible; thereafter there was little to prevent undersellers from matching price cuts with corresponding reductions in bread quality. So that, though the full-priced bakers might offer best white bread, the typical underseller's loaf was roughly of Standard Wheaten quality, though its inferiority was disguised by alum.[138]

The pressure to undersell, and so if possible to achieve a higher throughput, intensified during the periodic flour wars, as the gluts produced by the northern steam mills,[139] and from the late 1840s, the outputs of London's own flour factories, were vented. So intense was competition from mid-century that a new breed of metropolitan baker emerged – the 'cutter' or 'ha'penny under' man – who undersold even the undersellers, though at the further expense of bread quality.

Against such pressures, the vested trade did its best to achieve stability. Bread qualities and prices were collectively agreed, district by district, by the masters' societies.[140] So that London was a patchwork of different bread markets, that can be roughly grouped into zones:

London Bread Zones, c1853

> *1st-rate bakers*: in the City, Strand, Holborn, and West End. Selling quality bread at about 2d to 3d per 4lb loaf above the 2nd-rate price, but offering home delivery and credit to the respectable classes.
>
> *2nd-rate bakers*: in many 'middling' districts. Selling white bread of reasonable quality (mostly second-grade flour) but rarely offering delivery and credit.
>
> *3rd-rate bakers*: East End, Blackfriars Road, New Cut, populous Westminster. Selling poorer quality bread (with much third-grade flour mixed in), whitened by alum, at 1d or so below the 2nd-rate price; also household bread. No delivery, no credit.
>
> *Cut-price bakers*: intruding wherever they could. Under-cutting even the 3rd-rate bakers.
>
> Sources: *The Times* 2.11.1853, p 8, col f; Dodd p 192; *Northamptonshire Herald* reporting London bread prices throughout 1854; also later evidence from PP XLVII (3080) 1, HMSO 1862, pp 40–1, 114, 261, 278, 287.

Thus the principal item in the cost-of-living of London's poorer classes varied significantly in price according to where they lived (a grievance of the poor in Chelsea, for instance, who in September 1854 had to pay 9d a loaf, compared to the 7d or even 6d charged at Shoreditch);[141] but as a rule prices reflected bread quality, and therefore the amount of nutriment derived, by sedentary workers especially.[142] By 1862, 1st-rate bakers had about one-sixth of the metropolitan trade; 2nd- and 3rd- rate together had about two-thirds, and cutters about one-sixth.[143]

An expansion of throughput, from one, to two or even three batches per oven, was limited progress, involving no technical advance. Since the chief impediment to factory–scale production was the demand for warm bread, and for a cooking–service, further advance was feasible only where cold bread was acceptable, and where public bakehouses were established under municipal aegis. The compensation for eating bread cold, was the apparent economy achieved, both in consumption (being less palatable, less was eaten, especially by children) and in price, if the bakery achieved economies of scale, and passed on the benefits to its customers.

Cold bread and co-operativism were closely linked, especially where bakehouses were established as adjuncts to large-volume mills. A substantial proportion of the flour produced might be baked on site, for delivery to subscribers' homes, at less than the price demanded by the private trade.

Often, the apparent profiteering of commercial bakers gave powerful impetus to the formation of a co-operative. For instance, in April 1795 workers in the Royal Dockyard marched into Portsmouth, demanding cheap bread of the bakers: those who refused to sell loaves for 6d had their shops gutted. The same happened in 1796. In protest, the Portsmouth bakers stopped trading, whereupon the dockyardmen organized their own co-operative, putting up £800 to build a small windmill and bakehouse, from which flour and bread were delivered to members' houses on a ticket system. The Dockyard Union had 880 members in 1802.[144]

In 1800 the Privy Council was struck particularly by the success of the Birmingham Union, which thrived by selling bread cheaply. In June 1797, for instance, the co-operative was selling its quartern loaf for 6.25d compared to the 10.5d charged that month for wheaten bread in London. The Union committee conceded that the quality of its bread had fallen somewhat since the dearth of 1795–6, but claimed that most of the saving was due to its enterprise in buying wheat: although wheat was more expensive at open markets around Birmingham than at Mark Lane, the Union gave cash in exchange for a discount, whereas the London bakers, in thrall to the millers, bought their flour on credit. However, the London bakers doubted that that was the whole story. In 1800 the Master of the Worshipful Company visited Birmingham to test the claims, and found that the Union's loaves weighed less than those of the local vested trade, so that the price per lb was actually the same, and if quality was taken into account, then the Union's quartern was 2d over the trade price; compared to the even better London loaf, it was 3d over (be that as it may, the Birmingham Union continued to flourish, supplying 18 per cent of the city's bread, and in 1815 making and distributing a profit of 20 per cent).[145]

The loaves of the Bristol Union, too, were said to be of poor quality and underweight; it was alleged that the co-operators escaped prosecution only because the chairman of the venture was also the City chamberlain (a connexion that helped, too, in winning profitable contracts, such as one to supply inferior bread to the French prisoners held in the city).[146]

Bread companies on similar lines were established at Sheffield (by the freemasons), Hull, Wolverhampton (with 15,000 members), and in other cities. Whatever the quality, their bread was cheap, which often had the effect of lowering bread prices all round.[147] But most of those mills-cum-bakehouses, or embryonic bread factories, disappeared in the collapse of the co-operative movement after 1815. Co-operativism revived somewhat in the 1840s, and widely during the Crimean War, when the price of bread soared; the co-operatives surviving to the 1860s, however, were concentrated mainly in the north, and more concerned to supply flour to home-bakers than enter the commercial bread market on any large scale.

What popular capitalism attempted in England, private capital achieved at Glasgow. Glaswegians seem to have preferred the economy of cold bread – moreover, Scottish bread differed from English: it was made by a different process that was better-suited to large-scale production. The accounts of a Glasgow baker suggest the mass production of bread there before the end of the Napoleonic Wars; by the 1860s there were half-a-dozen 'splendid' bread factories in the city. It was claimed that Mr Thompson's establishment at Crossmyloof was the largest bakery in the world: its 38 ovens processed up to 800 Sacks of flour weekly (implying an average turnover of more than £100,000 per annum). The principle of mass-production was copied in other Scottish cities, and at Carlisle, where Carr's bakery employed hundreds of workers in model conditions (though biscuit-making was their principal business, and factory methods already were usual in that trade).[148]

However, the Scots' bread factories, and Carr's, like a number of large private bakeries at Birmingham, achieved economies of scale chiefly through the efficient deployment of labour. Even in those model factories, the mechanization of bread production had barely begun, though by the 1860s, the necessary technology existed.[149] A practical dough-making machine, patented by Eberneezer Stevens, appeared in 1862: but although it was adopted by many institutional bakeries (hospitals, prisons, the armed forces), the Stevens' machine found little acceptance in the trade at large.[150] In 1851 Angier March Perkins, a prolific inventor, patented a water-heated oven, which improved upon the established side-flue system by circulating boiling water, rather than hot air, round the back of the oven, thus keeping the temperature constant while economizing on fuel. In 1865 Perkins' son, Loftus, introduced a sophisticated stopped-end tube version of the water oven. Perkins' chief client was a London baker, W H Nevill, whose enterprise was in marked contrast to the backwardness of the metropolitan trade at large. But Nevill specialized in selling cold bread to chandlers (patronized by the poor, more for the facility of credit than the quality of their goods), and so he was not constricted, as were other bakers, by neighbourhood demand. By 1863 he had eight Perkins' ovens and was building four more; by 1878 he had 68 of the latest design, and a throughput of 5000 Sacks weekly, far in excess of any previous British output.[151] In the 1860s too, Dr John Dauglish perfected his wholly-mechanized method of bread-production, in which the use of yeast was eliminated, by injecting carbonic acid gas into a machine-made dough. The time taken from start to oven was thereby reduced from 16 hours or so, to 26 minutes. And, whereas a typical bakery might produce 200,000 lbs of bread annually, one Dauglish machine made ten times that amount, or twenty times, with double-shift working. But at Dr Dauglish's untimely death in 1866, the future of the process, and of his Aerated Bread Company, was far from certain.[152] Ordinary Londoners disdained the bland taste of yeast–free bread; the loaves, distributed from central-site factories (at first from the Peak Frean plant at Dockhead Bermondsey, later from Dr Dauglish's own establishment in Islington) to grocers throughout the capital, were cold on arrival, and (with the costs of carriage and of a retail margin added) expensive. The principal market for aerated bread, at the inception of the enterprise, was that (not necessarily large, though vociferous) portion of the middle class attracted by hygienic production, and the very blandness of the loaves, which suited weak digestions.

Labour

Given the impracticability of large-scale production wherever consumers demanded warm bread, and a 'cultural' resistance to machinery (labour-saving devices were deemed, by masters fearful of competition and men anxious for their jobs, to be 'unbrotherly'[153]), baking was, in 1870 as anciently, labour-intensive work.

The typical establishment of a small bakery, with a weekly through-put of up to seven Sacks, comprised the master helped by his family and an apprentice, and perhaps a journeyman. In a bakery working two or three batches daily, and making some sideline products, such as fancy breads, rolls, and morning goods, an additional one, two, or three journeymen might be employed.[154]

Hours were long, often almost unending. The process of commercial bread making in England was such that activity (making the 'sponge', overseeing fermentation, kneading the dough, dividing and baking, drawing and stacking the loaves) came in bouts, divided by breaks for food and sleep, around the clock for five or six days a week; with one or two of the men working on Sunday morning also, if the bakery opened to cook customers' brought in food. Overall, though with breaks included, an average working week was 100 hours; but where double batches were baked daily, the men might never leave the bakehouse, until Saturday night, when they were freed briefly to spend their pay on drink and other diversions.[155] The life of a London journeyman baker was 'a species of slavery'.[156]

Often, the working environment was squalid. Although rural bakeries usually were sited above ground, and so were reasonably ventilated and naturally lit, in the cities and in London especially, most were in basements. All bakeries were vulnerable to vermin, cockroaches especially. The pollution of bread by vermin, or by the sweat and expectorations of the men, horrified the enlightened.[157]

The work was especially hazardous to health. As Table 3.9 demonstrates, in an age when working men died young, bakers died younger than most.

Table 3.9   Average ages at death in London, 1848*

Bakers	49 years 0 months
Tailors	49 years 3 months
Shoemakers	50 years 0 months
Carpenters	52 years 4 months
Weavers	57 years 9 months

Source: PP 1847–8 LI (362) 367, HoC 29.5.1848, p 369.

* For comparative purposes, it must be assumed that men in all five crafts began work at the same age, and did not transfer from other trades.

And the living were prone to heat exhaustion, pneumonia, or severe colds, chest and lung damage (through breathing in flour dust), heart failure and apoplexy (from physical exertion, especially when making dough), and also a peculiar and painful rash on the hands ('bakers' itch'). Of 111 bakers examined by Dr Guy in 1848, none were 'in what might be termed robust health': 70 per cent complained of some disease or another (as against 36 per cent of brickmakers, 25 per cent of bricklayers' labourers, 26 per cent of carpenters, 19 per cent of scavengers, and 18 per cent of silk printers), and almost half had had a severe illness.[158]

Generally bad working conditions, and the exploitation of workers, especially at the bottom end of the trade, prevailed until 1870 and beyond, with little effective redress. Legislation was enacted in the 1860s to shorten the working week of apprentices and labourers under 18, and to set minimum standards of cleanliness and ventilation, but enforcement was left to local authorities, who suffered no penalty if they failed to carry out their prescribed duties. The early bakehouse acts, for the most part, were ineffective.[159]

The hazards of the trade, and particularly, the likelihood of a short working life, or one frequently interrupted by illness, had been recognized by relatively generous rates of pay. However, total earnings appear to have reached a plateau in the 1820s (see Table 3.10).

Table 3.10 Journeymen's weekly earnings

Year	Cash Payment	Board value	Total
London			
1779	approx 8s	full board: 7s	15s
1797	14s	part board	
1799	16s	part board	
1801–4	26s	part board	
1824	foreman: 30s	bread, flour, and beer	
	2nd hand: 14–20s	bread, flour, and beer	
1860s	underseller's 2nd hand: 18–19s	4s	22–23s
	1st-rate baker's 2nd hand: 21–26s	5s	26–31s
Country			
1824	foreman: 12–14s	full board: 12s	24–26s
	other: 6–8s	full board: 12s	18–20s
	Uxbridge journeyman: 21s	bread: 3s	24s

Sources: G: Ms 7801 1/2; PP IV/I (74) item 43, HoC 27.4.1804, Preface, p 5 – Loveland; VI (212) 465, HoC 8.4.1824, p 4 – Turner; XLVII (3080) 1, HMSO 1862, pp 73, 82, 120, 232, 251.

In addition to ordinary pay, the men could benefit from 'Sack money' – the pence given by the miller for the return of his sacks. In London, that bonus usually went to the foreman, but in the provinces it might be given to the hand. Sack money might add 1s 6d weekly.[160]

Weekly pay rates disguise a fall in the hourly earnings of undersellers' men. Not only were they paid less than their counterparts in the trade, they were worked harder. In 1848 there were 'many cases' of two men and a strong lad working three or even four batches daily, baking 30 or 40 Sacks of flour a week, against 25 Sacks from three men at the end of the war.[161] Also, since undersellers did not deliver, the men had no release from the bakehouse during the day; moreover, they were thereby deprived of further and important, if undeclared, earnings – they could not benefit from what was called 'the making system', that is the doctoring of customers' bills. This time-honoured subterfuge probably augmented a journeyman's weekly wage by about 7s 0d; that at least was the amount by which Mr Spiking of Dover Street increased his men's wages, in an apparently successful attempt to stifle the practice (and save on the delay and paperwork involved in answering customers' complaints). An even higher figure of 12s weekly was suggested. 'Making' was so ingrained and widespread that Mrs Rundell (first published in 1807, revised and reprinted till 1859) advised her readers that their cooks should give the roundsman a ticket for every loaf purchased, and pay only on the tickets attached to the bill; but it was alleged that many cooks and housekeepers were in league with the bakers, so that any such system could be overwhelmed.[162]

Even so, the apparent levelling-off, or fall, in average earnings, the hours of work and conditions, and the exceptional risks to health, did not deter an increasing number of men (and some women) from entering the trade. Nationally, from 1831 the number of bakery workers (including masters, but perhaps or probably excluding their families, wives especially) increased closely in step with estimated wheat bread demand, so that labour productivity was remarkably constant as is clear from Table 3.11.

However, national aggregates conceal marked differences of 'density' by region, as Map 1, derived from county data given in the occupational census of 1851, shows (though county numbers aggregate usually lighter rural with heavier urban concentrations). The main regional features were as follows.

Metropolitan London, in 1851, had one bakery worker to every 195 inhabitants. Three southern counties had higher densities: Berkshire (1:180), Middlesex excluding metropolitan districts (1:180), and Oxfordshire (1:185). The heaviest urban density was at Reading (1:84).

Roughly speaking, the concentration of bakery workers in the west and north Midlands was about the same as in London and the Home Counties. At Birmingham, the ratio was 1:360. But that is explained in part by the pattern, established by the co-operative there, of large-scale bread production. By the 1850s there were six large bread mills in the

Table 3.11   Labour productivity of British bakers c1831–71

Decade	Mid-decade estimate of bakers*	Average decadal wheat need for bread** m qrs	Qrs per baker
1831–40	40,051	9.8	242
1841–50	53,018	11.5	217
1851–60	62,605	13.9	222
1861–70	67,413	15.8	234

* Number of bakers calculated from: PP XXVII (9587) 1, HMSO 1844, pp 29, 38; LXXXVIII/I (1691–I) 1, HMSO 1852–3; LXXXVIII/II (1691–II) 1, HMSO 1852–3; LIII/I (3221) 1, 265, HMSO 1863; LIII/II (3221) 1, HMSO 1863; LXXI/I (872) 1, HMSO 1873. A figure for all bakers in 1831 has been estimated by assuming the same proportion of males aged 20+ as in 1841. Thus census year figures are – 1831: est 36,000; 1841: 44,102; 1851: 61,934; 1861: 63,276; 1871: 71,549.

** See Chapter 8, decadal averages.

city, one of which had shelf storage space for 2000 loaves (about 15 ordinary batches). Two of the mills regularly reached a weekly throughput of 500 Sacks each (giving each a turnover of something like £75,000 a year, on average, in that decade). Even so, it was estimated in 1851 that the plants had only a quarter share of all the city's bread, whereas the ordinary bakers had a half, the rest being home-baked.[163]

The average density in Lancashire was 1:476 and in Cheshire 1:563, reflecting the fact that in rural districts, conversion to wheat-eating, and bought-bread, came late. But in Manchester and Salford the ratio was 1:276, in Liverpool 1:267, and in Chester 1:188, though 1:500 was about average for the cotton towns.

Despite its industrialization, Yorkshire had the lightest density of all English counties, with the East Riding at 1:633, the North Riding at 1:1092, and the West Riding lightest of all, at 1:1135. There was an astonishingly low density of bakery workers in cities such as Bradford (1:1793), Halifax (1:1030), Leeds (1:989), Sheffield (1:421), and Wakefield (1:1100). That low penetration may reflect a preference for home-baking, encouraged by the local cheapness of fuel, though the latter was not necessarily a factor, when poorer families customarily made their own dough, but took it to public bakehouses for baking. Supply may have been as important an influence as demand, if firstly, the longevity of the soke in several Yorkshire cities obstructed the development of commercial milling, and therefore impeded the accumulation of capital that elsewhere was deployed to finance the development

Map 1   Baker density, 1851

   1 baker per 300 or less inhabitants

   1 baker per 301–600 inhabitants

   1 baker per 601 or more inhabitants

of commercial baking; and secondly, if men refused to work in the poor conditions, and for the relatively low wages, of the baking trade, when there were more attractive opportunities in many other industries.

A shortage of manpower probably explains the preponderance of women in the bakery workforce of the West Riding and several other counties which is apparent from Table 3.12.

Table 3.12 Women as proportion of all bakery operatives*

	%
Westmorland	85
West Riding of Yorkshire	68
North Wales	62
South Wales	61
Cumberland	51
Shropshire	31
Cornwall	30
North Riding of Yorkshire	23
Lancashire	21
Monmouthshire	19
Durham	14
Devon	14
Staffordshire	12
Cheshire	12
Northumberland	12

* Where at or more than the national average of 12 per cent, 1851

In Scotland as a whole there was a high density of bakery workers: 1 to 284 people (a pattern established by 1831). And that aggregates highland counties, where bakers were few, with the central zone and its major cities, where, for instance, the ratio at Edinburgh and Leith was 1:151, at Greenock 1:189, Dundee 1:203, and Glasgow 1:209.

In the Glasgow factories, conditions were better, hours shorter, but hourly productivity greater, because of the different process used. A 'quarter sponge' was allowed to ferment (patent rather than brewers' yeast was used) for 12 to 14 hours and then made into a 'half sponge': this needed only 90 minutes to two hours to complete its fermentation, after which the dough was made, moulded, and baked. The Scots' method therefore was suited to clearly demarcated 12-hour shifts, the men working six a week, at collectively negotiated rates of pay. The 12-hour day gave a disciplined framework, eliminated the need to board or lodge the men, and so freed space for more ovens. It was calculated that a man working the Glasgow shift could produce 182 loaves whereas in London, a man working a 20-hour day (with breaks for sleep and food) produced only 132: thus day-productivity at Glasgow was 38 per cent greater.[164]

Not only was there a high density of bakers in much of Scotland, but a recurring surplus of men who, having completed their apprenticeship, went to seek work in London: Scotland was known as the 'nursery' of the trade.[165] The metropolitan labour pool also was routinely supplied by trained bakers from the West Country and Germany. The migratory pattern was so well established that the prospect of a career in London was instrumental in attracting lads to a Scottish apprenticeship: consequently, Scots masters could use youthful labour to substitute to a larger extent for wage-paid men. For instance this is confirmed by the occupational census of 1851 from which the data in Table 3.13 are taken.

Table 3.13   Proportion of male bakers in each age group, 1851

Age Group	GB %	Scotland %
to 19	22.1	32.2
20–39	48.5	48.4
40–54	19.3	14.0
55+	10.1	5.4
Total	100.0	100.0

Migration alone kept the London labour pool full to overflowing after 1815. Had the indigenous workforce wished to keep a closed shop (of which they were accused in the later 18th century[166]), their defences were undermined by the abolition of the Statute of Apprentices in 1814 and of the London assize in 1815, and by the further crumbling of the Worshipful Company's powers after the introduction of the metropolitan bread act of 1819. A ready supply of labour precluded the organization of effective trade unions throughout the century in review. Moreover, though the craft had its claimed 'mystery', bread-making demanded no rare skill (except perhaps in the class trade), so many might consider the craft. And bakery did have its attractions: the journeyman did not have to supply his own tools; the work if onerous was regular and indoors; and the exceptionally high level of illness meant jobs fell vacant, temporarily or permanently, at an unusually frequent rate. On Saturday nights, bakers met in their 'own' public houses, which also functioned as 'houses of call' or labour exchanges, facilitating hiring and mobility.[167] Moreover, access to mastery was quite easy.

Mastery

Because of its character as a public service, for centuries under official regulation, and otherwise often regulated to the same effect, wherever possible, by the bakers themselves, the trade offered relatively little scope for profit.

Thus in 1768 it was estimated that, on a weekly throughput of seven Sacks of flour, the London baker's costs, income, and surplus were as listed in Table 3.14.

Table 3.14 Bakers' income and costs: London, 1768

INCOME:	
Allowance per Sack	10s 0d
less expenses (fuel, yeast, salt, candles, etc)	2s 11d
LEAVES	7s 1d
× 7 Sacks per week	
= Income per annum:	£128 18s 4d
DEDUCT per annum:	
House rent	£14 0s 0d
A journeyman's cash wages @ 6s pw	£16 18s 0d
Maid's cash wages	£4 0s 0d
Housekeeping for 5 in 'family' @ £15 each	£75 0s 0d
Implements inc repair, clothes, taxes, etc	£16 0s 0d
TOTAL DEDUCTION	£125 18s 0d
Left for Interest on Capital and cover for losses on bad debts, pa	£3 0s 4d

Source: G: Ms 7801 2/2.

Taking together the cost of living of the master, his wife, a child, and the maid, to be £60, adding the maid's wages, the full benefit of the house, and say £10 from the miscellaneous item, the baker's spent income might be put at £88, with only £3 left as profit.

A similar exercise, done in 1779 (and reproduced in Table 3.15), for a baker with a weekly throughput of eight Sacks of flour, shows:

Table 3.15   Bakers' income and costs: London, 1779

INCOME:	
Per annum per 8 Sacks weekly:	
Allowance at 10s per Sack	£208 0s 0d
COSTS:	
Per week per 8 Sacks:	
Yeast	10s 6d
Salt	3s 6d
Wood	9s 4d
Wages for one journeyman at 8s plus his board at 7s	15s 0d
Board etc of apprentice	7s 0d
House rent @ £16 p a	8s 6d
Maid servant: 2s p w + board @ 6s	8s 0d
Boarding etc for Master and Wife	15s 0d
Implements including repair	2s 0d
TOTAL WEEKLY COST	£3 18s 10d
PER ANNUM	£204 19s 4d
Left for interest on Capital and cover for losses on bad debts, etc, p a	£3 0s 8d

Source: G: Ms 7801 1/2.

Again, taking together the cost of living of the master, his wife, and the maid, in this case £67 in total, and adding the full benefit of the house at £16, this baker's spent income might be put at £83, with £3 again as profit. This baker also received £18 4s 0d annually for boarding the apprentice.

Those are estimates prepared by the Worshipful Company of Bakers to show that the London trade did not make an overlarge living, and so they might be expected to err on the lower side. Also they are estimates of income and profit from bread alone. The baker might make a significant extra profit from morning goods, fancy breads, and other things. For instance, in 1827 a Fleet Street baker obtained 40 per cent of his profit from pastries and small goods.[168] The baker also earned by baking the dishes that customers brought in: in the 1779 case cited above, an estimated one shilling a day, something about £18 a year. Even so, the warning given in a guide to the London trades, published in 1747, would seem confirmed:

> The Baker is none of the most profitable Trades; he is so much under the Direction of the Magistrate, that he has no great opportunity of making himself immensely rich ...[169]

During the Napoleonic wars, the baker's living became highly precarious, when the inflated costs of yeast, salt, wood, candles, and journeymen's wages, had to be paid out of his fixed allowance. It was calculated that between 1798 and 1804 the amount left for a metropolitan baker's living fell by 44 per cent per Sack of flour processed; out of which he had to find his rent, which typically had increased from £40 to £60.[170] Though the metropolitan allowance was increased in 1805 (a benefit, however, that was soon eroded by further inflation), and though bakers earned extra amounts from rolls, fancy breads, and from cooking the dinners of the poor, many suffered considerable hardship. Some preferred to ply their trade for assured pay in the armed forces, others abandoned the craft.

The circumstances of bakers in many provincial towns were even less favourable than in London. A Select Committee of 1813 heard that at Bristol, bakers were more prone to fail than other tradesmen; at Worcester, three had closed in the last four years, leaving 14 or 15; in the last month alone, two or three had failed at Exeter (out of 40); since the start of the war, thirty had been 'broken' at Leicester, and of those remaining, not six were 'worth a shilling'. Proportionately, village bakeries may have been worst hit: at Wilton near Salisbury, four out of seven had closed; while at Wheatley near Oxford, of four bakers 'one of them is in prison, and his family on the parish, and another had his goods siezed'. To survive as a provincial baker, it was said, a man had to have other and more profitable interests: as a miller, or corn factor, or general chandler.[171]

The circumstances of provincial bakers improved at the end of the war. Those in assized jurisdictions were relieved in 1813, by Parliament, which ended the power of magistrates to fix the local bakers' allowances, and itself assumed the responsibility, granting the same as allowed to the London trade; that was generous, especially so when with peace, the value of money increased (as a result, the 'country' allowance was reduced marginally in 1824). But relatively few bakers were direct beneficiaries of that boon: their powers reduced, most magistrates discontinued the assize, especially so once the abolition of the London assize showed the cast of government policy (the few remaining country assizes were abolished in 1836).

However, price evidence suggests that, wherever they could, bakers kept to the allowances last granted under the assize system, of roughly

2d a loaf: of which (again roughly) 1d would be absorbed in costs (excluding flour) and 1d left for the baker's living (including rent and, as applicable, taxes). Thus a provincial baker with a throughput of say eight Sacks (640 quartern loaves, old weight) weekly, might expect a gross annual revenue of about £280, giving a living of £140, from bread (such earnings being supplemented by other baked goods and various enterprises). Self-regulation was more easily achieved in the provinces, given that smaller markets offered less scope to intensive marketing and estate-building, as practised by competing millers in London. Where it was not necessary to compete, it seems that millers believed it necessary not to compete: rather than encouraging underselling, they preferred to sustain the bakers' margins (which better assured the payment of flour bills). Also, in smaller markets, bakers were likely to be bonded by ties of kinship and close acquaintance, and so disinclined to 'unbrotherliness'. Even in unassized jurisdictions, where supposedly market forces ruled, it was common for bakers to collectively agree their prices, either openly (by operating a voluntary assize) or informally (as at Bath, after the discontinuation of its assize); the practice was so widespread that parliamentary witnesses and newspapers routinely cited 'the bakers' price' at a place without further comment. Prices could differ significantly between place and place at any time, but such variations may represent different qualities of bread. Provided there was no evidence that bakers' agreements were maintained by threat or fine (contrary to the combination acts), they seem to have been tolerated by authority.[172]

Collective agrements might break down, as at Plymouth in 1821, where loaves were sold at 2d or 3d below the 'regular' price, though they were said to be underweight. Also, interlopers from elsewhere could try to undersell the agreed price of a locality, but then the vested trade might make corresponding cuts until the danger was past, or else prevail on the millers to deny flour or credit to the intruder.[173]

In addition to their ordinary earnings, bakers could, like millers, make profit on their stocks. Some (though probably an exceptional, entrepreneurial, minority) bought grain on Mark Lane during the turbulent war years, and may have made handsome gains, but there were few such opportunities in the 1820s and 1830s, when wheat was falling. However, expectation of fresh, sustained, increases in 1847 lured many to take large positions in wheat and flour. The anticipated rise petered out, however (breadflour advanced only 7 per cent, taking the average prices for 1846 and 1847), and many bakers were caught by the subsequent fall (of 26 per cent, averaging 1847 and 1848).[174]

Given meagre profits, why did men seek mastery? Some may have hoped to emulate the business skills of the more successful wartime undersellers, though the opportunity to do so clearly diminished after

1815. In any case, a man so disposed could find many trades more conducive than baking: commercial milling for one. Even to the less ambitious, the gain in earnings, above those of a first-hand, were not large: a cash wage of say 30s weekly, which with food, drink, and perks, might be parlayed into £100 per annum, could be as much as a master would earn, after deducting his rent and bad debts; and in London at least, the trade was so competitive that all might be lost.

Certainly some bakers appeared to do well, even after the war. An Ascot baker, for instance, was able to substantially extend his premises, and, in the course of an unusually long working life, buy or build eight cottages for rent.[175] A Peckham baker bought a freehold property in Surrey for £1200, though he went bankrupt in 1848, probably after injudicious speculation in wheat or flour.[176]

. Often, however, the rationale of mastery may not have been wholly material: advancement to mastery was a phase in the reproductive cycle of the trade. Quite literally so, when hours and conditions, especially in second- and third- class bakeries, militated against a journeyman marrying. Typically, marriage and mastery went together, and often the one assured the other, where a journeyman married the daughter or widow of an established baker. Mastery provided accommodation, above the shop, in which to live in domesticity; the baker's wife often served customers and managed the accounts; their children would help in the work.[177]

Others came into mastery through inheritance, as the continuity of family names in the trade indicates.[178] Otherwise, if a man without a patrimony intended to marry outside the trade, he would either set up his own bakery or else buy a going concern, in preparation and perhaps as a pre-condition. The very lack of profit in baking meant that the cost of entry was relatively low, a minimum in the 1860s as in the 1740s, of £100.[179] Above that, investment would vary according to the length of the bakery lease, the weekly volume (if a going concern was acquired), and the quality of the trade, whether respectable or not: £1000 being roughly the upper limit, and £500 perhaps, the average.[180]

If he was abstemious and careful with his money, a journeyman might save £100 over perhaps eight years, at a rate of say five shillings weekly (which was not hard to do when hours and conditions left little opportunity to spend, except on Saturday nights), and that might be supplemented by his gains on the making system.[181] If he needed to borrow, however, he was unlikely to turn to normal channels, given that the very low rate of return on capital, and the well-known insecurities of the trade, deterred lenders. The usual practice was to borrow from a miller. In the 1820s, for instance, David Johnston took over a Peckham bakery with twelve years remaining on the lease, and a throughput of eight Sacks weekly, for £750; to raise which he borrowed £500 at 5 per cent from a miller (he was given the rest by his prospective mother-in-law).[182]

A miller was ready to lend so as to secure custom for his flour; as security, generally he held the baker's lease, and a policy on his life. Should the baker fail, the miller might put in a manager in his stead, though with evident reluctance (only thirty of the 1706 London bakeries of 1815 were managed by 'millers' men', though numbers increased after 1824).[183] A 'millers' man' was allowed from 5s to 7s per Sack of flour processed, from which he paid all his costs.[184]

Not only did the millers lend start-up money, they also provided virtually the whole of the baking trade with its working capital, by extending credit, normally at three months, though often extended. Such credit provided an underseller with a positive cashflow. In the first-class trade, however, much of the advantage was passed on to customers, who were given credit on like terms, similarly to secure business. So completely did credit rule, that by the end of the 18th century London bakers took in their weekly supply of flour without knowing its price. However, when wheat and flour prices fell, in the 1820s and 1830s, the levels of required working capital were much reduced, and some bakers at least were able to free themselves of debt.[185]

Had the commercial millers not financed the baking trade, indeed, had they been returned by law to their hireling status, it is unlikely that the trade could have expanded as it did, to meet the needs of an increasing population. The strictures imposed by authority upon the bakers are examined next.

Notes

1. I am grateful to Dr Collins for this observation.
2. Bennett & Elton Vol 1, chapters I–V, especially pp 22–23, 168–9, 223, letter from HSW in *The Times* 27.10.1855; Walsh cit David p 42; David p 155 et seq; Dodd p 181.
3. Copley: Cottage Comforts; Rundell: New System; Acton: English Bread Book.
4. Letter from HSW in *The Times*, 27.10.1855, p 7f.
5. Copley p 60; David p 158; Edward Smith: Practical Dietary pp 44–5; Timbs p 249.
6. Oddy in F M L Thompson (ed), Vol 2, p 255.
7. See Chapter 2.
8. David p 155 et seq; Sheppard & Newton Chapter 11; PP XLVII (3080) 1, HMSO 1862, p 109: the capacity range of commercial ovens was from 120 to 180 quartern loaves.
9. Crell & Wallace (eds), Vol XVIII, p 219.

10. Edward Smith: Practical Dietary pp 44–5; Timbs p 249; HoC Sessional Papers vol 131 Cd 4983, 10.2.1800, p 6.
11. Orbell: thesis p 48; D Davies cit E P Thompson: Moral Economy p 101; D Davies cit Hammonds: V L p 110; Silvester p 18.
12. Thwaites: thesis p 219; HoC Sessional Papers vol 131 Cd 5056, 9.6.1800, p 5; David p 99.
13. Edlin pp 154–8.
14. PP IV part I (74) item 43, HoC 27.4.1804, p 6 – Loveland; Thrupp p 36; Copley p 59; Acton cit David p 185; PP 1831–2 VII (697) 253, p 156 – McEwen, p 166 – Digby.
15. Richardson: thesis p 126, citing Defoe and Cobbett.
16. Thwaites: thesis p 219; Eden pp 108, 282; D Davies p 118; Ashton: Changes p 177; Burnett: P & W pp 17–19.
17. G: Ms 7801 2/2 – letters 1813; PP V (186) 1341, HoC 6.6.1815, Appendix 8; Eden pp 108, 282, Thwaites: thesis p 219; Davies cit Richardson: thesis p 54, n 3.
18. PP XLVII (3080) 1, HMSO 1862, pp 57, 162.
19. PP IV part I (74) item 43, HoC 27.4.1804, p 4 – Loveland, p 9 – Farr; PP III Reports I (82) 401, HoC 3.6.1813, pp 7–8 – Urch, p 9 – Stacey, p 6 – Langston.
20. PP IV part I (74) item 43, HoC 27.4.1804, p 8 – Kirkman, p 9 – Grose Smith; III Reports I (82) 401, HoC 3.6.1813, p 10 – Everet, p 8 – Urch, p 9 – Stacey.
21. Extrapolated from PP IV part I (74) item 43, HoC 27.4.1804, Appendix, correlated to London bread price for that year.
22. Author's calculation.
23. Copley p 60.
24. J Davies p 37; Dodd p 167.
25. Mrs Beeton cit David p 162.
26. David p 185 et seq.
27. Barker, Oddy & Yudkin p 28; PP XXV (161) 1, HoC 14.4.1863, p 346; XXVIII (3416) 1, HMSO 1864, pp 228, 230, 231, 234, 243.
28. Acton p 82.
29. Dodd p 181; D Davies cit E P Thompson: Moral Economy p 101.
30. Orbell: thesis pp 47–8.
31. PP XXXII (13) 805, HoC 13.2.1865, for later army figures.
32. PP XLVII (3080) 1, HMSO 1862, p 135 et seq.
33. Abingdon RO: Church Records Box 3, Packet 27; Eden p 255.
34. Orbell: F & P p 141; idem: thesis p 339.
35. Calculated from PP 1804 IV/2 (118) item 9, HoC 6.6.1804; X (169) 543, HoC 20.3.1815.
36. Bennett & Elton Vol III p 171.
37. M D Freeman p 17.
38. Orbell: F & P p 147; Bennett & Elton Vol I p viii, Vol III chapters VIII, IX and X; see documents relating to Bramhall et al v Manchester Free Grammar School, MCL-A, MC: M516/1/1–92; papers re dispute over grinding corn at Carr Mill in Pendle Forest, MCL-A, MC: L1/12/34/1–48; Cornwall RO: Liskeard 358, 359; Sinclair pp 230–1.
39. Bennett & Elton Vol II p 193; Vol III pp 106, 154–5, 165, 171; Sinclair p 231 n.
40. Orbell: thesis p 128.

41. M D Freeman p 9; Orbell: thesis p 340.
42. Orbell: thesis p 54.
43. Bennett & Elton Vol II pp 247–5, 315; Orbell: thesis p 54; Dodd p 176.
44. M D Freeman pp 167–8, 172–92.
45. HoC Sessional Papers vol 131 Cd 5080, 1.7.1800, p 4 – Bush, p 7 – Pratt.
46. Bennett & Elton Vol III p 173.
47. Silvester p 15.
48. Acton pp 87–8; Dodd p 183.
49. Accum p 127.
50. [Egmont] p 19 n.
51. Atwood p 11; Charles Smith p 23; M D Freeman p 284; Orbell: F & P p 146; idem: thesis p 55; Silvester p 9; *Gentleman's Magazine* cit Bennet & Elton Volume III p 170; G: Ms 7799 – Pelham's observations.
52. Orbell: F & P p 162; Tann: Ag H of E & W Vol VI p 414.
53. M D Freeman pp 208–9.
54. Gras p 157 et seq.
55. M D Freeman p 300.
56. Clapham II p 299; PP VIII/II (465) 1, HoC 21.7.1836, Q 15266 – Frean.
57. See Chapter 6 Section 3.
58. See Chapter 6 Section 1.
59. M D Freeman p 286 et seq.
60. Acton p 89, Drummond & Wilbraham p 341; HoC Sessional Papers Vol 131 Cd 4983, 10.21800, p 15 – Urquhart, p 20 – Kingsford, p 22 – Dunkin, p 24 – Killick, p 34 – Scott; Orbell: thesis p 38.
61. HoC Sessional Papers Vol 131 Cd 4983, 10.2.1800, p 21 – Pilcher, p 27 – Perry.
62. Thomas Jefferson cit Kuhlmann p 36; PP 1814–15 V (26) 1035, HoC 23.11.1814, p 37 – Solly, p 102 – Parker; VIII/II (465) 1, HoC 21.7.1836, Qs 15266, 15271 et seq – Frean.
63. The account does not state the conversion rate: if a simple conversion of 8 bushels of flour = 1 quarter was used, rather than a conversion allowing for a 75 per cent extraction rate, then the proportion may be somewhat understated.
64. HoC Sessional Papers vol 131, Accounts 18.11.1800, nos V and VI.
65. PP 1814–15 V (26) 1035 p 151.
66. Silvester pp 14–21.
67. Anon: Lying Detected p 34.
68. Orbell: thesis p 124.
69. PP 1814–15 V (26) 1035, p 87 – Kingsford.
70. HoC Sessional Papers vol 25 Cd 3213, 14.6.1774, Report.
71. Bennett & Elton Vol III p 292.
72. Girdler p 105.
73. G: CoCo Reports 1810–15, No 13 – p 5; Corp PD 32.8 p 20 – Lovell.
74. G: Fo Pam 894, p 14.
75. HoC Sessional Papers vol 131 Cd 5080, 1.7.1800, p 18 – Pratt; Orbell: thesis p 138; PP III/I (259) 417, p 8 – Payne; G: Fo Pam 894: p 3.
76. Burke p xii.
77. See Chapter 4 Section 5.
78. eg: M D Freeman, Orbell, Tann in Ag H of E & W VI, and Westworth: Albion Steam Flour Mill.

79. Dodd p 176; CLRO: PD 32.8, 27.10.1796, p 7 – Wyatt, p 12 – Woolhead, p 17 – Lovell; M D Freeman p 20; Orbell: thesis p 351; G: Ms 5177 – Court Book 13, 27.9.1813; G: Common Council Reports 1810–15, no 13.

80. Orbell: thesis App 16; Tann: Ag H of E & W VI p 409; M D Freeman p 316; Westworth p 382.

81. Westworth pp 383–4.

82. Sackage estimated relative to that of 1798–1814, See Chapter 5 Section 6.

83. HoC Sessional Papers vol 131 Cd 5080; 1.7.1800, p 2 – Scott, p 4 – Bush; Cd 4983, 10.2.1800, p 35 – Scott; Dumbell p 93; M D Freeman pp 205, 317; Westworth pp 389–91; Bennett & Elton Vol III pp 289–91.

84. Bennett & Elton Vol III pp 291–2; Westworth pp 392–5; Shaw pp 1723–4.

85. Shaw pp 1723–4.

86. G: Fo Pam 894, pp 7–8; CLRO: MS 119.2, 113.3.

87. G: Fo Pam 894; Wells pp 1, 42 n 12, 45, 214–8; G: Ms 7801 2/2 – petition for the London Company; HoC Sessional Papers vol 131 Cd 5080, Privy Council 1.7.1800; Burke p xii (5); 39 & 40 Geo III c 97; PP I/I item 11, HoC 1.4.1801 and successive annual accounts up to XI (86) 19, HoC 25.3.1811; Girdler p 70 et seq.

88. Orbell: thesis pp 149, 170.

89. Tann: Co-op p 47 et seq; Orbell: thesis Chapter 9.

90. HoC Sessional Papers vol 131 Cd 5056, Privy Council 9.6.1800; Cole pp 13–14; Tann: Co-op p 47 et seq; idem in Ag H of E & W VI, p 409; Orbell: thesis Chapter 9.

91. Westworth pp 382–8; PP V (186) 1341, HoC 6.6.1815, p 12 – Smith; V (426) 1, HoC 17.4.1821, p 13 – Gill.

92. HoC Sessional Papers vol 131 Cd 5056, Privy Council 9.6.1800, p 3 – Clifford; Horne p 29.

93. Orbell: thesis pp 62, 332, 334–5; PP V (426) 1, HoC 17.4.1821, p 13 – Gill; HoC Sessional Papers volume 131 Cd 5056, Privy Council 9.6.1800, pp 2–5.

94. PP V (186) 1341, HoC 6.6.1815, p 49 – Phare, p 58 – Fothergill; V (426) 1, HoC 17.4.1821, p 13 – Gill; V (612) 1, HoC 2.8.1833, p 116 – Merry.

95. Dodd pp 180–1.

96. Bennett & Elton III pp 242–3, 256, 258, 263–70; M D Freeman p 9.

97. Holyoake pp 232–3.

98. Cole pp 84–93.

99. Potter p 68.

100. See Chapter 6 Section 3.

101. See Chapter 6 Section 1.

102. Kanefsky cit Perren: 1990 p 422; M D Freeman Appendix I , p 340.

103. Marx: Capital Vol I p 358; Marx drew on PP XLVII (3080) 1, HMSO 1862, eg p 13: 'There is probably no branch of trade supplying a vast and constant demand which has so completely remained in its primitive condition . . .'.

104. Adam Smith p 65.

105. PP III/I (82) 401, HoC 12.3.1813, p 11 – Everet; III/I (259) 417, HoC 3.6.1813, p 14 – Shepherd, p 28 – Beaver, p 37 – Johnson; ref Aunt Drusilla Fawley's shop in *Jude the Obscure*, Chapter II; D Davies p 118;

Eden pp 108, 282; Burnett: P & W pp 18–19; Ashton: Changes p 177; Thwaites: thesis p 219.

106. Thwaites: thesis p 221.
107. See Chapter 4.
108. Thwaites: Dearth & Marketing p 121.
109. HoC Sessional Papers volume 25, Cd 3213.
110. PP V (186) 1341, HoC 6.6.1815, p 147.
111. Copley cit David p 175; Eden p 335.
112. Holmes in Minchinton (ed) p 97; Dorset RO: B2/25/1.
113. HoC Sessional Papers vol 131 Cd 4983, 10.2.1800, pp 18–19 – Kingsford.
114. See Chapter 4 Section 2.
115. PP VIII/II (465) 1, HoC 21.7.1836, Q 17500 – Hayes; HoC Sessional Papers vol 131 Cd 4983, 10.2.1800, pp 18–19 – Kingsford.
116. PP VIII/II (465) 1, HoC 27.4.1836, Q 17501 – Hayes.
117. Read p 16.
118. Burnett: P & W pp 18–19.
119. Richardson p 39.
120. West Sussex RO: Add MS 18, 338–18, 341: ledgers of a Cuckfield baker, especially Jan-Feb 1859.
121. Dodd p 189; XVII (3080) 1, HMSO 1862, p 13.
122. G: Pam 16570; Worshipful Company of Bakers of London pamphlet, 1982; Thrupp p 2; Edward A Freeman p 168; Southampton Records I, Southampton Corporation 1963 p 27; C Moore: Brief Notes; Anon: Incorporation of Bakers of Glasgow, p 1.
123. Thrupp p 72; G: Ms 7801 2/2 – notes as to Laying Open the Trade; G: Ms 5177 Court Book 10, 2.2.1778, 15.3.1778, 11.3.1783.
124. Defoe: Complete English Tradesman.
125. PP V (186) 1341, HoC 6.6.1815, pp 40–6 – Wake, p 52 – Gray.
126. Thrupp p 70; G: Ms 7798A; G: Ms 5177 – Court Book 10, 11.3.1783; Court Book 11, 3.4.1785; Court Book 12, 5.2.1798.
127. G: Ms 7798A – Trade Minutes of Master Bakers, esp 18.8.1783, 15.10.1783, 15.3.1784.
128. PP VI (212) 465, HoC 8.4.1824, p 5.
129. Girdler p 88.
130. PP V (186) 1341, HoC 6.6.1815 – Grose Smith.
131. PP V (186) 1341, HoC 6.6.1815, p 13 – Wood; VI (212) 465, HoC 8.4.1824.
132. PP V (186) 1341, HoC 6.6.1815, p 102 – Bell; p 10 – Report.
133. G: Fo Pam 894 pp 11, 16–17.
134. See Chapter 4.
135. PP IX (345) 227, HoC 22.5.1818, p 17 – Hill; XLVII (3080) 1, HMSO 1862, p 52 – Wright.
136. PP IX (345) 227, HoC 22.5.1818 – Hill; VI (212) 465, HoC 8.4.1824 – Gray, Huntsman.
137. PP VI (212) 465, HoC 8.4.1824 – Turner, Gray.
138. PP IX (345) 227, HoC 22.5.1818, p 17 – Hill VI (212) 465, HoC 8.4.1824, p 14 – Huntsman.
139. PP V (186) 1341, HoC 6.6.1815 – Phare.
140. PP VI (212) 465, HoC 8.4.1824, p 4 – Turner, pp 7–9 – Gray; Walsh p 281.

141. Letter in *The Times* 9.9.1854.
142. See Chapter 2.
143. Burnett: P & W p 112, citing PP XLVII (3080) 1, HMSO 1862, p 180.
144. Patterson, A Temple: Portsmouth p 84; Culverhouse pp 27–8.
145. PP V (186) 1341, HoC 6.6.1815 – Preface, App 8; HoC Sessional Papers vol 131 Cd 5080, 1.7.1800, p 27 – Loveland; Cd 5056, Privy Council 9.6.1800, p 13 – Clifford.
146. PP III/I (259) 417, HoC 3.6.1813, pp 44–5 – Urch.
147. Tann: Co-op p 56.
148. PP XXVII (6239) 323, HMSO 1863, p 328; XLVII (3080) 1, HMSO 1862, pp 104, 117; Dodd pp 194–5; Adam pp 101–3.
149. Dodd pp 196–8; DNB – Dr John Dauglish.
150. PP XLVII (3080) 1, HMSO 1862, pp 126, 131–2, 142, 150, 152, 166; Acton p 30; Haydn's Dictionary of Dates: 'Bread'; CLRO: Gaol Committee Misc Papers No.4 537C (Stevens' catalogue).
151. Muir pp 10–12; PP XLVII (3080) 1, HMSO 1862, p 131.
152. PP XLVII (3080) 1, HMSO pp 61–2, 206–27; DNB – Dr John Dauglish.
153. Thrupp p 115.
154. Burnett: P & W 3rd ed p 122; Thrupp p 99; PP V (212) 465, HoC 8.4.1824, p 7 – Gray, p 13 – Huntsman, p 16 – Bayne; PP XLVII (3080) 1, HMSO 1862, p 120 – Peacock.
155. PP XLVII (3080) 1, HMSO 1862, especially pp 104–28; PP 1831–2 VII (697) 253, HoC 6.8.1832; Read p 20.
156. Johnston p 91.
157. PP XLVII (3080) 1, HMSO 1862, throughout; PP XLVII (175) 261, HoC 31.3.1865 – Preface; PP LXVI (394) 373, HoC 6.7.1866 – Preface; Acton p 29 et seq.
158. The Family Oracle of Health vol 1 (1824 6th ed) p 144; PP 1847–8 LI (362), HoC 29.5.1848, p 369; PP XLVII (3080) 1, HMSO 1862, pp 8, 204; 1831–2 VII (697) 253, HoC 6.8.1832, p 158 – McEwen, p 163 – Maton; VI (212) 465, HoC 8.4.1824, pp 158, 163; G: Pam 1093 pp 4–5.
159. PP I (Bill 54) p 133, HoC 25.6.1863; XLVII (175) p 261, HoC 31.3.1865; LXXVI (394) 373, HoC 6.7.1866.
160. PP VI (212) 465, HoC 8.4.1824, p 8 – Gray, p 15 – Bayne, p 19 – Swaine.
161. Read pp 17–18.
162. PP XLVII (3080) 1, HMSO 1862, pp 73, 82, 120, 232, 251; Campbell p 276; Maton p 2; Rundell (1859) p 10.
163. Dodd pp 196–8.
164. PP XLVII (3080) 1, HMSO 1862, pp 112–4.
165. PP 1847–8 LI (362) 367, HoC 29.5.1848, p 371 – Dr Guy.
166. G: Ms 7801 2/2 – notes for petitions against throwing open the trade.
167. PP XXVIII (6239) 323, HMSO 1863 p 115 – Bennett; Campbell, Appendix; Johnston p 89; PP XLVII (3080) 1, HMSO 1862, p 9.
168. Alexander p 125.
169. Campbell p 275.
170. PP IV/I (74) item 43, HoC 27.4.1804, p 11.
171. PP III/I (82) 401, HoC 12.3.1813, p 6 – Culverhouse, p 9 – Urch, p 10 – Stacey, p 11 – Everet, p 13 – Langston; III/I (259) 417, HoC 3.6.1813, p 14 – Shepherd, p 23 – Gray.

172. Somerset RO: DD/NE 22; Neale: Economic Conditions; *The Times* 19.9.1854; *Bridgwater Times* 14.9.1854, 21.9.1854.
173. West Devon RO: W 684 (letter from a freeman to the Mayor, 25.10.1821); *Buckinghamshire Advertiser* 5.9.1854; *The Times* 13.9.1854, 19.9.1854; *Bristol Times* 9.9.1854.
174. Read p 19.
175. Pearce typescript (Reading Central Library, Local Studies Collection B/ TU/LON).
176. Johnston p 146.
177. Thrupp pp 69, 121; PP V (186) 1341, HoC 6.6.1815 – Wright; XLVII (3080) 1, HMSO 1862.
178. Thrupp p 121 et seq.
179. Campbell: The London Tradesman, Appendix; Anon 'Bread Riots at Oxford 1867'.
180. Turton p 83.
181. Maton p 9.
182. Johnston pp 113–5.
183. PP V (186) 1341, HoC 6.6.1815 – Grose Smith; Read p 15.
184. Read p 15.
185. PP VI (212) 465, HoC 8.4.1824, pp 5, 11.

CHAPTER 4

The Assize of Bread

The nature of bread supply and the character of the baking trade in Britain were shaped by the assize of bread, wherever it operated up to its abolition in 1836.[1] And even where an assize was not set, the system influenced the trade, either because its principle and methods were approximated by voluntary agreement or because they were consciously refuted; that broader influence, *pro* or *contra*, was felt long after abolition.

The assize was one part of a comprehensive framework of regulation that affected the provision of bread and breadstuffs. The other chief elements, summarized in other chapters, were: the Poor Law; the Corn Laws; the statute and common laws against forestalling, ingrossing, and regrating; and an enabling power, vested in authority, to intervene directly in the market at times of crisis.

> In ancient times . . . it was usual to attempt to regulate the profits of merchants and other dealers, by rating the price both of provisions and other goods. The assize of bread is, so far as I know, the only remnant of this ancient usage . . .[2]

That Parliament's attention should still be focused upon bread and breadstuffs, when otherwise the regulation of price and profit had been left (explicitly or tacitly) to market forces, signifies the unique importance of 'the staff of life'. The assize of bread might be seen as a symbol, and as an instrument of appeasement, lest the hungry rebel. For, as a miller observed: 'an infuriated mob may be sooner collected on the subject of bread, than on any other; and, when once put in motion, be made the tool of the disaffected to an unlimited extent'.[3] Fear of such consequences, if never absent, was periodically enlivened by foreign example: for instance, Lord Liverpool, who had witnessed the fall of the Bastille, 'constantly fretted lest hunger' ('or national bankruptcy or a licentious press') 'should spark off a French-style revolution. . .'[4] Behind official policy was an awareness that might be formulated as a definition: *a staple is that which must be supplied lest a society break down.*

While other responses to domestic dearth, such as direct intervention in the wheat trade, and the Poor Law, addressed the threat of famine, the assize of bread had a particular economic significance. Its premise was that the demand for and supply of bread did not and could not interact as in other markets, since there was no parity of sovereignty between buyer and seller. Average per capita consumption of the staple was, of necessity, highly inelastic, and, given the difficulty of substitution, when the price of grain rose, the ordinary consumer had no option but to pay. That dependency, it was feared, gave every opportunity to suppliers acting in collusion, to charge as they pleased, without fear of a consequential fall in demand.[5] Therefore, because the trade in bread did not constitute a market proper, it could not be left to market forces. Thus the 'moral economy' of bread.[6]

While the assize was intended to protect the interest of all bread buyers, most especially it was meant to defend the poor, who relied on the staple largely or entirely.[7] And in that respect, the assize exemplified the Christian ethic. However, while the assize defended some of the poor, it was irrelevant to many others who were not buyers, but received bread (or breadstuffs) as payment-in-kind or by other means.[8] And the assize concerned bread alone: the prices of wheat and flour were unregulated; thus the system had no direct relevance to those who baked their own bread; and since it dealt only with loaves bought from bakers, it was originally and principally a feature of urban administration. Above all, the bread acts were framed with London much in mind (and several concerned London alone). That London should receive special attention is understandable in any circumstance: it was the capital, under the direct observation of parliamentarians, and strongly represented by its Corporation, by its own MPs, and by those of its citizens who sat for 'country' constituencies. But, London also was the chief bread market in Britain, and indeed, as its population soared, the largest bread market in the world, the principal concentration of those wholly or mainly dependent upon the baker for their chief sustenance.

One consequence of this urban and metrocentric emphasis was that, although the bread acts encompassed loaves made from the flours of other grains, in practice, as the papers of parliamentary committees indicate, the assize was concerned chiefly with the sale of wheat bread.[9]

Successive bread acts were intended to prevent both the overt and covert exploitation of dependency; in the first case to ensure that the price of a loaf was manifestly fair, and in the second, that bread was pure (as defined by law), that full weight was given, and that the types of bread were properly identified. Penalties for infraction were severe. Often, the legislation concerning standards was and is subsumed under the title of the Assize of Bread, a natural elision since usually the same acts concerned both aspects of regulation; strictly, however, 'Assize of Bread' refers only to pricing. Standards were specified by further bread acts after 1836.

Given the inevitable and often sizeable and frequent fluctuations in the cost of wheat, authority did not try to prevent changes in the price of bread; what was intended was that such changes be manifestly fair. But a dual fairness was intended: the assize was meant to be fair to the buyer and fair to the baker, who was to have an adequate reward for his work (without which the supply of bread would be threatened). The baker was, in effect, treated as a public servant and paid a fixed fee to cover his costs and provide him a living, which allowance was added to the prevailing price of breadstuffs. In principle, therefore, his income was assured independently of the price of wheat (or flour): ostensibly he neither gained nor lost by the swings of the market.[10] However, a system which had been quite simple to operate in the 13th century was, at the start of the 18th century, in disarray.

4.1 THE MODERNIZED ASSIZE

It was popularly supposed that King Alfred instituted the assize of bread, but the earliest known authorization is an ordinance of 1202.[11] An explication, concerning the pricing and standards of ale as well as bread, was issued in 1265.[12] Over following centuries, various amendments to that statute increased the amount of penalties, and the bakers' allowance, to keep them roughly abreast of inflation, but the main text was unchanged.[13] With the result that, in its language generally, and in the terms used to describe types of bread, by the start of the 18th century the statute had become 'so obscure and impracticable in these Times, that many Doubts and Difficulties have arisen, and daily do arise'. The meaning of the Act might be guessed at by magistrates, or approximated by local custom, but in many places the assize had been abandoned. As a result, 'covetous and evil-disposed Persons taking Advantage of the same' had 'for their own Gain and Lucre, deceived and oppressed her Majesty's Subjects, and more especially the poorer Sort of people . . .'[14]

Much of the once comprehensive system of medieval price regulation also had been left to decay, and indeed, those parts of the 1265 Act that dealt with beer were not revived.[15] But, alarmed by the threat of famine and disorder in 1709, Parliament chose to rescue the assize of bread from desuetude. A new and comprehensive bread act was passed, framed in current English, and setting out 'a plain and constant Rule and Method' that all magistrates were to observe.[16] Changes in the market were recognized and appropriate measures incorporated. Thus, the Assize of Bread no longer was an antiquity, lingering only where tradition persisted, but, revised and restated, it was to be a chief instrument of social appeasement and economic regulation in the 18th century.

The new Act (8 Anne c.18) and its subsequent amendments and additions[17] abandoned the nine designations of bread referred to in the old statute,[18] whose character was lost in obscurity, and introduced contemporary terms to describe three permitted grades of wheat bread: White (the best), Wheaten (a middling grade), and Household (brown or more often grey, bread). Provision also was made for breads made from other grains.

In the past, bread had been sold at fixed price-points, so that the weight of loaves at each price had been varied according to the prevailing cost of wheat. That had allowed finer shading, in ounces and drams, than could be achieved by price variations, when the smallest coin in circulation was the penny. But, with the introduction of copper coinage in the late 17th century, it was possible to shade price to the nearest farthing. From the baker's point of view, fixed weights varying in price were more efficient: it was easier to judge an unvarying dough weight, and to use moulds. The Act allowed magistrates to set the assize either by weight or by price (their preference being decided, probably, by the amount of small coin in circulation in their jurisdictions at any time).[19] The new fixed weights were denominated in terms of measure: Peck, Half Peck, Quarter Peck (or quartern) and Half Quartern. However, the traditional fixed-price pennyweight and twopennyweight loaves were to continue everywhere. For assize purposes, all weights were to be avoirdupois, and all measures Winchester standard.

Until 1709 one uniform bakers' allowance had been set by Parliament. But the new Act, recognizing that costs (especially rent, fuel, and journeymen's wages) now varied considerably from place to place, transferred the responsibility for determining the allowance to the local magistrates, so that account could be taken of varying local circumstances.

In its operation, the Act was meant to be simple. In any locality the prevailing price of a bushel of wheat was reported by the clerk of the market (or in London, by the mealweighers), to the magistrates who, adding the bakers' allowance, then referred to an official table (a ready reckoner) and found the true weight or price of each type of bread. Those prices then were declared publicly as the lawful maximum to be charged throughout the jurisdiction, and prevailed until any significant change in the cost of wheat prompted a new assize. Not only was the method simple, the populace could see that it was fair, for it had only three components: the price of wheat in the local marketplace; the bakers' allowance, openly declared and usually unchanged for decades;

and the bread yield of a bushel of wheat (which always could be substantiated by home-baking, and in any case was stipulated by Parliament, not by the bakers).

However, the 1709 Act foreshadowed increasing complications. Recognizing that in London especially bakers now bought meal and even ready-dressed flours, magistrates were given discretion to set the assize by the price of meal or flour, rather than by wheat. In principle, that normally meant cheaper loaves, since the price of commercial flour, relative to that of wheat, was declining on trend; but it increased confusion as to the true cost of breadstuffs.[20] Such confusion soon multiplied.

4.2 MARKET CHANGE AND MANIPULATION

Though Parliament acknowledged that the mechanization of flour production had changed the roles of miller and baker, in London certainly, it did not grasp the consequences. The new legislation implied (at least it did not address the contrary) that the price of flour would bear some unchanging relationship to the price of wheat. That would prove to be far from the case. Leaving aside the self-interest of millers, flour prices could vary – in summer for example, if drought stopped the watermills – even if the price of wheat was constant. If flour was milled in the jurisdiction, the millers' difficulties might be informally assessed and accounted for. But, when a place relied heavily on 'imported' flour, such checking was impossible. Also, given increased intranational trade, wheat might be brought to market from areas outside the jurisdiction, and represent much greater variety of quality, so that the 'true' price became more elusive, especially if much of the wheat was sold directly to millers, and did not enter official reckoning.[21] That large-scale millers and buyers avoided the open market does not necessarily imply that they wished to conceal their transactions from the magistrates or public – it was sensible to avoid unnecessary market tolls and middlemen's fees – but it did make regulation more difficult, and 'justice' less manifest.

An indication of changing circumstances came in 1735, when the London bakers represented that the bulk of the flour they now received made loaves of a quality midway between the statutory White and Wheaten grades; they complained that their allowance was thereby squeezed, since the assize table assumed flour of the lower quality and price. The bread committee of the House of Commons gave them redress by informally approving an understanding between the London Corporation and the Worshipful Company that the new grade could be assized according to a specially prepared, though unstatuory, table.[22]

But while there was flexibility in response to the market, there was rising concern at the amount of wheat being consumed. In part, that increasing consumption reflected a broad shift toward wheat bread from other grains and foods;[23] in part too, it represented an accelerating increase in population, in London particularly. From 1750, after decades in which Britain had been a net exporter of wheat, importation resumed; wheat prices began to rise; and there were years of scarcity and unrest, especially in semi-industrial districts.[24] Further, the probability of increased dependency on imports implied a drain of bullion, most alarmingly of gold to France, Britain's global rival. In response, Parliament brought in a new, comprehensive, bread act.

The 1757 Act (31 Geo II c.29) reflected both continuity (in that it embodied old principles) and change: it was not concerned solely with the mechanism by which bread should be fairly priced (though the previous method was confirmed), it also was intended to manipulate consumption, by fostering economy. The Act was concerned chiefly with London, though its enabling provisions were national in scope.

While recognizing that the improved Wheaten quality sold in London had effectively replaced the statutory White and Wheaten grades, Parliament was concerned to promote sales of Household bread, a grade largely neglected by the millers and bakers, who asserted that there was no demand for it.[25] To overcome such resistance, the quality of Household bread was to be improved.[26] Even so, since the better quality Household bread would use flour of roughly an 80 per cent extraction rate, compared to the 70 per cent or so required for the improved Wheaten bread, it was expected that considerable economies could be achieved if metropolitan consumption were to divide, more or less equally, between the two.[27]

So the 1757 Act abolished the old White and Wheaten grades (though White rolls – or pennyweight and twopennyweight loaves – might still be made, if magistrates permitted), while formally acknowledging the improved Wheaten type, and also readjusting the assize table in favour of the new Household bread. It stipulated that the price of Wheaten bread always be 25 per cent more than that of Household, or that the Household loaf should weigh 25 per cent more than the Wheaten, according to whether they were priced or assized (to aid identification they were to be impressed with a W or H respectively). The higher price of improved Wheaten bread in London – an eighth above the level laid down in the 1709 Act – was recognized in a new assize table, while the price of improved Household bread was also put at one-eighth above that of the previous coarser sort. But the new price of Household bread did not fully reflect the wheat/flour cost of its improvement, so that the relative cut in its price would be subsidized by the trade. However, since the pricing of the Wheaten type gave bakers a higher than average allowance, it was presumed that they would be compensated exactly, given the projected 50/50 split of sales.[28]

Also, the framers attempted to address the difficulties of fairly assizing in a more competitive, intranational, market.[29] In explanatory notes issued for the guidance of magistrates, a formula to find a true average was offered: they should take the prices of the first and second grades of wheat, add double the price of the third grade, and divide by four.[30] And a formula was offered by which wheat and flour prices might be related.[31] But, recognizing the unwillingness of certain magistrates to burden themselves with the task of assizing bread, especially if there was as yet little commercial baking in their districts, there was an opt-out clause: magistrates could choose not to set an assize (so leaving the price of bread to 'market forces'), though at any time (for instance, during dearth) they could resume their powers.

The effects of the 1757 Act reverberated for the rest of the century. In all their principal aims, its promoters were disappointed. The attempt to shift half of London's consumption to the improved Household type failed utterly. The public refused to give up the Wheaten loaf, and bakers had no incentive to encourage them to do so, rather the reverse: any substitution of Household for Wheaten would be at their expense. They could maintain their mark-up only if they charged the new price for the former, coarser, Household quality, which it was alleged some did, further confirming their customers' detestation of 'brown bread'.[32]

However, in the provinces, where Wheaten bread of the 1709 specification was still common, and where coarse Household bread also was sold, it seemed that the 1757 Act arbitrarily increased the prices of both by one-eighth: in the short-term the Act provoked or further inflamed unrest; as the framers later acknowleged, it would have been prudent to have chosen different names for the new types.[33] In the longer-term the Act helped to improve the quality of the bread eaten outside London from the 1709 to the 1757 standard, quite contrary to the economising intentions of Parliament. And, as in London, the better allowance on Wheaten, and poorer allowance on Household, bread gave bakers an incentive to make the former, and discontinue the latter.[34]

Also, the intention to provide magistrates with effective formulae for averaging wheat prices and determining flour prices was, as even the promoters of the Act recognized, something of a forlorn hope.[35] The price of first grade wheat, for example, did not necessarily represent higher expense, since the best quality grain usually was heavier and more absorbent, so that more flour and bread could be made from it; nor did third grade wheat necessarily represent an economy, since in some years at least, it might be unfit for bread-making.[36] Moreover, because a decreasing proportion of wheat was sold in the open markets (and virtually none in Scotland[37]) such prices as were obtained often would be unrepresentative.[38] And in the growing number of places where commercial millers dominated, and where the price of flour governed real costs, the conversion formula offered to magistrates was far from exact: apart from seasonal variations, there were many qualities of commercial flour, not made to uniform standards, and it was impracticable to assay them.[39]

Thus those chief needs of a regulatory system – common denominations exactly specified and easily inspected – were in important respects lacking. The problem was compounded where local, customary, weights and measures were used for purposes of trade: when the assize was set they had to be converted, often inexactly, into the avoirdupois and Winchester scales.[40]

In practice, therefore, the assize was imposed in a somewhat arbitrary and often muddled way. At Rye, for instance, a distinctly casual 'assize' was set, not by the price of a bushel but by a cartload of wheat, and at infrequent intervals; nor were the assizes there recorded, as the Act required, in a special book (at least, none such has survived) but *inter alia* in the General Quarter Sessions Book.[41] At Oxford, where it was the University's ancient privilege to set the assize for the city, the Vice Chancellor ignored 31 Geo II, keeping to the repealed 8 Anne: one result was that illegal White loaves still were made and sold there until 1769.[42] To add to the confusion, the freedom given to magistrates to opt out made the 1757 Act a peculiar hybrid: up to its 20th Clause it was, in effect, an enabling measure, whereas, from its 21st, when the penalties for light weight, adulteration, and misdescription were set out, it was mandatory everywhere, or supposed to be. The confusion had to be removed by further legislation.[43]

The shortcomings of the 1757 Act never were adequately overcome, though several attempts to do so would be made. Had demand stabilized, perhaps the legislators would have had better success, but in the second half of the 18th century the total demand for commercial wheat bread was rising rapidly, not only because national population was increasing, but because the occupational and locational balance was shifting too. That the proportion of the population engaged in manufacturing, commercial, and clerical work, had increased, and that accordingly the demand for wheat bread had risen, was recognized when three significant measures were passed during the dearth and unrest of 1771–3. First, the internal trade in grain, and in wheat especially, was freed from impediment by the repeal of the statutes against engrossing, forestalling, and regrating (described by E P Thompson as a signal victory for *laisser faire* 'four years before Adam Smith's work was published').[44] Thus the supply of wheat to towns was facilitated, if at the expense of consumers in the growing districts. That change was closely related to official expectation that the rising demand for wheat bread would in future exceed domestic output in all but years of abundance, so that Britain must become more dependent on imports. The Corn Law of 1772 recognized probable dependency by permanently lowering the tariff barrier to imports. But it was judged essential to moderate the demand for imported wheat by making further attempts to enforce a greater economy in bread consumption: the policy of 1757 more efficiently and forcefully executed.

A first essay in that direction had been made when rioting had recurred in 1766, mostly in the areas disrupted in 1756–7.[45] It was recognized that the rise of commercial milling had weakened the operation of the assize.[46] Members of the bread committee of the House of Commons argued that, since the market and public policy were at odds, the market must be straitened and made conformable to law. They proposed that only one type of wheat bread be sold for general consumption, and that that should be the improved Household loaf. It was conceded that finer types of bread might be specially licensed by the magistrates, but only for fair days and public celebrations.[47] But the proposal was not carried into law, partly perhaps because the authoritarians then lacked an effective spokesman.

That lack was remedied by the return, from an illustrious career in the colonies, of Governor Thomas Pownall. In promoting a more lenient import policy, Pownall also stressed the need to economize on bread consumption. He accepted that Household bread, even of the improved type, was too coarse for town dwellers, and that it offered no economy, since per pound weight it gave less nourishment than whiter bread, so that more had to be eaten to obtain the same sustenance.[48] But he argued that the improved Wheaten type was too fine, and thus 'wasteful'. Therefore he proposed a new type (roughly equivalent to the Wheaten bread that the 1709 Act had specified) to be known as Standard Wheaten bread. Its quality would be halfway between the improved Wheaten and Household types. And because it would be made of all the edible grain less bran and pollards – an extraction rate that Pownall put at 75 per cent exactly – the quality of the flour could be easily assayed. Thus the difficulty of the magistrates, in finding the true quality and right price of flour, would be overcome. Further, and considering London chiefly, Pownall argued that the average price of a loaf could be reduced if the trade were laid open, allowing others than the incorporated bakers to compete.[49] But the Worshipful Company lobbied successfully,[50] and the result was a compromise. The main provision of the bread act of 1773 (13 Geo III c.62) was that the Standard Wheaten loaf (to be marked SW) was introduced not as a replacement to, but as a third grade between, the Wheaten and the Household types; its availability would be determined by magistrates locally, who were encouraged to set an assize for it (for which purpose they were issued with a special table). However, Clause VIII of the Act betokened further regulation, should local authorities think fit: justices, at their Quarter Sessions, were empowered to prohibit for three months (or longer, by renewal) the baking or selling of Wheaten bread (thus making Standard Wheaten the best available quality) providing that the trade was given one month's notice, so that old flour could be used up and the new brought in. The Worshipful Company accepted that the final bill and Act were not materially prejudicial or inconvenient, and urged the City bakers to make the Standard Wheaten bread; in turn, the Committee dropped its threat to lay open the trade.[51]

The Bread Act of 1773 (13 Geo III c.62) was no more successful in reducing the metropolitan demand for Wheaten loaves than that of 1757: the new Standard Wheaten type was decisively rejected by the populace, and the Lord Mayor and aldermen, fearing unrest, acquiesced in their judgement.[52] It was hardly compensation for failure in the chief market that authorities elsewhere, notably at Oxford, took advantage of Clause VIII, banned Wheaten bread, and made Standard Wheaten the best type available in their jurisdictions.[53] Pownall judged that he (and Parliament) had been thwarted by the commercial millers who, since they made more profit per Sack from Wheaten flour than Standard Wheaten often declined to supply the cheaper grade. He came to the conclusion, therefore, that the bread laws could not be used as an instrument of manipulation, directing demand toward more economical bread, unless the trend of several decades was arrested and reversed. In 1774 Pownall proposed that, in effect, millers should once again be, like bakers, 'public servants', and granted an allowance (a toll of five per cent) and he recommended that flour, like bread, should be assized. But this course was deemed too radical, especially once the supply crisis of the early 1770s had passed, and the proposal languished.[54]

Therefore, in practice, the regulation of bread depended increasingly upon the judgement and partiality of local authorities. Now, the general provisions of the 1757 Act were muddled, and were further complicated by the specific measure of 1773. The imprecision of the formulae for finding the true costs of wheat and flour, the increasing proportion of breadstuffs traded off-market, the powerful influence of unregulated millers, and the bakers' differential allowances all made the local authorities' task more difficult. Meanwhile there was a general apprehension amongst consumers that a curtain had fallen, obscuring truth from inspection, and allowing every evil of monopoly and profiteering to be supposed. So, if the objective of manifest fairness was still tenable, it could be achieved only by increasingly arbitrary means. For example, a magistrate might choose to discount the reported average price of wheat or flour, and set the assize at a lower level. In the past some such arbitrariness had been accepted, on the understanding that when prices were high the magistrate might favour the poor and squeeze the bakers, and when they were low, incline in the other direction, so that in the long run there would be fairness to all. But magistrates now might lean far more in one direction than the other. For instance, the London bakers claimed that over the 326 weeks between 12 November 1770 and 9 June 1777 the metropolitan assize had been set 'accurately' in only 83 weeks, too generously in 105 weeks, but hard against them in 138 weeks, and they computed the cost to their livings as £111,666.[55] In effect, the authorities reimbursed to the public part of the higher allowance on Wheaten bread. But, because a squeeze on the bakers put indirect pressure on the millers' prices, a proportion of the flour formerly sent to London was diverted to more lenient jurisdictions elsewhere, threatening a supply crisis.[56] Similar juggling with the bakers' allowance can be detected, from marginalia in the assize books, at Worcester and elsewhere.[57] Constant manipulations may have increased the popularity of certain mayors and magistrates, but they indicate a system under strain.

4.3 THE ASSIZE IN WARTIME

The sense of crisis lessened, however, thanks to the unanticipated, indeed astonishing, increase in the domestic output of wheat;[58] and it was, perhaps, indicative of easier circumstances, after decades of difficulty and dispute arising from the assessment of wheat and flour costs, that the London Corporation and the Worshipful Company settled their differences in 1792. Together they devised a version of the 1757 table that related the prices of wheat and flour, ratios that, naturally, were approximations; the important step was that the Corporation agreed to keep to the table consistently at each setting of the assize. Thus the 'voluntary table' seemed to promise a period of better relations between the civic and the trade authorities, whose co-operation was fundamental to the working of the regulatory system.

However, the agreement did not survive the dearth of 1795–6, when the then Mayor again set the assize arbitrarily against the bakers,[59] and when the trade reacted by petitioning the Prime Minister for relief, threatening to close their ovens.[60] Alarmed that the bakers, if they carried out their threat, would curtail the supply of bread in the capital, and so precipitate the most dangerous disorder, Pitt promised the delegation redress: as a result the threat was withdrawn, and in 1796 the Worshipful Company promoted a bill to end the variation of their allowance, at the *diktat* of Lord Mayors, and reintroduce a fixed sum, set by Parliament (which, to cover increased costs, they put at 11s 8d per sack, as against their traditional but often ephemeral 10s 0d).[61] The Corporation, for its part, argued that the assize could not operate with accuracy or justice unless the price of flour was taken from weekly returns, from all the metropolitan bakers, of the actual amounts they had paid, rather than from the unreliable averages calculated by the mealweighers. After prolonged negotiation, the Corporation and the Company agreed to a compound bill incorporating both principles. Also, it was agreed that, as the metropolis had expanded greatly since 1757, the barely-regulated bakers of the suburbs ought to be placed under the respective jurisdictions of the Lord Mayor and Worshipful Company: a clause was added to the bill expanding the area of the assize to a radius of 10 miles from the Royal Exchange.[62]

All those provisions were included in the consequent statute known as the 'City Act' (37 Geo III c.98), to which was annexed a version of the voluntary table of 1792, now given the force of law. A further Act was necessary in the following year to systematize the method of making weekly returns (this Act also allowed the London bakers an additional 4d per Sack to offset the new tax on salt).[63] An amending Act of 1805 took account of further increases in costs, and raised the metropolitan allowance to 13s 4d per sack net of salt tax.[64]

During the dearth of 1799–1801, the assize system was supplemented by special acts of Parliament, intended to manipulate the market until the crisis was past. In 1800 the bread committee of the House of Commons examined the possibility of limiting sales to the Household grade, but having heard testimony from doctors, bakers, and millers, concluded that there would be no saving, since the people would eat more of the coarser bread to obtain their normal nourishment. Instead the committee accepted the trade's advice that consumption could be cut by at least a twelfth and perhaps up to a third, in London especially, if bread was sold cold, at least 24 hours after baking, and other warm foods, such as herrings and potatoes, were promoted. This was the principle enshrined in the 'Stale Bread Act' of 1800, described by the Webbs as 'surely the most extraordinary panacea ever propounded for a starving people'.[65] But, for a while, it had effect. An immediate fall in consumption of one-sixth was claimed, but it is doubtful if this was sustained;[66] and it was reported that many bakers would not observe the Act.[67] Resistance no doubt increased when the no-sale period was extended from 24 to 48 hours in August 1800 (which stipulation remained in force in London until the statute lapsed in December 1801).[68] Pressed to further action, in January 1801, and taking advantage of clause VIII of the 1772 Act, the Lord Mayor banned the sale of Wheaten bread in the metropolis, so that the Standard Wheaten grade was the best available;[69] while in 1801 also the bread committee of the House of Commons reluctantly reversed its previous judgment, and proposed that only brown, or else mixed-grain, bread be commercially baked and sold. The 'Brown George' Act, which was meant to operate between 1 February and 6 November 1801, proved a fiasco: the slurry-like loaves either stuck together or fell into pieces. Within weeks the emergency statute was acknowledged a fiasco,[70] and was largely ignored in London, though Standard Wheaten bread continued to be made and sold.[71] More extensive intervention by the Corporation was mooted, including schemes to open municipal granaries, and to buy or build mills[72] but none of these plans came to fruition and instead the ill-fated London company, a private capital venture, was established.

Regulation of various kinds may in some degree have helped to tide London (and other cities) over the worst of the crisis, which intensified as wheat-growing districts witheld much of the meagre harvest, and were encouraged to do so by the Lord Chief Justice, Kenyon. He accepted the argument that engrossing, forestalling, and regrating were still offences at common law:[73] thus he gave effectual authority to magistrates to enforce the local sale of the wheat grown in their jursidictions. Chiefly, London was saved by the world market, as importers (encouraged by government guarantees against loss) brought in 90 per cent of its needs[74] though at stupendous prices. The assize had little effect: even though the bakers were squeezed hard, such savings were fractional compared to the component cost of wheat and flour; however, it did demonstrate the public spirit of the authorities.

Whereas Parliament paid the closest attention to London, generally bread regulation in the provinces was at the discretion of authorities locally. Clause VIII of the 1772 Act was a ready stand-by, implemented, for example, throughout Buckinghamshire in 1795, so that Standard Wheaten bread became the best grade sold there;[75] where Clause VIII already was in force, as at Oxford, the assize was manipulated (by taking unrepresentatively low wheat prices) to squeeze the bakers and force down bread prices, in 1801.[76] The trade at large was 'sacrificed on the altar of public interest',[77] and resentment was most intense when bakers in neighbouring jurisdictions were dealt with more leniently.[78] The toughness of certain magistrates is understandable, however: they had a responsibility to the poor to keep prices as low as they could; fair bread prices and social order were synonymous; and given the immense increase in Poor Law expenditure in many counties, the less charged per loaf, the less the burden on heavily-taxed ratepayers. But the calculation was fine, for if the bakers were pressed too hard they might put up their shutters until authority relented (an effective and effectual strike);[79] and aggrieved bakers, millers, and factors could make the assize unworkable by refusing to buy in the market (private transactions were not recorded, except in Scotland). Such may have been the case at Plymouth, where the assize had to be suspended at some time after 1805, to be resumed in 1812, and was certainly so at Portsmouth, where the assize was discontinued in 1806.[80]

Elsewhere, the trade had long been left to market forces, either for want of administrative machinery, or from conviction that an unregulated market served the public better, or because in the past there had been few bakers in a jurisdiction, and increasing numbers had not prompted change. Roughly speaking, and with some exceptions, the assize was set in the older corporate towns, where incorporated societies of bakers were closely involved in its administration, and not set in the newer, rising industrial centres.

The patchwork of jurisdictions, some assized and others not, some committed to 'cheap' bread, others favouring the trade, itself checked initiatives for a national policy, for most of the war. In 1797 country bakers formed county federations and organized a petition, calling for a single national allowance, to be fixed by Parliament, on the lines of the new City Act, but they were rebuffed;[81] however, a revived campaign finally bore fruit in the Country Bakers' Act of 1813. That Act restored the fixed Parliamentary allowance to bakers outside London; generously, perhaps, they were allowed the same 13s 4d per Sack net of salt tax. Magistrates were required to set Wheaten bread by the price of the best wheat or flour, and Standard Wheaten and Household by second-rate prices, rather than unfairly aggregate both qualities of breadstuff. The potential effect on bread prices prompted magistrates in several jurisdictions, including Bristol and Bath, to suspend the assize and let market forces rule.[82] Others, perhaps, shied from interpreting what was now a kaleidoscopic assortment of laws, comprising not only the new Act, but surviving fragments from otherwise repealed statutes. Culverhouse, a baker, put together a compendium to aid country magistrates and the trade: a glimpse will show how complex the assize law had become.[83]

Sentiment against the assize, in official circles, and among the public-spirited, was encouraged by the belief that the system encouraged profiteering. Those allegations are considered next.

4.4 PROFITEERING

Those who believed that the Assize laws licensed profiteering[84] made four main allegations. First, that the baker gained a hidden profit by using ready-made flour. That was asserted in 1753 by 'A Journeyman Baker' and repeated in 1767 by an anonymous pamphleteer (probably Lord Egmont[85]), who noted that most bakers now bought ready-made flours from millers rather than dress their own. He concluded that whatever portion of the allowance formerly had compensated the baker for the task of sieving, he now pocketed as undue profit. But Egmont overlooked the fact that formerly the baker had the benefit of the bran and pollards, the value of which had been intended as an addition to his allowance. Now the miller benefited from them, which was appropriate, given that he did the sieving.

Second, it was alleged that the baker made an unwarranted profit from extra loaves. The Assize tables were calculated on the assumption that a 280 lb Sack of flour would make 80 quartern loaves (347.5 lbs of bread).[86] But it was known that a baker might get 82 or 83 loaves from a Sack (though the yield depended on the quality of the flour[87]); so that it could be claimed, since all costs were covered by the allowance for 80 quarterns, that these possibly two or three extra loaves represented pure profit.[88] But Parliament had been aware of this likely surplus: it was allowed to offset the risk of failed batches, underweight loaves in any batch, flour spillage, and to compensate for the generous division of the dough necessary to assure a fullweight loaf. Given that, in the past, as a safeguard against underweight, the bakers had given 13 loaves for the price of 12 ('the bakers' dozen') – a safety margin of 8.3 per cent – the above margin of 2.5 per cent or so seems modest.

Third, it was noted that the baker made more money from Wheaten than from Household bread. He did, but Parliament intended that he should, since it had been assumed that, if the baker made equal quantities of each, his higher profit on the Wheaten would subsidize the Household, making the latter as cheap as possible.[89] In practice, in London at least, virtually no Household bread was sold, so in principle the trade could make more profit than the average intended.[90] But since successive Lord Mayors more often than not depressed the allowance by taking unrepresentatively low wheat and flour prices, on balance the trade gained little, if anything.

The fourth charge was that profiteering must have been rife, since some bakers were able to undersell the majority.

For a while after the passing of the City Act, underselling was virtually extinguished in London.[91] But unintentionally, that Act had opened a loophole. Previously, the cost of flour had been judged from average wheat and flour prices certified by the mealweighers, but the City Act required all bakers individually to report what they had actually paid. The price of a Sack, however, was set on the assumption that the baker would want credit; a baker prepared to pay cash could command a discount, which, with the high prices and uncertainty of wartime could be 10s 0d or more.[92] Given a yield of 80 quarterns per Sack, such savings would approximate to 1.5d a loaf, and supposing a further halfpenny was saved by selling only for cash in the shop, the baker would have a discretionary margin of say 2d, so that he could undersell the Assize by a halfpenny or a penny and still make an enhanced profit. In principle, the cash-paying baker ought to have declared the true price paid, but this obligation was evaded on the ingenious premise that when the miller made out the bill, he did not know that his customer would offer cash, and it was the bill that was returned to the authorities. By exploiting this anomaly, an underseller could provide his customers with a good loaf at a saving, and still make a sizeable, and in some cases a huge, profit. Whether that amounted to profiteering depends on the view taken of the opportunity cost of using cash, at a time when the return for investing it, or lending it to others, was high; in any case the public were beneficiaries too, since their bread was somewhat cheaper. And the other side of the argument, that the baker who did not cut his prices must have made an untoward profit, was unsubstantiated and probably in most cases untrue, since such a baker almost certainly depended on credit, and so obtained no saving on the invoiced flour price. Moreover, since the traditional baker was likely to give credit to his own customers, and deliver to their homes, his higher price, compared to that of the underseller, represented the cost of a service given.

Though the practice of false invoicing might seem outrageous, the competitiveness and acumen of the undersellers would be favourably viewed by the bread committee of the House of Commons, when it considered the burning issue of the metropolitan assize.

4.5   ABOLITION OF THE ASSIZE

In its last decades the assize system affected the interest of far more people, not only quantitatively but as a proportion of the total population, than at any previous time. It now concerned the principal food of those artisans and labourers, and their families, who previously had purchased wheat (or flour) and baked their own bread, as well as the much-expanded populations of most (though not all) cities and towns. As to London, where once, at most, the assize had affected

55,000 people or so,[93] now it impinged on the standard-of-living of a million or more.[94] As far as ordinary people were concerned (especially those closest to the bread-line, and therefore more readily disaffected), the assize was a principal point of contact with authority, and perhaps, the keenest indicator of official concern and competence.

Yet, complex as they were, the later acts concerning the assize were inadequate to fairly regulate the price of bread, which now, in many places, substantially reflected the unregulated cost of flour. And given the freedom of the commercial millers, the attempts of authority to use the system as an instrument of market control had proved far less successful than expected. Generally, the best that magistrates could do to manipulate the price of loaves downwards, was to squeeze the bakers' allowance; but though that impoverished the trade, it had only a fractional effect on the price of bread, especially during the war, when the costs of wheat and flour rose to previously unimagined heights. And even that power was circumscribed by the City Act of 1797 and the Country Bakers' Act of 1813. Moreover, the multiplicity of statutory provisions confused even those responsible for their implementation: in 1813 it was discovered that the magistrates of Norwich, taking the acts separately rather than in combination, were granting a double allowance to the bakers under their jurisdiction.[95]

It was widely recognized that, if the system were to serve the public purpose, the price of flour must also be assized, and that the commercial miller should be demoted from the rank of capitalist to that of hireling, being given, like the baker, a fixed allowance, or like his parochial counterpart, paid a fee.[96] Needless to say, the commercial millers consistently opposed such a reform, and made a telling case in their own defence. The flour market no longer was wholly local in character, but substantially intranational, with wheat from many parts coming to the mill, and flour going out to far off markets. No local magistrate could comprehend the diversity, nor the complexity, of the trade, especially when account was taken of imports, storage, mixing, settling times, and the vagaries of transport movements and costs. If the trade was forced to conform to the structure of administration, what, the millers asked, would be the fate of those rising industrial cities that depended heavily on 'imported' flour? And who would supply the fixed and working capital that now drove the trade, if the miller no longer had a profit motive?

Conceivably, an assize of flour could have been established for the whole country, policed by a nationally organized if locally appointed inspectorate, on lines roughly similar to the system of monitoring the grain markets for the purposes of the Corn Laws. But the corn markets were open and public, while the millers objected on principle to inspectors entering their mills, which were private property.[97] Such invasions of privacy were, of course, routine in the baking trade, where local officials and trade beadles had lawful access to any part of the bakehouse at any time. But that was an ancient right; the millers seem to have been persuasive, in arguing that, in a free country, the invasive powers of authority ought not to be extended.

Even at the height of war, during severe domestic dearth, and with unprecedentedly high prices, Parliament could not be drawn to intervene in the flour trade. Given this circumspection, the alternative reform, that of abolition, gained in attraction.

Matters were brought to a head by the London bakers. The increase in their parliamentary allowance in 1805 had been eroded by inflation, and the grant, in 1813, of the same allowance to the country bakers, whose costs were lower, increased the pressure for further relief. But the London trade now was divided, between a traditionally-minded majority, and the forceful minority of undersellers, who advocated abolition. Only against its better judgement did the Worshipful Company endorse a new petition for an increased metropolitan allowance; at which the Corporation announced that it would promote a rival bill, seeking the outright abolition of the London assize.[98] There would be no compromise, as there had been in 1796–7: both petitions were referred to the bread committee of the House of Commons, which began an exhaustive review of the issue.

The nub was whether the assize could be made to work effectively. But the committee, like the Corporation, found no way around the problem of the unassized flour market.[99] And as to the principle that the bread market was like no other, since, without the protection of authority, the buyer was helpless against exploitation of his dependency, the committee was persuaded that the sheer number of bakeries guaranteed competition, if competition was unfettered. The success of London's more adroit undersellers provided confirmation, as did evidence from unassized provincial towns. The committee can be criticized for a relative lack of curiosity about the possible flaws in the 'free' market. Testimony from the unassized jurisdictions was accepted uncritically, by post.[100] An assumption that competition would encourage men (or groups) with capital to enter the London trade, to operate on a large-scale, was not weighed against the record of the Albion Mill and the London Company.[101] To this extent at least, C R Fay rightly detected a presumption in favour of *laisser-faire*. However, his conclusion that 'in 1774 the legislature would have approved the baker's indifference to fluctuations of price' but 'the liberalism of the next generation, sharpened by memories of recent famine, saw in this security an offence against nature',[102] goes too far. The same committee had recently

granted the country bakers their bill, and in 1815 the House also passed
the most illiberal of corn laws; Hilton shows that behind the scenes the
government welcomed abolition as an expedient balance to Protection,[103] additional evidence of which comes from the records of the
Worshipful Company and the Corporation. While Lord Sidmouth
advised the bakers that the government was a disinterested party, he, the
Prime Minister and the Chancellor of the Exchequer, privately assured
the City's representatives of their personal commitment to abolition.[104]
Perhaps, above all, ministers, and other members of Parliament, hoped
to escape a controversial responsibility for bakers' profits and bread
prices.[105]

   The abolition of the assize in the country's chief bread market further
undermined the case for regulating the price of bread elsewhere.
Magistrates generally took advantage of the opt-out clause of the 1757
Act to discontinue their local assizes.[106] So that, by the end of the
1820s, there were few provincial places of consequence where the Assize
still was set: generally, it lingered in once great but now reduced
boroughs, perhaps more as an exercise of ancient privilege than as a
practical measure. When in 1824 the House of Commons reviewed the
country bakers' allowance, it was hard put to find witnesses, and so
relied largely on the experience and hearsay of London bakers.[107] The
1813 allowance was now, with deflation, unjustifiably high, and so was
marginally reduced, but the effect was limited. In 1835, in response to a
government circular, only 35 places reported that they were still assized
(and of those, several had not had an assize set for years); some may
have supposed that the question referred to the enforcement of quality
standards).[108] The evident desuetude of the system prompted Parliament
to clear away its last vestiges in 1836.[109]

   However, where bakers were disposed and able to act collectively,
local price agreements were operated in lieu of official regulation, both
in unassized jurisdictions before, and in many and probably most places
after general abolition. In some places, as at Lewes c1815, and in
Glasgow from 1801 to 1834, such arrangements were quite open and
formal, being described as 'voluntary assizes'.[110] They seem to have
been tolerated by authority providing they were not reinforced by threat
or fine, which would have infringed the combination acts.

   So ordinary was 'voluntary' price fixing that, in 1815, the Worshipful
Company of London assumed that, although the official metropolitan
assize was abolished, it could itself maintain the system throughout
London: officers of the Company were to collect the returns of flour
prices, and a committee was formed to set a 'recommended' price. But a
freedom that might be tolerated elsewhere was hotly opposed in the
capital, by members of the Corporation and others who had brought

about abolition. The Company was warned not to defy the explicit will of Parliament, and advised by counsel that its 'voluntary assize' constituted *prima facie* evidence of a combination. The scheme was discontinued before the end of the year. However, after a long anarchy of unrestrained competition, district bakers' societies would establish local collective pricing, in many parts of the capital.

Outside London, the principle of the assize, that the public should have a fair price and the baker a fair living, persisted widely, for decades after the official system was discontinued.

4.6 SUBSTANDARD BREAD

Defenders of the assize system warned that its dismantling would lead to a reduction in average bread quality if there was unrestrained competition in the trade.[111] However, the select committee of 1814–15, which recommended the abolition of the metropolitan assize, was reassured by undersellers that no such degradation would follow, since the quality of their own bread was wholly comparable to that of the full-priced trade.[112] And in any case, the 1815 Act[113] restated the requirements that loaves be pure, of full weight, and correctly described; in London, as in every other part of the country, whether bread was assized there or not, measures to defend standards remained in force.

Penalties under the bread acts always were severe: for instance, fines of £10 which might, at a magistrate's discretion, be levied on each deficient loaf, or the baker might be imprisoned with hard labour for a month or more.[114] But the vigour of policing depended upon the local authority: it was perhaps strictest at Oxford and Cambridge, where until 1836 the universities punctiliously exercised their ancient right to administer the bread laws in those cities; and formidable in London, up to *c*1820, wherever the writ of the Worshipful Company ran.[115] Elsewhere the inspection of loaves and bakers' premises was a civic duty, the performance of which varied with the commitment of those appointed, and with custom.[116] But in most places, even where the institutional machinery of inspection creaked, there were common informers to act as the eyes and ears of the magistrates: generally, their reward was a portion of the fine.[117] Inspection and punishment fell almost entirely on the bakers, rather than millers, because when the bread laws first were framed the miller had been the baker's hireling.[118] But, when the bulk of flour was used to bake commercial bread, an indirect control of millers' standards was exercised, at least in theory.

Apart from the machinery of law enforcement, the public were armed with their own senses of taste and sight. Most malpractices were detectable by the consumer. For instance, shortweight might be discovered either by weighing, or, by those used to buying bread every day, possibly by feel and look.

Where weight-variable loaves were prescribed,[119] so that the amount of bread sold for say 6d might vary considerably from time to time, errors in calculating the necessary amount of dough per loaf may have been common; such 'honest mistakes' were less likely to occur when the weights of larger loaves were fixed. Even so, difficulties in achieving a homogenous mixture, and the impossibility of achieving even heat distribution in the oven, might mean underweight loaves in a batch,[120] which it was illegal to sell (the baker could use them to feed his own household, or give them free to the poor).

But weight was a complicated matter. All loaves lost weight after baking (as the steam went out): the old quartern (prescribed weight 4 lb 5.5 oz) would on average lose an ounce on the first day, and half-an-ounce daily thereafter.[121] A prudent baker would compensate for such natural weight loss by using marginally more dough; but a fraudulent baker might use marginally less, and underbake, so that there was more 'unfused' water trapped in the loaf, which added to its weight when drawn from the oven. Such loaves had to be sold and consumed quickly, since, as the unfused water evaporated, they staled and lost weight more quickly.[122] Also, at time of sale, underbaked loaves were likely to feel clammy; and if they had a high unfused water content, they would be slurry-like. Such bread might be sold through chandlers' shops, to the poorest class of consumer whose need for credit overrode other considerations; otherwise, the alert consumer could take his or her custom elsewhere.

If wheatflour was surreptitiously adulterated with the flours or meals of the coarser grains, then the sour tang of rye, or the nutty taste of barley, and particles of fibre (inevitably in the case of barley or oats), and a more dense texture would be difficult if not impossible to disguise. And, in their natural state, such loaves would be darker in colour, or clammy. Even if bread of that kind evaded detection in the shop, consumers might find it less digestible, and whether or not they complained, they could again transfer their custom. Similarly, if best wheat flour was adulterated with the quality used for Household bread, the brannish taste of the latter could hardly be concealed. And loaves made of Standard Wheaten flour were, in their natural state, distinguished by their greyish, sallow, colour and bluish 'bloom'. Hence the whiteness of a loaf was, to the public at large, the guarantee of its purity.

But the public could be deceived. A small amount of alum (three or four ounces to every 280 lb Sack[123]) would whiten poorer quality wheat flours or flours made of the cheaper red rather than white wheat grain (though in quality, reds were the equal of whites[124]), and mixtures including them, to give loaves the appearance of best Wheaten bread.

Many writers on food and household management offered advice to the public on how alum might be detected,[125] but such tests were complicated, time-consuming, and involved expense;[126] nor were they wholly reliable (impurities of common salt, also used in bread-making, would give a false result[127]). A professional analyst might assay a loaf for a fee, but relatively few consumers could afford such a cost, and in any case, so large was the quantity of bread consumed that any such tests, being occasional and random, could apply only to an infinitesimal fraction of the volume. Thus, of all the adulterants, alum was the most insidious. Perhaps the best safeguard against its use lay in the self-interest of the full-priced trade, in deterring undersellers from whitening cheaper wheat flours in order to lower their prices; in 1796 the Worshipful Company suggested that alum users should be transported.[128] However, that recommendation was not pursued, probably because, in the exigencies of wartime and dearth, alum was an indispensible aid: as a drying agent, it could 'save' wheat that otherwise was unfit for human consumption, and, by shortening the 'settling' time of flour, it allowed millers to release stocks quickly, at times of need. Reading between the lines, it would seem that authority turned a blind eye to its use while the long emergency lasted.[129]

After the war, and the abolition of the metropolitan assize, the law concerning shortweight was reformed, as a result of the notorious Crisp case. Crisp led a band of paid informers, who bore so heavily on the bakers of metropolitan Surrey and Kent that in 1818 their victims went to the considerable trouble and expense of petitioning Parliament for redress. Crisp and company, relying on the ordinary loss of loaf-weight over three days or so, presented staling loaves to selected (and perhaps, gullible) magistrates, and thereby secured convictions (and for themselves, a portion of the fines). Also, it seems, they took protection money from other bakers, who rather than suffer the expense of hiring counsel, or of having their reputations sullied, succumbed to blackmail. Before the bread committee of the House of Commons, however, the bakers argued convincingly that their loaves were of fullweight when sold.[130] And to relieve the honest trade of exploitation by Crisp and his kind, a new metropolitan bread act[131] was quickly passed, which stipulated that loaves thought to be deficient must be weighed before a magistrate within 24 hours of their baking. But that measure erred too far towards leniency: the time limit being too short to allow the whole process of entering, searching, seizing, making complaint, issuing a summons, and presentment.[132]

Returning to the problem, Parliament passed new metropolitan acts (the provisions of which were extended to the country as a whole in 1836), that abolished the ancient practice of selling by the loaf, in favour of selling by amount: all bakers were to have scales in their shops, and weigh bread before the customer. If a loaf was deficient, then the shortfall should be made up by cuttings from another; to make the system simple, the prescribed weights were rounded off, 4 lb being the commonest (succeeding the 4 lb 5.5 oz quartern loaf).[133] Thus the principle of the law, regarding shortweight, shifted from *caveat vendor* to *caveat emptor*. However, that principle could not apply to adulteration with alum.

During the hearing of 1818, Crisp also threw out allegations of adulteration, mentioning alum, pearl ash, ground stone and gypsum; but as to cases, he could cite only abuses he claimed to have detected at Leicester some years before, and in the south, only one instance at Greenwich (the use of ground stone to bulk out flour).[134] Given that he and his men had recently preyed on dozens of bakers around London, with the sole purpose of finding actionable evidence, and that they knew exactly what to look for, had adulterants been in any wide use in those counties surely plentiful evidence would have been produced. It was not. And Accum, who cited the Crisp case in his work on adulteration, otherwise relied on the private testimony of 'several bakers', until at the proof stage of his book, a brief report of a solitary court case, in which a baker was fined £5 for having alum in his possession, could be inserted.[135]

However, adulteration was widely suspected, and public fears were periodically enlivened by alarmist 'exposures', such as that published in 1824 by James Maton, a much-travelled journeyman.[136] And, almost certainly, the incidence of adulteration did increase (or revert to wartime levels) during the 1820s, and in London particularly. There were three main causes. First, the powers of the Worshipful Company, as the agency of inspection and enforcement, waned rapidly after the abolition of the metropolitan assize and the passing of the 1818 Act.[137] Second, the metropolitan market was inundated with flour from the northern mills (steam-mills especially), which typically was made from 'Stockton' or second-grade wheat, and often of a relatively high extraction rate: whether used solely or mixed, loaves made from such flour would have been, in their natural state, of greyish colour, and rejected by the public. Third, the use of Stockton flour, and other cheaper grades, was unavoidable when undersellers, making cuts of 2d or 3d, came to dominate London's bread trade:[138] there was no other way for them to survive.

Thus alum became an essential of the trade, to such an extent that millers, as a commonplace, doctored their flours, so that even the best quality bakers might have no option but to make adulterated bread.[139] An analysis of London loaves, carried out between 1851 and 1854 by Dr Arthur Hill Hassall, and published in *The Lancet*, showed that all in the sample contained alum (even those 'guaranteed' to be pure); in some it was present in large amounts.[140]

There was doubt as to the effect of alum on health. Medical opinion was sharply divided, between those who claimed the susbstance was harmless, and those who, like Ure, warned that habitual ingestion, or the taking of a large amount at any time, must prejudice the functions of the stomach.[141] In 1862 Dr Septimus Gibbon testified that the effect of frequent intake on children could be constipation, diarrhoea (which could be fatal to infants), or ulceration.[142] Today, a moderate intake of alum is considered harmless: for instance, it is used to clarify the public water supply, and as an ingredient of baking powder.[143]

A common objection was, that by using alum, the bakers defrauded the public.[144] And certainly, ordinary people were deceived. But fraud implies an unwonted, as well as an unwittingly granted, gain; and by and large, it would seem, people got what they paid for – loaves made from disguised cheaper flours were sold at correspondingly cheaper prices. Second-grade or Standard Wheaten flours were in no sense nutritionally defective: they lacked only for colour; but given the rigid prejudice (in London at least) against anything other than white bread, a prejudice still common even late in the century in review.[145] only alum could bring such valuable food into general use. In that sense therefore, alum achieved what the bread acts of the 18th century could not: it allowed the maximum and most efficient use of Britain's wheat output (and the fullest use of economical imported grades).

Notes

1. The standard account of the assize of bread in industrializing Britain is that published in 1904 by the Webbs; the subject has been treated briefly by Boyd Hilton (Corn, Cash and Commerce) and the authors of general works on bread, and in its local aspect, at Oxford, by Ballard (1905) and by Wendy Thwaites: Assize of Bread.
2. Adam Smith p 65.
3. [Dumbell] p 12.
4. Hilton: Political Arts p 148.
5. 8 Anne c.18: preamble.
6. E P Thompson: Moral Economy.
7. 8 Anne c.18: preamble.
8. See Chapter 5 Section 2.

9. Ashley p 149.
10. Sheppard & Newton Chapter 5; Ross p 332 et seq.
11. Pownall p 11, Adam Smith p 82; Atwood p 2; Culverhouse p 16.
12. 51 Henry III.
13. Ordinances of Edward I and Edward II; 12 Henry VII; 34 Elizabeth I; Book of Assize published by Order in Council 1638; 13 Charles I.
14. 8 Anne : preamble.
15. S & B Webb: Assize p 196.
16. 8 Anne c 18: preamble.
17. 1 Geo I c 26; 3 Geo II c 29; 12 Geo II c 13; 22 Geo II c 46.
18. Ross p 333.
19. Kirkland pp 18–19. The relevant decisions of the magistrates are probably a good reflection of the supply of small coin in any locality at any time. For instance, at Worcester the old weight-variable loaves were used until September 1782; the price-variable larger loaves from then till September 1790; weight-variable loaves were again in use until December 1801, and price-variable loaves thereafter, apart from a brief reversion to weight variation for part of 1807 (Worcester RO: Shelf B10: Wheat Books, 7 vols, 1779–1820).
20. Atwood p 25; 'A Journeyman Baker' pp 6–19.
21. E P Thompson Moral Economy p 93.
22. G: Ms 7801 2/2; CLRO: Mss 171.8; Read pp 14–15.
23. See Chapter 7.
24. D E Williams p 58; Barnes pp 31–2.
25. G: Ms 7801 2/2 – Charles Smith's evidence on the Assize of Bread, 1768.
26. [Sanderson] p 5; [Egmont] p 2.
27. [Egmont] p 27.
28. [Egmont] p 25; HoC Sessional Papers vol 25 Cd 3064, 16.4.1767; [Dickenson] pp 2–3.
29. [Egmont] p 6.
30. [Dickenson] p 1; [Sanderson] p 2.
31. [Dickenson] p 3; [Sanderson] pp 5–6.
32. [Egmont] pp 27–8; HoC Sessional Papers vol 25 Cd 3144, 21.12.1772; G: Ms 7801 2/2 – Charles Smith's evidence on the Assize of Bread, 1768; Pownall p 10; E P Thompson, Moral Economy p 81.
33. [Sanderson] p vii; HoC Sessional Papers vol 25 Cd 3064, 16.4.1767; Atwood p 11; S & B Webb: Assize p 203; D E Williams map p 63.
34. [Egmont] p 27.
35. [Sanderson] p iv.
36. G: Ms 7798B – untitled, undated, note on calculating the price of wheat.
37. Adam Smith pp 66, 84; 12 Geo II c.13; 3 Geo III c.6.
38. G: Ms 7798B – letter from Edward Grose Smith to Lord Sidmouth, Mr Vansittart, and Mr Lygon, 19.2.1813.
39. Pownall pp 14–15.
40. E P Thompson, Moral Economy p 102.
41. East Sussex RO: Rye MS 2/9.
42. Thwaites: Assize pp 174–5.
43. 32 Geo II c.18; 3 Geo III c.11.
44. E P Thompson, Moral Economy p 89.
45. D E Williams map p 65.
46. Charles Smith p 31.

47. HoC Sessional Papers vol 25 Cd 3064, 16.4.1767.
48. DNB – 'Pownall'; Pownall p 5 et seq.
49. G: Ms 5177 – Court Book 10, 10.5.1773.
50. G: Ms 5177 – Court Book 10, 10.5.1773; G: Ms 7801 1/2 – brief to counter laying open of trade; G: Ms 7801 2/2 – note of arguments against laying open of the trade; G: Ms 7801 2/2 – Charles Smith's observations written 25.9.1774.
51. G: Ms 5177 – Court Book 10, 5.7.1773, 6.9.1773; HoC Sessional Papers vol 25 Cd 3144, 21.12.1772; Wells pp 13–14.
52. HoC Sessional Papers volume 25 Cd 3144, 21.12.1772; Cd 3213, 14.6.1774.
53. Thwaites: thesis p 345.
54. G: Ms 5177 – Court Book 10, 15.3.1779; HoC Sessional Papers volume 25 Cd 3213, 14.6.1774; Pownall pp 21–2, 32 et seq.
55. G: Ms 5177 – Court Book 10, 2.2.1778; Thrupp p 31.
56. Barnes p 35.
57. Worcester RO: Shelf B10: Wheat Books, 7 vols, 1779–1820.
58. Detailed figures are given in Chapter 7.
59. G: Ms 7801 2/2 – observations on a bill to repeal two Acts, undated.
60. G: Ms 5177 – Court Book 11, 14.10.1795, 30.11.1795; Culverhouse p 26.
61. G: Ms 5177 – Court Book 11, 22.8.1796, 3.10.1796, 28.11.1796.
62. G: Ms 5177 – Court Book 11, 28.11.1796, 6.2.1797, 3.4.1797.
63. S & B Webb: Assize pp 208–12; Thrupp pp 20, 31; G: Ms 5177 – Court Book 12, 7.5.1798, 2.7.1798; 38 Geo III c.lv.
64. PP IV/I (74) item 43, HoC 27.4.1804; 45 Geo III c.xxiii.
65. S & B Webb: Assize p 212.
66. See Chapter 5 Section 6; HoC Sessional Papers vol 131 Cd 4983, 10.2.1800; Cd 5080, Privy Council 1.7.1800, p 29 – Loveland; Wells pp 217–20.
67. G: Ms 5177 – Court Book 12, 26.10.1801.
68. CLRO: 431C.
69. CLRO: 431C.
70. 41 Geo III; HoC Sessional Papers vol 131 Cd 5116, 17.12.1800; Wells p 223; PP V (186) 1341, HoC 6.6.1815, p 43 – Wake.
71. HoC Sessional Papers vol 131 Cd 4990, 6.3.1800, p 18; G: Ms 5177 Court Book 12, 13.6.1800; CLRO: 431C.
72. Wells p 247.
73. G: A.3.5 no 32 – Trial of John Rusby.
74. Wells pp 195–201; Galpin pp 23, 213, 256.
75. Bibliotheca Buckinghamiensis, Aylesbury 1890, p 18.
76. Ballard p 630.
77. Culverhouse p 26.
78. Somerset RO: T/PH/hmy 3 [C/2936]; PP III/R I (82) 401, HoC 12.3.1813.
79. PP III/R I (259) 417, HoC 3.6.1813, pp 18–19 – Houlditch.
80. West Devon RO: W 648 – handbills dated 9.5.1802 and 1.9.1813; Temple Patterson: Portsmouth pp 84–5.
81. Somerset RO: T/PH/hmy 3 [C/2936]; S & B Webb: Assize p 212.
82. PP V (186) 1341, HoC 6.6.1815, Appendix 8; Somerset RO: DD/NE 22 – draft letters or speeches.

83. Culverhouse: Arrangement of the Bread Laws.
84. Several gentlemen with a bent for mathematics 'exposed' large latent profits enjoyed by the trade: see Atwood: Review; Heslop: Observations; and Hodson: Present Scarcity.
85. [Egmont]: Important Considerations.
86. Paragraph 3 of the introductory comments to the Assize Table attached to 31 Geo II c.29.
87. Some bakers claimed never to get more than 80 quarterns per Sack: see PP IV Part I (74) 43, HoC 27.4.1804, p 4 – Vere.
88. See Hilton: C C C, p 27.
89. [Egmont] p 27.
90. [Sanderson] p vii; [Egmont] p 27.
91. It was claimed that only three metropolitan undersellers survived the 1797 Act: PP VI (212) 465, HoC 8.4.1824 – Turner.
92. CLRO: Corp PD 32.8 – Woolhead; Maton p 7; PP V (186) 1341, HoC 6.6.1815, pp 13–16 – Wood, p 17 – Davis, p 26 – Jones, p 47 – Phare.
93. Professor Wrigley's estimate of the metropolitan population c1520: P C W p 162.
94. See Appendix 7.
95. G: Ms 7801 2/2.
96. HoC Sessional Papers volume 131 Cd 4983, 10.2.1800, p 40 – Heslop; [Dumbell] p 43.
97. G: Fo Pam 895, p 5.
98. G: Common Council Reports 1810–15, No 13 – Ms 5177 – Court Minute Book 13, 9.5.1814, 29.11.1813, 7.2.1814, 4.4.1814.
99. PP V (186) 1341, HoC 6.6.1815, Preface.
100. PP V (186) 1341, HoC 6.6.1815, Appendix 8.
101. See Chapter 3 Section 2.
102. Fay p 87.
103. Hilton, C C C pp 26–30.
104. G: Ms 5177 – Court Minute Book 13, 4.7.1814; CLRO: Misc MSS 282.1, 6.6.1814.
105. See Hilton: Political Arts pp 155–6.
106. S & B Webb: Assize pp. 207–8
107. PP VI (212) 465, HoC 8.4.1824.
108. PP XXXVII (128) 601, HoC 3.4.1835.
109. 6 & 7 Will IV c.37.
110. PP V (186) 1341, HoC 6.6.1815, Appendix XX; Gourvish: Note pp 854–5.
111. PP V (186) 1341 6.6.1815, p 51 – Phare, p 90 – Harvey.
112. PP V (186) 1341, HoC 6.6.1815, p 40 – Wake, p 47 – Phare, p 52 – Gray.
113. 55 Geo III c.xcix.
114. See for instance 31 Geo III c.29, clause XXI.
115. There seems to have been little enforcement in Westminster, which had its own authorities, but where civic duty seems to have been largely ceremonial. See S & B Webb: E L G Part 1, Chapter IV.
116. See the records of Barnstaple, eg North Devon RO: no 3992 Sessions Book Vol 22.
117. 32 Geo II c.18, clause II.

118. eg G: Fo Pam 895 Committee of Millers and Mealmen in the vicinity of London − Observations on two Bills, 1800.
119. See above p 100.
120. PP IX (345) 227, HoC 22.5.1818, p 7 − Berryman.
121. PP IX (345) 227, HoC 22.5.1818, p 9 − Fisher, p 11 − Harrow.
122. PP IX (345) 227, HoC 22.5.1818, p 19 − Turner, p 16 − Hill.
123. Accum p 127.
124. PP V (186) 1341, 6.6.1815, p 63 − Surrey.
125. M D Freeman p 36.
126. eg Rundell, 1859 ed, p 177.
127. Accum p 141.
128. G: Ms 5177 − Court Minute Book 11, 5.12.1796.
129. [Dumbell] p 84.
130. PP IX (345) 227, HoC 22.5.1818, throughout; V (426) 1, HoC 17.4.1821, p 4.
131. 59 Geo III c.cxxvii.
132. G: Ms 5177 − Court Minute Book 13, 9.7.1819, 29.11.1819, 7.2.1820, 17.4.1822.
133. 60 Geo III c.i; PP V (426) 1, HoC 17.4.1821; PP II (493) 691, HoC 19.4.1821; 1 Geo IV c.iv; 3 Geo IV c.cvi; 6 & 7 Will IV c.37.
134. PP IX (345) 227, HoC 22.5.1818, pp 20−1.
135. Accum pp 127−34; see also Burnett: P & W 3rd ed p 91.
136. Maton, Tricks of Bakers Unmasked.
137. G: Ms 5177 − Court Book 13, 9.7.1819, 29.11.1819, 7.2.1820, 17.4.1822.
138. PP XLVII (3080) 1, HMSO 1862, pp 35, 36, 39, 40, 41, but see also pp 130, 248.
139. PP XLVII (3080) 1, HMSO 1862, pp 130, 132.
140. Hassall pp xiv, 159−64; Walsh p 281.
141. Accum p 135; PP XLVII (3080) 1, HMSO 1862, pp 37−8; Ure: Dictionary, cit Acton p 10; Hassall p 160.
142. PP XLVII (3080) 1, HMSO 1862, pp 276−7.
143. Encyclopaedia Britannica 1986, volume 1, p 303.
144. Burnett: P & W 3rd ed p 88.
145. PP XLVII (3080) 1, HMSO 1862, p 48.

CHAPTER 5

Consumers and Consumption

The first four chapters of this book have discussed the dependence of the population on wheat bread, the reasons for this dependence, the changes in production which enabled the market (and non-market) demand to be met, and the regulation of the market. A further topic, to be dealt with in Chapter 6, is the way in which grain was brought to market, and the development of a national market. Much of the remainder of the book is concerned with analysing the volume and value of bread consumption, and establishing estimates of this consumption on an annual basis.

In this chapter, the average *per capita* consumption of wheat bread during the century in review, 1770 to 1870 will be assessed and estimated.

Estimated levels of consumption will be expressed as yields from wheat. Taking the main (parliamentary) grades of bread, the approximate yields per Imperial quarter of wheat were officially considered to be: Wheaten 426 lbs, Standard Wheaten 449 lbs, and Household 484 lbs.[1]

Those yields will be used throughout this chapter, wherever the grade can be identified or reasonably guessed.

Annual *per capita* bread consumption will be expressed as a percentage of an Imperial quarter (%Q).

For example, a person eating 1 lb of Wheaten grade bread daily thus consumed 365 lbs a year, which, if divided by 426 (the number of lbs of Wheaten bread obtained on average from an Imperial quarter of wheat), gives 86%Q.

As a preliminary, two main classes of consumer will be considered: those who bought most or all of their bread (Section 5.1) and those who obtained some or all of their bread by other means (Section 5.2).

Section 5.3 considers the contemporary view that the average individual's intake of wheat bread was unvarying with the amount usually put at one quarter per head per year. This will be tested, so far as data allow, with particular reference to gender, socio-occupational group, and location in sections 5.4 to 5.6. My own estimates of *per capita* consumption are in the last section of this chapter.

5.1 BUYERS

Those who bought their bread might be sub-divided into sovereign and non-sovereign consumers, according to the nature of their demand.

Sovereign consumers (roughly speaking, the middle classes) could buy substantial quantities of bread for themselves and their households. For them, however, bread was a want, a commodity like any other. And though their incomes were such that changes in the price of bread ought to have little affected their purchasing, in practice they were able (and strongly encouraged, by writers such as Mrs Rundell, Mrs Copley, Miss Acton, and 'Lady Bountiful'[2]) to pursue economies assiduously. Those with the means and staff to do so could spurn the commercial baker and make their own bread; they might prefer brown bread to white (but not only for economy, perhaps also for its purging properties); they might, especially in times of dearth, and in response to the King's appeal,[3] economize on their bread consumption. Their demand might be idiosyncratic, if like Parson Woodforde they disliked bread, or like John Howard, they were frugal on principle.[4] In sum, it might be argued (as an extension to Engel's Law), that the less spent on bread as a proportion of outgoings, the greater the command that could be exercised, for material or immaterial reasons, over that expenditure.

While conversely, those who depended largely or solely on bread had the least command over their expenditure. Many lacked the means to make their own bread;[5] most refused to economize by substituting a cheaper grade for white, or by eating less: the amount they consumed was relatively invariable, and they were obliged to pay the prevailing price. Even in 1800, and 'notwithstanding the great price of bread', the poor paid 'with Cheerfulness' (if Thomas Loveland, Master of the Worshipful Company of Bakers, is to be believed).[6] Newmarch later summarized the common wisdom, that 'everything is given up before bread, and . . . bread being the staff of life, it must be had by the people whatever the price may be.'[7]

To summarize points discussed in earlier chapters, such dependency may have been justified and confirmed by the cost-efficiency of wheat bread, 'physically' and nutritionally, especially to those performing sedentary work; that such benefit was reinforced by the economies of commercial milling and baking, with consumers defended against exploitation either by the assize system, or by its voluntary equivalents, or by competition; that when wheat bread was expensive, the prices of other grains rose in alignment, and the cost of other foods may have been greater, so that substitution was difficult.

The relative economy of wheat bread, compared to other foods, probably varied considerably from place to place, depending on local supplies and the efficiency of the market. But possibly the case of Manchester, during the French wars, is not untypical. A handbill of 1818 shows that, since 1788, though the price of flour had risen by 138 per cent, oatmeal had risen almost at parity (increasing by 136 per cent), and potatoes had risen more (by 175 per cent). Though the price of milk had increased only 100 per cent, butter was up by 433 per cent. Also, it was asserted that meat followed or rose faster than wheat, a contention apparently borne out by the Manchester comparisons, where beef had increased by 143 per cent and mutton and pork by 167 per cent.[8]

At times, however, the market would have been in suspension, if and where wheat became unavailable at any price (the circumstances of 'absolute dearth' discussed by Dr Wells).[9]

Also, the demand for wheat bread may have influenced, or been influenced by, spending on other basics. One example is expenditure on alcoholic drinks. Some complained that wages that ought to have been spent on food were squandered in alehouses; conversely, Bagehot observed that an increase in bread prices was followed almost at once by a fall in the sales of drink. Official measures were taken to limit the manufacture and consumption of alcohol in times of dearth.[10] Also, the effect of fluctuating bread prices on the purchase of mass manufactures, textiles particularly, was observed and reified into a fundamental principle, by James Wilson.[11]

The possible interaction of bread dependency and household rent is less clear-cut. Urban rents may have been invariable for the term of a tenancy, but Rodger summarizes studies by Englander, Dennis, Pooley, and Jackson, to show how short average tenancies might be: five to six months at Glasgow, for instance; 40 per cent of Liverpool's population moved home within the year; address changes were most frequent among the unskilled, unmarried, newly wed, and migrants, but less frequent where there was continuity of employment and earnings.[12] Such flits may have been perfectly proper, but in how many cases did people disappear, as in Lant Street, on the verge of quarter-day?[13] And did the incidence of non-payment of rent vary with the price of bread?

Inevitably, the issues of price and income elasticity merge. Perfect inelasticity was relatively assured where labourers, who formerly had been paid a stipulated amount of bread daily, were instead paid the prevailing cash value of that amount[14] (though they may not have spent all their money on bread). It was claimed that wages both rose and fell more slowly than prices;[15] and it was to correct the adverse phase of that cycle that the Reverend David Davies proposed the minimum assured wage, geared to the prevailing price of bread, and supplemented from the rates:[16] a principle that, however awkwardly and variously, was implemented under the Speenhamland system. However achieved, Richardson notes the remarkable inelasticity of rural labourers' wheat bread consumption in the counties he studied.[17]

From Table 5.1 it appears that labourers' wages in Norfolk, which fluctuated roughly with the price of wheat in wartime, did not fall proportionately once prices fell and 'sound money' was restored.

Table 5.1   Norfolk labourers' average weekly wages on a light-land farm, 1804/13 – 1834/43

| | Weekly cash wage | | Buying power (bushels of wheat at local prices) |
	s	d	
1804–13	10	7	1.05
1814–23	10	0	1.24
1824–33	9	11	1.31
1834–43	9	10	1.50

Calculated from: Bacon p 144.

However, the circumstances of piece-paid workers, in the textile trades for instance, were markedly harsh during the wartime years of high bread prices.[18] But whether the effects on consumption were offset by working even harder, and/or by involving other members of the family, or by subventions from charity and the dole, and whether bread consumption remained constant, when all else was sacrificed, is less clear. Later, the effects of falling incomes and rising prices upon the bread consumption of textile workers was measured in small studies. The investigation commissioned by William Nield, Mayor of Manchester,[19] of the circumstances of 19 families of textile workers in 1836 and 1841 (when the prices of 12 lbs of flour averaged 21d and 29.5d respectively), shows that the better paid and continually employed Manchester workers, and their families, increased their volume of bread/flour consumption by 9.5 per cent (from roughly 6.3 to 6.9 lbs of flour *per capita* weekly) despite the 39 per cent rise in price, while the families of customarily less well paid, and in 1841 unemployed or underemployed, Dukinfield workers reduced their bread/flour consumption by 10.6 per cent (from roughly 4.7 to 4.2 lbs). Income was not necessarily the regulator: at Manchester it remained constant, but overall expenditure rose (even though rents fell), and as can be seen, the increased price coincided with increased consumption. In the case of the poorest families, chiefly at Dukinfield, expenditure in 1841 exceeded income, suggesting that the respondents were drawing on savings, insurance, charity, or parish relief.

That higher bread prices and recession (though obviously an uneven recession) went together was not coincidental, in the liberal view: as the price of bread increased, so it was argued, ordinary people cut back on purchases of other goods, and so created unemployment and underemployment in mass-manufacturing.

However, at the onset of the Cotton Famine of the 1860s, the local price of bread did not change significantly: the slump was caused by the exogenous shock of the Amercian Civil War. Dr Edward Smith's survey of Lancashire cotton workers, in 1862,[20] shows that the average annual *per capita* bread consumption of the unemployed or underemployed fell from 97%Q to 81%Q (that is, by 16 per cent), though the fall was most pronounced among unmarried workers (the average for females fell from a very high 140%Q to 102%Q, though their proportionate consumption of other foods, potatoes especially, fell far more).

Both the Nield and the Smith surveys appear to confirm a causality indicated in reports by the successive committees on agricultural distress in the 1820s and 1830s: that a, and perhaps the, critical determinant of bread consumption was whether a worker, his wife and possibly his children, were fully employed, underemployed, or unemployed.[21] The determinant of consumption then may not have been income as such, but the incidence of exertion. In the bleakest assessment, an underemployed or unemployed worker might survive on reduced rations, since the body's minimal energy demand would be only that needed to maintain the basic functioning of the metabolism (though his family, if already inured to mere existence, may have been unable to endure any further reduction in their consumption).

Thus there could have been a response, albeit indirect and perhaps lagged, of non-sovereign demand to a rise in prices. A conviction that the demand for bread must have been price elastic to some degree led Caird, in the 1850s, to suggest that a high price might reduce consumption by 10 per cent or so, and later he amplified the point, by proposing that 'every ten per cent of additional price on the loaf, diminishes the consumption by at least one per cent'. But he had no evidence of such an effect; indeed his own enquiries among the bakers of Whitechapel and along the Harrow Road confirmed the view of Newmarch, that bread consumption was not at all affected by price increases. And, when prices rose, the real test was the cost of possible substitutes: when Caird enquired in 1868, for instance, potatoes were scarce and dear; moreover, since 1850 the cost of meat and dairy produce had risen by 50 per cent, while on average the price of bread had remained the same.[22]

Relative cost might mean also that when the price of bread fell, its consumption fell too, as people took the chance to vary their diets by buying other foods (if their prices had fallen too), though early evidence of bread as a 'Giffen good' (a good for which demand falls as its price falls) is sparse.[23]

Information about individual consumers, or groups, is too limited and discontinuous to allow tracking of price or income elasticities of demand (and any estimation of income elasticity of demand is especially fraught, given the complication of family, as opposed to individual, earnings). Even Edward Smith's comparison of cotton workers' consumption in ordinary and depressed times was too limited for firm conclusions.[24] At market level, however, there is one fairly, if not entirely, reliable measure of commercial bread consumption. That is the volume of Sacks of breadflour sold within 10 miles of the Royal Exchange between 1798 and 1814, compiled from bakers' returns. But, if Sack volume is related to estimated population, and to the prevailing price of bread, no clear pattern emerges. The relevant data are in Table 5.2.

Over sixteen wartime years, apparent *per capita* demand rose in seven years, in five of which the loaf price was lower, but in two of which it was higher, than in the previous year; in nine years when demand fell or was static, the price of bread was higher in seven years, but lower in two. If 1800 and 1801 are removed from the latter group, because bread demand was exceptionally and artificially depressed by operation of the Stale Bread Act, then in seven years when demand fell, the price of bread was higher in five but lower in two. Also, overall, it will be seen that the amount of change in Sackage, related to the size of swing in the bread price, varied considerably.

Those calculations concern commercially-baked bread only: given that the trade was squeezed during the war, variations may simply reflect a greater or lesser incidence of home-baking. And the demand of sovereign and non-sovereign buyers is aggregated, together with the consumption of non-buyers supplied by their employers. Also, the estimates of the 10-mile metropolitan radius zone population are crude, especially in non-census years, presuming a straight-line trend, which is a large presumption for a capital city, especially in wartime. The most that might be safely deduced from the pattern is that there appears to have been more likelihood that demand would respond inversely to price, in some degree, than otherwise, a likelihood borne in mind in later calculations. However, the market was not the only factor in bread supply and consumption. Non-buyers are discussed next.

5.2   OFF-MARKET SUPPLY

Many consumers were not directly dependent on the market, at least for some of their bread. Traditional methods of supply, of the kind found in

Table 5.2 Bakers' Sackage related to bread prices, metropolitan 10-mile radius zone, 1798–1814.

Mayoral year ending*	Est pop '000	Sacks reported	Sack *per capita*	year on year %	Price of bread per 4 lb	year on year %
1798	1020	745,720	0.731	–	7.7	–
1799	1040	791,670	0.761	+4.1	9.6	+24.7
1800	1060	740,387	0.698	−8.3	15.3	+59.4
1801	1081	703,340	0.651	−6.7	15.5	+1.3
1802	1100	757,953	0.689	+5.8	9.5	−38.7
1803	1121	789,363	0.704	+2.2	8.7	−8.4
1804	1140	783,606	0.687	−2.4	9.7	+11.5
1805	1161	693,055	0.597	−13.1	13.1	+35.1
1806	1180	754,251	0.639	+7.0	11.7	−10.7
1807	1201	749,453	0.624	−2.3	10.8	−7.7
1808	1222	761,495	0.623	0	11.6	+7.4
1809	1242	734,332	0.591	−5.1	13.7	+18.1
1810	1263	773,814	0.613	+3.7	14.7	+7.3
1811	1285	797,620	0.621	+1.3	14.0	−4.8
1812	1307	737,883	0.565	−9.0	17.0	+21.4
1813	1329	830,657	0.625	+1.1	15.7	−7.6
1814	1351	821,607	0.608	−2.7	11.4	−27.4

* 9th November.

Sources: Sackage returns from PP V (186) 1341, HoC 6.6.1815, Appendix 5. Estimates of population in 10-mile radius zone: see Appendix 7.

the 16th and 17th centuries,[25] still were common between 1770 and 1870, among groups whose circumstances were defined by social and legal as well as economic relationships.

First, there were those communities that fed themselves. In 1800, as Everitt says of 1500, 'there were probably still many villages whose food was grown entirely within the confines of the parish', even if a considerable amount more was grown for sale elsewhere.[26] Thwaites' study of 18th century Oxfordshire shows that much of the wheat produced (and the barley for beer and the oats for livestock) was consumed on the farm by the tenant, his family, servants, and outworkers.[27] Ann Kussmaul suggests, from her study of marriage patterns, that the incidence of living-in, having fallen during the 17th century, rose to a new peak in the mid-18th century, before the final decline.

Even in 1851, servants in husbandry constituted 30 per cent or more of the combined numbers of servants and labourers, both male and female, in Cumberland, Westmorland, Durham, Yorkshire, Nottinghamshire, Derbyshire, Leicestershire, Cheshire, Shropshire, Devon, and Cornwall.[28]

Even where full board no longer was supplied, and where farmers relied chiefly on day workers, frequently bread and beer were provided, if only at certain times of the year. Clearly it was sensible for the farmer to supply his employees at the lowest cost to himself: there was no point to sending grain to market in order to buy it back at prices inflated by the cost of carriage, factors' margins, and market fees, nor in having the workers themselves pay market prices and thus demand higher wages. Arthur Young noted, during his six weeks' tour of 1767, that board or victuals were given in kind at eight out of 33 places; during his six months' tour of 1770, he noted the practice at 55 places out of 94. Day workers were given bread in kind throughout the year, or in the winter months only, or at hay-making or harvest-time. Eden cites similar instances at 13 places. Smout has shown that in the later 18th century the married Scots' farmworker, with children, could not have survived had he depended on his cash wage alone; in most cases such men were 'paid' a stipulated quantity of oats (and sometimes wheat), which was constant irrespective of market prices. In other places, cash wages were set and changed with some reference to the prevailing price of bread.[29]

When bread was not given in kind, often grain, flour, and/or bread would be sold at a discount to the market price, and even where the practice was not normal, it might be introduced in years of dearth; then, even large-scale farmers who normally sent most of their output to distant markets, felt an obligation (or were made to feel it, either by magistrates or the populace) to supply their locality at preferential prices. Of course, recipients were purchasers, but it is convenient to classify them, with others supplied off-market, as non-buyers. Eden notes either direct-discounting, or funded supplies, or both, at Dunstable, New Windsor (Berkshire), Hawkley with Newton Valence (Hampshire), Ealing in Middlesex, Frome and Minehead (Somerset), Farnham (Surrey), and Seend in Wiltshire. It was prevalent too in Dorset.[30]

In the 1840s, direct-discounting was still common at least in Scotland, Devon, and Oxfordshire, and Edward Smith, in 1864, recorded instances in Devon and Cornwall, and Somerset: in those cases, however, the amount supplied, though enough for the labourer himself, was not sufficient to feed his family. In wheat-growing parts of Wales, however, Smith noted direct-discounting of bushels of wheat to be ground for family use, while the man took his food at the farm.[31]

Similarly, it was no loss to the farmer to supply rural neighbours, or callers at the farm, with wheat at a gate price that showed him a profit, but still was below the market price of a bushel. Alternatively, in 'local exchanges', one farmer might trade with another (wheat for meat, for instance) at a discount to the market and without need of scarce coin.[32]

Of course, many of those buying at a discount could be classified as semi-sovereign consumers, where they had the option of buying from one farmer or another, or either at the farm gate or in the marketplace. But it is convenient for analysis to aggregate them with those who perhaps or probably had no option but to purchase from their employers, all such sales being off-market; and discount transactions were different again from the marketplace or contract trades, wherever they were used to vent inferior grades of wheat that otherwise would have found no ordinary sale, at least as human food.[33]

Formal methods of payment-in-kind and direct-discounting often were supplemented by the custom (and, as it was believed, the ancient folk-right) of gleaning. Eden notes the gleaning of fields after harvest at Roade in Northamptonshire, where the poor made a great deal by it: 'several families will gather as much wheat as will serve them for bread the whole year . . .' Some farmers tried to suppress the practice, since the line between gleaning and pilfering was blurred; also, greater efficiencies in harvesting, as the 19th century progressed, may have reduced this free yield. However, Salaman recalled that, in his own village of Barley, Hertfordshire, there were three families that obtained most of their needs from gleaning. In the vicinity of Saffron Walden,

> cottagers would walk from miles around with their sacks of gleanings from the harvest fields to seek out [Billy Bragg, the village miller, who] would give his full attention to those small sacks, reducing their contents to good flour, to be taken home to cottage bakehouses.[34]

Second, many forms of rural transaction were replicated among industrial and commercial workers, with the one obvious difference that the employer was not a producer but a buyer. Traditionally, articled men were employed on contractual terms that often included full board, while most apprentices were boarded. Though living-out was becoming as common in the cities as in the countryside, in the baking trade at least (which for obvious reasons may be unrepresentative) bread was commonly given in part payment of wages.[35]

Among the unarticled indoor trades, it is clear from Mayhew's London enquiry of 1849–50 that most workers in the sweatshops, and others in the clothes' and boot and shoe trades, were given bread (and cheap coffee or tea) as they worked; many of these supplies were meagre, but among the dressmakers and milliners, generous quantities of good bread were given. And of course, merchant seamen were fed (often with bread as well as biscuit, at least for the first days of a voyage) by their masters. In a majority of cases, perhaps, the amounts of bread were not stipulated exactly by contract (unlike the practice of the articled trades), but specified as 'breakfast' or 'dinner', so that the master might vary the amounts and quality given. Nonetheless, a great number of indoor workers, it seems, effectually obtained their own bread (if not bread for their families) by such means.[36]

The practice of paying bread in kind seems also to have extended to clerks, since banks and other commercial houses placed large contracts with bakers for rolls and loaves.[37]

In some respects, the infamous truck system was an extension of payment-in-kind. Certain employers, the Guests for instance, sold flour at a discount to their workers, and though the tommy shop (which operated a system of credit sales) at the Dowlais iron works in Wales was shut in 1823, it reopened five years later 'at the request of the men'. Where a token system operated, discounts might be obtained (at least in theory) from nominated shops. And though the many abuses of truck impelled Parliament to legislate against the system, exceptions were made of those industries operating in isolated parts, where retail outlets were few. The Truck Act of 1831 did not extend to the construction trades (which included railway building), and some 'voluntary' forms of payment in kind continued in the textile industries, and among nailers, miners, ironworkers, and the Portland quarrymen.[38]

Among the largest class of living-in workers, domestic servants, bread (at least) was guaranteed as a part of board: such workers made up 16 per cent of the British workforce in 1871.

Third, bread was supplied 'free' to all those in the armed forces, in institutions, workhouses, and prisons (though not to the inmates of bridewells, who provided their own).

Thus, throughout the century in review, a considerable proportion of the population, and of the poorer classes especially, were to some (and perhaps to a large) extent insulated from the market, as far as their chief food was concerned. Reliable quantification is impossible given that not all in a category may have been non-sovereign consumers; or that payment in kind may have been intended for the worker but not his family; or that such arrangements may have been periodic and not permanent; and when the amounts given varied from place to place. Also, those supplied with grain and flour probably had to pay for milling and/or baking, or else sold their entitlement and bought bakers' bread with the proceeds, and so became semi-sovereign consumers.[39]

Nor did reliance upon an employer necessarily insulate non-sovereign consumers against the market, if the quantities given fluctuated, if the

worker was dismissed or put on part-time working, or if the employer
failed. But then, in common with semi-sovereign consumers, the non-
sovereign could be saved by various forms of intervention. They can be
briefly summarized.

At local level, the voluntary principle was strong. A rise in bread
prices (or the effect on the poor of a harsh winter, or of a disaster such
as a flood) might prompt a special subscription, usually raised under the
patronage of local notables, as at Oxford, where contributions from the
Duke of Marlborough and others 'seem to have been made at every
inclement season'; in the dearth of 1795 the Duke and Lord Harcourt
ploughed up the greater part of their parks to raise grain for the
distressed. In the same year there was a general subscription for the
city's poor, while the assized price of bread was held artificially low, and
the bakers compensated by a donation, headed by the corporation's gift
of 100 guineas.[40] Such schemes supplemented the usual relief offered by
private, church, and semi-public charities and bread funds, to the aged,
ill, widowed, or otherwise over-burdened.

Where voluntary help was not forthcoming, or not enough, magistrates had formidable powers of intervention, to suspend the ordinary
workings of commerce, and prevent grain (or flour or bread) leaving
their jurisdictions. Otherwise, they might redress local shortages by
seeking supplies from elsewhere, often at public expense. Where
magistrates were dilatory, they could be prompted to their duty by the
clamour of the people, and the threat or actuality of mob violence.[41]

Even when direct action to protect or secure supplies was not called
for, magistrates in practice had considerable freedom to moderate rises
in prices, by the manner in which they set the Assize of Bread.

At national level, supply crises prompted revision of the bread acts
(as in 1709, 1757, 1772, and 1797), to widen the scope given to
magistrates in the public interest. And Parliament operated the Corn
Laws, sanctioning lowered tariffs to allow the importation of foreign
grain at times of high prices. When domestic wheat was held back in the
growing districts, such imports were directed chiefly to the larger towns
and cities, to make good the magnified deficit there. And in the worst
crises, during the Revolutionary and Napoleonic wars, government took
further, exceptional, action to accelerate the flow of imports.

Finally the Poor Law (except in Scotland) sustained those who could
not sustain themselves. Bread was the staple of the workhouse, but its
role in outdoor relief is less clear-cut: it was rarely given to the able-
bodied.[42] However, the usual forms of outdoor relief – cash, or rent
money, or less frequently, the supply of fuel or clothes, especially
shoes[43] – might all be considered as subventions that, either directly or
indirectly, enabled the applicants to buy their bread. Cash payments, for

instance, were known as 'bread money' in places.[44] Even after the Poor
Law Amendment Act of 1834, considerable numbers still received
outdoor relief, often supplemented in emergency by food doles financed
by public or private subscription. Bread seems to have been the chief
food provided by subscription schemes: even where, in obedience to
official injunctions, soup was given, usually an amount of bread was
added: soup alone could provoke a riot.[45]

5.3   GENERAL ESTIMATES OF CONSUMPTION

Though, as Dr Collins has commented, 'contemporary estimates of
wheat consumption per head were at best notional (being seldom based
on first-hand knowledge or systematic enquiry)',[46] there was substantial
consensus (accepted by Charles Smith, Eden, and Young, among others)
that the average wheat-eater consumed the product of one quarter
(Winchester or Imperial) of wheat a year.

The 'one quarter' rule-of-thumb may have been more easily accepted
in the earlier part of the century in review, when it was still possible to
conceive of a roughly homogenous population; and more open to
dispute later on, especially as the proportion of the urban and
sedentarily-occupied populations increased.

In 1800 Turton distinguished between the amount of bread consumed by the poor, 'where it is their chief food', and that consumed by
the better off: taking all classes into account he put the national *per
capita* consumption at 85%Q. Much the same estimate runs through
Jacob's calculations, made in 1827-8: he allowed 13,700,000 quarters
to a population of 15.4m, or 86%Q (arriving at his volume by assuming
that all people were wheat-eaters, though in 1836 he supposed a
significant potato-eating population). Dodd, in 1856, suggested an
average of five bushels of wheat, or about 63%Q for the UK as a whole,
but his figure, of course, is diluted by the inclusion of Ireland. In 1868
Caird estimated the *per capita* daily consumption of bread in Ireland as
0.25 lbs, which, if it was of Standard Wheaten type, would approximate
to 20%Q, while he put consumption in Britain at 1.25 lbs, or 102%Q.
But one estimate, made in 1824, was very low: it put the bread
consumption of 'ordinary people' at 0.75 lbs to 1.0 lb per day;[47] if that
was Standard Wheaten bread, then the band suggested was from 61%Q
to 81%Q. Porter, with little enthusiasm, summarized the range of wheat
consumption estimates, up to 1851, as from six to eight bushels, or 75-
100%Q.[48]

The lowest official figure, proposed as the target for reduced bread
consumption during the dearth of 1800-1, was one quartern loaf per

week per person, 'which had been found, by Experiment, to be sufficient.'[49] Assuming that Wheaten bread was meant, that represents a minimum bread consumption of about 53%Q, which to those dependent on bread would represent a starvation ration.

5.4 GENDER AND AGE

However imprecise the general estimates of consumption, authority had to be exact when issuing bread to those it fed. Officially prescribed diets indicate the contemporary judgement of ordinary need, and so suggest a norm. And they represent something like the actual consumption of large 'institutional' populations (though prescriptions may not have been followed exactly, there was a degree of official monitoring). Also, they give the official view of the different requirements of men, women, and children, in various conditions of employment, and in relation to their consumption of other foods. If only from the historian's viewpoint, it is fortunate that in 1864 the Home Office rejected the 'scientific' diets proposed by Dr Edward Smith, in favour of its own 'pragmatic' assessment of need, roughly representative of expectations in the outside world.[50]

Taking the prescribed diets listed in Appendix 6, the mean averages of bread consumption for adult men and women were as shown in Table 5.3.

Table 5.3 Prescribed diets: bread consumption by gender

	Men	Women	Gender ratio*
Armed Forces	102%Q	–	–
Prisons	104%Q	85%Q	82%
New Poor Law	77%Q	65%Q	84%
MEAN	94%Q	75%Q	83%

* women's consumption as percentage of men's

The medians in each case (averaging variations within a case, where appropriate, so as not to double count what was, effectively, one prescription severally applied) were 102%Q for men (median of 25 case-groups) and 83–85%Q for women (median of six case-groups). However, the medians under-weight the New Poor Law prescriptions. Taking means and medians together, a roughly balanced average of the prescribed diets for adults would be men 95%Q, women 80%Q.

This implies a gender ratio of 84 per cent, which gives an overall adult average of 87%Q.

Apart from one age-specific reference in Edward Smith's survey of Lancashire (indicating that 'two aged persons' ate somewhat less bread than single adults, but perhaps no less than parents with families[51]), little attention was paid to the diets of the elderly. Such lack of attention may be because 'aged' was a relative term, when the median age at death of the 1771 birth-cohort (in England and Wales) was 35 for men and 37 for women, and of the 1831 birth-cohort, 44 and 46 respectively,[52] and when for most people, age brought no release from labour.

As a rule, the Poor Law scales allowed as much for a child as for a woman, while Edward Smith counted each child under 10 as half-an-adult;[53] but both are unreliable guides to actual consumption rates, when need increased with the child's age. More exact indications of the bread needs of children, male and female, come from dietaries collected by Porter (complicated by the inclusion of some adults) and the bread given at the Foundling Hospital, cited by Dodd.[54] The average of the former is 77%Q; of the latter 59%Q. If the 'adult-factor' in Porter's estimates is allowed for, a reasonable mean for children under 15 would be 65%Q. This gives children's consumption as about three-quarters of that of adults.

The average *per capita* prescribed bread diet for all ages can be indicated by relating the above estimates to the age constitution of the country. Although the proportion of children under 15 in the population varied in the century in review, for order-of-magnitude calculations those variations have no significant effect: if the proportion of children under 15, within the population as a whole, is put at 36 per cent, against adults at 64 per cent, then the average *per capita* consumption of children and adults aggregated together, as represented by the pre-scribed diets – 'the prescribed norm' – was 79%Q.

5.5 SOCIO-OCCUPATIONAL GROUPS

Evidence of bread consumption by the population at large (see Appendix 6) comes from three main types of source: surveys (such as those undertaken by Davies, Eden, and Edward Smith), informed estimates (by Sir Charles Smith, McCulloch, and others), and *ad hoc* reports and anecdotes. The reliability and representativeness of such data is questionable: even the more 'scientific' surveys were not entirely methodical, and concentrated deliberately on the circumstances of the poorest classes, generally in years of greatest adversity; moreover, hardship may have been exaggerated, if respondents were unwilling to divulge all their sources of food (the rewards of poaching for example, or gleaning).

Compared to the relative consistencies of the prescribed diets, the levels of bread consumption recorded or alleged in the reports vary greatly; nor at first sight does the information seem much more manageable when categorized by three broad socio-occupational groups. However, when each group is averaged, as in Table 5.4, there is a semblance of order.

Table 5.4   Reported diets: average of bread consumption by broad socio-occupational groups

	Mean	Median
Rural labourers and their families:	86%Q	81%Q
Urban labourers, artisans, and their families:	80%Q	81%Q
Middle and lower-middle classes:	62%Q	58–61%Q

If, making a crude extrapolation from the socio-economic analysis of Colquhoun (for England and Wales, 1803),[55] the proportion of the above groups is put at: rural labourers and their families, 47 per cent; urban labourers, artisans, and their families, 34 per cent; and the middle and lower-middle classes, 19 per cent then the mean average bread consumptions given above would aggregate to 79%Q. This is exactly the aggregate of the prescribed diets ('the prescribed norm'). A similar crude extrapolation from the Baxter/Perkin analysis (for England and Wales, 1867)[56] gives the proportion of the groups as: rural labourers and their families, 26 per cent; urban labourers, artisans, and their families, 46 per cent; and the middle and lower-middle classes 28 per cent, which puts the aggregate at 77%Q, also a close fit.

However, it cannot be assumed that group consumption averages were constant throughout the century in review, though the limited evidence suggests, as would be expected, that the average of middle and lower-middle class consumption was constant. And there is no *prima facie* evidence of significant fluctuation, over the century, in the bread consumption of urban labourers, artisans, and their families. However, the urban data are heavily tilted toward sedentary workers, whose absolute need presumably was less than that of labourers, though their family consumption may not have been much less overall, since children could more readily participate in work calling for nimble fingers rather than strength, and so be bread winners in their own right, adding significantly to the family budget and intake. Of course, such trades were subject to long-run as well as short-term depressions: Mayhew describes the progressive effects of the over-supply of labour in the London trades he observed[57] (with effects similar to those seen in commercial baking). Trade slumps may have had a savage effect on bread consumption,[58] but generally the effect of underemployment or unemployment, on those whose consumption already was frugal, was more likely to force economies in everything but bread. Smith's Lancashire survey[59] indicates that average bread consumption dropped from 97%Q to 81%Q (that is, by 16 per cent) during the Cotton Famine, but the fall was most pronounced among unmarried workers (the average for single females fell from a very high 140%Q to 102%Q). Overall, the bread eaten by the unemployed represents a bare adequacy. The 'bottom line' might be taken as the New Poor Law dietary average of 71 per cent[60] (though some like Betty Higden may have preferred to starve rather than enter a workhouse[61]).

But probably there was a long-run variation in average consumption by rural labourers and their families: the evidence suggests that during the century their bread consumption described a U-curve. There may have been a slight fall on trend in the intake of rural labourers from the 1760s[62] to c1790, when Davies put *per capita* consumption at about 99%Q.[63] What followed was relatively well pronounced: a drop to an aggregate 77%Q in the Eden tabulations,[64] reflecting the dearth of 1795–6 and the obvious hardship of many of his respondents, especially in the southern and eastern counties.

During and after the war, it seems clear from the reports of successive committees, that the critical determinant of bread consumption was whether a labourer (and his wife and possibly his children) was fully employed, or underemployed or unemployed. In the latter circumstances, families were kept alive by Poor Law subventions, so that the plight of the hedger's family[65] was exceptional, when the average Old Poor Law dole amounted to perhaps 66%Q.[66] And probably most rural labouring families compensated for falls in their bread consumption by using potatoes, at least as a winter supplement.[67] In the bleakest assessment, it would be possible for men to survive on considerably reduced rations if, by being underemployed or unemployed, they had a markedly lower energy need. Rural bread consumption in certain counties may have fallen below the regular allowance given in prisons, as a Wiltshire magistrate, testifying in 1831, was 'sorry to say'.[68] Serious rural unemployment and underemployment especially in the southern and eastern counties was gradually (and often harshly) resolved by migration. However, the circumstances of those remaining brightened considerably from 1853:[69] with relatively full agricultural employment, and increased opportunities for regular work for women, both income and energy need *per capita* would have increased. Edward Smith's monumental survey[70] (undertaken in 1863) does suggest that the bread consumption of agricultural labourers and their families was, on average, higher in *per capita* terms than it had been in previous decades: the mean of 111%Q is substantial. Also, some increase may be due to the partial replacement of potatoes by bread. My conclusion is, therefore, that the average consumption of this group fell from about 100%Q *c*1790 to about 80%Q from *c*1795 to *c*1853 (roughly indicated by the reported data), and then rose steeply to about 110%Q (on the evidence of Edward Smith).

Smith's survey also suggests that there was no lingering difference in consumption levels between those parts of the country where wheat had long been the staple, and those where wheat had replaced other grains and foods. This is clear from Table 5.5.

Table 5.5 Agricultural families' consumption (all computed as adults) by Collins' regions, 1863

'Traditional' wheat-eating regions			'Converted' wheat-eating regions		
I	–	132%Q	IV	–	115%Q
II	–	128%Q	VI	–	137%Q
III	–	143%Q	Wales	–	168%Q
V	–	132%Q	Scotl'd	–	138%Q
MEAN	–	134%Q	MEAN	–	140%Q

Extrapolated from PP XXVIII (3416) 1, HMSO 1864.

For Collins' regions see Map 6.

The high level for Wales does suggest that past high-consumption levels of barley bread (or muncorn) were carried over into wheat-bread eating; and that would be understandable especially if the wheat bread was coarse. Similarly, the northern aggregate disguises continued use of mixed flours – maslin in Northumberland for instance – though overall 'barley and rye constitute no noticeable part of the dietary in England, and *white* bread is universally preferred.'[71]

5.6 URBAN CONSUMPTION

Urban bread consumption would differ from rural by decade, given the rural U-curve discussed in the previous section. Also, average consumption ought to have differed between towns according to their social composition. Thus, Birmingham, with a high proportion of artisans in the population, should have had a higher aggregate bread consumption than a small country town like Exeter, almost devoid of industry,[72] or a principal port such as Bristol, where, since many men were serving at sea, the proportion of women and children in the population was higher than average. Such differences are indicated by contemporary evidence (see Table 5.6).

Table 5.6   Indicated urban bread consumption

	Average *per capita*
Birmingham, *c*1800	75%Q
Exeter, *c*1820	64%Q
Bristol, *c*1820	53%Q

Calculated from HoC Sessional Papers vol 131 Cd 5056, 9.6.1800, p 13 – Clifford; PP II (255) 101, HoC 8.7.1820, p 33 – Floud, p 31 – Ogden.

Such social factors ought to have been compounded in multifarious London. But London's consumption rate would be further complicated by seasonal residents, and large, probably fluctuating, numbers of people passing through; moreover, the metropolitan consumption of batch bread may have been beneath the representative average, even for towns, given the degree of availability of near-breads and fancy breads, in catering as well as retail outlets.

Maitland estimated that in 1756 London's total flour consumption was equivalent to 77%Q.[73] In 1800 Charles Pratt, a leading mealman, gave the consumption of London and its environs as 20,000 quarters of wheat a week,[74] which assuming a population base of 1,100,000 is roughly 95%Q. In 1820, Harvey calculated that London consumed 20,000 Sacks of flour weekly,[75] which assuming a slightly higher post-war extraction rate, and a population base of about 1,600,000 gives 91%Q for all wheat products. London's consumption of commercially-baked batch bread (the types assized) can be computed from the bakers' official returns of 1798–1814, already cited.[76] The data are reproduced in Table 5.7.

There are caveats of course. The assumption of a constant population trend line for a capital, and especially for a capital in wartime, can readily be challenged. And the recording and return of the data depended on the bakers themselves, who even if they participated with a will, may have made many mistakes.[77] Even so, the London returns

Table 5.7 Consumption of batch bread in the metropolitan
10-mile radius zone, 1798–1814

Mayoral year ending*	Est pop '000	Sacks reported	Converted to bread** '000 lbs	Lbs per head	Converted to %Q***
1798	1020	745,720	278,154	273	64%Q
1799	1040	791,670	295,293	284	67%Q
1800	1060	740,387	276,165	261	61%Q
1801	1081	703,340	262,346	243	57%Q
1802	1100	757,953	282,715	257	60%Q
1803	1121	789,363	294,431	263	62%Q
1804	1140	783,606	292,287	256	60%Q
1805	1161	693,055	258,511	223	52%Q
1806	1180	754,251	281,335	238	56%Q
1807	1201	749,453	279,545	233	55%Q
1808	1222	761,495	284,036	232	55%Q
1809	1242	734,332	273,905	221	52%Q
1810	1263	773,814	288,631	229	54%Q
1811	1285	797,620	297,512	232	54%Q
1812	1307	737,883	275,229	211	49%Q
1813	1329	830,657	309,836	233	55%Q
1814	1351	821,607	306,461	227	53%Q
			MEAN	242	57%Q

* 9 November
** at a Wheaten conversion rate of 4 lbs of bread from 3 lbs of flour (giving 373 lbs of bread per Sack).
*** at the Wheaten rate of 426 lbs of bread per Imperial quarter. The use of Standard Wheaten, or even coarser flour, in 1800–1 would be offset largely by a lower bread-to-flour yield.

Source of Sackage Returns: PP V (186) p 1341, HoC 6.6.1815, Appendix 5.

provide market information of a sort and detail rare for the period. They suggest a 'norm' of something like 64–67%Q, that declined (as would be expected, given periodic scarcity, patriotic self-denial, and government intervention) to about 49-55%Q. Of course, these figures represent only commercially-baked bread: allowance has to be made for some amount of home-baked bread. Although home-baking may have become quite unusual in the City and Westminster, it could well have been significant in the suburbs, and especially in the semi-rural parishes on the edge of the zone; and there was probably a quantitative decline, and certainly a fall in density, of the metropolitan trade during the war, owed to the pressure on bakers' margins and the alternative attractions of craft-service in the armed forces. Thus, even in the centre, there would have been a degree of pressure to resume home-baking, in households that had ovens (and, perhaps, staff). And the same pressure on margins no doubt made it more attractive for surviving bakers to make and sell unassized breads, using best flour: such alternatives would to some extent have substituted for batch bread.

By the middle of the 19th century, when home-baking in the metropolis was certainly uncommon, Eliza Acton put London's average *per capita* bread consumption at the equivalent of 63%Q.[78]

5.7 AVERAGE *PER CAPITA* CONSUMPTION

Though the *per capita* consumption of wheat bread was highly inelastic, average levels for the country as a whole, during the century in review, must aggregate the customary demand levels of different groups, and take some account of varying circumstances.

As shown above, the 'prescribed norm' of 79%Q per head (aggregating men, women, and children) is consistent with crude socio-occupational aggregates of 79%Q for c1803 and 77%Q for c1867. But the components of that demand, differentiated by three broad socio-occupational groups, were markedly different, as is indicated also by urban data. Given that, over the century in review, the proportion of 'lighter' to 'heavier' bread consumers was increasing, and that the consumption levels of rural workers declined somewhat, before rising again after Repeal (the rural U-curve), a national aggregate should allow for some variation by decade. Also, to the extent that higher bread prices reflected lower full-time employment, and therefore a somewhat reduced energy need, some slight variation, roughly on Caird's lines,[79] can be made within each decade, while allowing for adjustment to inflation.

Those variables individually are quite elusive, and combining them is, essentially, a matter of judgement. My own estimates are given in Table 5.8.

In this chapter, I have considered *per capita* consumption of wheatbread across different sections of society and produced average figures on an annual basis for the period 1770 to 1870. These figures will be used as a component of estimates of aggregate consumption of wheat bread in Chapter 7.

As stated earlier, another objective of this chapter has been to consider the one quarter rule-of-thumb used by contemporaries includ-

Table 5.8 Estimated average *per capita* consumption by wheat-bread eaters, 1771–1870

1771	86%Q	1805	77%Q
1772	85%Q	1806	80%Q
1773	86%Q	1807	80%Q
1774	85%Q	1808	80%Q
1775	85%Q	1809	80%Q
1776	85%Q	1810	79%Q
1777	85%Q	1801–10 average	79%Q
1778	85%Q		
1779	84%Q	1811	79%Q
1780	84%Q	1812	77%Q
		1813	77%Q
1771–80 average	85%Q	1814	78%Q
1781	84%Q	1815	79%Q
1782	84%Q	1816	79%Q
1783	83%Q	1817	77%Q
1784	83%Q	1818	77%Q
1785	83%Q	1819	78%Q
1786	83%Q	1820	79%Q
1787	84%Q	1811–20 average	78%Q
1788	82%Q		
1789	82%Q	1821	77%Q
1790	82%Q	1822	78%Q
		1823	78%Q
1781–90 average	83%Q	1824	75%Q
1791	82%Q	1825	75%Q
1792	82%Q	1826	75%Q
1793	81%Q	1827	77%Q
1794	80%Q	1828	77%Q
1795	77%Q	1829	74%Q
1796	77%Q	1830	74%Q
1797	79%Q	1821–30 average	76%Q
1798	80%Q		
1799	77%Q	1831	75%Q
1800	75%Q	1832	75%Q
		1833	76%Q
1791–1800 average	79%Q	1834	76%Q
1801	75%Q	1835	76%Q
1802	80%Q	1836	76%Q
1803	80%Q	1837	75%Q
1804	79%Q	1838	74%Q

Table 5.8 concluded

1839	73%Q	1856	75%Q
1840	74%Q	1857	77%Q
1831–40 average	75%Q	1858	78%Q
		1859	78%Q
1841	74%Q	1860	77%Q
1842	74%Q		
1843	75%Q	1851–60 average	77%Q
1844	75%Q		
1845	75%Q	1861	76%Q
1846	74%Q	1862	77%Q
1847	75%Q	1863	77%Q
1848	75%Q	1864	77%Q
1849	76%Q	1865	77%Q
1850	77%Q	1866	77%Q
		1867	76%Q
1841–50 average	75%Q	1868	77%Q
		1869	78%Q
1851	78%Q	1870	78%Q
1852	79%Q		
1853	78%Q	1861–70 average	77%Q
1854	75%Q		
1855	75%Q	1771–1870 average	78.4%Q

ing Eden and Charles Smith. The data in Table 5.8 make clear that this rule-of-thumb is too high when applied to *per capita* wheat bread consumption alone, but it may be a reasonable estimate when combined with an allowance for 'marginal products' such as fancy breads, rolls etc. This is discussed further in Appendix 8.

Although *per capita* consumption of wheat bread was stationary, or declining slightly, over the course of the century in review, a growing population made an increase in supply essential. In the next chapter attention is focused on the means by which supply expanded to meet this rising demand.

Notes

1. See Appendix 3.
2. Rundell: New System; Copley: Cottage Comforts; Acton: English Bread Book; Timbs: Lady Bountiful.
3. G: A.8.5 no 24 of 51; Cunningham p 709 n 4.

4. Drummond & Wilbraham p 252; Ignatieff p 50.
5. See Chapter 3 Section 1.
6. HoC Sessional Papers vol 131 Cd 4983, 10.2.1800, p 15.
7. Caird: ODF p 19.
8. Hammonds: TL pp 306–7; for wheat–meat link see PP V (612) 1, HoC 2.8.1833, Q 2687 – Oliver; VIII/I (79) 1, HoC 4.3.1836, Appendix 9; O'Brien 1985, graph p 780.
9. Wells pp 42–50.
10. Barnes pp 38, 41.
11. See Chapter 1.
12. Rodger p 29.
13. Pickwick Papers, Penguin ed p 521.
14. PP V (612) 1, 2.8.1833, Qs 403, 4040, 5330; VII/I (79) 1, 4.3.1836, Qs 1988, 3973; Sinclair pp 262–3.
15. PP V (612) 1, 2.8.1833, Qs 3849, 4025–8, 4038.
16. D Davies p 115 et seq.
17. Richardson p 17.
18. Hammonds: Town Labourer p 109.
19. Nield: Comparative Statement.
20. PP XXV (161) 1, HoC 14.4.1863, Appendix V.
21. PP V (612) 1, 2.8.1833, Qs 2393, 2976, 5328.
22. *The Economist* 10.11.1855; Caird: ODF pp 19, 33.
23. PP VIII/I (79) 1, HoC 4.3.1836, Q 3927 – Morton.
24. PP XXV (161) 1, HoC 14.4.63, Appendix V p 326.
25. Walter in Walter & Schofield (eds): Famine, Disease and Social Order.
26. Everitt in Ag H of E & W IV p 466.
27. Thwaites: thesis Part IV; see also Peto and Peto in Rotberg & Rabb (eds): H & H p 309; Livi–Bacci pp 49, 100.
28. Kussmaul: Servants pp 20, 97.
29. Extrapolations from Young: Six Weeks, Six Months; Eden, the places being Dunstable and Leighton Buzzard in Bedfordshire, Winslow (Buckinghamshire), Petersfield (Hampshire), St Albans, Ashby de la Zouche and Leicester, Cockerington (Lincolnshire), Brixworth and Roade (Northamptonshire), Lichfield, Coventry, and Inkborough (Worcestershire); Clapham Vol I pp 121–2; Shammas p 93; PP XXVIII (3416) 1, HMSO 1864, p 244; T C Smout: 'Exploring the Scottish Standard of Living'; Adam Smith p 53; PP XXVIII (3416) 1, HMSO 1864, pp 244, 271.
30. Eden: State of the Poor; Richardson p 407.
31. PP IX (471) 125, HoC 20.7.1842, pp 69, 133, 166; XXVIII (3416) 1, HMSO 1864, pp 244, 271.
32. Everitt in Ag H of E & W IV, p 466; see Pelto and Pelto in Rotberg & Rabb (eds), H & H, p 309; Livi–Bacci pp 49, 100; Thwaites: thesis Part IV.
33. PP IX (668) 1, HoC 18.6.1821, p 81 – Capper, p 186 – Edwards; II (255) 101, HoC 8.7.1820, pp 16–17 – Durrant, p 18 – Harvey.
34. Eden: State of the Poor; Young: France p 8; Hammonds: V L p 109; Salaman p 533; Ketteridge & Mays p 52. Peter King ('Customary rights', Ec HR, August 1991) has calculated that from the 1790s to the 1830s, gleanings contributed from about 3 to 14 per cent of the earnings of agricultural labourers' families in England and Wales (p 474).
35. Shammas: 1983 p 93; PP XLVII (3080) 1, HMSO 1862 throughout.

36. Thompson & Yeo (eds): Unknown Mayhew pp 247, 264, 309, 372, 524.
37. HoC Sessional Papers vol 131 Cd 4983, 10.2.1800, p 18 – Crichton; XLVII (3080) 1, HMSO 1862, p 176 – Dwarber.
38. 1 & 2 Will IV c.37; PP IX (471) 125, HoC 20.7.1842, pp 1, 3, 5, 34, 51, 64, 86, 88, 93, 108–10, 122, 142, 148, 152–5, 160, 163; XIII (530) 425, HoC 28.7.1846, p vi, Q 202, 735, 2051; XV (609), HMSO 1845, pp 72, 74, 77, 247, 270, 299; V (612), HoC 2.8.1833, p 15; Clapham I pp 409–10; II p 456; Elsas p 77; Orbell thesis: p 142 et seq; Blackman: Development p 111; Cole p 17.
39. PP VIII/II (465) 1, HoC 21.7.1836, Q 10379.
40. Thwaites: thesis p 228; Green in Stainer (ed), pp 109, 232, 233.
41. Wells p 74.
42. PP XXVII (44) 1, HoC 21.2.1834, p 8.
43. PP XXVII (44) 1, HoC 21.2.1834 pp 8, 11.
44. PP XXVII (944) 1, HoC 21.2.1834, p 16.
45. HoC Sessional Papers vol 131 Cd 5056, 9.6.1800, p 9 – Clifford; eg riot at Exeter, *The Times* 16.1.1854.
46. Collins p 97.
47. *The Family Oracle of Health* Vol I, cit Drummond & Wilbraham p 396.
48. Turton p 161; Jacob pp 89–91; Dodd p 167 (Dodd's estimate may also reflect his metrocentric viewpoint); Caird: Our Daily Food pp 34–5; Porter p 537.
49. HoC Sessional Papers vol 131 Cd 4990, 6.3.1800, p 5.
50. Drummond & Wilbraham p 440.
51. Appendix 6, case 6.15 b.
52. Anderson in F M L Thompson (ed) Vol 2, p 26 (based on Wrigley & Schofield).
53. See Appendix 6, case 6.16.
54. Appendix 6, case 4.
55. Appendix 6.
56. Appendix 6.
57. Thompson & Yeo (eds): Unknown Mayhew.
58. See Appendix 6, case 6.9.
59. Appendix 6, case 6.15.
60. Under the new Poor Law, the average of the bread rations laid down in the national guidelines for workhouse inmates in 1855 (see Dodd p 145) was, assuming standard Wheaten bread, 77%Q for men and 65%Q for women; ie an average of 71%Q, assuming a gender ratio similar to that in prisons of 84 per cent.
61. *Our Mutual Friend* pp 566 et seq, especially p 571.
62. Appendix 6, cases 5.1, 5.2.
63. Appendix 6, cases 5.3, 5.4.
64. Appendix 6, case 5.5.
65. Appendix 6, case 5.8.
66. Hammonds: VL pp 184–5 give the Old Poor Law dole in 1831 as one gallon of bread per head plus one gallon over per family (at Speenhamland one gallon loaf weighed 8 lb 11 oz). Assuming that 70 per cent of the indexed dole went on food, and 80 per cent of food was bread, and assuming a family of six, then 34 lb of bread would be consumed weekly, or 5.7 lbs per head. This is 66%Q, assuming standard Wheaten bread.

67. Eden (p 166) shows the case of a Cumberland labourer's family which spent 8 per cent of its budget on potatoes in the winter, but only 3 per cent in autumn.
68. cit Ignatieff p 175.
69. Giffen p 391.
70. Appendix 6, case 5.17.
71. PP XXVIII (3416) 1, HMSO 1864, p 267. 6.5d per family. Davies' correspondents collected expenditure details from 20 other wheat–eating places in England:
72. Bohstedt p 93.
73. Extrapolated from Charles Smith, Example 2, p 190.
74. HoC Sessional Papers vol 131 Cd 5080, 1.7.1800, p 21 – Pratt.
75. PP II (255) 101, HoC 8.7.1820, p 18 – Harvey.
76. See Table 5.2, and see Appendix 7 for population estimates.
77. Thrupp p 34; PP V (186) 1341, HoC 6.6.1815 – Hobler.
78. Acton E B B p 10.
79. Caird thought that a 10 per cent increase in the price of the loaf would reduce consumption by at least 1 per cent. See Caird ODF p 19.

CHAPTER 6

Wheat Supply

To sustain a highly inelastic *per capita* demand for wheat bread, supply had to be determined by the market, rather than by the shortfalls and surpluses of local production. And, needless to say, to meet a huge increase in the aggregate demand for wheat bread, over the century in review, a matching expansion of supply was essential.

That was achieved, first, by the development of bulk freight transportation, especially through the extension and improvement of the inland navigation (Section 6.1). An extensive and more efficient inland navigation, together with an increased coastways carrying capacity, allowed the intranational (and international) trade in wheat and flour to respond, efficiently and flexibly, to market demand at national, regional, and local level (Section 6.2); as it helped to unlock the output potential of domestic agriculture, which was supplemented at first periodically, and then permanently, by imports (Section 6.3).

6.1 TRANSPORT

Transport was the link, the buckle, uniting the supply of, and demand for, breadstuffs. Although, even *c*1800, many agrarian communities were self-sufficient in grain, the principal cities and towns, and the rising industrial districts, depended almost entirely on breadstuffs brought from elsewhere. Three aspects of transport will first be outlined: cost, access, and capacity.

Before the rail age, breadstuffs moved cheaply on water, dearly on land. In 1796 it cost 6d to transport a 280 lb sack of flour the 73 miles by river from Reading to central London. The same journey over land, although only 40 miles, cost 4s 6d. Sea transport was cheapest of all: 6d would get a sack the 200 miles from Kings Lynn in Norfolk to London.[1]

Crudely calculated, those charges represent rates per ton-mile of 0.24d coastways, 0.66d by river, and 10.8d overland, or ratios of 1: 2.75: 45. That relationship of coastways and inland water charges is roughly consistent with other estimates, but the cited cost of overland carriage is considerably above Jackman's rough average (of from two to four times the inland navigation, and from four to eight times the coastways, costs).[2] However, actual charges and therefore ratios could vary greatly over time. On the Thames, a main artery of the breadstuffs trade, in the 1760s the extortions of the lock-keepers were so steep, and the state of the navigation so poor, that goods were diverted overland, possibly at little extra cost.[3] As Professor Chartres observes, restrictive practices and deterioration of the navigation were commonplace.[4] Also, the premium paid for overland conveyance would have been somewhat less, after allowance for the port handling costs and tolls imposed on water-borne goods.[5] Nonetheless, the usual cost efficiency of water transport, and of coastways carriage especially, is clearly indicated.

Given which, Britain's insularity conferred an outstanding economic advantage. Compared to France, for example, a larger proportion of Britain's land surface was accessible by sea: Dr Szostak, taking Britain south of the Firth of Forth, has calculated a ratio of 55 square miles of land surface per mile of coast, compared to 134 square miles for France.[6] Moreover, the northern and southern coasts of France were divided from each other, and economically distinct.

The traditionally close association of Britain's market economy and the sea is suggested by the location of the chief concentrations of demand. Of the total inhabitants of the twenty English towns for which Professor Wrigley gives a population estimate for c1750, 84 per cent lived in seaports (more than half of them in London).[7]

But not all of Britain's coast was amenable to a regular or substantial seaborne trade: parts were too rocky or too silted; or too distant from centres of population, or lacking in tradeable goods.

Conversely, the island was penetrated by water highways reaching far inland. In principle at least, the Thames, Severn, and Trent were navigable for most of their lengths; there was a navigation through a network of waterways, from Kings Lynn to Cambridge; Norwich was an important port.[8] All such were served by river craft, and some, even a distance inland, such as Gloucester, were thriving seaports too.[9] Also each port, quay, and riparian wharf might have a hinterland of sizeable extent, served by tributaries or feeder roads.

However, up to the 1830s, the inland waterways and their immediate hinterlands were not linked in a comprehensive interior network:[10] their chief connexion was exterior, to and from the sea. So that a 'breadstuffs supply map' of Britain shows a patchwork, comprising a 'water zone' – including much but not all of the coastland, and the discrete inland navigations, with their immediate hinterlands – and a 'land zone', where there was no ready access to bulk capacity water transport (see Maps 2 and 3 on pages 168 and 169). In principle, breadstuffs moved cheaply within the water zone, and expensively, if at all, in the land zone. Nor was the water zone confined to Britain: it could be as economical to send grain down the Vistula to Danzig, transfer it to ships, and land it in London[11] – or to bring hard wheat down the Dnestr to Odessa, then on via the Bosphorous, Mediterranean, Atlantic and Channel – as to drag a cartload of English wheat through several miles of Midland mire.[12]

Of course, there were exceptions. Defoe observed, for instance, that the farmers of Chichester and district sent their ground meal by sea; but they took their wheat no less than 40 miles to Farnham (from whence it could be sent via the Wey navigation to London);[13] perhaps, as they used their own carts, they did not count the cost. And Arthur Young noted that in Suffolk and Essex grain commonly was carried 25 miles to market.[14]

Where commercial carriers were used, and so cost incurred, overland carriage may have been preferred for various reasons. In ordinary circumstances, a cargo of wheat in good condition might go by the slowest, if cheapest, means; but damp wheat, which was prone to heat or rot, had to be conveyed quickly if it was to be marketable at all. And at any time, a supplier might choose the speediest, though costliest, means of transport to catch a rising market, or to obtain earlier settlement. Particularly careful calculation was necessary when sending flour or meal, given their propensity to stale, especially in summer. And in summer also, there was the added hazard that the rivers might dry out, or in winter that they might flood or freeze, stranding perishable cargo in transit. In such circumstances, overland carriage was the safest and surest option, and so the most economical, considering the commodity value at risk.[15]

But, crude as they are, the concepts of 'water zone' and 'land zone' are useful guides to the structure and expansion of the trade in breadstuffs.

The inland water zone expanded rapidly during the 18th and early 19th centuries, as river navigations were improved and extended, and as the canals were dug.[16] Estimates of the length of navigable waterways in Britain are listed in Table 6.1.

The estimates indicate that the navigable length of Britain's inland waterways more than doubled between 1660 and 1760, and then roughly tripled between 1760 and 1830, though as noted, such gains, especially before 1770, have to be treated cautiously given the likelihood of deterioration. Also, the key indicator of commercial usefulness is not so much the length of, but the area served by, the navigations. Willan depicts a zone of up to 15 miles from a navigation (implying that most of lowland Britain had access to water transport as early as 1600–60),[17] but that may significantly over-state the areal effect where wheat, a bulky commodity, had to be carried. Much would depend, for instance, on the suitability of feeder roads and the diffusion of wharves with adequate loading facilities. Thus, maps 2 and 3 here give a more conservative impression of the expanding water zone.

Table 6.1 Estimated total length of the inland navigation,
1660–1830, in miles

	England & Wales	Scotland	Great Britain
1660	684 (a)	(e)	684
1725	1,181 (a)	(e)	1,181
1760	1,398.5 (b)	(e)	1,398.5
1780	1,750 (c) + 400 (d)	(e)	2,150
1800	2,690 (c) + 400 (d)	(e)	3,090
1820	3,190 (c) + 400 (d)	(e)	3,590
1830	3,875.5 (b)	215 (b)	4,090.5

Sources and notes:
(a) Willan cit Turnbull cit Szostak p 55.
(b) Duckham in Aldcroft & Freeman (eds) p 109.
(c) Ginarlis (estimate of canals and improved river naviagations) cit Feinstein
     1978 p 62.
(d) 400 miles added to Ginarlis' estimates to represent unimproved river
     navigations, giving rough consistency with Duckham's totals.
(e) Assuming a negligible length of inland navigation in Scotland until the
     completion of the Caledonian Canal in 1822.

The areal expansion of the water zone was paralleled by increases in
transport capacity. The tonnage employed in the coastways trade of
England and Wales more than doubled between 1709 and 1770 (from
92,929 tons to 211,031 tons), and then (with Scottish vessels included)
quadrupled to 863,959 tons in 1826.[18] The average annual volume of
all grains carried coastwise almost tripled between 1780–6 and 1819–
27, with wheat increasing from 62,974 tons to 169,663 tons.[19] The rate
of expansion of the water zone, and the increase in carrying capacity, is
indicated also by Professor Feinstein's calculations of the gross stock of
domestic reproducible fixed capital represented by canals and waterways, docks and harbours, and ships.[20] The total (at 1851–60
replacement cost) rose from £21m in 1760 to £48m in 1800 and to
£81m in 1830.

As the canals and river navigations developed, the number of barges
grew to about 25,000 by the middle of the 19th century,[21] and their size
increased with the lengthening of the locks and broadening of the
waterways (the planned width of canals doubled from 7 ft to 14 ft[22]).
Canal design and development impacted directly on the river navigations, especially as the inland waterways were linked; thus, after the
opening of the Thames & Severn and Oxford canals, the upper Thames
navigation was steadily improved to accommodate barges of 70 tons
(roughly double the capacity of c1770 and before[23]). However, a 70 ton

barge going against the stream needed 50 to 80 men, or from five to twelve horses.[24] to haul it, and that in turn called for a continuous towing path. Though parts of the Thames were served by private paths (for the use of which riparian owners charged often sizeable tolls) the objective of a free and continuous path from Putney to Lechlade was still far from achievement in 1811, despite powers of compulsory land purchase granted to the Thames Conservancy Board by successive acts of Parliament.[25]

If the Thames is representative, then millers were prominent in opposing improvements to river navigation, despite their interest in efficient transport. Paradoxically, since the river was their principal source of motive power, they had an overriding interest in such old-fashioned features as flash-locks, which, if kept closed till a powerful head of water had built up, could then be opened, releasing a torrent. Such locks impeded and imperilled river craft directly, and indirectly, since they increased the scour of the river, which, excavating the bed and banks, carried down mud and debris that formed into shoals, further constricting the navigation.[26]

Since the efficient conveyance of cargo within the water zone depended upon a mix of transport, capacity also was increased by the improvement of feeder roads. A cartload (five Winchester quarters) of wheat weighed roughly one ton, the maximum weight permitted on unsurfaced roads by an Act of 1621 (though a further Act of 1667 allowed a weight of 30 cwt in summer).[27] As roads improved, greater maxima were permitted (60 cwt in 1741, 120 cwt in 1765), while the number of horses could be reduced from seven in 1662 to five in 1751. Even then, legal maxima barely reflect the full improvement, since an unsurfaced road used by a succession of wheat waggons, in wet weather especially, could easily mire and become impassable. The increasing length of turnpiked roads offers a rough though by no means exact approximation to the improvement: in 1750 3000 miles of main roads were under turnpike trusts; in the 1830s, 20,000 miles of all kinds of roads.[28]

The contribution of the railways to the movement of bulk freight was small until the network had expanded significantly (only c1850 did rail mileage exceed the total length of navigable waterways[29]), until more powerful locomotives had been introduced, and until the companies integrated and simplified their goods business.[30] As Bagwell has observed, the goods traffic on most canals 'reached its greatest volume many years after the arrival of the railway in the district'.[31] Moreover, steam also improved the cost-efficiency of the navigations (where tugs replaced horses and hauliers).[32] Hawke estimates that in 1865 27 per cent of the wheat grown in England and Wales was transported by rail.[33] For the grain trade, the speed of rail conveyance may have been of little importance when cost was the usual consideration, and both the coastways and inland carriers competed intensely;[34] however railways did offer access, where lines unlocked the remaining land zone (as in Wales and Scotland), and rail also replaced water, where canals were bought out (approximately one-third of the canal network had been taken over by 1865).[35] But the assured speed of rail conveyance could be an inestimable advantage in the flour and meal trade, in summer especially, since cargoes could be sent without fear of staling. Millers were prominent backers of new lines (indeed, flour was the first cargo carried on the Liverpool & Manchester railway in 1834).[36]

Transport largely determined the nature of the wheat and bread markets at any place, the topic considered next.

6.2 THE NATIONAL MARKET

Whereas in the 'land zone' communities were likely to depend heavily on whatever types and qualities of grain were locally grown, and in whatever amount from year to year, in the water zone wheat of various qualities (and if required, other grains), and also wheat flour, chiefly fine and bran-free, were readily obtained.[37] As access to water transport improved, formerly land-locked markets previously monopolized by local growers, were 'cracked open',[38] though openness worked both ways. For instance, inclusion in the water zone did not necessarily moderate the extremes of local glut and dearth:[39] in glut a market might be deluged with wheat and flour from other parts, threatening local producers with ruin, albeit benefiting consumers. In dearth, however, a district could be drained of wheat and flour, if higher prices were available elsewhere.[40] Thus, in the water zone, not only was the monopoly of supply 'cracked', so too was the monopoly of demand; at least, that would have been the case had not commerce been constrained. The flow, or threatened flow, of breadstuffs out of a district might be checked, at an extreme, by the action of the mob in blocking the way, seizing cargoes, or menacing the carriers.[41] More often, either to avoid unrest, or to contain it, the trade in breadstuffs was lawfully impeded.

The Tudor statutes against forestalling, engrossing, and regrating[42] had been abolished, virtually, by an act of 1663; but, as the water zone expanded, clamour for their reintroduction increased, and during the scarcity of 1766 local authorities were given fresh enabling powers to enforce them.[43] But, as Dr Penry Williams has observed of the 16th century,[44] so in the 18th century: an artificial check to the commerce in breadstuffs, when operated locally, had the effect of diminishing supplies, as cargoes were directed to 'uncontrolled' markets or as farmers held back stocks, in expectation of a rising, and therefore 'realistic' price. Recognizing that these 'internal corn laws were counter-productive', Parliament finally repealed them in 1772. Even so, as Adam Smith remarked, the old laws, and the protection that they seemed to offer, exercised a powerful hold on the popular imagination; magistrates too hoped for their reinstatement, as symbols of appease-ment if not as warrants of supply.[45] Thus in the dearth of 1795–6, Eden noted a considerable agitation in Herefordshire for instance, in favour of the old restraints, and re-enactment was supported by Lord Mountmorres, Girdler, and others.[46] During the dearth of 1799–1801 the Lord Chief Justice, Kenyon, gave authority to those magistrates who, appealing *force majeure* and citing common law, acted against forestallers, ingrossers and regrators.[47] Pitt was dismayed at such endorsement of 'dangerous notions', which indeed were contrary to explicit statute, but given the circumstances of the time, he declined to act.[48]

Such impediments threw the burden of dearth onto the towns and cities. And if urban magistrates sought to contain the resultant price explosion, either by intervening against speculators, or as in the case of London, for instance in 1795–6, by manipulating the Assize of Bread in favour of the poor, then as in the past they ran the risk of intensifying scarcity. Indeed, metropolitan vulnerability had increased: traditionally, when much of the intranational trade in breadstuffs had been carried coastways, London had dominated, and to an extent monopolized, the market. But, by the end of the 18th century, the rise of new urban centres served by the water zone gave a greater freedom to suppliers: substantial quantities of flour could be diverted, conveniently by canal, to other cities.[49] That the millers also held back supplies to drive up prices, was widely alleged, though Turton, inspecting 150 mills in 1799–1800, found no proof.[50] Certain contemporaries recognized that the answer to national shortage was not local price control, but improved supply. One long-term solution proposed was that there should again be public metropolitan granaries (as there had been before the Great Fire of London), so that the surplus of glut might be bought up and stored, at a charge on the rates, and then released in years of dearth by the authorities, thus meeting need and checking speculation.[51] That option was closely examined, but not pursued (Burke, for one, argued that such granaries would be a ready target for the mob in years of high prices).[52] Another solution, a chartered company to challenge the commercial millers, was tried but failed. The third option was to rely upon imports. Thus in 1800–1 the London market, which ordinarily was chiefly or wholly supplied with domestic wheat (or flour made from it) depended for 90 per cent of its need on imported wheat (and some imported flour).[53] Since the total demand of London (for home as well as commercial baking, and for marginal wheat foods) was put at 1,000,000 Sacks of flour annually[54] (the equivalent of roughly 750,000 Quarters of wheat) the metropolis consumed approximately 60 per cent of all the wheat and flour imported into Britain in those crisis years. If most of the rest was consigned to other cities, then the burden of dearth was shifted almost entirely: the scale of imports suggests that virtually all the wheat that could be grown in 1800 and 1801 would have been consumed in the growing districts.

Given London's ancient standing as an international as well as intranational market-place, such shifts probably had occurred in times of dearth in past centuries. But the crises of the late 18th and early 19th centuries, and especially those of 1795–6 and 1799–1801, showed starkly that not only London, but substantial populations elsewhere in Britain now depended for their breadstuffs on the long-distance trade. As the inland water zone had expanded, large concentrations of population could be sited at a distance from the sea.[55] Thus, of the total inhabitants of the 27 English towns for which Professor Wrigley gives population figures for 1801, only 73 per cent lived in seaports, compared crudely to the estimated 84 per cent of c1750; and in the eight inland cities where estimates can be compared, population had increased by 153 per cent.[56] Adam Smith argued elegantly that the latent food-producing potential of previously underpopulated regions was thereby realized,[57] which may have been the case with meat, dairy, and vegetable foods. But it was not so with breadstuffs.

Rough calculation suggests that the demand for breadstuffs in the new industrial zones far exceeded the supply capacity of local agriculture. To take Lancashire: supposing an average annual *per capita* consumption of one quarter of wheat (as bread and marginal products), or its net nutritional equivalent in barley, rye, and/or oats, then the demand of Lancashire's population in 1801 would have amounted to 673,000 quarters. Assuming a net yield of wheat per acre of 20 bushels (and for simplicity, assuming that the yields of inferior grains corresponded to their net nutritional value), then that demand would equal the output of 269,200 acres, which, supposing a four-year rotation including two grain crops, required a dedicated land-stock of 538,400 acres. Dr Turner has estimated that there were 103,710 arable acres in Lancashire in 1801:[58] thus the county's demand was, very roughly, five times its own output capacity, a dependency confirmed by a contemporary estimate. According to a committee of millers, in 1800 five-sixths of the breadstuffs (grain or flour) consumed in Lancashire came from other parts of the United Kingdom or from abroad.[59] In Scotland's 15th District (which included Glasgow, Greenock, and Paisley), by 1805 demand exceeded local output by a multiple of two, three, or more, according to the state of the harvest.[60] And even had the industrial counties been able to raise most of their own breadstuffs, they would have encountered a milling crisis, because of competition for water-power. To take Lancashire again, Dr Orbell has shown that the textile trades pre-empted inland mill sites, so that grain had to be ground at the ports, using either tide or wind-power (the Mersey Mills at Warrington were the largest milling complex in the country); otherwise, ready-made flour was imported coastways or by canal from the southern and eastern mills that also supplied London.[61]

There was also a qualitative as well as quantitative dimension to the intranational (and international) trade. Wheat is not and was not a homogeneous commodity, but differs by strain (there are, today, at least 30,000 varieties[62]) and by quality (whether a plump and heavy grain, allowing a proportionately and quantitatively large extraction of first-rate flour, or thin and light, yielding less and perhaps uneconomically little, saleable flour). It also differs by strength (gluten content); by age (older, drier grain generally being preferred for milling and baking) and condition (whether well-kept or deteriorating, whether cleaned or still mixed with dirt); and by pigment ('white' wheats being preferable to 'reds', which, if not treated with alum, gave bread a brownish tinge, easily confused with the appearance of bran). And quality as well as quantity varied significantly according to the growing and harvesting conditions at any place in any year. Such variety is reflected in market prices. The rule of thumb was that best wheat fetched double the price of inferior,[63] and that span might be exceeded. At Bodmin, a small market, a wide variety of wheat was offered in late 1816; to take the not untypical transactions of 17th November, the lowest price of wheat there was 17s per quarter, and the highest, 43s.

Since Tudor times at least,[64] wheats of breadstuff quality had been classified roughly into three grades, according to their flour-making value: best or superfine or 1st; average or fine or 2nd; and ordinary or 3rd, the latter grade shading into a fourth – wheats that, being wholly unfit for human consumption were generally not recorded in the market returns, though they might have some value as animal food or for starch manufacture (perhaps the cheapest wheat sold at Bodmin was of that sort[65]).

Because all three breadstuff grades were likely to be available in the water zone, they could be mixed to a standard quality. Mixing greatly extended the supply of breadstuffs, since it allowed the widest use of the second grade, and especially third grade wheats that by themselves may have been unsuitable for breadstuffs (at least, bread made from their flours alone would have been less saleable in towns); and mixing eked out the supply of firsts, which used alone produced bread of unnecessarily high quality and expense (for the mass market) but when mixed, contributed a good rise, texture, colour, and taste, to the usual white loaf. From the Middle Ages, most of London's bread had been made from the flour of mixed wheats (as the implicit qualities of the loaf-types itemized in the Assize law indicate), though up to 1757 'White' bread, made mostly or entirely from first-rate wheatflour, was available. Mixing for the metropolitan trade had traditionally been the speciality of 'meal men', who purchased consignments of ground meal (or flour) of different qualities, and sold their own mixtures to the bakers; as commercial flour production developed, the millers themselves undertook the work (and risk), so that progressively the two trades merged. Otherwise, the baker himself either took different qualities of wheat for milling, or bought meal or flour, and then mixed them to his own particular standards. The art of mixing, or mealing, assured the greatest efficiency, economy, and consistency of bread production.[66] Charles Smith described mixing as 'an inconceivable advantage'; and Thomas Pownall (in other respects, no friend of the trade) observed:

> there is not a Trader more beneficial to the Publick than the Mealman ... He is become absolutely necessary to the permanent and equal Supply of great Towns.[67]

A typical mixture for Wheaten bread (cited in a pamphlet issued in 1757, for the guidance of magistrates when setting the assize) was one part first-rate to one part second-rate to two parts third-rate – with indicative prices suggesting price ratios of 100 for first-rate: 92 for second-rate: and 83 for third-rate.[68] Roughly the same price ratios obtained at Mark Lane in October 1828,[69] and also at various markets in the summer of 1834 (mean ratios of 100:91:81), as shown in Table 6.2. The latter table shows too how closely aligned prices were throughout the water zone, indicating the fluency with which wheat cargoes could be moved.[70]

The bread acts, by requiring common types of stipulated quality (irrespective of whether such loaves were or were not assized) further encouraged mixing and therefore the intranational trade in wheat throughout the water zone. Also, commerce in wheat grain overlapped the trade in ready-milled and mixed flours. So that probably much of the grain, as well as flour, imported into Lancashire was of better quality than the average of the local growth, though native sorts might be mixed in. Similarly, at rising Glasgow, the locally-grown second and third grades were mixed with best wheat 'imported' from the southern

Table 6.2   Wheat prices per Imperial quarter at the principal ports, cJuly 1834

	Best	Average	Inferior
Belfast	48s 3d	43s 11d	39s 8d
Bristol	48s 8d	44s 0d	39s 4d
Dublin	48s 10d	44s 0d	39s 2d
Glasgow	48s 6d	44s 0d	39s 6d
Gloucester	48s 8d	44s 0d	39s 4d
Liverpool	48s 0d	44s 0d	40s 0d
London	48s 6d	44s 0d	39s 6d
MEAN	48s 6d	44s 0d	39s 6d

Calculated from PP VII (517) 1, HoC 25.7.1834, p 320 (Q 4014).

and eastern counties of England, though it is apparent from Table 6.3 that the proportions varied greatly from year to year.

There were substantial mills at Glasgow, two of which were owned by

Table 6.3   Accounts of James Liddell, baker of Glasgow*, showing the ratio of 'imported' (bought from merchants) and 'domestic' (bought from farmers) wheat, 1811–16

| Year | Volume | | Value | |
	% Merchant	% Farmer	% Merchant	% Farmer
1811	28	72	35	65
1812	60	40	65	35
1813	79	21	87	13
1814	44	56	48	52
1815	42	58	50	50
1816	44	56	41	59

Calculated from SRO (WRH): CS 96/3526–7.

* Clearly Liddell was a baker on a large scale, or else he factored to others in the trade. His wheat purchases in 1813 amounted to £4769. The main wheats bought from merchants were English, Canadian, and Danzig types, mostly white; usually, he bought reds from farmers.

the bakers' incorporation, but nonetheless, a significant amount of English ready-made flour was sent c1800.[71] A probable explanation is that watermill sites in and around Glasgow were, as in Lancashire, at a premium (especially for textile processing).

A particular trade developed between the West Country and the south coast (Sussex and Hampshire, including the Isle of Wight). Inferior wheat from Devon and Cornwall was shipped to the southern ports, mixed with better qualities, and then returned, usually as flour. Opportunities for milling in the south-west were constricted, as elsewhere, by other industry: many of the population centres were linked to tin and clay mining, industries which pre-empted water supplies; and when water was released from their workings, not only had it lost much of its force, it was full of rubble and grit, which damaged the wheels of mills downstream. But the relative lack of industry at Exeter allowed mixed grain to be returned there for local milling.[72]

6.3   HOME OUTPUT AND IMPORTS

The commercial growing of wheat in Britain was influenced not only by the quantity but by the quality of wheat bread demanded, and by the nature of the intranational trade; also, since it was public policy that the poor should not starve, supply comprised fluctuating proportions of home output and imports, even in years when, officially, Protection was in force. Therefore, qualitative aspects of supply are best considered as a whole (the quantitative consequences are assessed in the next chapter).

The development of British agriculture was a continuous process; however, it is now 'widely accepted' that in many areas, considerable changes in means and methods were introduced over a relatively short period, c1650–1750, and analyses indicate substantial gains in land and labour productivity.[73] A brief retrospective (aided by later information) helps to show the continuing relevance of such developments to bread, during the century in review.

The timing of the 'agricultural revolution', in the case of wheat at least, seems odd: taking the national market as a whole, there is little to indicate a pressing need for innovation before c1750. England's population was roughly static, and though London was growing rapidly (so that metropolitan demand for all corn, as food and drink, may have increased from 500,000 quarters c1600 to more than 1,400,000 quarters c1700[74]), wheat appears to have been in considerable over-supply, to judge from the downward trend of its price between c1650 and c1750, and from the steep rise in exports that occurred in those years.[75]

Possibly, such over-production was the by-product of a shift to livestock husbandry, if increased amounts of manure fertilized the tilled acreage.[76] Or, as argued by A H John and E L Jones, innovations in arable husbandry may indicate a determined struggle for competitive advantage in an adverse market (the 'pie-slicing thesis'), especially on the part of those farmers whose proceeds from livestock inadequately compensated them for falling grain prices. To offset smaller grain margins, it is argued, they therefore increased their output, using the new techniques of intensive husbandry. The incentive to improvement may have been greatest where lighter soils were farmed with greater labour efficiency and therefore at less cost, thus explaining the paradox that, as prices continued to fall, commercial wheat-growing spread throughout Norfolk and inward from the eastern seaboard generally, to districts which, having the advantage of water transport, also had easy access to the London and export markets. Other farmers may also have concentrated on increased grain, and especially wheat, output if they were constrained by social as well as physical considerations.[77]

However, the pie-slicing argument is not clear-cut. It might be surmised that wheat producers, in aggregate, would have adjusted to over-supply in the course of a century. Clearly some did (the wheat-growers of the Hertfordshire Chilterns for example, and those farming heavy Midland clays[78]), but more seem to have endured long adversity (as did their successors after 1815) rather than diversify. Also, the advantage to those who did adopt the new techniques might be considered in the round. If, for instance, an improver converted from a three-part system of wheat, fallow, and lenten corn, to a four– or five–course rotation, with only one wheat crop per cycle, then *ceteris paribus* he would sacrifice wheat acreage. To compensate for which, yields would have had to increase by some 33 per cent or 66 per cent respectively, simply to achieve break even. Nor would the accountancy be much improved by lenten corn (since a similar sacrifice of acreage probably was incurred), nor by the relatively small direct worth of the intervening roots and grasses. Even higher gains in output would be needed to repay the initial and recurring costs of improvement.

If the volume argument is fraught, the history of bread may supply an alternative explanantion of the timing and nature of change: that the 'agricultural revolution' was not quantity-driven but quality-led. Not only was metropolitan demand increasing, but the nature of that demand was changing. If breads made from coarser grains had been acceptable to poorer Londoners in earlier centuries, by 1616 it would seem that only wheat bread would serve: in that year, the Grocers' Company complained that none would eat barley or rye, nor even a maslin of two-thirds wheat content.[79] And progressively, the quality of the wheat bread eaten by the masses improved, a process forced on by the mechanization of flour production and the rise of the commercial miller: the brannish Household grade was generally spurned, and the middling Wheaten sort was up-graded, to the high standard officially recognized in 1735, when the metropolitan assize table was adjusted. By c1750, London's demand for high quality wheat would have been of the order of 675,000 quarters annually (assuming that on average each of Professor Wrigley's estimate of inhabitants[80] consumed one quarter annually), compared to relatively small amounts early in the 17th century (when the 'White' grade, later recognized by the 1709 Act, was probably a luxury). The demand for good quality, rather than inferior, wheat in provincial towns, if lagged would have followed, given the effect of the bread acts in imposing 'metropolitan' bread standards on the rest of the country.

Thus the 'quality wheat' market expanded substantially; and at the same time, supplies of that sort from one important source declined. Polish wheat, shipped via Danzig, was valued throughout Europe for its bread-making properties, chiefly its relative 'hardness', or higher gluten content; it was mixed with 'soft' wheat to give well-risen loaves of light texture. However, the Danzig trade was seriously affected by successive wars in central Europe and by plague; both depopulated many parts of Poland, reducing the number of cultivators and constricting the opportunity for reciprocal commerce. Between 1670–9 and 1710–19, shipments from Danzig more than halved, creating a vacuum in the 'quality' market throughout Europe, that British producers strove to fill.[81]

All the wheats then grown in Britain were 'soft' or 'softish', with gluten contents as low as 8 per cent by weight. The flour of the softest wheat would produce a low-raising bread, certainly of lighter texture than barley bread, but with little or no greater rise than rye. Such bread might be good to taste, but its density was a disadvantage, especially on the London, and on the export, markets. As a rule, the gluten content of wheat increases in direct relationship to the prevailing heat and dryness of summers; and wheat of 12 per cent gluten content could be produced in Britain, given suitable conditions, such as sheltered sites, relatively low summer rainfall, and relatively high temperature. Such wheat still fell short of a Danzig 'strength' (say 13.5 per cent gluten content), but, by being somewhat softer, it was 'tastier'.[82] The demand for a higher gluten-content wheat, in itself, might explain the extension of commercial wheat-growing in England's southern and eastern counties, even overriding considerations of soil-type. And such expansion was facilitated by improving access to water transport.[83]

The bread trades imposed a second 'quality preference' on the grower: the demand for a plump and thin-skinned wheat grain that when milled gave the highest extraction of white flour and the least bran. The best flour-yielding quality, and higher gluten content, usually coincided, since the crop benefited in both respects from warmer and drier ripening conditions; but in addition, good flour-producing wheat called for dedicated husbandry, involving most of the 'revolutionary' arts, to bring soil up to the highest standard. One prescription given by Edlin, in his manual of bakery, as the established and common opinion of farmers, millers, and bakers, specified a clay soil that had been well marled and limed, and then enriched by the repeated ploughing-in of root crops and other vegetation, which when putrefied created the most fertile growing medium. His prescription stipulated too that a drilling machine be used when sowing, to deposit the seed exactly two inches below the surface, so that crop quality was not compromised, either by exposure and drift, or else by 'suffocation'.[84] Other prescriptions, for clays or lighter soils, involving carefully chosen rotations, manuring, drainage, the use of coarse sand or ash or chalk, would tend to the same result: the production of wheat which, having the best milling properties, was most readily saleable at premium prices especially in London, and on the continent.

Although Houghton's figures are not consistently reliable, and though a number of factors could affect a regional price (such as local demand and supply, the cost of transport, and the degree of market regulation), his data strongly suggest that a substantial premium was paid for quality (averaging all types sold) in and around London at the end of the 17th century, compared to prices obtaining elsewhere (the differentials being broadly consistent with the bands for first, second, and third grade wheats). Houghton's figures are shown in Table 6.4.

Thus the macro-regional means are in the ratio 100:91:82. Except, perhaps, where the natural dispensation was so generous that few of the finer arts of husbandry were needed, quality interposed an absolute discipline: if wheat was to be saleable on the London market, then every skill and artifice was called for in its cultivation. Quality imposed a gate, the entrance to relatively high prices and returns, that was shut to the inferior producer. Thus, amounts of wheat of a quality that formerly might have been sold in London probably were redirected, flooding instead smaller provincial markets, and driving down prices there.

However, 'quality' and 'quantity' were not wholly distinct. First because wheat of good quality implied a 'hidden gain' in greater weight per bushel. If a farmer could improve the quality of his wheat from 'inferior' (at perhaps 50–51 lbs per Winchester bushel) to first-rate (at 57 lbs or more), his real output increased by 15 per cent or so,[85] though his bushel yield was constant (Dundas, in 1794, put the weight of inferior wheat at one-third less than best, though probably he cited extreme cases[86]). Second, volume might increase substantially, because soil prepared to such prescriptions was likely to yield more bushels

Table 6.4 Average prices per quarter of wheat
by region, 1691–1702

	s	d
Home	47	0.25
London	44	4.25
MEAN	45	8.25
South	42	0.75
East	41	0
MEAN	41	6.375
South West	38	9.75
Midlands	36	10.5
North	36	0.75
MEAN	37	3.0
ALL ENGLAND	40	5.5

Source: Houghton cit Gras p 119.

(unless the farmer sowed lightly, so as neither to prejudice quality nor exhaust the soil). But such volume gains might better be seen as the consequence, rather than the cause, of conversion.

Adoption of the new husbandry may have been justified even when wheat was not a lead crop, if improved qualities of barley, especially, yielded a worthwhile return. Barley might lead in places such as Gloucestershire, where a neighbouring county (in that case Hereford-shire) produced a wheat surplus that fully satisfied the regional demand.[87] And generally, where conversion was wheat-led, soil improvement would add to the quality and quantity of barley and oats, as also, if access to water transport was the trigger, cheap bulk carriage would enhance the marketability of those grains too.

If, so far as wheat was concerned, before c1750 the 'agricultural revolution' was quality-led, thereafter quantity had equal priority, as the national demand for Wheaten bread increased. Thomas Pownall attributed that increase to the rising class of artisans, tradesmen, and clerks, who now depended on the white loaf and would accept nothing less. That the balance of wheat supply and demand altered, between c1750 and c1775, is clearly indicated by the rising trend of prices, the fall in exports, recurring disorders, the bread acts of 1757 and 1773, and the new corn law of 1772. A run of bad harvests contributed to domestic scarcity, but it was considered that, even in an average year, Britain would in future depend to some extent upon imports.[88]

And yet (though with periodically severe strain) British agriculture proved able to supply a sufficiency of wheat. Its potential to do so was not exhausted even after Repeal. In 1854–6, when the world market was deranged, partly by the effects of the Crimean War, the demand for wheat breadstuffs was met chiefly from an enlarged domestic output: on the basis of calculations made by Caird, in those years Britain may have been 90 per cent sufficient, and might have remained so after the war, had not 'unnecessary' importation resumed.[89] It did not seem unreasonable to the *Liverpool Courier*, in 1855, to suppose that Britain's wheat acreage could be increased by a further 15 per cent (if farmers were encouraged by a state subsidy), to assure complete sufficiency.[90] Though, in the 1860s, Britain imported from a quarter to a third of her needs, that dependency was less an indicator of necessity than of public policy, justified by comparative advantage.

Agricultural innovation continued through the later 18th and 19th centuries: for example, in the development of new strains of wheat designed to suit various growing conditions. Some thirteen strains of wheat were known *c*1695. No less than eleven new strains were tried in Norfolk in 1841, in a controlled experiment recorded by R N Bacon: the most successful of them yielded 48 per cent more by weight than the least.[91]

Also, the wheat output of a district might increase sizeably if, as husbandry techniques developed further, other grains were sacrificed, or reduced in importance, within rotations. Brown and Beecham note that in Nottinghamshire, by the 1840s, 'it was possible to take three crops of wheat in a six-year course, alternating corn with fallow, clover, and beans', and dispensing with barley; such displacement often was associated with the intensive improvement of lighter soils.[92] And outputs could increase wherever new reaping techniques, for instance, and better pest and blight control, were introduced.[93] But in addition, and perhaps chiefly, an increasing supply of commercial breadstuffs was assured by the substantial expansion of the water zone, and related improvements to the existing navigations and in carrying capacities. Canals, especially, gave economical access to good or satisfactory wheat lands that previously had been excluded from commercial exploitation. Thus, the fivefold increase in the volume of wheat traded at Norwich corn market, between 1805 and 1843, and the amounts exported from King's Lynn, partly reflect the digging of new navigations in Norfolk from 1818.[94] Less defined developments, such as the gradual improvement of the Thames navigation (which opened access to larger barges and speeded journey times) also greatly increased potential annual carrying capacity. Where hitherto land-locked districts were opened to water transport, the effects might roughly be described as either an 'infilling', as remaining pockets were converted to wheat-led regimes (in the south-eastern counties especially), or as broad areal expansion, where the water zone advanced like a tide. This can be seen from Maps 2 and 3.

The bread trades imposed a detectable pattern upon the market, and therefore on the regional nature of wheat growing. In principle, those districts producing first-rate and second-rate wheats 'exported' their surplus; while those which, with a less favourable dispensation of terrain, soil, and climate, produced third-rates, retained most of their output, and 'imported' better qualities for mixing (as outlined in the previous section), thus producing marketable breadstuffs for local consumption. In the upper Thames valley there seems to have been a mixed trade, with locally-grown wheat being sent down-river, and perhaps firsts coming up for mixing and milling; however, it is hard to disaggregate the Thames trade by type, since much of the wheat sent up-river, certainly as far as Reading, was milled there and then returned to London as flour.[95]

There is no hard-and-fast rule by which first-rate, second-rate, and third-rate growing districts can be demarcated, since, the natural dispensation apart, good husbandry could transform ordinarily unfav-ourable land, just as bad methods could exhaust the best. However, as a rough generalization, represented by market classifications, firsts pre-dominated in the intranationally marketed output of the south-eastern counties (Hampshire including the Isle of Wight, Sussex, Kent, Essex, rural Surrey and Middlesex, Hertfordshire and parts of Suffolk), and seconds in the output of the east Midlands, and of the eastern seaboard from parts of Suffolk north to Fife. The respective contributions of those two regions to the intranational trade can be glimpsed in Table 6.5 which is taken from accounts of the quantities brought coastways to London in 1810–13.

However, since great amounts of wheat also were brought into London by inland navigations, as some (and still much in 1750[96]) came overland, and because ready-made flour is excluded, the coastways evidence does not necessarily indicate the balance overall.

To confirm the principle that most thirds were held in the regions where grown, Rushton's accounts show that, at least in 1810–13, virtually no wheat was brought coastwise to London from the west, though some amounts (as well as seconds) may have come down the Thames and its tributary navigations.

The relative qualities of the wheat commercially grown in the three regions is roughly substantiated by price relationships (using Irish wheat as a surrogate for British thirds). The comparative prices obtaining at London in the summer of 1814 (see Table 6.6) typify the relationship.

Map 2   Transport zones *c*1770.

Based on maps in Aldcroft and Freeman, eds, pp 102, 179; Langton
and Morris, eds, p 81.

'Land Zone' in black. 'Water Zone' in white.

Map 3   Transport zones *c*1830.

Based on maps in Aldcroft and Freeman, eds, pp 110–111, 195;
Langton and Morris, eds, p 85.

'Land Zone' in black. 'Water Zone' in white.

Table 6.5 Total amount of wheat brought coastways to London, 1810–13

Region	Winchester Quarters	% of total
South-East		
South coast	3,909	–
Kent	117,291	9
Essex	425,903	33
Sub-total	547,103	42
Eastern		
Norfolk/Suffolk	343,993	26
Lincolnshire	114,172	9
Yorkshire	86,932	7
North-east	81,597	6
Scotland	116,941	9
Sub-total	743,635	57
TOTAL	1,290,738	99
From elsewhere/unplaced	17,446	1

Calculated from: William Rushton's Accounts of the London trade, cit PP 1814–15 V (26) 1035, HoC 23.11.1814, p 151 et seq.

Table 6.6 Prices at Mark Lane, 14.6.1814: shillings per Winchester quarter

	General range	Very best
South-east		
Essex/Kent	54–66	80
Eastern		
Cambridge/Lincoln	46–58	66
Yorks/Norfolk/Suffolk	52–60	68
Scotch	46–58	60
Western		
Irish	46–52	56

Source: PP 1814–15 V (26) 1035, HoL/HoC 23.11.1814, p 7 – Ruding.

Taking the middle price of the general range, it will be seen that the value, and implicit quality, ratios of the output of the three regions was 100 for the south-east to 88 for the east to 82 for Ireland (here representing the west), which roughly approximate to the ratios given more than a century earlier by Houghton. As to the very best qualities, those from the east and west were most likely to be used for bread, but those from the south-east probably were reserved for high-quality pastries or rolls.[97]

Tracking intranational trade flows from price data, in the early part of the century in review, is difficult, since variations may reflect the vestiges of differential regional pricing, especially the distinct characters of land zone and water zone markets. How much local market autonomy remained in the middle-to-late 18th century has been debated, but at least, there were significant exceptions to increasing homogeneity.[98] Taking county returns for the first week of April (usually the least turbulent time of the market year), from 1771 to 1777 inclusively, on average there was a 40 per cent span (roughly 2s per bushel) between the highest and lowest county means. The Midland counties (Warwickshire, Derbyshire, Northamptonshire), though also Gloucestershire and Westmorland, were top of the price table in different years, while seaboard counties (Sussex, Devon, Cornwall, Yorkshire, and Northumberland) were bottom.[99]

But by 1815, given the great expansion of the water zone, local price data more surely reflect the comparative significance of intranational trade, and its relationship to local agriculture.

I have analysed aggregated returns from the monitored markets in the twelve maritime districts of England and Wales. Table 6.7 shows that the mean price in the eastern region was, as would be expected (given a lower average quality and worth of locally-grown wheat) somewhat less than the mean for the south-east; but the mean for the western region, where local qualities and prices were generally poorest, was considerably higher (11.5 per cent more than in the south-east, and 15 per cent more than in the eastern region), which indicates the 'importation' of first-rate and second-rate wheats into the west, in such quantity as to thrust average prices so high.

The importation of better quality wheat (and flour) transformed the marketability of local thirds, which formerly may not have been saleable, but sufficed for payment in kind to farm labourers: mixing raised them to the rank of commercial breadstuffs. However, as the market returns indicate, most thirds were sold privately, direct to millers. At a time when contemporaries thought that, nationally, perhaps a half or three-quarters of commercial wheat was traded off-

Table 6.7   Average price per Winchester bushel, 5.11.1814 to 18.2.1815.

	s	d
South-east*		
London	64	4
2nd District (Suffolk, Essex)	57	9
12th District (Dorset, Hants)	62	11
MEAN	61	8
Eastern*		
3rd District (Norfolk)	56	9
4th District (Lincs, East Yorks)	59	6
5th District (N'land, Durham)	62	10
MEAN	59	8
Western		
6th District (North-west)	60	0
7th District (Lancs, Cheshire)	69	3
8th District (North Wales)	72	1
9th District (South Wales)	69	2
10th District (Severn, Wye, S'set)	75	4
11th District (Devon, Cornwall)	67	0
MEAN	68	9

* Regional demarcations differ somewhat from those in following tables.

Source: PP X (133) 511, HoC 6.3.1815.

market in various ways, the proportion thus sold at Bristol may have been 95 per cent.[100]

The third-rate of quality, predominant in the west, shaded into an 'inferior' classification, signifying wheat that was ordinarily unusable as a breadstuff, but might be sold for biscuit flour, or for example, as animal feed, or for starch and paste manufacture. Sales of 'inferior' wheat were not recorded, either for the purpose of the corn laws or of the assize of bread. It is probable that, given generally less favourable growing conditions, the west, and especially western Scotland, produced a higher proportion of inferior wheat than the other two regions.[101]

Thus Caird's map[102] can deceive. Though generally the best wheat was grown east of his line, much was produced to the west. This is apparent from Table 6.8.

The estimates suggest that, in the south-east, wheat acreage was near to its practicable limit in 1801, whereas in the eastern region especially, much potential remained. However, the west (the largest area) produced more wheat than either of the other two regions, and its share of output appears remarkably constant. But, in between the years for which estimates are given, there may have been significant fluctuations in regional shares, especially c1815–20, and after Repeal. The considerable expansion in tillage between c1801 and c1815, encouraged by the prospect of high wheat rents,[103] coincided with governmental interventions (for instance, the Brown George Act of 1801), and more effective and constant local prohibitions of the Wheaten grade of bread; therefore, millers and bakers could use a greater proportion of thirds in their mixes. After the war, such demand contracted (though it could revive where undersellers competed at the lowest prices, in London especially).[104]

The post-war distress experienced by many wheat-growers, especially those farming marginal land, persisted at least till 1836, as testimony to the select committees on agriculture shows. The longevity of the crisis is in part a measure of their tenacity; adverse market forces could not, it seems, undermine their commitment to wheat.

Such persistence may in part be explained by the scale and nature of the investment needed to make land suitable for a wheat-led regime. Conversion to the new husbandry required much horse-power, to haul the huge quantities of marl and lime, and plough, and cart away the crop; it called for specialized tools and acquisition of the skills to use them; wherever possible, the regime required the integration of livestock (as consumers of roots and grasses, and the bran and pollards of wheat, and of other cereals, as producers of manure, and as providers of foods and raw materials either for own-use or sale). Conversion could involve substantial changes in organization and infrastructure: alterations in manning, the building of cottages for workers living out, new or improved barns for storage and threshing (and, from the 1780s, a threshing machine), perhaps a mill, improved farm roads, and the expenses of enclosure, hedging and ditching.[105] It might call for new lines of distribution and of credit. All of which represented a considerable commitment of effort and capital by agriculturalists[106] that surely few would readily sacrifice.

But also, conversion to new means and methods implied a spreading of risk. Given the variety of crops raised, and integration of livestock, it followed that wheat did not predominate in a wheat-led regime, though it would normally be the largest single source of income.

Sinclair's estimates of the output value of crops are listed in Table 6.9.

Table 6.8 England and Wales: estimated regional shares of wheat output

Date and region (a)	% of wheat acreage (b)	% of net bushel volume (c)	% weighted breadstuff output (d)
1801			
South-east	28	28	31
East	26	27	27
West	46	45	42
late 1830s			
South-east	23	25	28
East	29	29	30
West	48	46	42
1866			
South-east	23	23	26
East	34	34	34
West	43	43	40

Notes and sources:
(a) Regions comprise:
   South-east: Bedfordshire, Berkshire, Dorset, Essex, Hants, Herts, Kent, Middlesex, Surrey, and Sussex.
   Eastern: Cambridgeshire, Durham, Huntingdonshire, Lincolnshire, Norfolk, Northumberland, Suffolk, East and North Ridings of Yorkshire.
   Western: all other England, and all Wales.
   Regional shares of national area: South-east: 17 per cent; Eastern 23 per cent; Western 60 per cent.
(b) Acreage shares calculated from:
   1801: M. Turner: 'Arable in England & Wales: estimates from the 1801 Crop Return', tables 1 and 2. The ratios of recorded wheat to recorded arable acreages have been applied to Dr Turner's estimates of total arable acres, to approximate wheat acres per county. The ratio for Derbyshire has been applied also to Nottinghamshire, and the ratio for Caernarvonshire also to Anglesey.
   Late 1830s: Kain & Prince: The Tithe Surveys of England & Wales, table 7.2. The proportion of wheat acres to total county acres per region has been applied to counties for which no data exists.
   1866: PP LX (3727) 1, HMSO 1866, pp 8–10.
(c) Net bushel volume estimated as follows:
   1801: Yield ratios of 100:101:97 for the south-east, east, and west respectively, being the mean of yields in 1800 and 1801 in the English counties (excepting Lancashire) given by M Turner: 'Agricultural Productivity in England in the Eighteenth Century: Evidence from Crop Yields' pp 507–8.
   Late 1830s: Yield ratios of 100:90:87 for the south-east, east, and west respectively, being the mean of yields given by Kain & Prince, table 7.2.
   1866: Yield ratios of 100:99:97 for the south-east, east, and west respectively, being the mean of yields given for English counties in 1861 by the *Mark Lane Express*, cit Agrarian History of England & Wales VI pp 1048–9.
(d) Assuming weight/quality ratios per bushel of 100:92:83 for the south-east, east, and west respectively ; no allowance has been made for inferior wheat weight/quality.

Although values could fluctuate greatly, the relative proportions, certainly between the cereals, remained roughly the same: it was the rule of thumb that wheat, on average, commanded twice the price of barley and three times that of oats.[107] And, since the opportunity to commercially raise garden and orchard produce was largely confined to farms closest to urban centres, for most agriculturalists, wheat offered the best return. But the new husbandry lessened exposure to the swings of the wheat market.

If wheat was the lead crop of a three-part system, then dependency on it might be almost total: as one farmer observed, wheat had 'two Years Rent dependent on it; that is, the fallow year and that in which it grows', while the lenten corn raised in the third year would 'seldom bear a Reckoning, otherwise than a Subsistence for our Horses and other Cattle'.[108]

Such a dependency, of 67 per cent or more, might be compared to Arthur Young's calculation (citing a double rotation of 8 years, including two wheat crops) that wheat contributed only 37 per cent of income (though as it directly accounted for only 28 per cent of costs, it was still the most profitable product).[109] Also, Young's calculations were based on high wheat (and other grain) prices: the income from other products, being generally less variable, was a safeguard against falling returns from cereals. As William Jacob put it:

> the turnips are converted into mutton and wool, much will depend on the price of mutton and wool for the first year. The second [year] comes the barley, that depends upon what the brewers and distillers give for the barley. The third year comes the clover, if they fat bullocks or fat sheep on them, they must look to the price of beef, butter or cheese for the profit. Then the fourth year comes the wheat, we know that the farmer in former times has looked for his remuneration to the wheat; but suppose he gets but half the price of the wheat, supposing he gets an additional price on barley and oats, or a high price for meat, wool, butter, cheese and bacon, the farmers would still go on with that system, seeing that the wheat occupies but one year in four.[110]

The risk comparison may mislead, of course, if the three-part farmer had various, though perhaps not integrated, interests. And the merits of conversion, even at reduced risk, may have appeared differently to different landowners. Probably, those whose land was rented out on long tenures had less reason to invest in conversion, if the appropriate and necessary return would take a generation or more to come through; whereas, if common land was enclosed, and then brought up to prescription, it could be let without delay at appropriate market rents.

Only after Repeal, it seems, did the tenacity of many growers weaken. In 1853 it was estimated that only three-quarters of the breadth

Table 6.9   Value per acre by crop, *c*1820

£15	garden and orchard produce
£11	wheat
£8	barley, potatoes, or flax
£7	oats
£6	rye, beans, or peas
£4	turnips
£2	grass, hay, or pasture
£0	fallow

Source: Sinclair p 17.

of former years had been sown, though many 'lost' acres clearly were 'recovered' during the Crimean War (an estimated 3.8m wheat acres in 1854 corresponds exactly to McCulloch's 'guesses' for 1839 and 1846). Contraction resumed thereafter: in 1867 Caird estimated that the wheat acreage was 8 per cent less than that of 1850, and that of Scotland may have halved between 1856 and 1870.[111] However, the impact of Repeal upon British wheat-growers may have been qualitative, as much as quantitative.

Foreign wheats can be classified according to their gluten content, as shown in Table 6.10.

Table 6.10   Gluten content of foreign wheats

Polish (Danzig)	13.5%
North American: Virginian	11.5%
New Orleans	13.5%
Russian: Odessa soft	12.0%
Odessa flinty	14.55%

Sources: Edward Smith: Foods pp 172, 179; idem: Practical Dietary pp 31–2; David p 45; Hassall p 134 (citing an analysis by Dumas); Acton Chapter VI.

Sicilian grain also was hardish; while in normal to good years, French wheat was judged supreme, since the grain naturally combined hardish properties with softish taste.[112]

Flours of the hard or hardish wheats produced more bread: thus Mrs Rundell recorded that one stone (14 lbs) of American (New Orleans) flour could produce 21.5 lbs of bread compared to the 18.5 lbs she expected from British flour. But generally, imported hard wheats or flours were mixed with British breadstuffs to achieve an ideal combination of strength and taste: 'they help each other in the working together'.[113]

However, the wheats cited were not wholly representative of imports. In former years of scarcity, considerable amounts of softer and 'thin' wheats had been imported, chiefly it seems to sustain the cities and industrial districts of the west and north-west. For instance, in the summer of 1814, the prices at Mark Lane for American, Danzig, and (similar) Konigsberg wheats ranged from 54s to 76s per Winchester quarter, comparable to the best British varieties (56s–80s), but other imports were priced on average 12.5 per cent below the general range of British wheats (40s–60s per quarter, compared to 46s–66s).[114] During the period 1792–1814 inclusively, of a total importation of 11,923,000 Winchester quarters of grain or its approximate equivalent in flour, about 40 per cent was soft and inferior (judged by its source), as against roughly 60 per cent hard. And if imports of generally inferior wheat and flour from Ireland are included, the balance becomes 47 per cent soft and generally poor, to 53 per cent hard.[115]

After Repeal, softer and poorer wheat from northern Russia, Scandinavia, Germany, and the Low Countries was imported regularly, and not only, as before, in response to domestic dearth. Thus imports might be classified into two qualitative sorts: hards, which were essentially complementary, because they had no native equivalent and 'strengthened' domestic grain when mixed with it, and softs which competed directly with home-grown seconds and thirds. Unfortunately, demarcation of the two sorts becomes difficult, since official statistics give only country of origin. Before Repeal, it is not unreasonable to suppose that the bulk of imports from Russia were soft wheats from the north, and the bulk of imports from the United States were hard wheats from the south. However, after Repeal the proportion of hards from Odessa certainly, and of softs from America's eastern seaboard possibly, increased substantially, and so may have greatly affected the overall balance (to take 1864–66 inclusively, for example, 47 per cent of imported wheat grain came from Russia and the United States).[116]

More detailed research on the quality of imports may help to better understand the impact of Repeal upon the wheat-led regimes of the various regions.[117]

However, all regions may have suffered similarly from one aspect of Repeal: the likelihood of unnecessarily large importations. Intelligence as to the likely or actual availability of foreign wheat was quickly received in the 18th century, when most supplies came from north-western Europe or the Baltic. With favourable winds and seas, crop and market information could be transmitted to London within days (and cargoes could follow rapidly). But as the range of potential supply extended to North America, the Mediterranean, and the Black Sea hinterland, so the time needed to send intelligence (as well as the grain itself) lengthened. By the fastest means and routes, it took three weeks to transmit news from Odessa and up to six weeks from various parts of America. So that if, at the beginning of the harvest year, a London merchant wished to guard against an anticipated domestic deficiency, by importing quantities of wheat from the Great Lakes before the waterways froze, he made his decision blind as to the price his agent must pay; or else he contracted early for fixed quantities without knowledge of the likely domestic yield. Thus it was quite possible to flood the British market, to the detriment of home producers. This gave an added uncertainty to the market until, in the 1860s, the telegraph and cable dissolved distance.[118]

Notes

1. CLRO: PD 32.8 – Report of Common Council Committee on the High Price of Flour, 27.10.1796, p 7 – Wyatt, p 12 – Woolhead, p 17 – Lovell.
2. M Freeman in Aldcroft & Freeman (eds) p 12; Armstrong & Bagwell in Aldcroft & Freeman (eds) p 160; Szostak p 50; M D Freeman p 54.
3. Thacker volume I, p 118.
4. Chartres in Ag H of E & W V–II, p 467.
5. M Freeman in Aldcroft & Freeman (eds) p 16.
6. Szostak p 59.
7. Calculated from Wrigley: PCW p 160; see Turnbull p 539.
8. Defoe: Tour Vol I pp 49–52, 65–74.
9. *The Times* 15.4.1856: the first British cargo sent to St Petersburg at the end of the Crimean War went from Gloucester.
10. M Freeman in Aldcroft & Freeman (eds) p 4.
11. Norman Davies volume I, Chapter 6.
12. Wordie in Ag H of E & W V–I pp 319–20.
13. Defoe: Tour pp 150, 155, 158.
14. Young cit Perren in Ag H of E & W VI p 219.
15. Thacker vol I, p 146.
16. Clapham I p 78; Thwaites: thesis p 257 et seq; see maps in Aldcroft & Freeman (eds) pp 102, 110, 179, 195; see M Freeman: 'Transport' in Langton & Morris eds p 80 et seq.
17. Willan: River Navigation pp vi, 32, 68.
18. Armstrong & Bagwell in Aldcroft & Freeman (eds) pp 143–5.
19. Armstrong & Bagwell in Aldcroft & Freeman (eds) p 155.
20. Feinstein 1978 p 42. Since Professor Feinstein's calculations and the orders of magnitude above both derive from Ginarlis' estimates, they are not wholly independent.
21. Bagwell p 21.
22. Freeman in Aldcroft & Freeman (eds) p 4.
23. Thacker volume I, p 118.

24. Thacker volume I, pp 148, 177.
25. Thacker volume I pp 109, 123, 133, 137, 153, 164.
26. Thacker vol I pp 12, 123, 146.
27. Albert in Aldcroft & Freeman (eds) p 56.
28. Albert in Aldcroft & Freeman (eds) p 58.
29. See Bagwell pp 81–2.
30. Gourvish: Railways pp 26–7, 31.
31. Bagwell p 12; see also Holderness in Ag H of E & W VI p 88.
32. Thacker vol I, p 187.
33. Hawke cit Perren p 422.
34. M D Freeman p 77; Bagwell p 98; Gourvish: Railways p 30.
35. Gourvish: Railways p 30.
36. M D Freeman p 77.
37. HoC Sessional Papers volume 131 Cd 5080, p 7 – Pratt, p 13 – Appendix resolution 2; Orbell: thesis pp 2, 38–9; M D Freeman p 10.
38. Adam Smith p 234; Mathias cit Turnbull p 537.
39. J S Mill pp 64–6; Ashton: I R p 68; Dodd p 175.
40. Barnes pp 31, 34.
41. Barnes p 32; Albert in Aldcroft & Freeman (eds) pp 58–60; Wells part II.
42. 5 & 6 Ed VI c.14; 5 Eliz I c.12.
43. Barnes pp 39, 41, Chapter XIII.
44. P H Williams p 187.
45. Adam Smith pp 170, 235–8, 241.
46. Eden p 204; Mountmorres: Impartial Reflections; and Girdler: Observations.
47. G: A.3.5 no 32 – Trial of John Rusby.
48. Galpin p 24; 31 Geo III c.30; PP I/2 item 16, HoC 24.6.1801, p 8.
49. CLRO: Corp PD 32.8, p 3.
50. Girdler: Observations, introduction; [Turton] p 83.
51. Anon: A Proposal for Supplying London with Bread, at a Uniform Price.
52. Burke p 27.
53. HoC Sessional Papers vol 131 Cd 5080, p 21 – Pratt.
54. CLRO: Corp PD 32.8, p 24 – Pratt; HoC Sessional Papers vol 131 Cd 5080, p 9 – Pratt.
55. Turnbull p 539; Thwaites: thesis p 195.
56. Calculated from Wrigley: P C W p 160.
57. Adam Smith pp 180–1. The broad question as to whether infrastructure precedes or results from population expansion is discussed in Rotberg & Rabb (eds): H & H, by Ester Boserup p 185 et seq, Julian L Simon p 227, and R C Floud p 245.
58. Turner 1981 p 294.
59. Orbell: thesis pp 4–5, 60; M D Freeman pp 286–8; G: Fo Pam 895 28.4.1800, p 6.
60. PP III (154) 181, HoC 31.5.1805, p 16 – Macdowall.
61. See above, p 52.
62. David p 9.
63. PP III (154) 181, HoC 31.5.1805, p 15 – Giles.
64. 12 Henry VII cit PP V (186) 1341, HoC 6.6.1815.
65. PP II (255) 101, HoC 8.7.1820, pp 16–17 – Durrant, p 18 – Harvey; IX (668) 1, HoC 18.6.1821, p 91 – Capper, p 186 – Edwards; VII (517) 1, HoC 25.7.1834, p 324 – Page.

66. Walsh p 275.
67. PP II (255) 101, HoC 8.7.1820, p 17; HoC Sessional Papers vol 131 Cd 4983, 10.2.1800, especially testimonies of Kingsford, Pilcher, and Dunkin; Charles Smith pp 23–4; Pownall p 32.
68. [Dickenson] p 1.
69. *Royal Leamington Spa Courier*, 13.10.1828.
70. Clapham Vol I pp 303–4; A.B. Robertson: Foundation.
71. Anon: The Incorporation of Bakers of Glasgow, p 19; Observations of Committee of Millers and Mealmen, 28.4.1800, p 6 (G: Fo Pam 895); Adam Smith pp 34, 87.
72. Benney p 16; Observations of Committee of Millers and Mealmen, 28.4.1800, p 6 (G: Fo pam 895); PP II (255) 101, HoC 8.7.1820, p 33 – Floud; PP V (612) 1, 2.8.1833, Qs 3465, 3466.
73. E L Jones in Floud & McCloskey I, p 66; Glennie: Hertfordshire p 56; Bowden in Ag H of E & W V–II p 9; J V Beckett pp 1–10, 16.
74. Taking Gras' estimate of London's *per capita* consumption of all corn (as food and drink) to be 2.5 quarters annually, and applying that to Professor Wrigley's estimates of the metropolitan population: Gras p 77; Wrigley: P C W p 162.
75. Gras pp 110–13; Ag H of E & W V–II, pp 851, 856; V–I pp 334–5 – Wordie; Ormrod p 22 et seq; Outhwaite: Dearth & Government Intervention p 392; J V Beckett p 30; Glennie: Hertfordshire p 56.
76. J V Beckett pp 30–1.
77. E L Jones in E L Jones (ed), pp 161–7; John in Pressnell (ed) pp 130–2; Glennie: Hertfordshire p 56; Clay I p 130.
78. Wordie in Ag H of E & W V–I pp 328, 336; E L Jones in E L Jones (ed), p 166.
79. Gras p 38.
80. Wrigley: P C W p 160.
81. N Davies I pp 275–6; John in Pressnell (ed), p 131; idem in E L Jones (ed), p 179; PP 1814–15 V (26) 1035, HoL/HoC 23.11.1814, p 8 – Ruding, p 33 – Mills, p 102 – Parker.
82. Edward Smith: Foods pp 172, 179; idem: Practical Dietary pp 31–2.
83. Ag H of E & W IV, pp 492, 505 – Everitt; V–I, pp 286–7 – Short; pp 324, 328, 334, 336, 345 – Wordie; V–II pp 19–20 – Bowden, p 466 – Chartres; Willan: River Navigation maps pp vi, 32, 68; idem: The Inland Trade pp 14–25; Gras pp 62–3.
84. Edlin pp 4–7; Bacon p 88; see also Sinclair pp 277, 280; Ashley p 143; Ag H of E & W V–I, p 173 – Thirsk, pp 216–7 – Holderness.
85. PP II (255) 101, HoC 8.7.1820, p 17 – Durrant.
86. In 1795 Report reprinted as PP VII (517) 1, App I p 371, HoC 25.7.1834.
87. Thirsk in Ag H of E & W V–I, p 173.
88. Holderness in Ag H of E & W VI, pp 92 et seq; Barnes p 42 et seq; HoC Sessional Papers vol 25 Cd 3144, 21.12.1772; Pownall p 6 et seq.
89. Letters from Caird in *The Times*, 10.11.1854 and 26.11.1856.
90. *Liverpool Courier* 3.1.1855.
91. Overton in Campbell & Overton (eds) p 290; Bacon p 248.
92. Ag H of E & W VI, pp 282–3 – Brown & Beecham, pp 37, 39, 41, 72 – Prince, pp 218–9 – Holderness; E L Jones: Development pp 14–15; J V Beckett p 31.

93. Brown & Beecham in Ag H of E & W VI pp 291–2.
94. Bacon pp 4–9, 87.
95. Thwaites: thesis pp 257, 272–3; idem: Dearth and Marketing p 12.
96. Chartres (ed): intro to Agricultural Markets and Trade, p 9.
97. PP 1814–15 V (26) 1035, HoL/HoC 23.11.1814, p 7 – Ruding.
98. Granger & Elliott p 262; Chartres in Ag H of E & W V–II p 459; Perren in Ag H of E & W pp 217, 231.
99. Extracted from the *London Gazette*, reports for first week of April 1771–7 inc.
100. PP II (255) 101, HoC 8.7.1820, pp 16–17 – Durrant, pp 17–18 – Harvey, pp 31, 37 – Ludlow, p 48 – Wray, p 61 – Wynn. For methods of private sale see M D Freeman pp 300–1; Everitt in Ag H of E & W IV pp 466, 506 et seq, 531 et seq; Chartres(ed): intro to Agricultural Markets and Trade p 5; Perren in Ag H of E & W VI pp 238–43.
101. Sinclair p 74; PP III (154) 181, HoC 31.5.1805, p 16 – Macdowall; II (255) 101, HoC 8.7.1820, p 16 – Durrant; IX (668) 1, HoC 18.6.1821, p 81 – Capper.
102. eg in Ag H of E & W VI p 75.
103. J V Beckett in Ag H of E & W VI pp 620–2.
104. PP III (184) 479, HoC 11.5.1813 p 3; 1814–15 V (26) 1035, HoL/HoC 23.11.1814, p 19 – Wakefield; II (255) 101, HoC 8.7.1820, p 16 – Durrant.
105. Slicher van Bath p 100; Wrigley C C C p 38; Campbell & Overton (eds) pp 35, 115, 172–3, 183, 323; Sinclair p 274; Chambers & Mingay, citing Ernle, p 72; J V Beckett pp 20–1; Clapham I p 103; John in Pressnell (ed), p 132.
106. Ashley p 137; Barnes pp 103–7; Brown & Beecham in Ag H VI pp 287–8; Feinstein in Cambridge Economic History of Europe VII–I, pp 48–50; Thomas p 732.
107. PP 1814–15 V (26) 1035, HoL/HoC 23.11.1814, p 21 – Wakefield, p 26 – Birkbeck, p 59 – Custance.
108. William Ellis cit John in Minchinton (ed): Essays, p 227; idem in Pressnell (ed) p 129.
109. Calculated from PP 1814–15 V (26) 1035, HoL/HoC 23.11.1814, pp 63–4. For calculation of typical grain profits see Bowden in Ag H of E & W V–II pp 85–93.
110. PP VIII Part I (79) 1, HoC 4.3.1836. Qu 183.
111. *Norfolk Chronicle* 6.8.1853; *The Economist* 2.7.1853; Holderness in Ag H of E & W VI p 128; Caird: ODF p 40.
112. PP VII (517) 1, HoC 25.7.1834, Q 4017 – Page.
113. Kingsford cit Orbell: thesis pp 9, 11; HoC Sessional Papers vol 131 Cd 4983, 10.2.1800, p 34; Cd 5080, 1.7.1800, p 23 – Pratt; Rundell 1807 p 363.
114. PP 1814–15 V (26) 1035, HoL/HoC 23.11.1814, p 7 – Ruding, p 33 – Mills.
115. Calculated from PP X (169) 543, HoC 20.3.1815.
116. Herlihy p 204 et seq; Gatrell pp 103, 130; LXV (46) 1, HoC 14.2.1867, p 6.
117. see E L Jones p 17.
118. Market reports in the *New York Daily Times*, 11.10.1855, 8.11.1855, 6.12.1855.

CHAPTER 7

Measuring Wheat Consumption

British governments during the century in review did not attempt to measure what they did not administer, subsidize, or tax; and since it was not official business, at the national level, to know what amount of bread, at what price, the British consumed, comprehensive data were not collected, nor official statistics published. Such respect for commercial privacy was criticized as negligent.[1] Even when deciding matters of literally vital national interest (such as the level of wheat imports needed to offset wartime dearths) the government had to rely, chiefly, on the roughest guesswork.

To some extent, the lack of data on bread consumption was remedied by the exertions of those private individuals who conducted food surveys for their own purposes: the Reverend David Davies, for instance, to support his argument for a minimum 'bread wage', and Sir Frederick Morton Eden, when examining the potential for mass insurance against unemployment and sickness. Official surveys began only at the end of the century in review, with the comparatively extensive projects undertaken by Dr Edward Smith in the 1860s, as part of broad enquiries into public health. However, informed observers from Sir Charles Smith to Caird made general estimates of bread consumption. And authority had to make exact judgements of ordinary or minimal need when establishing dietaries for those in its employment, care, or custody.[2]

Government did take an official interest in prices: from 1771, of the average prices of the grains sold in monitored markets, so as to operate successive corn laws; and at local level, up to 1836, wherever an Assize of Bread was set, of the average prices of grain or flour, by which to determine (and then record) the maximum lawful prices of loaves.[3] Also, the volume and (at least notional) value of imports and exports were recorded.[4]

In this and the following chapter I have brought together sources frequently used by historians of the period, along with some less familiar material, to establish order-of-magnitude estimates of the volume and value of wheat bread.

7.1 MEASURING THE TREND TO WHEAT

G E Fussell observed that there are two 'obvious' approaches to the task of measuring the volume of wheat demand: either to work from *per capita* consumption estimates, multiplied by population, but allowing for the use of other cereals; or to work from estimated net national wheat output, adjusted for imports and exports.[5] Obvious as both approaches may be, each raises problems, of material, interpretation, and integration. And though, ideally, the methods ought be insulated from the other to allow for cross-checking of results, in practice they are mutually dependent.

Supply-side estimates

Although much work has been done on the measurement of domestic wheat output, reliable data, of acreages and yields, exist only for certain years (and even then are rarely comprehensive) and may not be representative of an immediate ('circa') period; also, apparent long-run trends can conceal large intervening variations.

William Jacob, Comptroller of Corn Returns, estimated that the volatility of wheat harvests, over a 12-year period, was as shown in Table 7.1.

Table 7.1 Britain: estimated wheat output
('000 quarters), 1816–27

	Gross output	Net of seed*
1816	9,000	7,700
1817	11,700	10,400
1818	12,000	10,700
1819	12,500	11,200
1820	16,000	14,700
1821	12,600	11,300
1822	13,500	12,200
1823	11,000	9,700
1824	11,500	10,200
1825	12,700	11,400
1826	13,000	11,700
1827	12,500	11,200
MEAN	12,333	11,033

* Jacob allowed a constant 1.3m quarters for seed.

Source and calculations from William Jacob: Tracts relating to the Corn Trade and Corn Laws, 1828, p 88 et seq.

Jacob's estimates indicate that gross output could be up to 30 per cent above (as in 1820) and 27 per cent below (as in the 'catastrophic' year of 1816) a mean expectation, and net output 33 per cent above or 30 per cent below average: the highest net output was almost double the amount of the lowest.

Fluctuations in domestic output might be offset (and to some degree indicated by) the amount of imports, net of exports, released into home consumption. However, the workings of the world market were not perfect, and estimates of need were crude (Pitt the Younger lamented the paucity of reliable statistics[6]), so that imports might often over-represent the deficiency of any year.

And before Repeal, storage, rather than importation, usually was the chief additional variable. Wheat could be stored for many years, in suitable conditions, without deterioration and with little loss to vermin (in 1834 it was estimated that the annual loss of granary-stored wheat was between 1.1 per cent and 2.7 per cent, with 2 per cent as the rough average[7]). Reports attached to the Crop Returns of 1801 show that it was usual to have, at the end of each harvest year, about 25 per cent of annual consumption in store (enough to cover the months of October, November, and December, until the first tranche of the new crop could be threshed and marketed). Of course, in ordinary circumstances, that three-month reserve would be rolled over from year to year, but after poor harvests it would be drawn on first (and perhaps make importation unnecessary), while in glut it probably accumulated. In addition to such stocks, which typically might be held threshed or unthreshed on the farms, there were the reserves held by millers and merchants, and whatever imports were locked in bond.

William Jacob calculated that, over the same period of 1816–27 inclusively, the stock in hand at the start of each harvest year was as shown in Table 7.2.

Vamplew notes that the estimated period in bond of foreign wheat, between 1829 and 1848, ranged from two up to seventy-six months.[8] The problems posed by output swings and storage effects ought to be answered by sales data. In a fresh approach to supply-side calculations, Dr Fairlie used the reported sales figures of the monitored markets as a base, and added net imports, for each year.[9] However, such recorded transactions represent only a fraction, and an unknown and probably fluctuating fraction, of the total trade in wheat, to compensate for which Dr Fairlie used a multiplier of 4 for the period 1829–41, a multiplier of 14/5 for 1843–64, and a multiplier of 4 for the years 1865–76.[10] Because little is known about the operations of the market, and the multipliers are so large, the results need the support of, rather than act as an independent check upon, agricultural estimates.

Table 7.2 Britain: wheat held as stock on hand at the start of each harvest year ('000 quarters)

	Net domestic output	Stock on hand	Combined total	Stock as % of combined total
1816	7,700	6,150	13,850	44.4%
1817	10,400	3,442	13,842	24.9%
1818	10,700	4,211	14,911	28.2%
1819	11,200	4,094	15,294	26.8%
1820	14,700	3,967	18,667	21.3%
1821	11,300	7,324	18,624	39.3%
1822	12,200	6,997	19,197	36.4%
1823	9,700	7,327	17,027	43.0%
1824	10,200	4,944	15,144	32.6%
1825	11,400	2,956	14,356	20.6%
1826	11,700	2,357	14,057	16.8%
1827	11,200	1,768	12,968	13.6%
MEAN	11,033	4,628	15,661	29.6%

Calculated from William Jacob: Tracts relating to the Corn Trade and Corn Laws, 1828, p 88 et seq.

Apart from difficulty in assessing the bushel-volume of supply, quality may also pose a problem. If the proportion of wheat grades varied little, from year to year, then their typical weights might be averaged, and that average treated as a constant; but in the 18th century especially, as commercial wheat-growing spread westwards and northwards, probably the proportion of seconds and thirds within total output increased, so that the weighted output of wheat breadstuffs would not have risen to the same extent as acreage multiplied by yield. Howeover, the problem may be less or negligible in post-1800 calculations, given that fairly constant output proportions between the regions had by then been established.[11]

Demand-side estimates

The method used for calculating volume is broadly that used by Sir Charles Smith c1760,[12] and other contemporaries, as later described by G E Fussell, and employed by E J T Collins to establish 'spot estimates' of the grain-eating equivalent populations in 1801, 1850, and 1900.

The procedure has been: to take the population of Britain in each year from 1771 to 1870, and from that to calculate annual 'wheat-eating equivalent populations', by a simple polarization technique; each wheat-eating equivalent population is then multiplied by an estimate of the average annual consumption of wheat bread *per capita*, derived from contemporary data, to arrive at the amount of wheat bread consumed per year, which is expressed as the volume of wheat necessary to make that amount of bread.

Example

> Year: 1821.
> Population of Great Britain: 14.1 million
> x estimated 68% = wheat-eating equivalent population of 9.6m
> x estimated 77% quarter of wheat to make the average amount of bread consumed *per capita* that year, gives the national volume as 7.4m quarters of wheat consumed as bread.

The rest of this section is concerned with deriving the estimates of the wheat-eating equivalent population; figures for the aggregate volume of wheat consumed as bread are established in Section 7.2.

National population is the surest component in demand-side calculations. Population after 1801 is, of course, derived from the Census and inter-censal annual estimates. England's population up to 1800 is taken from the Wrigley & Schofield estimates. The populations of Wales and Scotland before 1801 have been crudely estimated, but potential error is unlikely to radically affect the rounded British total.[13]

The wheat-eating equivalent population, c1759–64, calculated by Sir Charles Smith, has been accepted as the baseline; Dr Collins' spot estimates for 1801 and 1850 are also accepted.[14] The linking trend between those dates, and its projection beyond 1850, has been judged by assessing contemporary estimates, contributory factors such as the growth of urban population and the expansion of the transport infrastructure, and by cross-checking with estimates of domestic wheat output, adjusted for imports and exports. In the latter case, for calculation of the wheat-eating equivalent population, I have used the rule of thumb that average *per capita* consumption of wheat was one quarter a year, an amount that allows for the variable consumption of other wheat products, such as fancy breads, morning goods, biscuits, and the pastry of puddings and pies, in addition to batch bread.[15]

The weakest element in the calculations is the allowance to be made for the use of other grains as staples. To estimate other-grain consumption, Sir Charles Smith used a polarization technique. He calculated the net domestic output of wheat, rye, barley, and oats, and the proportion of each consumed as human food; divided the latter by his estimates of *per capita* consumption of each of the grains (assuming dependency) and thus arrived at grain-eating 'equivalent' populations, cross-checked to his estimate of the population of England and Wales. Since the consumption of other grains was known by observation to vary considerably by region, he subsequently broke down his national aggregates, estimating the demand for each grain against his calculations of regional populations.

The polarization technique clarifies the amounts, but also obscures the nature, of grain consumption, especially in that 'middle ground' where individuals ate a mixture of cereals, for example in the form of muncorn and maslin bread. If quite a large number of people ate wheat as their chief food, but also ate other grains as supplements, they should really be classed as wheat-eaters, but their number is reduced by polarization, to a totally dedicated 'equivalent' core. On the other hand, the smaller amounts of other grains eaten by many such people are represented as the staple of a minority: the problem of reification. Thus there is room for dispute, as there was c1760, as to the size of the actual, predominantly wheat-eating, population.[16]

The problem of accounting for other-grain consumption appeared to diminish as the 18th century progressed: by 1800 contemporaries assumed far larger wheat shares, and later historians improved on their estimates. Ashley believed that c1800, 95 per cent of the population of England and Wales subsisted on wheat ('the almost universal bread corn of the whole people, of all classes and occupations'); Fussell estimated 90 per cent. If those estimates and the 'one quarter rule' were accepted, calculation would rest largely and with comparative safety upon the census population of 1801 (and, given little variation in *per capita* consumption, on the populations of subsequent censal years, and graded increases between).

That estimates of 90 per cent and 95 per cent wheat dependency were hardly borne out by the researches of Davies and Eden, for example, or by official reports made in 1795–6 and 1800–1, might be explained by the freak circumstances of dearth years. But that assumption has been challenged by Dr Collins, who, drawing on various contemporary sources, has estimated that in 1800–1 the wheat-eating equivalent population of England and Wales was only 66.4 per cent, and that of Great Britain only 57.8 per cent, and has argued that, though 1800 was an untypical year, the 'normal' wheat-eating fraction in wartime was unlikely to have exceeded 70 per cent in England and Wales and 60 per cent in Britain as a whole.[17]

Dr Collins also has suggested, tentatively, that the wheat-eating equivalent populations in 1850 were 88 per cent for England and Wales and 81 per cent for Great Britain (and in 1900, 97 per cent and 95 per cent respectively), indicating that at mid-century there were still significant pockets of other-grain consumption;[18] in which case, estimating the trend of total wheat consumption between c1800 and c1850 (especially the rate of change, whether gradual, or slow at first and then accelerating), calls for continuing attention to the problem of other grains, and therefore in part still relies upon estimates of agricultural output, rather than discrete calculation. However, certain broad non-agricultural factors offer helpful if inexact indications of the trend and its pace.

From the testimony of bakers and others, wheat bread and white wheat bread particularly, was overwhelmingly predominant in London.[19] and the close connexion of wheat bread and urban living elsewhere is demonstrated by surviving records of the assize of bread. There were exceptions: Young observed that, in 1768 the commercial bakers of Leeds made oat bread, those of Newcastle-on-Tyne rye bread, and bakers elsewhere in the north sold breads of mixed grain flours,[20] while at York in 1813, not only wheat breads but also maslin, rye, and a coarse 'rubble' bread were assized;[21] also, home bakers, especially in northern towns, may have made bread of other grains. Overall, however, given a normal connexion between wheat and town living, increasing urbanization is a partial indicator of accelerating demand: the proportion of the population of England and Wales living in towns of 10,000 inhabitants or more, increased from 17 per cent c1750, to 24 per cent in 1801, to 44 per cent in 1851 (and 69 per cent in 1901).[22]

In addition to town-dwellers, artisans working in villages and country districts are likely to have demanded more digestible white wheat bread, even rioting if they were denied it.[23] Taking Professor Wrigley's estimate for England only, the 'rural non-agricultural population' increased from 1,910,000 c1750 (33 per cent of total population) to 3,140,000 in 1801 (36 per cent).[24]

The trend to wheat-eating among the rural agricultural population most probably reflected the expansion of wheat growing, from the south-east outwards, especially where labourers were given wheat grain, flour, or bread in kind, or at a discount. The expansion of the inland water zone, and the particular concentration of canal construction in the war period, c1793–1815, together with the scale of enclosures, gives a very rough indication of the scale and pace of change. Conversely, as Dr Edward Smith observed, local specialization in inferior grains probably assured continuing dependency on barley and oats, with payment-in-kind 'locking' labourers and their families to their traditional diets.[25] However, estimates of the 'grain dedication' of rural agricultural populations are complicated, especially between c1815 and c1836, by the role of the potato, where it displaced inferior grains, until wheat flour became universally available.

Information from the occupational censuses, as to the number of bakers by region, suggests that after 1831 commercial wheat bread was still not easily obtained in much of Yorkshire, and in parts of Lancashire.

Price may also have some bearing on the trend to wheat: when low, at least it represented no impediment to wheat bread consumption; when very high, it suggests there may have been 'absolute dearth' in parts of the country,[26] which would have checked or reversed the trend, if briefly.

With such broad influences in mind, the trend to wheat dependency over three sub-periods – from c1770 to 1801; from 1802 to 1850, and from 1851 to 1870 – will be assessed.

c1770–1801

A decade before the start of the century in review, Sir Charles Smith published his polarized estimate of 'bread corn' consumption in England and Wales (see Table 7.3).

Table 7.3 Bread corn consumption c1759–64: England and Wales

| Grain | Amount consumed per capita | | by number of people | gives bread corn volume of Win Qrs |
	Win Qr	bu		
Wheat	1	0	3,750,000	3,750,000
Rye	1	1	888,000	999,000
Barley	1	3	739,000	1,016,125
Oats	2	7	623,000	1,791,225

Source: Sir Charles Smith: Three Tracts p 140.

Given that he put the national population at six millions (the Wrigley & Schofield estimate for England in 1759 is 6,063,000), Smith's 'wheat-eating equivalent population' represented 62.5 per cent of the total (for convenience, such calculations will be expressed as '%W', thus 62.5%W). The corresponding proportions for the other grains were: rye 14.8 per cent, barley 12.3 per cent, and oats 10.4 per cent.

Smith's further regional breakdown is listed in Table 7.4 and the regions he used are shown in Map 4.

Table 7.4   Grain-eating equivalent populations by region *c*1764

REGION (see Map 4)	Wheat %	Barley %	Rye %	Oats %
I	89.3	1.8	8.9	–
II	75.5	24.5	–	–
III	67.5	15.5	15.3	1.7
IV	27.1	17.4	16.1	39.3
V	31.8	4.2	32.0	32.0
VI	10.9	47.2	42.0	–

Source: Sir Charles Smith: Three Tracts p 185.

From those consumption estimates, Sir Charles then calculated the national domestic output of the grains, allowing for imports and exports at 1759 levels, and making allowance for other uses. Table 7.5 gives his calculation for wheat.

Smith's calculations were at once challenged by Arthur Young:

> The different proportion between the eaters of wheat, rye, barley, etc is conjectured; the number of people is conjectured; the quantities otherwise applied are imagined, and to appearance at random . . .[27]

In 1768, Young estimated that the output of wheat and rye together was 9,198,585 Winchester quarters.[28] If, by reference to prices, Young's

Table 7.5   England and Wales: wheat volume *c*1759

	Winchester quarters	Converted to Imperial quarters*
Consumed as bread	3,750,000	3,629,000
Other purposes	90,000	87,000
Consumed at home	3,840,000	3,716,000
Exported	210,771	203,972
Consumed & exported	4,050,771	3,919,972
Imported, deduct	4,168	4,034
Annual growth (net)	4,046,603	3,915,938

* Winchester quarters are converted to Imperial by multiplying by 31/30.

Source: Sir Charles Smith: Three Tracts p 140.

Map 4 Sir Charles Smith's regions.

From Sir Charles Smith, p 183.

estimate for rye is identified and removed, an output of roughly 7,665,000 Winchester, or 7,418,000 Imperial, quarters of wheat is left, double Smith's estimate. But, whereas Sir Charles had put the population of England and Wales at 6,000,000, Young thought it to be 8,500,000. Even so, his mammoth output figure, reduced by say 5 per cent for other uses, and then adjusted for imports/exports in 1768, would represent 90%W, a proportion higher than his own estimate of the norm at the end of the century (80%W).

To make ends meet, as it were, Young estimated the breadth given to wheat and rye together as 3,066,195 acres (which might be compared to the estimates for c1750 of Chartres and Holderness, of 2,629,000 acres and 2,300,000 acres respectively),[29] and a yield of 24 bushels per acre, an estimate rejected explicitly by Holderness (whose own calculation is 16 bushels net) and implicitly by Chartres (18 bushels[30]); however, Allen and O'Grada incline towards Young (referring to similar yield estimates he made in 1771).[31] But since the renovation of the Thames navigation did not begin until 1770, and the chief canals had yet to be dug, it is hard to believe that farmers nationally would have produced such amounts, without easy connexion to the main market, although those served coastways, or within a close overland distance of London, may have done so.

While Fussell, a 'wheat optimist', broadly endorsed Young, Ashley inclined to Smith, because of the esteem in which he was held by contemporaries and his close experience of the trade as a miller 'in a large way of business':[32] thus his estimates ought to have been well-conjectured. Dr Collins has questioned Smith's estimate for rye consumption, and also doubts that as many as one-third of the population of northern England depended on wheat.[33] Also, he points out that definition is blurred, when, especially in western and northern Britain, cereals were eaten in a wide variety of forms, so that the true consumption of inferior grains especially, may be under-estimated. The first objection has been countered by the estimates of Chartres and Holderness; the second is difficult to answer, given the problem of disaggregating the grain content of muncorn and maslin breads, of accounting for inferior wheats used for local subsistence, that did not enter the market returns, and of estimating the flows of intranational trade. The third objection also is hard to resolve. For my purposes, however, such regional difficulties might be left, and only the national aggregate considered. With the caveat that much must be guesswork, Professor Chartres has broadly accepted Smith's estimates, though he has uplifted net output somewhat; however, Professor Holderness' estimate for c1750 is lower. As a result, Smith's calculation of wheat output, on which his calculation of consumption depends, has the *post hoc* merit of representing, almost exactly, the mean of those two recent estimates as can be seen from Table 7.6.

Table 7.6   England and Wales: net wheat output

	'000 Imp qrs
Smith, *c*1759	3,916
Chartres for *c*1750	4,249
Holderness for *c*1750	3,600
Mean of Chartres and Holderness	3,925

And, with estimates so close, the variable of wheat quality alone could blur them to rough equivalence. Therefore, I will take Smith's estimate, of 62.5%W for England and Wales, *c*1759–64, as my baseline.

Recurring bad harvests (1756–7, 1764–74[34]) coincided with rising demand, as the proportion of those in sedentary occupations ('manufacturers', artisans, and clerks) rose,[35] a phenomenon closely if not entirely linked to the growth of the urban population (on a straight-line trend, comparing *c*1750 to 1801, the population of English towns with more than 5000 inhabitants would have increased by 210,000 between 1761 and 1770, representing most of the estimated increase of 258,000 in the entire national population[36]). The resulting strain on supply is indicated by the rising price of wheat (from roughly 29s per quarter in 1759 to 44s approximately in 1770), falling net wheat exports (from an annualized 257,000 quarters 1751–60 to 40,000 quarters 1761–70), frequent unrest at times turning to riot,[37] and the concern of Parliament, represented by the Bread Acts of 1757 and 1773, the aborted bill of 1766–7, and the reform of the Corn Laws in 1772, when it was accepted that in most years Britain would be partly dependent on imports.[38]

Thus it is probable that the polarized proportion of wheat-eaters in 1770 was no greater than in 1759–64, though a constant 62.5%W implies a higher satisfied demand, in England and Wales, of about 250,000 quarters annually, a quantitative rise of 6.3 per cent. To include Scotland, *c*1770, I have assumed that the wheat-eating equivalent population there could not have represented more than the 10 per cent estimated by Dr Collins for 1801,[39] but probably not less, given the beginning of commercial wheat growing on the central plain, and the nearness to the sea of the larger Scottish towns and industrial centres. The total for Britain is shown in Table 7.7.

Table 7.7 Estimate of the wheat-eating equivalent population, 1770

	Total population	WEEP*
England and Wales	6,700,000	4,187,500
Scotland est	1,400,000	140,000
BRITAIN	8,100,000	4,327,500

* WEEP = wheat-eating equivalent population.
(that is, 53%W for Britain as a whole).

The pessimism reflected by the Corn Law of 1773,[40] which was meant to permanently lower the barrier to foreign wheat, proved to be misplaced. Whereas, in the critical four years from 1765 to 1768 inclusively, Britain had imported a net 1,279,000 quarters of wheat grain and flour, in the eighteen years during which the new Act operated, the net import was 921,000 quarters: annualized, only 16 per cent of the previous crisis level.[41] The price of wheat fell in 1775, and reached its 1774 level in only two years from then until 1794. The price of flour fell further.

After 1770, the accelerating expansion of the water zone, and increasing carrying capacity, helped to realize the wheat-growing potential of Britain. As the market indicators suggest, until 1794 supply kept pace with the demand of a fast-increasing population (the estimated population of England rose by 26 per cent between 1771 and 1794, with the urban, 'rural non-agricultural' and 'rural agricultural' sectors possibly increasing in alignment[42]).

To protect new and further investment in wheat-led regimes, the 'liberal' Corn Law of 1773 was reversed in 1791 by a protectionist measure that restored the barriers to imports (except from Ireland and Canada, a distinction found in every corn bill until 1846).[43] But shortly after the return to protection, Britain's vulnerability was starkly exposed, by the dearths of 1795–6 and 1799–1801.

Arguably, vulnerability had increased not only in relation to the growth of national population, but additionally, as the result of a continuing shift to wheat dependency. Such a shift might be hypothesized thus. First, whereas London had been overwhelmingly dependent on wheat since the early 18th century, in other towns, in the north and west at least, and even as late as c1770, a significant proportion of the population, the poor especially, may have depended chiefly on inferior grains; but the expanding water zone probably allowed a near complete conversion to wheat thereafter. The effect would have been greatest in the rising manufacturing towns of Lancashire, in Glasgow and district, and probably in the west Midlands, where barley and oats had been, and may have continued to be, the principal staples of surrounding rural populations. Second, again because of better transport, and also due to the spread of commercial baking, probably a great majority of rural artisans and their families, whose frustrated demand for wheat bread had, at an extreme, led to riots in 1756–7, 1766, and 1771–3,[44] now could be satisfied by an improved supply. Third, as wheat-led regimes were adopted by agriculturalists in more parts of the country, it is likely that wheat displaced other grains as the chief breadstuff of their labourers and families, a shift reinforced by off-market supply.

Such shifts should be reflected regionally. Unfortunately, the rural survey organized by the Reverend David Davies in 1787–93 is on too small a scale, and too random in its geographical spread, to offer convincing proof: the most that can be said is that it does not contradict the supposition. Table 7.8 relates Davies' evidence to Sir Charles Smith's regions.

Table 7.8 Davies' evidence on the predominance of wheat, 1787–93

Region	Number of places	Circumstance
I	7	All wheat-predominant
II	8	7 wheat-predominant, 1 not
III	3	All wheat-predominant
IV	3	2 wheat-predominant, 1 not
V	4	2 wheat-predominant, 2 not
VI	2	Both relying on barley and oats
TOTAL	27	21 wheat-predominant, 6 not.

Source: D Davies: Labourers in Husbandry

Overall, Davies noted that wheat bread 'has been constantly growing more and more into general use among the lower classes of people', and put the proportion of 'wheat-eaters' in England and Wales at 75%W in 1795.[45]

Eden's survey[46] spans one average year and two years of dearth (1794–6). His rural England can be divided into three bread zones (see Map 5):

I – wheat-bread dependent, with commercially-baked bread available in rural areas, signified by the citing of a loaf price in at least one place per county.

II – more various, where Eden quotes prices for wheat, rye, barley and/or oats, though in most places wheat seems to have been the chief breadstuff. However, in Nottinghamshire and Northumberland mixed bread was common, while potatoes were said to be the labourers' chief food at Tanfield in County Durham and in parts of Somerset.

III – Cumberland, Westmorland, and the western part of Yorkshire, where oats predominated.

Scotland is cursorily reported, as depending chiefly upon bannocks made of oatmeal, though potatoes were now the principal food of the Highlands, and an important part of the labourers' diet in East Lothian.

Eden makes it clear that many of the poor faced, if they had not as yet experienced, hunger. But, in 1795–6, government and Parliament acted vigorously to deal with deficiency through various measures, chiefly the expansion of the Poor Law system, roughly on Speenhamland lines, through the southern and eastern counties, where the rural populations were heavily dependent on wheat. Dr Collins, after detailed analysis of local reports made during the crisis of 1799–1801, gives regional cereal-eating equivalent populations for six regions of England (which I have numbered I–VI: see Map 6), and of Wales and Scotland. His data are listed in Table 7.9.

Possibly the estimates for regions I, II, and III over-state wheat-eating in that year, since the authorities promoted several stratagems to reduce consumption and encourage substitution, while the estimate for region VI may understate the importance of wheat in northern cities, towns, and semi-rural industrial zones (especially given the wheat component of maslin and muncorn breads). However, the aggregate estimate of 57.8%W for Britain is supported by an official projection of domestic output in that year[47] added to the volume of imports.

As Dr Collins acknowledges, there are considerable difficulties in taking 1801 as a representative year. Given his estimate, if Sir Charles Smith's calculations are taken as the baseline, the proportion of wheat dependency may have increased little above the 53%W of c1760, though the quantitative effect would be large: 4.3m 'wheat-eaters' rising to about 6.2m, an increase of 44 per cent.

However, contemporaries suggested considerably higher average proportions. Young, though not quite the super-optimist of former years, put the normal wheat-eating equivalent population of England and Wales, c1800, at 80%W, and also doubted if dearth had much reduced it (when asked by the bread committee of the House of Commons if, in a year of high wheat prices, perhaps a third of the

Map 5 Eden's regions.

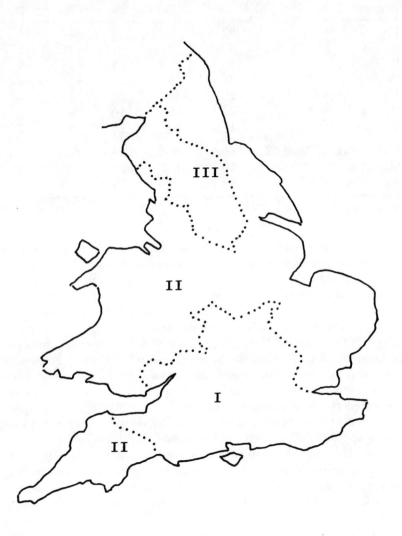

I – Commercially-baked wheat bread widely available in rural areas.
II – Intermediary zone: wheat and other grains, some commercial baking.
III – Oats predominate.

Derived from Eden, State of the Poor.

Table 7.9   Regional cereal-eating equivalent populations, 1801

Region	Wheat %	Barley %	Oats %	Rye %	Pulse %
I	97	2	1	−1	−1
II	90	9	−1	1	−1
III	96	4	−1	−1	−1
IV	45	55	−1	−1	−1
V	70	17	12	1	−1
VI	25	18	50	6	1
Wales	15	60	20	5	−1
ENGLAND & WALES	66.4	16.9	14.8	1.8	0.1
SCOTLAND	10	10	72	–	8
BRITAIN	57.8	15.5	23.6	1.5	1.3

Source: Collins p 105.

population used barley or oat bread, he replied that that was an exaggeration, though 'what it would be without Parochial Assistance, is another thing'): also he pointed out that other grains too were deficient both in quality and quantity, and so offered no saving (in 1800 a stone of oat flour in Westmorland cost as much − 4s 6d − as a stone of wheat flour in Suffolk); therefore, he argued, grain consumption was less all round. 'CG' exceeded Young, suggesting 85%W. If those estimates are restated for Britain (allowing Scotland as 10%W), then the national wheat-eating equivalent population would have been 69–74%W. Turton, a 'pessimist', suggested 75%W for England and Wales (which, converted as above would give 65%W for Britain). In 1801, Benjamin Capper estimated normal wheat bread consumption in England and Wales at 6,648,314 quarters. If his estimate is put on the same footing as the others, by taking all wheat consumption into account (using the rule of thumb: one quarter of wheat per head annually), then, given his assumption of a population of 9,500,000, 86%W is indicated, or 74%W, if Scotland is included. However, the official estimate of normal consumption, set out in the Sixth Report of the House of Commons' Committee on the High Price of Provisions, gives a more conservative 67%W for Britain,[48] indicating 6.7m to 6.9m wheat-eaters.

The official estimate fits quite closely with Professor Holderness' calculation that c1800, the output of wheat in England and Wales was 6.1m quarters,[49] when allowance is made for high imports.

If the official estimate is accepted as representing normality, Dr Collins' 57.8%W for 1801 would indicate an exceptional fall in wheat

Map 6 Collins' regions.

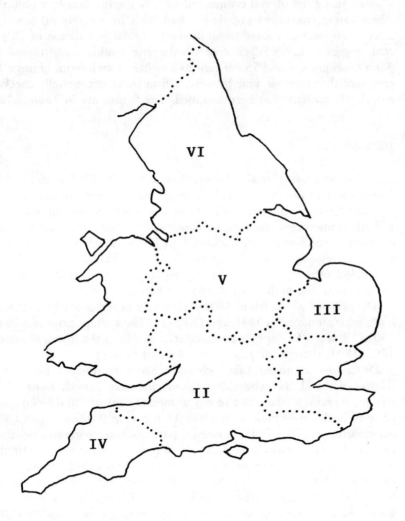

From Collins, p 105

dependency, during the dearth, of 16 per cent. That a fall of such an order, or greater, did occur is indicated by Dr Collins' observation, that of almost 500 towns and villages replying in 1800 to a government circular, 'most claimed a reduction in wheat consumption of between 30 and 50 per cent.'[50]

Also, using the official estimate of 67%W implies that by c1800 the wheat-eating equivalent population had risen by roughly 60 per cent since 1770 (which, related to an increase in total population of 28 per cent suggests that 45 per cent of the rise could be attributed to population growth and 55 per cent to a switch from inferior grains). To represent that increase year by year, a firm trend occasionally checked by relative scarcity, has been assumed. The figures are in Table 7.10.

1802–50

By a combination of push (the shock of dearth in 1795–6 and 1799–1801) and pull (unprecedentedly high prices, the accelerating extension of inland navigation, especially after the 'canal boom' of the mid-1790s), domestic wheat output continued to rise. The enclosure of commons (which in principle allowed the fastest return on investment in wheat-led regimes) proceeded apace; the General Enclosure Act of 1801, and 1,482 other acts passed during the Napoleonic period, altogether put an extra one million acres into cultivation.[51]

The price of wheat fell in 1802–4, but rose again in 1805 and stayed high, with pinnacles in 1810 and 1812–13. The average price of wheat, 1802–15, was 85s per quarter compared to 74s in the first war period 1793–1801, though the paper currency had inflated.

Dr Collins' argument, that high prices had a depressive effect on the relative demand for wheat throughout the war period, must carry weight, especially when, due to governmental controls on distilling, the price of barley rose by less: in 1802–15 it averaged 42s as against 40s per quarter in 1793–1801. However, parliamentary witnesses doubted any readiness to switch to barley,[52] and in the dearth of 1810 the government took exceptional steps to defend wheat consumption, at the expense of British (and French) war objectives. Since the outbreak of hostilities, each side had prohibited trade with the other, though both governments had issued licences of exemption in special cases. By 1809, and despite the Berlin decrees, the will to trade had become irresistible: four bountiful continental harvests in 1806 to 1809 had piled up surpluses, much to the dismay of European farmers, while Britain now suffered another severe deficiency. Therefore, during 1810 licences were distributed prolifically, making sanctions all but meaningless. In 1810

Table 7.10 Britain: estimated wheat-eating equivalent population,
1770–1801

Year	%W	Total pop m	WEEP* m
1770	53	8.1	4.3
1771	53	8.1	4.3
1772	53	8.2	4.3
1773	54	8.2	4.4
1774	54	8.3	4.5
1775	56	8.3	4.6
1776	57	8.4	4.8
1777	57	8.5	4.8
1778	58	8.6	5.0
1779	58	8.7	5.0
1780	59	8.9	5.3
1781	59	8.9	5.3
1782	60	9.0	5.4
1783	60	9.0	5.4
1784	61	9.1	5.6
1785	61	9.2	5.6
1786	62	9.3	5.8
1787	62	9.3	5.8
1788	63	9.4	5.9
1789	63	9.5	6.0
1790	64	9.6	6.1
1791	64	9.7	6.2
1792	65	9.8	6.4
1793	65	9.9	6.4
1794	66	9.9	6.5
1795	62	9.9	6.1
1796	62	10.0	6.2
1797	66	10.1	6.7
1798	67	10.2	6.8
1799	67	10.3	6.9
1800	59	10.4	6.1
1801	57.8**	10.5	6.1

* WEEP = wheat-eating equivalent population.
** Dr Collins' estimate.

Britain imported 1,567,125 quarters of wheat, almost all from France
and French satellites and allies; set against the government's rough

estimate, of a total demand for wheat of about seven million quarters, that represented almost 25 per cent of Britain's consumption.[53] Subsequently, the external trade collapsed, largely because Europe's run of good harvests was over, and because American supplies to Britain were stopped by the war of 1812. Thus, just as the fortunes of war turned decisively, there was renewed fear of scarcity in Britain.

The ability of cash-paid workers to afford high wartime prices surely varied by occupation and district. Professor Flinn has observed that

> contrary to the very commonly made generalization that rapidly rising prices tended to erode real wages during the French wars, it seems that for many groups of workers – though Neale's Bath labourers seem to have been a particularly unfortunate exception – wage rates in general broadly kept pace with rising prices'.[54]

Off-market supply, and in some cases the truck system, may have insulated a large proportion of the workforce from the market;[55] and for the neediest in many parts, the much expanded Poor Law system assured a minimal subsistence. However, the increase in expenditure on Poor Law relief, from £4,268,000 in 1803 to £6,656,000 in 1813,[56] represents a fall in purchasing power, against the price of wheat, of 16 per cent, and when further deflated against the increase in population of England and Wales, of 27 per cent. Moreover, outdoor relief was not usually issued as food[57] (though payment of other household costs indirectly released money for bread).

Professor Holderness calculates that c1810, the net output of wheat in England and Wales was 7.4m quarters;[58] if the average of net imports from 1806 to 1815 is added, and 5 per cent deducted for other uses, that gives 7.45m quarters for human consumption, which, related to the population of England and Wales in that year represents 73%W. Allowing for an increasing wheat output in Scotland,[59] the British level may have been roughly 68–70%W.

Colquhoun estimated that the wheat output of the UK in 1812 was 9,170,000 quarters, and that the cereal-eating equivalent populations were: wheat, 56.25 per cent; barley 9.38 per cent; oats 28.13 per cent; rye 3.12 per cent; and beans and peas 3.12 per cent.[60] The inclusion of Ireland (33 per cent of UK population), so heavily dependent on inferior grains and potatoes, dilutes the wheat-eating population, so that the figure for Britain would be higher, but by no means so high as to substantiate Dr Burnett's claim that 'wheat had become the almost universal bread corn of England' by 1815.[61]

As a result of government interventions, in the period of nominal protection from 1791 to 1814 inclusively, net imports, including those from Ireland, totalled approximately 10,592,000 quarters: annualized, they increased to a level 863 per cent greater than that of 1773–90, when freer trade was official policy.[62] With peace, and the restoration of commercial relations, there was a well-founded fear (demonstrated by Dr Fairlie[63]) that cheap imports would inundate the British market, and undermine the much expanded commitment to domestic wheat; a threat that the 1815 Corn Law was intended to counter. But the new Corn Law, with its 80s floor, acted not as a deterrent to imports, but as a lure. In anticipation of the Act large amounts of foreign wheat were imported into bond; again, in 1816–17, when it seemed that 80s must soon be exceeded, more flooded in. The 1815 Act created a 'wheat mountain' of about six million quarters in store, that towered over the British market until the mid-1820s. Not only did so large a reserve ensure that the home price would stay below 80s (lest domestic producers be engulfed by its release), probably prices were pushed further down, since with stores so ample, annual output could be sold only for current use. Eventually, after the introduction of sliding scales, the mountain moved onto the market, by degrees, at lowish prices: by the early 1830s, the bonded granaries were almost empty.[64]

However, the apparent fall in prices after 1820 may deceive, given the return to hard currency (at a ratio to inflated wartime paper probably much greater than Ricardo and Peel allowed[65]). Real prices may therefore have acted as a check on the trend to near-universal wheat dependency in Britain. McCulloch estimated that in 1821 the staple-eating populations of the UK were: wheat 10.3m, barley and oats 7.0m, and potatoes 5.0m.[66] Again Ireland is a complication: the granivorous balance of 60 per cent wheat to 40 per cent for other grains may be lifted significantly for Britain. However, wheat seems still to have been rarely eaten in Wales, where barley bread was the staple, as part of a quite varied diet. But Jacob, when calculating consumption levels in 1828,[67] assumed that all Britons were wheat-eaters, a proposition which may have become truer, though by no means wholly true, as the 1820s progressed. The rate of growth of the urban population accelerated. Between 1821 and 1831 the populations of London and the next sixty British towns increased by almost one million (a rise of 25.8 per cent) when national population increased by 15.2 per cent, though of course that total includes northern cities where wheat-eating was not yet universal.

As to the countryside, the agricultural committees of 1833 and 1836 heard evidence indicating a strong trend to wheat, but by no means an overwhelming one. In 1833 there was less talk than in the early 1820s of scarcity affecting the poor: in Somerset, circumstances seem to have improved, thanks in part to farmers providing their employees with wheat at subsidized prices; in Shropshire, wages largely followed bread prices; a Norwich land agent considered that the labourer had never been so well off. In parts of Yorkshire, however, the diet of the poor had deteriorated since the war, largely it seems because wages and employment suffered from a decline in the profits made from wheat grown on marginal land. However, in Scotland, where payment-in-kind still constituted the larger part of earnings, labourers seem to have maintained their frugal standard, or even to have improved on it, as those in employment (especially day workers) now ate wheat bread, either as their chief or second cereal. In Cumberland, barley bread was still the staple (with potatoes, milk, and bacon featuring in the local diet), though some wheat bread either was bought, or baked by the families themselves; whereas in Cornwall, wheat bread had become usual, in place of barley, the grain being 'imported' from the Isle of Wight. Overall, it is difficult to separate the question of diet from regularity of employment; clearly in many places, especially where poor relief was constricted, there were considerable differences in the diets of those in work and those not.[68]

For England and Wales as a whole, a Liverpool corn auditor reckoned wheat consumption in 1833 at 12,000,000 quarters,[69] implying 84%W, but that was probably an over-estimate (Dr Kain's calculation of wheat output in England only, for 1836, is 9.25m quarters).[70] In 1841, Dudgeon put the proportions of wheat-eaters in England and Wales at less than 90 per cent, and in Scotland at about 40 per cent, implying 75–80%W for Britain. Porter in 1851 made no attempt to calculate the wheat-eating equivalent population (though he had useful information to offer on *per capita* consumption): deploring the 'most unaccountable prejudice' against data collection on so important a matter, he confined himself to the comment that now, except in years of scarcity 'no part of the inhabitants of England, except perhaps in the extreme north, and there only partially' used rye and barley, though an increasing number of them 'are in a great measure fed upon potatoes.'[71].

McCulloch estimated that the British population consumed 15m quarters of wheat in 1846 (76%W).[72] Repeal greatly confuses the position immediately thereafter, as imports flooded in and farmers cut back their wheat output, but, given low bread prices, Dr Collins' tentative estimate, that by 1850 the wheat-eating equivalent population of Britain had reached 81%W,[73] appears safe.

Summarizing and weighing the evidence, Dr Collins' 'spot' estimates for 1801 and 1850 might be linked as in Table 7.11.

Table 7.11 Britain: estimated wheat-eating equivalent population, 1801–1850

Year	%W	Total pop m	WEEP* m
1801	57.8	10.5	6.1
1802	65	10.6	6.9
1803	66	10.7	7.1
1804	67	10.9	7.3
1805	63	11.0	6.9
1806	63	11.2	7.1
1807	65	11.3	7.3
1808	67	11.5	7.7
1809	69	11.6	8.0
1810	65	11.8	7.7
1811	65	12.0	7.8
1812	63	12.2	7.7
1813	63	12.4	7.8
1814	65	12.6	8.2
1815	67	12.8	8.6
1816	65	13.0	8.5
1817	63	13.2	8.3
1818	65	13.4	8.7
1819	66	13.6	9.0
1820	67	13.8	9.2
1821	68	14.1	9.6
1822	69	14.3	9.9
1823	70	14.5	10.2
1824	71	14.7	10.4
1825	69	14.9	10.3
1826	69	15.1	10.4
1827	71	15.3	10.9
1828	71	15.5	11.0
1829	71	15.8	11.2
1830	71	16.0	11.4
1831	72	16.3	11.7
1832	73	16.5	12.0
1833	74	16.7	12.4
1834	75	16.9	12.7
1835	76	17.1	13.0
1836	77	17.4	13.4
1837	78	17.7	13.8
1838	77	17.9	13.8

Table 7.11 concluded

Year	%W	Total pop m	WEEP* m
1839	75	18.1	13.6
1840	75	18.3	13.7
1841	77	18.5	14.2
1842	77	18.7	14.4
1843	78	18.9	14.7
1844	79	19.2	15.2
1845	79	19.4	15.3
1846	76	19.7	15.0
1847	77	19.9	15.3
1848	80	20.2	16.2
1849	80	20.4	16.3
1850	81**	20.6	16.7

* WEEP = wheat-eating equivalent population.
** Dr Collins' estimate.

1851–70

The depressive effect of Repeal upon British wheat production continued, and may have intensified, in the early 1850s. But, buoyed by curbs
on the exportation of European wheat, and poor American harvests,
agriculturalists regained confidence: 1854 was, by contemporary
account, the *annus mirabilis* of British wheat production, though the
benefit to consumers was offset by the exhaustion of stored old wheat,
and allegedly, by profiteering.[74] McCulloch's estimate that the net
output of wheat in England and Wales in 1854 was only 10,590,000
quarters might be contrasted to the optimistic view of 'A Farmer',
writing to *The Times* in 1854, that 15,000,000 quarters was now an
average production.[75] The difficulty of aggregating output in a volatile
period may be reflected by Professor Holderness' calculation that the net
output of England and Wales c1850 was 11.7m quarters;[76] if to that is
added the low result of the Highland Society's census of Scottish output
in 1854, of 600,000 quarters,[77] then British output would be 12.3m
quarters; adding the average of net imports between 1846 and 1855
inclusively, and deducting 5 per cent of the whole for other uses, gives
15.3m quarters for human consumption. Related to the 1850 population that would indicate 74%W for Britain. McCulloch put British
consumption in 1854 at 15.5m quarters, equivalent to 72%W.[78]

Undoubtedly, there was scarcity, represented by high bread prices and reflected in urban unrest, during the Crimean War,[79] but I have found no indication of a 'forced' return to barley and oats (nor, so far as it still was grown, rye), though the prices of inferior grains rose less than wheat. There may have been a lowering of consumption all round, which in the case of wheat would typically mean less demand for marginal products (such as pastries, fancy breads, etc). That would reduce *per capita* consumption possibly 10 or 20 per cent below the estimate of one quarter per head per annum, used throughout for statistical continuity, and so lift the wheat-eating equivalent population. But such a resort may be unnecessary.

That the McCulloch and Holderness figures are perhaps pessimistic indicators for the post-Repeal period, is suggested by the Lawes and Gilbert estimates of UK wheat output from 1853. The six-year averages are shown in Table 7.12.

Table 7.12 Lawes and Gilbert indication of %W for Britain, 1853–70

Period	L&G adjusted averages m qrs	Average pop m	WEEP*
1853–58	18.2	21.9	83%W
1859–64	21.6	23.4	92%W
1865–70	21.3	25.1	85%W

* WEEP = wheat-eating equivalent population.

The result for 1859–64 seems too high. It can be compared to Caird's estimates of UK supply in 1862–66.[80]

The average British supply of 20,095,000 quarters, set against an average population of 24m, gives 84%W for Britain in 1862–66.

That level of wheat dependency reflects McCulloch's comment, in 1859, that 'wheaten bread is now universally made use of in towns and villages, and almost every where in the country', a view confirmed in 1864 by Edward Smith, though it still allows for significant usage of other grains, and oats especially, in Scotland, some remaining pockets of maslin consumption in the north, and the survival of 'black loaves' of barley bread in isolated parts of Lancashire.[81]

Advancing the trend from 81%W in 1851, and bearing in mind Dr Collins' 'spot' estimate of 95%W for 1900,[82] I have therefore assumed a modest increase in the British wheat-eating equivalent population, up to a level of 85%W by 1870 (see Table 7.13).

Table 7.13 Britain: estimated wheat-eating
equivalent population, 1850–70

Year	%W	Total pop m	WEEP* m
1850	81	20.6	16.7
1851	81	20.8	16.8
1852	82	21.0	17.2
1853	82	21.3	17.5
1854	82	21.5	17.6
1855	82	21.7	17.8
1856	82	21.9	18.0
1857	83	22.2	18.4
1858	83	22.5	18.7
1859	83	22.7	18.8
1860	83	22.9	19.0
1861	83	23.1	19.2
1862	84	23.3	19.6
1863	84	23.6	19.8
1864	84	23.9	20.1
1865	84	24.2	20.3
1866	84	24.5	20.6
1867	84	24.8	20.8
1868	85	25.1	21.3
1869	85	25.4	21.6
1870	85	25.8	21.9

Summary

The above order-of-magnitude estimates indicate that the 'wheat-eating equivalent population' rose from 53 per cent in 1770 to 85 per cent in 1870, implying a fivefold increase in numbers from 4.3m to 21.9m.

7.2 ESTIMATED VOLUME

The order-of-magnitude estimates of the wheat-eating equivalent population can now be multiplied by the estimates of annual *per capita* consumption of bread, expressed as a proportion of an Imperial quarter (%Q),[83] to find the amount of wheat consumed as bread in each year. The estimates are in Table 7.14, below.

Table 7.14 Wheat bread volume, 1771–1870

	WEEP ×	%Q =	Wheat consumed as bread (m Imp qrs)
1771	4.3	86	3.7
1772	4.3	85	3.7
1773	4.4	86	3.8
1774	4.5	85	3.8
1775	4.6	85	3.9
1776	4.8	85	4.1
1777	4.8	85	4.1
1778	5.0	85	4.3
1779	5.0	84	4.2
1780	5.3	84	4.5
1771–80 ave	4.7	85	4.0
1781	5.3	84	4.5
1782	5.4	84	4.5
1783	5.4	83	4.5
1784	5.6	83	4.6
1785	5.6	83	4.6
1786	5.8	83	4.8
1787	5.8	84	4.9
1788	5.9	82	4.8
1789	6.0	82	4.9
1790	6.1	82	5.0
1781–90 ave	5.7	83	4.7
1791	6.2	82	5.1
1792	6.4	82	5.2
1793	6.4	81	5.2
1794	6.5	80	5.2
1795	6.1	77	4.7
1796	6.2	77	4.8
1797	6.7	79	5.3
1798	6.8	80	5.4
1799	6.9	77	5.3
1800	6.1	75	4.6
1791–1800 ave	6.4	79	5.1
1801	6.1	75	4.6
1802	6.9	80	5.5
1803	7.1	80	5.7
1804	7.3	79	5.8
1805	6.9	77	5.3

Table 7.14 continued

	WEEP	×	%Q	=	Wheat consumed as bread (m Imp qrs)
1806	7.1		80		5.7
1807	7.3		80		5.8
1808	7.7		80		6.2
1809	8.0		80		6.4
1810	7.7		79		6.1
1801–10 ave	7.2		79		5.7
1811	7.8		79		6.2
1812	7.7		77		5.9
1813	7.8		77		6.0
1814	8.2		78		6.4
1815	8.6		79		6.8
1816	8.5		79		6.7
1817	8.3		77		6.4
1818	8.7		77		6.7
1819	9.0		78		7.0
1820	9.2		79		7.3
1811–20 ave	8.4		78		6.5
1821	9.6		77		7.4
1822	9.9		78		7.7
1823	10.2		78		8.0
1824	10.4		75		7.8
1825	10.3		75		7.7
1826	10.4		75		7.8
1827	10.9		77		8.4
1828	11.0		77		8.5
1829	11.2		74		8.3
1830	11.4		74		8.4
1821–30 ave	10.5		76		8.0
1831	11.7		75		8.8
1832	12.0		75		9.0
1833	12.4		76		9.4
1834	12.7		76		9.7
1835	13.0		76		9.9
1836	13.4		76		10.2
1837	13.8		75		10.4
1838	13.8		74		10.2

Table 7.14 concluded

	WEEP	×	%Q	=	Wheat consumed as bread (m Imp qrs)
1839	13.6		73		9.9
1840	13.7		74		10.1
1831–40 ave	13.0		75		9.8
1841	14.2		74		10.5
1842	14.4		74		10.7
1843	14.7		75		11.0
1844	15.2		75		11.4
1845	15.3		75		11.5
1846	15.0		74		11.1
1847	15.3		75		11.5
1848	16.2		75		12.2
1849	16.3		76		12.4
1850	16.7		77		12.9
1841–50 ave	15.3		75		11.5
1851	16.8		78		13.1
1852	17.2		79		13.6
1853	17.5		78		13.7
1854	17.6		75		13.2
1855	17.8		75		13.4
1856	18.0		75		13.5
1857	18.4		77		14.2
1858	18.7		78		14.6
1859	18.8		78		14.7
1860	19.0		77		14.6
1851–60 ave	18.0		77		13.9
1861	19.2		76		14.6
1862	19.6		77		15.1
1863	19.8		77		15.2
1864	20.1		77		15.5
1865	20.3		77		15.6
1866	20.6		77		15.9
1867	20.8		76		15.8
1868	21.3		77		16.4
1869	21.6		78		16.8
1870	21.9		78		17.1
1861–70 ave	20.5		77		15.8

The table shows that the volume of wheat bread consumption rose fourfold, from 3.7m Imperial quarters in 1771 to 17.1m in 1870. There was particularly rapid growth in the period 1820 to 1860.

In accounting for this impressive rise in aggregate consumption over the course of the century in review, the most important factor was the increase of population. As shown in Section 7.1, there was also a compositional shift towards wheat bread and away from bread made with other grains: *per capita* consumption of wheat bread actually fell slightly from about 85%Q in the decade 1771–80 to 77%Q in 1861–70, so clearly it cannot account for any of the growth in aggregate consumption.

This completes the estimation of volume, though in the next chapter the figures will be combined with price data to calculate the aggregate value of bread consumption.

Notes

1. Leader in *The Times*, 18.10.1853, p 6; Porter p 538; Wilson: CL p 120.
2. See Chapter 5 Section 4, and Appendix 6.
3. National average grain prices cited by Mitchell p 736; for the Assize of Bread see Chapter 4.
4. Annual trade figures cited by Mitchell p 221.
5. Fussell: 1929 p 65.
6. Anon: A Proposal for Supplying London with Bread, p 8.
7. PP VII (517) 1, HoC 25.7.1834, p 225 – Palmer.
8. Vamplew: Corn Laws p 389.
9. Fairlie: 1969 op cit.
10. Fairlie: 1969 p 115 n 5.
11. See Chapter 6.
12. C Smith: Three Tracts.
13. Mitchell pp 7–12.
14. Collins: Dietary Change.
15. See Appendix 8.
16. C Smith p 182.
17. Collins pp 99, 105.
18. Collins p 114.
19. See Chapter 2.
20. Young: Six Months' Tour I p 90 et seq, II p 116 et seq.
21. G: Ms 7801 2/2 – letters relevant to the Country Bakers' Petition.
22. F M L Thompson in F M L Thompson (ed), vol I p 8.
23. D E Williams pp 58–9.
24. Wrigley: P C W p 170.
25. Edward Smith: Present State of the Dietary Question pp 15–16.
26. Wells pp 1–2.
27. Young cit Fussell p 67.
28. Young: Six Months' Tour Vol III p 326.

29. Young: Six Months' Tour p 326; Chartres in Ag H of E & W V–II p 444; Holderness in Ag H of E & W VI p 145.
30. Chartres in Ag H of E & W V–II p 444; Holderness in Ag H of E & W p 138.
31. Allen & O'Grada p 98.
32. Fussell p 67.
33. Collins p 106.
34. Ashton: Changes p 185.
35. Pownall: speech to House of Commons 14.4.1772, cit Barnes p 42.
36. Calculated from Wrigley: P C W p 162.
37. D E Williams: Morals, Markets.
38. Barnes p 42 et seq; 13 Geo III c.43; HoC Sessional Papers vol 25 Cd 3144, 21.12.1772; 13 Geo III c.62; Pownall p 6 et seq.
39. Collins p 105.
40. Barnes p 42 et seq.
41. Calculated from Mitchell p 221.
42. Wrigley: P C W p 170.
43. 31 Geo III c.30; Colquhoun pp 3–4; Barnes p 58.
44. D E Williams: Morals, Markets.
45. D Davies: Labourers in Husbandry, pp 31, 49.
46. Eden: State of the Poor.
47. HoC Sessional Papers vol 131 Cd 5126, HoC 31.12.1800, pp 5–6.
48. Young and 'CG' cit [Turton] p 161; Young: cit Salaman p 480; Fussell p 67; HoC Sessional Papers vol 131 Cd 4983, 10.2.1800, p 37; Capper pp 55–6; HoC Sessional Papers Cd 5126, 31.12.1800, p 5.
49. Holderness in Ag H of E & W VI p 145.
50. Collins p 104.
51. Galpin pp 28–9.
52. Galpin pp 57–73.
53. Galpin pp 83–118, 168–73, Appendix 8.
54. Flinn, Trends pp 407–8; Neale, Standard of Living; Hunt, British Labour History p 62.
55. See Chapter 5 Section 2.
56. Mitchell p 605.
57. PP XXVII (44) 1, HoC 21.2.1834, p 8.
58. Holderness in Ag H of E & W VI p 145.
59. McCulloch p 194.
60. Colquhoun p 89.
61. Burnett: P & W p 16.
62. Calculated from Mitchell p 221.
63. Fairlie: 1965.
64. PP V (165) 1, HoC 1.4.1822, pp 4, 88 et seq; Clapham I p 239; Dodd pp 161, 174; Jacob pp 88–91; PP V (612) 1, HoC 2.8.1833 p iv; VIII/I (79) 1, HoC 4.3.1836, Qu 30–49; Kemp: Reflections.
65. Barnes pp 203, 207.
66. cit Collins p 110.
67. Jacob: Tracts.
68. PP V (612) 1, HoC 2.8.1833, pp iv, viii; Q 4852, 2119–20, 2650, 2653, 2761, 2763, 3295, 6647, 6883; VIII/I (79) 1, HoC 4.3.1836, p 30 – Jacob; VIII/I (189) 225, HoC 15.4.1836, Q 5790, 5460,; VIII/II (465) 1, HoC

21.7.1836, Q 9649, 9651, 9652, 9880, 9881, 10378, 10379, 13525, 15084 et seq.

69. PP V (612) 1, HoC 2.8.1833, pp iv, viii, Qs 4852, 2119–20, 2650, 2653, 2761, 2763, 3295, 6647, 6883, 3431; see also PP VIII/I (79) 1, HoC 4.3.1836, p 30 – Jacob; VIII/I (189) 225, HoC 15.4.1836, eg Qs 5790, 5460; VIII/II (465) 1, HoC 21.7.1836, Qs 9649, 9651, 9652, 9880, 9881, 10378, 10379, 13525, 15084 et seq.
70. cit Prince in Ag H of E & W VI p 41.
71. Dudgeon cit Collins p 110; Porter p 538.
72. McCulloch cit Tooke V p 107.
73. Collins p 114.
74. Petersen pp 6–9, 20–4.
75. McCulloch cit Tooke V p 107; letter from 'A Farmer' in The Times 30.10.1854.
76. Holderness in Ag H of E & W VI p 145.
77. Morning Post 20.2.1855.
78. McCulloch cit Tooke V p 108.
79. Petersen: Thesis.
80. See Appendix 8.
81. Dodd p 166; Edward Smith: Practical Dietary p 48; Wentworth pp 302–4; Collins p 112; McCulloch p 194; PP XXVIII (3416) 1, HMSO 1864, Appendix VI pp 243–82.
82. Collins p 114.
83. See Chapter 5 for the derivation of the per capita figures.

CHAPTER 8

Value

Having estimated the volume of wheat bread consumed, the last step is to consider value.

Market forces both magnified and moderated the price effects of variable domestic harvests (as described in Section 8.1). And various questions arise when estimating the value of wheat bread (Section 8.2), and in attempting to put a value on bread made of other grains (Section 8.3). The new estimates of the volume and value of bread consumption are brought together and summarized in Section 8.4, the British Bread Table.

8.1 MAGNIFIERS AND MODERATORS

The open market price of wheat was notoriously volatile. Between 1772 and 1871 the year-on-year swing in the average price, as recorded in the monitored markets, exceeded 10 per cent in 55 years (see Table 8.1).

Table 8.1 Wheat price swing (+ or −), year-on-year

	Number of years
0–9.9 per cent	45
10–19.9 per cent	33
20–29.9 per cent	12
30 per cent or more	10

And the annual average prices conceal turbulence during the course of a year, especially in the period immediately before and after harvest. For instance, the average wheat prices computed from the *London Gazette* and cited by Mitchell[1] are 60s 5d for 1828, and 66s 3d for 1829.

But as the harvest of 1828 came in, actual Mark Lane price bands were as shown in Table 8.2.

By the Spring of 1829 the market had stabilized, so that between 16 March and 16 May the span was narrow and constant at 60s − 63s. By 29 June 1829 the span was 52s − 58s; after the next harvest it was (on 19 October and also on 9 November) 48s − 60s,[2] showing how wide

215

Table 8.2   Mark Lane price bands, October to
December 1828

Report Day	Shillings per Quarter
1828	
13 October	60–70
20 October	56–72
27 October	60–74
3 November	60–74
. . . .	. . . . .
17 November	56–70
24 November	54–66
1 December	56–68
8 December	68–70
15 December	70–74
22 December	65–70

price-spans (reflecting the range of wheat qualities – new and old, red and white, south-east or north-east or Irish) could be.

However, quoted prices reflect only open trade on official market days: they represented perhaps only one-quarter of all the domestic wheat traded in Britain, still less when imports are taken into account. Most of the wheat used for bread was bought off-market; prices may have been lower than those openly recorded (where bulk commanded a discount, and market fees were saved), or higher, if the wheat thus sold was generally of better quality;[3] or might bear no direct relationship at all (if bought forward at contract prices): there is no way of knowing. But, where large-scale purchasers were middlemen, who broke out consignments and sold smaller parcels to millers and bakers, it is probable that they charged at or close to the spot price prevailing at the time of the latter sale, which might take place either hours or years after the time of their own purchase.

The volatility of wheat prices lessened somewhat during the 19th century. This is clear from the data in Table 8.3.

Though currency values have to be taken into account, generally after 1821 quantitative price movements were within narrower bands, and the relative spread was less. This may well have followed from the wider availability of better and cheaper transport, and to some extent from the freeing of the external trade before, and especially after, Repeal; but in part it may represent a 'magnifier effect'. Given that, by one means or another, the individual growers of wheat retained a relatively fixed amount of their individual outputs to feed themselves, their families,

Table 8.3   Wheat price spreads, 1771–1870

Decade	Highest annual average price of qr wheat, s	Lowest annual average price of qr wheat, s	Spread: highest as multiple of lowest price
1771–80	54.25	34.67	× 1.56
1781–90	54.75	40.00	× 1.37
1791–1800	113.83	43.00	× 2.65
1801–10	119.50	58.83	× 2.03
1811–20	126.50	65.58	× 1.93

SUB-PERIOD:
Highest decadal cash difference: 70.83s
Average spread: × 1.91

Decade	Highest annual average price of qr wheat, s	Lowest annual average price of qr wheat, s	Spread: highest as multiple of lowest price
1821–30	68.50	44.58	× 1.54
1831–40	70.67	39.33	× 1.80
1841–50	69.75	40.25	× 1.73
1851–60	69.17	38.50	× 1.80
1861–70	64.42	40.17	× 1.60

SUB-PERIOD:
Highest decadal cash difference: 31.34s
Average spread: × 1.69

workforces, and neighbours,[4] then the effect of abundance or dearth would be exaggerated in the price (and especially the open market price) of wheat. Even relatively modest fluctuations in output would 'magnify' glut or scarcity in the towns and cities. Such an effect is suggested by the observations of Gregory King, Davenant, W S Jevons, and Bouniatian, all of whom developed formulae to show that fluctuations in grain output had a disproportionate effect on market price; as Professor Wrigley has shown, the key determinant is net yield, defined as the marketable surplus after deducting not only seed and fodder, but self-supply.[5] It follows that if self-supply, as a proportion of gross (or net) output declined over the century in review, thanks to considerably improved yields and productivity, then the magnifier effect would be moderated.

Furthermore, swings moderated as wheat neared the consumer, given intranational trade, which evened out local gluts and dearths, and storage, which lessened year to year variations in marketed volume. While it was natural for the public, much of the press, and many politicians, to suspect speculators of harmful machinations, John Stuart

Mill argued boldly for the market. In Book IV of *Principles of Political Economy* Mill praised capitalists for buying cheaply, storing, and then profitably selling wheat, since their self-interest helped 'to equalize price, or at least to moderate its inequalities.' Speculators had 'a highly useful office in the economy'; even if they artificially raised prices, volume would flow in and bring prices back down; and speculators had bad, as well as good, years. Mill's arguments did not persuade all: in the Crimean period there were fierce attacks on the 'few millionaires' who profited from the people's hunger, with calls for renewed state intervention.[6]

As well as moderators operating in the wheat market itself, there were restraints at work throughout the processing chain. The large-scale miller, with different varieties of wheat (and allegedly, alum) at his

Table 8.4   London average wheat and flour prices[7] in 1773

a) Flour per Sack: £2 3s 0d	Wheat per qr		
	£	s	d
1–3 March	2	14	6
3–8 March	2	10	3.5
8–10 March	2	12	5.25
10–15 March	2	8	4.5
15–17 March	2	11	0
17–22 March	2	11	7
22–24 March	2	10	11.5
24–29 March	2	13	1.75
29–31 March	2	12	10
31 March – 5 April	2	13	10.25
5–7 April	2	11	8.25
b) Flour per Sack: £2 8s 0d			
1–6 September	2	16	0
6–8 September	2	16	1.25
8–13 September	2	10	7.5
13–15 September	2	15	2
15–20 September	2	16	0
20–22 September	2	13	10.25
22–27 September	2	14	5.5
27–29 September	2	12	1.25
29 September – 4 October	2	9	11.25
4–6 October	2	10	7.25
6–11 October	2	7	7.25

disposal, could adjust his mixtures according to market circumstances. If millers acted collectively, they could set fixed prices for a season at a time, though the open market price of wheat oscillated. Thus, in 1773, the millers set a constant price for the Spring, and a constant price for the Autumn, though, in the first season, the highest average weekly price of wheat was 12.6 per cent above the lowest, and in the second, 17.6 per cent as can be seen from Table 8.4.

However, though the millers could stabilize flour prices by season, at least in relatively uneventful years, and so reduce the frantic element in short-term buying, in aggregate their prices usually reflected annual average wheat costs. This was bound to be so where a miller bought most of his grain for use in the current year, but even where he was using old stock, probably he kept a close eye on spot prices. Such a policy could hardly be avoided when consumers saw commercial flour and bread not as distinct products, but as particular forms of a universal commodity. Even when for a majority of people it was an unachievable or undesirable course, it was supposed that all could buy grain and have it ground and dressed (and then bake their own bread). As letters to newspapers testify, the public expected that when wheat was cheap, flour and bread should be cheap in proportion (though there was less tolerance of proportionate rises when wheat was dear), irrespective of when the individual miller had bought his grain and at what price.[8] Thus the price of flour (and bread) still responded to an increasingly fictitious external – the spot price of wheat – than to real costs.

That fiction was sustained by the assize system, which formally enshrined the old assumption of a commodity market. Whatever amount the baker actually had paid for his grain or flour, his bread price was set by the current spot market, and that price was enforced on all bakers within the same jurisdiction. Of course, this was not an unreasonable reflection of the circumstances of a small-scale baker, buying load-over-load, especially if he bought ready-dressed flours, which had a short 'shelf life'. In other respects, the assize might or might not moderate prices, according to the consistency with which the bakers' allowance was set (up to the introduction of the parliamentary allowance in London, in 1797, and elsewhere in 1813). If, for instance, the allowance consistently was 2d (1d for costs, 1d for profit) then when the flour cost per loaf was 10d, the end-price of bread would be 1s 0d; if the flour cost was 4d, the bread price would be 6d: thus the mark-up in the former case would be 20 per cent and in the latter case 50 per cent.[9] Therefore, the end-price of bread would never rise nor fall to the same extent as wheat or flour. The same applied in non-assized jurisdictions (as at Bath after 1815[10]) and throughout the country after 1836, wherever the bakers could keep to a fixed-sum mark-up. Elsewhere, in assized jurisdictions with no consistent allowance, or where competition forced down margins, prices could be much more volatile. And whether there was a fixed-sum mark-up, or a variable one there may have been a further 'shading off' of bread prices when costs were highest, if bakers wished to protect their sales volumes, or at least their windows.[11]

The assize system could also impact indirectly on the price of flour. Where magistrates took as their guide an untypically low wheat price, when setting the price of bread, the bakers would be pressed to demand correspondingly cheap prices of the millers, who had the options of complying, or of squeezing the bakers (risking their failure, and so bad debts) or of witholding or transferring supplies from a given jurisdiction, if they could. The assize also could affect corn prices, especially in the period when the country was divided into autonomous price districts. Corn merchants then were subject to contradictory pressures: from farmers, who hoped to keep prices just low enough so as not to trigger the release of bonded imports, and from bakers wanting to make them higher, to push up the assize. The volume in several of these districts was small enough to allow the carefully judged manipulation of a few local markets to produce whichever result was desired.[12] Under the sliding scale, and the single market structure, similar tensions and contradictions continued, though it was harder to manipulate their outcome. When speculators' margins were fine, their prospective profits might be eliminated by storage charges, if years of low domestic prices kept foreign wheat sealed up; on one memorable occasion in 1836, London holders threw nearly 2000 quarters of wheat into the Thames in protest at the adverse working of the sliding scale.[13]

8.2   MEASURING THE VALUE OF BREAD

To estimate value, average annual retail prices of wheat bread, at various places, have been aggregated, according to the amount of wheat needed to make the grades of wheat bread represented. That gives the 'retail bread value' (roughly corresponding also to the average cost of home-baking) of a quarter of wheat in each year. The value per quarter is then multiplied by estimated volume, to find the consumer-cost of the wheat bread consumed nationally, per annum.

Example

Year: 1821.
Aggregate 'retail bread value' of 1 quarter of wheat: 999d
x estimated volume of 7.4m quarters,
gives the value of wheat bread consumed that year as £31m.

Putting a value on bread volume raises several questions of interpretation.

How to value non-commercial bread

What the proportion of home-, to commercially-baked bread was at any time can only be hazarded. However, the proportions of commercial and home-made bread will not affect the computation of value if it is accepted that, overall, non-commercial costs approximated to commercial prices, supposing that the instances of economy in home baking (thanks to self-supplied grain or flour, and cheap or free fuel) were balanced by instances of diseconomy (costlier ingredients, wastage, etc), and supposing that often, when cheaper, home-made bread was of inferior quality to commercial bread (see Chapter 2). Moreover, grain supplied free or at a subsidized price would represent a cost to the provider, which ought to be accounted for in national estimates.

How to value price variables

The price of commercial bread was relatively uniform throughout the country (compared to the prices of other foods) even in the 18th century. This is clear from Arthur Young's tours, where the price of wheaten bread in the southern provincial areas and in the north was very similar to the prices then prevailing in London. Adam Smith agreed with Young on the near uniformity of British bread prices.[14] Nonetheless, there were differences from place to place, owing to:

1 – location: the prices of wheat and flour (and therefore bread) could vary between places in the land zone,[15] whilst they were relatively uniform throughout the water zone.

2 – the assize: the operation of the Assize of Bread created 'artificial' differences in bread prices between place and place, according to the policies of the magistrates; there were often further differences between assized and unassized jurisdictions. However, such differences might signify only different qualities of bread.

3 – discounting: even under the assize it was possible to discount the price of bread (providing that quality was not affected), but the practice was discouraged, certainly in London, where the bakers' corporation was formidable. After the abolition of the assizes, and with the weakening of bakers' societies especially in the cities, competitive pricing was frequently practiced; generally, however, prices reflected the quality of bread sold.

4 – overselling: with exceptions, the effect of truck was to raise the price of bread to those caught up in the system, perhaps by as much as 25 per cent. Thus it was possible, in any place, for dear bread to co-exist with cheap (especially where co-operatives and bread clubs were set up for the benefit of 'free' workers).

Overall, up to the 1840s, such variations can best be reflected and then aggregated by taking a relatively large selection of prices from various places. From the 1840s, by when distinctions between the land and water zones had disappeared, when there was no assize, and when the truck system was in decline, London prices probably represent the country as a whole, especially since they aggregate first-rate prices and various shades of discounting.

How to value bread types

Although contemporaries often referred to bread as if it were a standard product, in most places two or more types of bread were sold. They might be the parliamentary Wheaten, Standard Wheaten, and/or Household types, or licit or illicit sub-varieties. All had their different prices (or costs). And the same descriptions could mean different types of bread from place to place and/or from generation to generation. As Kirkland observed, price comparisons can be 'wholly misleading because the same description does not at different times represent the same quality of bread.'[16]

Little is known about the 'market shares' of these various types. Broad statements were made by witnesses to inquiries, largely circumstantial evidence is found in surveys, and there are occasional (though not always consistent) references in press reports and correspondence. A generalized summary might be: that the Wheaten type predominated in London until 1815, after when a middling type, approximating to Standard Wheaten bread ('improved' with alum), became common; that a Standard Wheaten type was usual in provincial towns and cities; and that coarser bread, of the Household type, or poorer, was normal in the countryside until it was steadily replaced by better qualities. But there are exceptions, impossible to measure, to all these generalizations.

However, in principle, it is not necessary to know the 'market shares' of the various types when calculating value, since their prices were heavily influenced by the wheat yield represented. Thus the approximate 'bread value' (V) of an Imperial quarter of wheat is arrived at by multiplying price and the known average yield of each type. Of course, even in ideal circumstances, there will be slight variations, given the different distributions of overheads, the effects of pricing to the nearest coin, and rounding-off when averaging. But the result should be close. Thus, for Oxford in 1815, V computed from Standard Wheaten bread (8.89d annual average price for 4 lbs x 449/4) was 999d, while computed from Household bread (8.54d annual average price for 4 lbs x 484/4) it was 1033d, a difference of only 3.4 per cent (which in most years would not affect a computation of national value, expressed to the nearest m). Even so, although V is a useful aggregate, especially when local bread yields can be identified, it is not an exact equation.

Price information

Extant sources used include, firstly, the official annual averages of the price of wheat in the monitored markets, which provide a broad guide to the cost of the principal ingredient. By correlating these prices to a representative allowance for millers' and bakers' costs, a rough 'end price indicator' can be estimated, to show how the trade margin varied as a percentage of costs (see Appendix 10).

There are also published records, special studies and sources that mostly, to the best of my knowledge, have not previously been tabulated. All these sources are discussed in Appendix 11.

From the price information assembled, an indicative figure for V (the bread value of an Imperial quarter of wheat) can be calculated, to represent roughly the average price (or cost) of bread nationally in any year.

Each local average annual bread price (per 4 lb) is multiplied by the appropriate yield for the bread type concerned, using the yields mentioned above[17]
Wheaten: 426 lbs (divided by 4)
Standard Wheaten: 449 lbs (divided by 4)
Household: 484 lbs (divided by 4).

Wherever possible, I have used Wheaten and Standard Wheaten rather than Household prices. Data from various places suggests that whereas Wheaten and Standard Wheaten yields were common and consistent over time, Household bread qualities varied considerably, though by what amount is unclear. Thus V calculated from a Household price might be significantly misleading, whereas V calculated from Wheaten or Standard Wheaten data should apply roughly to Household bread whatever the quality.

The calculations of V at various places in each year are then related to the national annual average price of wheat, and the guideline indicator of mark-up, to allow commonalities and deviations to be compared (and wherever possible, explained).

Following comparison, an estimate of national V is decided, judgementally, within the bounds of the evidence. In deciding V, clearly account must be taken of the 'weight' of each data source, according to the size of bread market it represents. For the largest market, London, I have assumed from Professor Wrigley's estimates that the population of the metropolis $c1770$ was about 750,000; further assuming that all Londoners were wheat-eaters, that population therefore represented about 17 per cent of the estimated national wheat-eating population (W) of that year. By 1801 the proportion would have been about 16 per cent. London may have become somewhat more important, proportionately, by the mid-19th century, declining thereafter, if the number of bakers in the metropolis and in the country as a whole are compared as in Table 8.5.

Table 8.5   London's share of the bakery trade

Year	% of bakers in London
1831	15.7
1841	20.7
1851	19.6
1861	19.5
1870(1)	18.2

From the 1840s London is the chief source used, given the probability that it represents prices in the country as a whole. However the series for Edinburgh/Leith (a market with a large and traditionally competitive baking trade[18]) shows somewhat lower prices generally, and therefore, to err conservatively, I have slightly discounted the London prices.

Calculations for each year, decade by decade, are shown in Appendix 12. The result of the calculations is an estimate of V, expressed in old pence (d), being the annual average price/cost of the bread (aggregating all types) produced from an Imperial quarter of wheat. V is then multiplied by wheat bread volume (QW) to give the 'market value' estimates, expressed to the nearest £m, that are shown in Section 8.4, the British Bread Table.

8.3   OTHER BREAD

The volume and value of breads made from other grains can be calculated in the same way as for wheat. The equivalent population of other bread-eaters is first calculated, then *per capita* consumption is estimated. Multiplying these two together gives an estimate of the volume of consumption. This is multiplied by price data to give figures for the total value of other bread consumed. Consumption data is scant and interpretation difficult. The sources and methods are outlined in this section, and the figures themselves in Appendices 13 and 14.

Other bread-eating populations

The numbers of those who principally ate grains other than wheat can be crudely estimated by the polarization technique used to calculate the numbers of wheat-eaters.

According to Sir Charles Smith, c1766[19] the population of England and Wales could be divided, as to principal breadstuffs, in these proportions:

Barley   12.3% ⎫
Oats   10.4% ⎬   37.5%
Rye   14.8% ⎭
[leaving: Wheat 62.5%]

Applied to a population estimate of 6.7 million for 1770,[20] that gives roughly:

800,000 barley eaters
700,000 oats' eaters
1,000,000 rye eaters.

If the population of Scotland, put at 1.4 million,[21] is added, in these (guessed) proportions:

1,000,000 oats' eaters
100,000 barley eaters
200,000 rye eaters
allowing a further 140,000 wheat eaters.

then the totals for Britain would be as shown in Table 8.6.

In Sir Charles Smith's time, rye was still an important breadstuff, but its cultivation and use declined rapidly in the late 18th century. Extrapolating from Collins,[22] by 1801 the other-grain populations were as listed in Table 8.7.

Rye apart, Dr Collins indicates increased 'dedicated' populations of barley eaters and rye eaters, a plausible phenomenon during the great

Table 8.6 Proportions consuming grain types, *c*1770

	of population of 8.1 million
900,000 barley eaters	11.1%
1,700,000 oats eaters	21.0%
1,200,000 rye eaters	14.8%
3,800,000 other grain eaters	46.9%

Table 8.7 Other-grain eating populations, 1801

	of population of 10.5 million
1,700,000 barley eaters	16.2%
2,500,000 oats eaters	23.8%
200,000 rye eaters	1.9%
4,400,000 other grain eaters	41.9%

dearth of 1799–1801. Even so, the cheaper prices per bushel of barley and oats did not necessarily represent better value, in terms of employable energy, and dearth prices caused hardship: the

> workers from Newport, in Pembrokeshire, who complained of the high price of bread in January 1801, stated that barley had risen at Cardigan to 11s 9d a quarter and oats to 30s a teal, whereas they were not able to pay for the barley and oats more than 10s and 14s respectively.[23]

By 1850, extrapolating from Dr Collins' estimate, the grain populations were as given in Table 8.8.

Table 8.8 Other-grain eating populations, 1850

	of population of 20.6 million
800,000 barley eaters	4.0%
3,100,000 oats eaters	15.0%
insignificant rye eaters	–
3,900,000 other grain eaters	19.0%

Thereafter, the dedicated eaters of other grains continued to decline in number, so that by 1900, on Dr Collins' estimate, barley eaters represented less than 1 per cent and oats' eaters only 5 per cent of the British population.

I have tried to connect these pinpoint estimates, in a way consistently inverse to the trend to wheat: estimated 'other grain' eating populations are given in Appendix 13.

Consumption of other grains

Sir Charles Smith put *per capita* consumption of other grains at levels higher than for wheat (approximating to their bread yields):

Barley   138%Q
Oats   288%Q
Rye   113%Q
where wheat was 100%Q[24]

though even rye could be eaten in vast amounts: Smith cites a case of labourers round Newcastle-upon-Tyne, whose consumption approximated to 263%Q.[25]

However, a quite different pattern of consumption is suggested by Eden's survey,[26] a generation later. His particularly detailed study of miners, craftsmen, and labourers in the north-west, shows that other-grains were constituents of varied diets which included amounts of milk and other dairy products, and meat: other-grains did not have the singular importance that wheat had in the southern and eastern counties. Such people were not limited to one grain, but most ate two (and sometimes three, including a little wheat), though these grains may have been mixed into one bread. The total amount of grains consumed there was less, *per capita*, than of wheat eaten in the south and east.

Take for instance the case of the Cumberland labourer with a wife and five children.[27] The annual grain consumption of this family was approximately 483 lbs of oatmeal and 640 lbs of barley (with an additional 25 lbs or so of wheat–flour). Combining the oats and barley, the total of 1123 lbs works out to 160 lbs per head of this family of seven. This can be compared to an average *per capita* consumption of wheat by the wheat-eating population (W) of 79%Q or so,[28] or about 380 lbs of bread: more than twice the weight of grain.

The apparent modesty of consumption by other-grain eaters can also be made by comparing expenditures. Of the 16 cases, over all the country, where Eden recorded other grains as predominant, breadstuffs accounted for 34 per cent of all expenditure (including rent, clothes, alcoholic beverages) while of his 14 cases where wheat bread predominated, the proportion was 55 per cent (a figure closely consistent with Davies).

Thus, two starkly different patterns of other-grain consumption emerge: on the one hand, *per capita* levels considerably in excess of 100%Q, and on the other (and a generation later) levels substantially below. Assuming that the determining factor was the availability of other foods, and relating the other-grain consuming regions of the 1790s to the known pattern of agriculture, it can be argued that, more often than not, other-grain eaters lived where milk, butter, and meat were plentiful and cheap. And even where that was not the case, the potato made rapid and deep inroads in the last decades of the 18th century.

The question of consumption is further complicated by problems of definition. This thesis concerns bread, and batch bread particularly. But some amount of barley, and a large amount of oats, were eaten in other forms, especially as porridges of various kinds;[29] while much of the 'bread' itself – often unleavened and hard, like the oatcake which was 'the principal bread used by the labouring classes' in and around Kendal[30] – might not be considered bread proper, or, if included, would encourage the inclusion of biscuits, fancy breads, puddings, pies and pastries, in the wheat 'bread' total.[31] That in turn raises the question: 'What was and was not a staple food?'

Since limited evidence does not allow a conclusion, instead I shall assume that *c*1770, the *per capita* consumption of other grains, in a form roughly recognizable as bread proper, was as shown in Table 8.9.

Table 8.9   *Per capita* consumption of other grains

	Sir Charles Smith's estimate of total consumption *per capita*	Assumed amount that was eaten as 'bread'
Barley	138%Q	120%Q
Oats	288%Q	140%Q
Rye	113%Q	110%Q

Then I shall assume that, taking the country as a whole, those levels of consumption fell significantly in the last decades of the 18th century, as other-grain eating 'retreated' to the mixed farming areas (though any calculation is complicated by polarization, when mixtures such as maslin and muncorn were popular), and as use of the potato increased greatly, till the levels that were reached by c1800 were 80%Q for each of barley, oats and rye. I assume further that those levels of consumption were sustained thereafter. The assumed reduction is listed in Table 8.10.

Table 8.10 Assumed reductions in *per capita* consumption: other grains

	Barley	Oats	Rye
1770s	120%Q	140%Q	110%Q
1780s	100%Q	110%Q	100%Q
1790s	80%Q	80%Q	90%Q
1800s on	80%Q	80%Q	(80%Q)

This is, of course, a crude reduction, with sharp switches at the ends of decades, but finer shading would suggest an accuracy not pretended to, and the coarse effect has small influence on the rounded, order-of-magnitude, end-totals.

Value

Young, on his six months' tour of 1768, recorded prices for various breads. When wheat bread was selling (according to type) for 1d to 2d per lb, he found loaves made from other grains priced as in Table 8.11.

Thus, better qualities of other-grain bread, and of mixed bread, sold for about the same price per lb as the coarsest qualities of wheat breads. And clearly, commercial bakers in the north, unlike most in the south, still catered to the demand for barley, oat, and rye loaves. But a large amount of other-grain bread must have been baked at home, and its price or cost is largely conjectural. First, because the national annual average prices for other grains almost certainly overstate the cost to most 'heavy' consumers. Often these grains kept a franchise because they were paid in kind, or sold at farm-gate prices at a considerable discount to the market; so that the production cost, rather than the distributed cost, with transport, market, and other charges added, is the truer guide. And that cost might be notional, where the principal use of the crops was as animal feed, for instance, or as 'fillers' in the rotation. Also, workers paid in kind in oats, say, may have sold part or all of their ration, and used the money to buy wheat bread from the commercial bakers.

Table 8.11   Price of breads in d per lb, 1768

Place	Barley	Oats	Rye	Mixtures
Leeds		1.60		
Kiplin (maslin)				1.24
Raby Castle			1.00	
Newcastle-upon-Tyne				
– best quality			1.00	
– worst quality			0.60	
Berwick				1.14
High Ascot	0.75			0.75
Penrith				0.50–1.00
Keswick				0.75
Kendal (clapbread)		0.75		
Holme		under 1.00		
Kabers		1.09		
Garstang		0.75–1.00		
Newcastle-under-Lyme (maslin)				1.00
Shenstone				1.00

Source: Young: Six Months' Tour Vol I p 90 et seq, Vol II p 116 et seq.

It is probable too that the open market in these grains, as breadstuffs, was far less fluent than the open market in wheat,[32] so that prices in producer localities might be significantly lower than elsewhere. As these grains travelled, their comparative cheapness eroded; and the differential was reduced further at each stage of processing.[33] For rye and barley, as in the case of wheat, it is reasonable to suppose that the cost of milling was offset by the value of the bran, the charge thus being subsumed in the price of the grain. But in the case of oats, where the yield of meal or flour was comparatively low, the charge for milling represented a substantial addition to the grain price.

In 1796, Eden recorded that at Kendal oatmeal of a quality good enough to make oatcakes was selling at 28d per stone;[34] in that year the national average price of an Imperial quarter of oats was 262d. Assuming a meal yield of 22.5 lbs per bushel,[35] or roughly 13 stones per Winchester quarter, the oatmeal yielded would have cost 364d, or 39 per cent above the grain cost. Nor were the prices of oatmeal consistent throughout the country – much depended on grain costs, the policy of the millers, and the durability of their grinding-stones. Even in Scotland, oatmeal was more expensive than wheat flour. In 1800 oatmeal sold at Edinburgh at the rate of 116s for 280 lbs, whereas the same amount of wheat flour sold locally for 105s, or about 8 per cent less.[36]

For the purposes of an order-of-magnitude calculation of value, applied to the volume scenario already sketched, I have assumed firstly that the milling cost of rye and barley was subsumed in the grain price, but that the cost of baking – allowing for some yeast and salt (even if fuel was free or cheap) and wear and tear – would represent an addition of 10s 0d per quarter on the grain price in any year.

Secondly that the cost of oats used as bread ought to be increased by 50 per cent to roughly represent the net charge for milling, and then that 5s 0d per quarter (allowing for salt and wear and tear) ought to be added.

Calculations of volume and value for each of the grains are given in Appendix 14. Decadal averages of the aggregate value of other breads are combined with estimates of wheat bread value in the British Bread Table (see the next section).

These order of magnitude calculations suggest that other-breads may have represented almost half of the total bread value estimated for 1771, but that their share declined thereafter, falling below a quarter of the total in the 1780s, rising somewhat during the great dearth of 1799–1801, then falling back to about a quarter share until the 1820s; thereafter, decline continued, hastened by potato consumption, until other breads were of little significance.

8.4 THE BRITISH BREAD TABLE

The estimated volumes and values of wheat bread (together with decadal average allowances for bread of other grains) are set out in Table 8.12 overleaf.

Table 8.12 The British Bread Table, 1771–1870

Year	Bread value per Imp Qr of wheat (d) ×	Volume of wheat used for bread (m Imp qrs) =	Wheat bread value at retail prices/ home cost (£m)
1771	692	3.7	11
1772	777	3.7	12
1773	777	3.8	12
1774	781	3.8	12
1775	765	3.9	12
1776	618	4.1	11
1777	703	4.1	12
1778	692	4.3	12
1779	586	4.2	10
1780	607	4.5	11
1771–80	700	4.0	12

Est annual average for other-grain bread: 8
Est annual average value of all bread: 20

1781	752	4.5	14
1782	786	4.5	15
1783	831	4.5	16
1784	797	4.6	15
1785	674	4.6	13
1786	629	4.8	13
1787	606	4.9	12
1788	719	4.8	14
1789	775	4.9	16
1790	820	5.0	17
1781–90	739	4.7	14

Est annual average for other-grain bread: 6
Est annual average value of all bread: 20

1791	752	5.1	16
1792	685	5.2	15
1793	775	5.2	17
1794	831	5.2	18
1795	1190	4.7	23
1796	1044	4.8	21
1797	887	5.3	20
1798	820	5.4	18
1799	1123	5.3	25
1800	1640	4.6	31
1791–1800	975	5.1	21

Est annual average for other-grain bread: 6
Est annual average value of all bread: 27

Table 8.12 continued

	Bread value per Imp Qr of wheat	Volume of wheat used for bread	Wheat bread value at retail prices/ home cost
1801	1721	4.6	33
1802	1031	5.5	24
1803	918	5.7	22
1804	1033	5.8	25
1805	1346	5.3	30
1806	1234	5.7	29
1807	1175	5.8	28
1808	1269	6.2	33
1809	1459	6.4	39
1810	1566	6.1	40
1801–10	1275	5.7	30
Est annual average for other-grain bread:			7
Est annual average value of all bread:			37
1811	1505	6.2	39
1812	1819	5.9	45
1813	1617	6.0	40
1814	1145	6.4	31
1815	999	6.8	28
1816	1179	6.7	33
1817	1539	6.4	41
1818	1294	6.7	36
1819	1117	7.0	33
1820	1044	7.3	32
1811–20	1326	6.5	36
Est annual average for other-grain bread:			9
Est annual average value of all bread:			45
1821	999	7.4	31
1822	842	7.7	27
1823	887	8.0	30
1824	1011	7.8	33
1825	1101	7.7	35
1826	955	7.8	31
1827	898	8.4	31
1828	988	8.5	35
1829	1044	8.3	36
1830	1022	8.4	36
1821–30	975	8.0	33
Est annual average for other-grain bread:			7
Est annual average value of all bread:			40

Table 8.12 continued

	Bread value per Imp Qr of wheat	Volume of wheat used for bread	Wheat bread value at retail prices/ home cost
1831	1035	8.8	38
1832	929	9.0	35
1833	838	9.4	33
1834	748	9.7	30
1835	661	9.9	27
1836	757	10.2	32
1837	871	10.4	38
1838	930	10.2	40
1839	1018	9.9	42
1840	955	10.1	40
1831–40	874	9.8	36
Est annual average for other-grain bread:			7
Est annual average value of all bread:			43
1841	965	10.5	42
1842	893	10.7	40
1843	751	11.0	34
1844	800	11.4	38
1845	763	11.5	37
1846	905	11.1	42
1847	1004	11.5	48
1848	788	12.2	40
1849	733	12.4	38
1850	691	12.9	37
1841–50	829	11.5	40
Est annual average for other-grain bread:			7
Est annual average value of all bread:			47
1851	688	13.1	38
1852	685	13.6	39
1853	831	13.7	47
1854	1060	13.2	58
1855	1120	13.4	63
1856	1121	13.5	63
1857	940	14.2	56
1858	769	14.6	47
1859	767	14.7	47
1860	895	14.6	54
1851–60	888	13.9	51
Est annual average for other-grain bread:			6
Est annual average value of all bread:			57

Table 8.12 concluded

	Bread value per Imp Qr of wheat	Volume of wheat used for bread	Wheat bread value at retail prices/ home cost
1861	923	14.6	56
1862	898	15.1	56
1863	795	15.2	50
1864	742	15.5	48
1865	763	15.6	50
1866	899	15.9	60
1867	1051	15.8	69
1868	956	16.4	65
1869	809	16.8	57
1870	833	17.1	59
1861–70	867	15.8	57

Est annual average for other-grain bread: 6

Est annual average value of all bread: 63

Notes

1. Mitchell p 756.
2. Prices cited weekly by the *Royal Leamington Spa Courier*.
3. PP III/I (82) 401, HoC 12.3.1813, pp 6–7 – Langston; II (255) 101, HoC 8.7.1820, p 17 – Harvey, Ludlow; see p 412; Thwaites: thesis pp 166–7.
4. See Chapter 5.
5. Wrigley: PCW Chapter 5, esp p 98.
6. J S Mill pp 67, 68–70; *Daily Telegraph* 21.9.1855; *Liverpool Courier* 3.1.1855.
7. HoC Sessional Papers vol 25 Cd 3213, 14.6.1774 – Appendix.
8. eg Petersen: B A thesis pp 43–51.
9. See Appendix 10.
10. Neale p 166.
11. eg the baker of Exeter whose plight was reported by *The Times* 9.1.1854 and *The Western Luminary* 10.1.1854.
12. PP II (255) 101, HoC 8.7.1820 p 7, Ellman p 21, Harvey p 28, Fothergill p 42, Wray p 48, Gladstone p 54.
13. Dodd p 174.
14. Young: Six Month's Tour; Perren in Ag H of E & W p 228 is a convenient summary of the earlier six week tour; A Smith p 34; HoC 22.2.1815 for London prices.
15. See the varying bread prices for towns in Essex and Hampshire given by Richardson, pp 45–6.
16. Kirkland p 5; see also Appendix 3.
17. See Appendix 3 for further details.

18. Johnston pp 31–42.
19. Charles Smith p 140.
20. Wrigley & Schofield give a figure of 6.277m for the English population in 1766; adding in Monmouthshire and Wales would give a total of roughly 6.7m.
21. Flinn ed, Scottish Population p 241.
22. Collins p 114.
23. D J V Jones p 326. The local teal was equal to four or five Winchester bushels: Ag H of E & W VI p 1152.
24. Charles Smith p 140.
25. Charles Smith, case 16, p 194.
26. Eden: State of the Poor.
27. Eden p 166.
28. See Chapter 5 Section 7.
29. eg: PP XXVIII (3416) 1, HMSO 1864, pp 281–2. The relatively high consumptions for other grains given by Colquhoun probably reflect uses other than bread: porridge, for instance.
30. Eden p 333.
31. See Appendix 8.
32. Indicated by, for instance, the different prices of oatmeal in various parts of the country.
33. See above, Chapter 2.
34. Eden p 335 et seq.
35. Collins p 108.
36. G: Fo Pam 895 (Committee of Millers and Mealmen in the vicinity of London), 1800, p 9.

Conclusion

The population of Britain tripled between c1770 and 1870: *prima facie* evidence of an industrial revolution, and also, prosaically, of the provision of an adequate, if unvarying and often sparse, mass diet in which the wheat loaf predominated.[1] The scale of the achievement is impressive: a roughly fourfold increase in volume and fivefold increase in value of wheat bread consumption during the century in review. And the proximate consequences were considerable, affecting the development of agriculture, commerce, transport, milling, and baking.

Some of the quantitative effects of bread dependency are readily measurable, others less so. Moreover, quantitative change occurred in a qualitative context. Not only did farmers, millers, and bakers produce more food, they produced a staple which, in aggregate changed, as wheat all but displaced the coarser grains, and as the quality of the wheat loaf itself improved, shifting (if often imperceptibly) from a coarser to a more easily digested bread, a shift reinforced by the practice of supplying bran-free flour, whenever possible, via the long-distance trade to market-dependent populations. If wheat is considered not as a homogeneous commodity, but is disaggregated into its commercial grades, then more light may be shed on the structure and dynamics of British agriculture, and intranational and international trade, both before and during the century in review.

Possible lines of future research also have qualitative as well as quantitative aspects. Three main topics might be suggested.

First, and perhaps as part of the fresh examination urged by Berg and Hudson,[2] further consideration of the dynamics of the industrializing economy, focusing especially on the effect of the price of bread on the demand for other food, goods, and services. In part, such research may usefully illuminate the role of the staple, especially one supplying much of the energy needed by an economy (in that respect, like coal or oil, bread was a primary fuel, when so much of industry depended on human muscle and dexterity).

Second, as suggested by Beckaert,[3] an enquiry into the influence of diet upon the course of industrialization, bringing qualitative as well as quantitative aspects into account. If the white loaf was as cost-efficient as coarser bread, given typical amounts of employable energy derived per penny, then clearly, the productivity gains achieved in agriculture were not, to some extent 'squandered' by the long-term shift from coarser to finer bread; the contribution of the 'agricultural revolution' to industrialization can therefore be reasserted.

Third, further examination of the effect of the Industrial Revolution upon the standard-of-living, and on the level of the population. That many groups of workers, and those unable to fend for themselves – those closest, literally, to the bread-line – were supplied off-market, may indicate that the price of the staple did not necessarily determine the level, nor trend, of population during industrialization. Also the premise of a suitable (if minimal) diet may also help in addressing the problem, posed by Floud, Wachter and Gregory, that while the height (and probably stature) of workers may have been constricted by the effects of the industrial environment yet they lived longer.

As this study has shown, bread may provide a key to several of the problems still posed by the era of continuity, chance and change.

Notes

1. See Wrigley: C C C esp p 35 et seq.
2. Berg and Hudson: Rehabilitating the industrial revolution.
3. Beckaert: Caloric Consumption.

Food Expenditure

Recently, Carole Shammas has reinterpreted food expenditure data (see Table A1.1). She begins by citing Gregory King, David Davies, Eden, Nield, and Purdy:

Table A1.1 Percentage of English household expenditure devoted to diet[1]

	All households	Poorest category of household
1695: All English families	60.7%	74.1%
1787–93: English agricultural labourers	72.2%	70.1%
1794–96: English agricultural & urban labourers	74.3%	69.0%
1836: Manchester working class	55.0%	–
1841: Manchester working class	69.3%	–
1837–38: English agricultural labourers	72.2%	–

While noting that the largest of the known samples was 127 families, and that therefore the statistical base is slender, Shammas argues that since these surveys were intended to point to crises of subsistence, and since they tended to exclude various miscellaneous expenditures, they themselves are probably too high; she concludes that, for all the labouring classes, the probable proportion represented by diet was between 50 per cent and 60 per cent.[2] Komlos has countered that by ignoring income features (not working on Sunday, etc) Shammas understates expenditure on diet, which should be about 75 per cent, close to Phelps Brown and Hopkins, and Gilboy, and identical to

Tucker. Shammas has defended her estimate.[3] The issue becomes more muddled if payment in kind is taken into account. However, whether 50 per cent or 75 per cent or 80 per cent is the better estimate, the calculations in all cases show the predominant importance of diet within total expenditure (a similar range of from 60 to 80 per cent, for a French 'model' family of the period, is cited by Olwen Hufton[4]).

Notes

1. Shammas: Food Expenditure p 91.
2. Shammas: Food Expenditure pp 92, 100.
3. Shammas: Reply to Komlos p 673.
4. Hufton in Rotberg and Rabb (eds): H & H, p 106.

Bread Expenditure

Table A2.1 Summary of some estimates of bread expenditure as a proportion of the visible means of families

Case	Estimate of bread expenditure
1760s: England[1]	44% of total family expenditure
1787–93: England, 21 localities[2]	55.8% of ordinary outgoings; 45.1% of total annual expenses
1788: Wales[3] (barley meal)	60% of weekly income
1789: England, south of the 'coal line'[4]	60% of weekly income
1794–6: England, 14 cases where wheat bread predominant[5]	55% of all expenditure
England, 16 cases where other bread predominant[6]	34% of all expenditure
c1787–96: average labourer[7]	40% of total expenditure
1800: a labourer's family[8]	approx 89% of earnings
1836: a reasonably prosperous working class family[9]	46% of total outgoings

To these numerical estimates can be added various statements, such as Engels' observations of the food of the Manchester working classes;[10] Jefferies' notes on the Wiltshire labourers' diets of the 1870s, which show little change from those reported by Davies and Eden almost a century before;[11] Eliza Acton's comment that 'it is no unusual

circumstance for the entire earnings of a poor hard-working man to be
expended upon *bread* only, for himself and his family' ('without their
being nourished as they ought to be, even then');[12] conclusions from
Edward Smith's dietary surveys, for instance that for indoor and
outdoor workers alike 'bread was undoubtedly the principal food of all
the groups he investigated';[13] and Davies' own conclusion that 'bread
makes the principal part of the food of all poor families, and almost the
whole of the food of all such large families . . .'[14]

Notes

1. Young 1767, cit Salaman p 497.
2. Extrapolated from D Davies.
3. A H Dodd, cit Salaman p 497.
4. Salaman p 497.
5. Extrapolated from Eden.
6. Extrapolated from Eden.
7. Gilboy's aggregate of Davies and Eden in Taylor, S O L p 4.
8. Correspondent to the Home Office, cit Hammonds T L p 24.
9. Longmate p 58.
10. Engels, esp p 100 et seq.
11. cit Mennell p 219.
12. Acton p 3.
13. Barker, Oddy, & Yudkin p 27.
14. D Davies p 21.

Wheat Bread Types

Wheat could be ground and dressed in an almost infinite variety of ways; the commonest types of flour were:[1]

whites: the finest dressing from the very best of the wheat, a flour which, if unmixed, was reserved for pastries and breakfast rolls;

best (or fine) households: the grade which, if unmixed, was used for the batch bread known as 'Wheaten' (confusingly, 'households' flour was of high quality, but 'household bread' was relatively coarse[2]);

seconds: which, if mixed with best households' flour, produced 'Standard Wheaten bread', and if unmixed, or mixed with some wheat meal, produced 'Household' bread;

wheat meal: a coarse grind of the entire grain excepting only the bran: then rarely used, unmixed, for bread;

whole meal: the whole of the grain including bran: then rarely used, unmixed, for bread.

In practical milling, there was no exact prescription of flour yields, since much depended on the weight and quality of grain, the mill machinery, and the art and judgement of the operator. On average a bushel of wheat weighing 60 lbs might be expected to produce from 47 to 52 lbs of flour of all descriptions (giving extraction rates of from 78 to 87 per cent),[3] though usually the miller would concentrate on producing one type only from each bushel. The extraction rates normally achieved by Mr Saunders, miller of Market Lavington in Wiltshire,[4] are reasonably representative. From 1 Winchester quarter of wheat weighing 58 lbs per bushel he extracted:

320 lbs of 'Wheaten' bread flour (69 per cent)
or 344.5 lbs of 'Standard Wheaten' bread flour (74 per cent)
or 373 lbs of flour suitable for 'Household' bread (80 per cent).

Converted to Imperial measure, at the official rate of 31/30,[5] the same yields are:

331 lbs of 'Wheaten' bread flour
or 360 lbs of 'Standard Wheaten' bread flour
or 385 lbs of 'Household' bread flour.

Nor was there a precise yield of bread from each flour, since again much depended on quality, or else on mixing, and the baker's art (and cunning); also bread lost weight the longer it stood after baking.[6] A safe rule was that bread weighed about 25 per cent more than the flour that produced it, though 33 per cent (4 lbs of bread from 3 lbs of flour) was common, especially from the most absorbent best flour.[7] Parliament crudely and repeatedly calculated (and ordained) that the weight relationships of the three main types of bread ought to be 8 Wheaten to 9 Standard Wheaten to 10 Household, but that had the effect of producing a Wheaten loaf too fine for provincial practicalities, and a Household loaf too inferior for London tastes. Ultimately,[8] the legislators settled on the sensible premise that one Winchester quarter of wheat ought to produce:

413 lbs of Wheaten bread
434 lbs of Standard Wheaten bread
468 lbs of Household bread

(the relationships therefore being roughly 8: 8.4: 9.1), which converted to Imperial measure meant that a quarter yielded roughly:

426 lbs of Wheaten bread
449 lbs of Standard Wheaten bread
484 lbs of Household bread.

These calculations somewhat understated the actual average yields, since it was officially allowed that the baker ought to have a margin to compensate him for flour wastage and underweight loaves (a risk almost inseparable from batch baking, when ovens did not have exactly distributed heat) and failed batches. The rule of thumb was that a 280 lb Sack of flour should produce at least two surplus quartern loaves to offset the baker's risk. The assumptions of contemporaries like Heslop,[9] and of some historians (including Boyd Hilton[10]) that this average was a rich source of profit rather ignore the real conditions of batch-baking.

Contemporary references to bread types have to be interpreted cautiously. The terms 'Wheaten', 'Standard Wheaten', and 'Household' were those normally used in 18th century London, and in official documents such as the assize tables. However, in bread as in much else, terms varied throughout the country: often, in the provinces, 'household' described a bread roughly comparable to 'Standard Wheaten',[11] though sometimes such bread was called 'seconds', from the flour partly or chiefly used in its making;[12] but in Essex 'household' described the best quality bread,[13] and by the 1860s, in many places such bread was known as 'fine households', from the flour used.[14] Officially, 'white' bread disappeared in 1758, when the best grade it designated was prohibited, but in ordinary speech 'white' meant 'Wheaten' bread; however 'wheaten' was a term sometimes used generically, to mean all types of bread made from wheat. 'Brown' bread was a loose colloquialism that might mean 'Standard Wheaten' bread (though it most often was a greyish white) or 'Household' grade, or bread made of mixed flours including some rye or barley, or rye or barley bread *per se*.

Notes

1. Acton pp 87–8.
2. [Egmont] p 19, note.
3. Extrapolated from the evidence of Wyatt, HoC Sessional Papers vol 131 Cd 4983, 10.2.1800, p 28.
4. PP III Reports I (259) 417, HoC 3.6.1813; for examples of other extraction rates see HoC Sessional Papers vol 25 Cd 3064, HoC 16.4.1767, Appendix; HoC Sessional Papers vol 131 Cd 4983, HoC 10.2.1800, pp 18, 20, 24, 39, 43; PP III Reports I (259) 417, HoC 3.6.1813 – Shepherd; PP V (186) 1341, HoC 6.6.1815 – Surrey; PP V (472) 1, HoC 10.7.1840 – Hassell.
5. PP VII (517) 1, HoC 25.7.1834, p 34.
6. HoC Sessional Papers vol 25 Cd 3064, 16.4.1767, Appendix; PP IX (345) 227, HoC 22.5.1818 – throughout.
7. HoC Sessional Papers vol 131 Cd 4983, 10.2.1800, p 13 – Loveland; Acton p 82; Rundell (1807) p 363.
8. 53 Geo III c.116 – introduction to tables.
9. HoC Sessional Papers vol 131 Cd 4983 p 41 – Heslop.
10. Hilton: C C C p 27.
11. PP VI (212) 465, HoC 8.4.1824 – Turner.
12. PP VI (212) 465, HoC 8.4.1824 – Swaine; PP 1864 XXVIII [3416] 1, HMSO 1864 CITE.
13. PP III Reports I (259) 417 – Patrick.
14. Edward Smith: Practical Dietary p 33.

Sedentary versus Active Occupations

Although occupational groups can be identified and measured with some accuracy from 1831, classification for earlier periods must depend on the estimates made by contemporaries. And even with census material to hand, it is notoriously difficult to make qualitative judgements about the kind of work undertaken in any category. In particular, the polarization of the occupied population the 'sedentary' and the 'active' is a matter of guesswork (and the problem continues: as Damon and McFarland's anthropometric study of American bus-drivers shows, a literally sedentary job can involve considerable physical exertion[1]). Terminology is also difficult and relative: 'sedentary' might mean 'on the whole, less active work', and 'active': 'on the whole more active work', but judgement as to where the line is drawn must be contentious.

The crudest impression of qualitative occupational changes during the century in review might be gained from a polarization that alleges that the Mitchell & Deane groupings[2] (taking males only) of 'agricultural, horticulture, and forestry', 'mining, quarrying, and workers in products of same', and 'building and construction', represent overall the more active, and others overall the less active, sorts of work; assumes that the proportions of less active workers in the first grouping and of more active workers in the second, balanced out; and that the first category corresponds roughly to Perkin's summary[3] of the King/Colquhoun (family) categories: 'freeholders (2)', 'farmers', 'mines, canals', 'labourers', and 'paupers, cottagers'. If so, the crude trend was as listed in Table A4.1.

Table A4.1   Crude trend of occupational emphasis, 1688–1871

	'Active'	'Sedentary'
King, 1688 (families):	77%	23%
Colquhoun,1803 (families):	46%	54%
Mitchell & Deane, 1841(males):	30%	70%
Mitchell & Deane, 1871(males):	31%	69%

On such a trend, it might be asserted that the 'sedentary' proportion of the occupied population increased to a majority about the turn of the century, and continued to increase. Though the sedentary proportion of occupied males levelled out at about 70 per cent, c1841, perhaps the sedentary total, including occupied females, continued to increase (especially when account is taken of domestic service and, in some respects, housework).

Notes

1. Damon & McFarland, Physique of Bus and Truck Drivers.
2. See Patrick Joyce in F M L Thompson (ed): The Cambridge Social History of Britain, Vol 2, pp 134–5.
3. Perkin pp 20–1.

Qualities of Wheat

Most of the wheat grown in Britain was soft and flavoursome and much of that imported was hard, its greater gluten content giving higher bread yields and better texture. *Ceteris paribus* the ideal flour is 'strong', made from a mixture of both hard and soft grains.[1]

Until the development of special strains in recent years, hardness or softness were imparted by the relative dryness of climate in the country where the wheat was grown. Table 6.10 above lists the gluten content of various foreign wheats, including Polish, North American and Russian. Sicilian grain also was hardish; while in normal to good years, French wheat was judged supreme, since the grain naturally combined hardish properties with softish taste.[2]

Hardness often, though not always, coincided with the 'red' sort of wheat, and softness with the 'white', though the only fixed difference between the sorts was that red wheat produced a somewhat darker flour.[3]

Most North American hard wheat was milled at source and shipped as flour, in barrels of 196 lbs (as a rule, importers broke open the barrels, dug out the compacted flour and rotated it in a cylinder till the clods were broken down; then the flour was repacked in sacks, for sale[4]). Imported American flour, though strongly resisted by some British millers, had keen proponents. The great corn merchant Claude Scott declared it to be 'the finest in the world'; Mrs Rundell (who, unlike Scott, had no personal interest in its sale) recorded that one stone (14 lbs) could produce 21.5 lbs of bread compared to the 18.5 lbs she expected from British flour; generally, though, American was mixed with native flour to achieve an ideal combination of strength and taste: 'they help each other in the working together.'[5]

Though the most remarked of the imports, however, American flour was scarce until the 1830s.[6] Most of the wheat grain, meal, and flour imported into Britain was from Europe, and though much of it was of middling to inferior quality, being harder (usually) it strengthened the native flours, especially if the British harvest had been damp, and the gluten content of the wheat was low.

Notes

1. Acton Chapter IV; HoC Sessional Papers vol 131 Cd 5080, 1.7.1800 – Pratt; PP II (255) 101, HoC 8.7.1820, p 43 – Fothergill.

2. Edward Smith: Foods pp 172, 179; ibid Practical Dietary pp 31–2; David p 45; Hassall p 134 (citing an analysis by Dumas); Acton Chapter VI; PP VII (517) 1, HoC 25.7.1834, Q 4017 – Page.
3. Freeman p 150.
4. Walsh p 276; Orbell: thesis p 9; Dodd p 185; HoC Sessional Papers vol 131 Cd 5080, 1.7.1800, p 19 – Pratt; see also Perren 1990 p 429.
5. eg Kingsford, cit Orbell: thesis pp 9, 11; HoC Sessional Papers vol 131 Cd 4983, 10.2.1800, p 34; Cd 5080, 1.7.1800, p 23 – Pratt; Rundell 1807 p 363.
6. Freeman p 38; Orbell: thesis p 6.

Consumption of Various Groups

CONSUMPTION: 'THE ONE QUARTER ESTIMATE'

1758. Sir Charles Smith, of England and Wales: each person eating 'one quarter of Bread-corn yearly'.[1]

1774. The cities of London and Westminster 'are computed to consist of 600,000 People, and every Person is calculated to consume One Quarter of Wheat in a Year, in Bread'.[2]

1797. Eden, of the labouring poor (men, wives, and children) of England and Wales: 'supposing each individual of them consumes a quarter of wheat in a year . . .'[3]

1800. Lord Hawkesbury of England and Wales: 'a quarter of wheat in the year for each man was the general calculation'.[4]

1800. Arthur Young: put consumption at 'about One Quarter per Head of Population of the Country among those who live upon wheat; and this seems the settled result of all Enquiries on the Subject'.[5]

1812. Western & Colquhoun estimated one quarter of wheat *per capita*.[6]

1846–54. McCulloch estimated consumption in Great Britain by 'adopting the supposed scale of an Annual Consumption of a Quarter of Wheat by each [wheat-eating] person'.[7]

1863. Dr Dauglish put the UK consumption of wheat at 30m Quarters, when the population was 29,245,000.[8]

These contemporary estimates are closely supported by Dr Fairlie's calculations of consumption per head in England and Wales[9] (see Table A6.1).

Table A6.1   Fairlie's estimates of *per capita* consumption

Year	Bushels per head	= %Q
1831	8.32	104
1841	8.72	109
1851	8.08	101
1861	8.16	102
1871	7.60	95
AVERAGE		102

CONSUMPTION: ARMED FORCES

%Q

Assuming a Standard Wheaten quality of bread:

1.1. *c*1765. Royal Hospitals at Chelsea and Greenwich:
allow 7 bushels of wheat a year;[10] assume when converted
into bread: 82
1.2. *c*1765. Army ration of 1.5 lbs of bread daily when
encamped:[11]   122
1.3. 1811. Army ration of 1 lb of bread daily (with 1 lb of
meat:)[12]   81
1.4. 1811. Navy ration of 1 lb of bread daily (as part of a
quite varied diet including meats):[13]   81
1.5. From 1850. Military prisons. 24 oz of bread a day:[14]   122
1.6. 1857. Army ration of 24 oz of bread a day (with 12 oz
of meat and 16 oz potatoes):[15]   122
1. AVERAGE   102

CONSUMPTION: PRISONS

	%Q	
	M	F

Assuming Household bread:

2.1. 1815. Gloucester Gaol. 1.5 lbs of bread per day
(with 1.5 oz oatmeal per day, and meats and potatoes
according to day of week):[16]   113
2.2. Until 1822. Millbank Penitentiary. 20 oz of bread
daily, as part of a varied diet:[17]   94
2.3. 1823. Millbank Penitentiary ('coarse brown
bread'),[18]
1.5 lbs daily for men: 113
18 oz daily for women: 85
2.4. 1843. Prison diets introduced by Sir James
Graham[19] (amount of bread per week):

			M	F
with hard labour:	Class II	168 oz:	113	
	Class III	140 oz	94	
	Class IV	168 oz	113	
	Class V	154 oz	103	
without hard labour:	Class I	112 oz:	75	
	Class II	168 oz:	113	

Class III	140 oz:	94	
Class IV	168 oz:	113	

2.4. AVERAGE   102

2.5. 1843. County Gaols.[20] Daily Bread.

i. Absolute Minimum (for term not exceeding 7 days,
or as punishment diet): 1 lb, both sexes: 76   76
ii. 7–21 days: men 24 oz: 113
            women 18 oz: 85
iii. 21 days to 6 weeks: men 20 oz   94
            women 18 oz: 85
iv. 6 weeks to 4 months: men 24 oz: 113
            women 18 oz: 85
v. 4 months and more: men 22 oz: 103
            women 18 oz: 85

2.5. AVERAGES   100   83

NB: the men's bread rate varied with the amounts of supplementary foods given; apart from minimum rations, the women's diet was unvarying.

2.6. 1857. Selected prisons.[21] Prescribed daily issue of bread.

		M	%Q F
Millbank Penitentiary.	Men 22 oz:	103	
	Women 20 oz:		94
	Punishment (both) 1lb:	76	76
Pentonville. Men 20 oz:		94	
Portland. Men ordinary diet 21.4 oz average:		101	
	Men increased diet 24.4 oz average:	115	
	Three-quarters diet 16.1 oz average:	76	
	Punishment diet 1 lb:	76	
Portsmouth. Men 27oz:		127	
Chatham. Men 27 oz:		127	
Dartmoor. Men 23.6 oz average:		111	
Defence Hulk, Woolwich. Men full diet 27 oz:		127	
Parkhurst, General and Junior Wards.			
	Men and youths 22 oz:	103	
Wakefield. Men 20 oz:		94	
Brixton. Females 20.9 oz average:			98
Fulham Refuge. Female convicts 17.14 oz average:			81
2.6. AVERAGE		102	87
2. OVERALL AVERAGE OF PRISON DIETS		104	85

CONSUMPTION: CHILDREN

| | %Q | |
| | M | F |

Assuming Standard Wheaten bread:

3: Dietaries from Porter.[22] All seem to relate to 1841.

3.1. Asylum with 9 superintendents and servants, and 158 female children, consuming 41,690 lbs of bread per year: — 55

3.2. Asylum with 290 inmates, chiefly children of both sexes, consuming 90,780 lbs of bread per year: —70—

3.3. Asylum with 139 inmates, chiefly young of both sexes, consuming 473 lbs of bread and flour each per year, approx: —105—

3.4. Asylum with 116 inmates, 10 of them adults, and 106 male and female children, consuming 33,488 lbs of bread per year: —64—

3.5. Large public establishment with 646 males, chiefly older boys, consuming 384.5 lbs of bread each per year: 85

3.6. Large establishment with 365 male, and 67 female, children younger than 7, consuming 309 lbs of bread each per year: —69—

The latter case indicates that where bread was the chief article of diet, even children of 6 and under could consume large quantities.

3. The average of Porter's six cases is: —77—

A smaller consumption by children (perhaps as the result of a more generous and various diet) was cited by Dodd:[23]

4. c1855. Foundling Hospital, London.

4.1. Children under 9 – 72 oz bread weekly: —52—

4.2. Children of 9 and older – 92 oz bread weekly: —66—

4. AVERAGE —59—

CONSUMPTION: CLASS AND OCCUPATION

%Q

5. Rural Labourers and their Families

Wherever possible, I have checked that these consumption figures are for wheat bread only, but it may be that in some cases other grains, either solus or mixed, are represented.

5.1. *c*1765: Dr Brackenbridge's estimate, that healthy labourers in the country ate 1 quarter of flour annually,[24] if household quality converted to bread at 3:4, say: 129

5.2. *c*1765: 2 farmers and their households in Essex, consuming 1q 1bu 1.5p of bread each p.a.,[25] if household quality say: 110

5.3. 1787 – Reverend David Davies' survey of six families in his own parish of Barkham, Berkshire[26] (weekly consumption of flour, say household, at 3:4 conversion):

a) family of seven, 7.5 gallons: 111
b) family of seven, 6 gallons: 89
c) family of six, 6 gallons: 104
d) family of five, 3 gallons: 63
e) family of five, 4.6 gallons: 95
f) family of four, 5 gallons: 130
Average of 34 persons: 99

5.4. 1788–94 – Davies' correspondents.[27] The average expenditure on flour per week in Barkham was 4s 6.5d per family. Davies' correspondents collected expenditure details from 20 other wheat-eating places in England: taking all together with Barkham the weekly family expenditure on bread and/or flour averaged 4s 10d per family, which, allowing for variations in price over the six years in which the data was collected, for bread as against flour prices, and for price differences at any time between localities, suggests that the Barkham average consumption per head approximated to the national average, thus for the 21 parishes: 99

5.5. 1794–6 – Eden's survey.

Eden took the 'Quarter standard' as a rule of thumb. The actual consumption of wheat bread by seven cited families of agricultural labourers was (lbs of bread per family per week); say household quality:

a) at Streatley, Berkshire; family of six, 68.5 lbs:[28]   122
b) at Kibworth Beauchamp, Leicestershire; family of seven, 42.0 lbs:[29]   65
c) at Ealing, Middlesex; family of six, 30.4 lbs:[30]   55
d) at Monmouth; family of ten, 49.5 lbs:[31]   54
e) at Roade, Northamptonshire; family of seven, 20.0 lbs: 31
f) at Banbury, Oxfordshire; family of four, 39.1 lbs:[33]   105
g) also at Banbury; family of eight, 78.2 lbs: 105
Average of 48 persons:[34]   77

The discrepancies are particularly large, and may be accounted for in part by the age of those in each family, in part by the timing of the individual enquiry, whether before or during the dearth of 1795–6, in part by the ease of gleaning, especially at Roade, and in part by the availability and use of other foods.

5.6. 1821. Isle of Ely. Labourers' families consuming on average 7 lbs of bread *per capita* per week:[35] if Standard Wheaten: 81

5.7. 1821. Aldburgh, Norfolk. Labourers consumed on average 8 lbs of bread corn per week:[36] if as Standard Wheaten bread: 92

5.8. 1823? – hedger's family: weekly bread allowance amounting to 1 lb 2.25 oz each;[37] if Household quality: 12

5.9. 1824 – Mrs Rundell's estimate of the needs of a cottager's family of 5 persons; 24 lbs of bread and flour weekly, if Standard Wheaten say:[38]   55

5.10. 1833 – Thanet; family of six, consuming about one quartern loaf per day;[39] if Standard Wheaten say: 59

5.11. c1836 – Mr Tufnell in the 2nd Poor Law Report estimated that agricultural labourers and their families ate approximately 400 lbs a year each of solid food, chiefly bread.[40] If bread is allowed at 80% of the whole, or 320 lbs, and as Standard Wheaten, then: 71

5.12. 1836 – Beaconsfield; the most eaten by labourers was 8 lbs of bread weekly;[41] if Standard Wheaten: max 93

5.13. 1839 – widow and four children receiving five 4 lb loaves weekly from the parish;[42] if Standard Wheaten: 46

5.14. c1839 – estimated that a man and wife with three children, two of them above 15, with an income of 30s a week, and living near a country town, consumed 26 lbs of bread weekly;[43] if Standard Wheaten: 60

5.15. 1843 – widow and child employed in agriculture consuming 1.5 gallons of bread weekly (properly 13 lbs of bread, or 6.5 lbs each);[44] if Standard Wheaten: 75

5.16. 1857 – estimated that the typical Yorkshire labourer consumed 40 oz of bread daily. This estimate was made by Letherby, who also estimated that labourers generally consumed the equivalent of 217%Q, a hopeless over-estimate, as Drummond and Wilbraham pointed out.[45] If Household quality: 188

5.17. 1863 – Edward Smith's survey of the diets of farm labourers and their families.[46] Arranged by Collins' regions. Breadstuffs consumed per adult per week; if Household quality:

I
Essex, 11.75 lbs: 127
Hertfordshire, 12.5 lbs: 135
Kent, 12.25 lbs: 133
Middlesex   –
Surrey, 12.25 lbs: 133

I – AVERAGE   132

II
Bedfordshire, 12 lbs: 130
Berkshire, 10.25 lbs: 111
Buckinghamshire, 12.25 lbs: 133
Dorset, 13 lbs: 141
Gloucestershire, 12.5 lbs: 135
Hampshire, 11 lbs: 119
Herefordshire   –
Oxfordshire, 11 lbs: 119
Somerset, 10.5 lbs: 114
Sussex, 12.75 lbs: 138
Wiltshire, 12.5 lbs: 135
Worcestershire, 12lbs: 130

II – AVERAGE   128

III
Norfolk, 12.5 lbs: 135
Suffolk,13 lbs: 141
Cambridgeshire, 14.25 lbs: 154

III –AVERAGE   143

IV
Cornwall, 9.25 lbs: 100
Devon, 12 lbs: 130

IV –AVERAGE   115

V
Cheshire, 11 lbs: 119
Derbyshire, 12.75 lbs: 138
Huntingdonshire, 11.5 lbs: 125
Leicestershire, 12lbs: 130
Lincolnshire, 12.25 lbs: 133
Northamptonshire, 11.5 lbs: 125
Nottinghamshire, 13.25 lbs: 144
Rutland, 11.75 lbs: 127

Shropshire,15.5 lbs: 168
Staffordshire, 11 lbs: 119
Warwickshire, 11.5 lbs: 125

V –AVERAGE   132

VI
Cumberland, 12.75 lbs: 138
Durham, 11.5lbs: 125
Lancashire, 11 lbs: 119
Northumberland, 15.25 lbs: 165
Westmorland, 12.5 lbs: 135
Yorkshire, 12.75 lbs: 138

VI –AVERAGE   137

ENGLAND – AVERAGE, 12.75 lbs: 138

WALES
Anglesey, 18.75 lbs: 203
North Wales, 14.75 lbs: 160
South Wales, 13 lbs: 141

WALES –AVERAGE   168

SCOTLAND, 12.75 lbs: 138

I have difficulty in following Smith's use of the 'two children under 10 = one adult' principle: his calculations do not seem consistent. However, re-expressing the above consumption per 'computed adult' as consumption per actual individual, to give due importance to children, and using Smith's 'family membership' figures as they stand, the actual average *per capita* consumptions are:

ENGLAND: 109

WALES: 131

SCOTLAND: 117

If these national averages are roughly weighted, according to total population, then the aggregate *per capita* consumption for agricultural labourers and their families was:

BRITAIN: 111

6. Urban Labourers, artisans, and their families.
6.1. *c*1765 – Jeweller of London and his household, totalling ten persons, seven of whom were apprentices, consuming

7 half-peck loaves of bread per week;[47] assuming 'Wheaten' sort:

6.2. *c*1765 – Printer of London and his household, totalling six persons, of whom four were apprentices, consuming 6 half-peck loaves of bread per week;[48] again, assume 'Wheaten' sort:

6.3. 1794–6 – Eden's survey. Assume all Standard Wheaten:
a) at Bristol, a labourer; family of four consuming 18 lbs of bread per week:[49]

b) at Portsmouth, a dockyard labourer; family of five consuming 41.2 lbs of bread per week:[50]

c) at Manchester, a dyer; family of two consuming 14.0? lbs of bread per week:[51]

d) at Leicester, a woolcomber; family of four consuming 23.7 lbs of bread per week:[52]

e) at Frome, Somerset, a cooper; family of seven consuming 70.1 lbs of bread per week:[53]

f) at Epsom, Surrey, a gardener; family of ten consuming 56.4 lbs of bread per week:[54]

Average (32 persons):

6.4. 1810 – a London compositor, family of four, consuming five quarterns of bread/flour per week;[55] if Standard Wheaten:

6.5. 1824 – London artisan, family of four, consuming 4s 0d worth of bread per week,[56] in a year when the average full price of 4 lbs of bread in London was 10.5d; if bought from an underseller at 8.5d then = 22.4 lbs:

6.6. 1825 – a miner, family of five, consuming 2.5 stones of bread per week;[57] if Standard Wheaten:

6.7. 1841 – a large trading establishment in the City of London; 114 persons, males and females, all adults, consuming 40,464 lbs of bread p.a.;[58] if Standard Wheaten:

6.8. 1841 – a poor widow of Southwark, with two young children, consuming in all six 4lb loaves a week;[59] if Standard Wheaten:

6.9. 1841 – case cited by Bosanquet, of a London man with a wife and five children; when he earned 30s per week, his family consumed twelve 4 lb loaves weekly;[60] if Standard Wheaten: when he earned 21s per week, his family consumed only five 4 lb loaves;[61] if Standard Wheaten:
Mean:

6.10. 1849–50. London: a woodworker; family of four, consuming 2 lbs of bread daily:[62] if Standard Wheaten:

74

106

52

95

81

68

116

65
81

60

70

81

79

92

79
33
56

41

6.11. 1849–50. London. Consumption of poorer artisans
and their families calculated by Thompson and Yeo: average
of 4 lb per head per week;[63] if Standard Wheaten: 46
6.12. 1849–50. London. A 'sweater' and his household: 4
adults spending 3s 6d weekly on bread:[64] at say 4.5d for
4 lbs of Standard Wheaten, so 10 lbs per head per week: 116
6.13. Nield's survey of 12 families follows
6.14. 1850 – minimum budget per week for a family of four
based on seven 4 lb loaves;[65] if Standard Wheaten: 81
6.15. 1863 – Edward Smith's survey of cotton-trade operatives in Manchester, Ashton-under-Lyne, Wigan, Black-
burn, Stockport, and Preston:[66]; assume all Standard
Wheaten:

IN ORDINARY TIMES (lbs of bread per week):
a) 11 single female workers, each averaging 12.1 lbs: 140
b) family of two aged persons, 14 lbs: 81
c) family of one adult and two children, 28 lbs: 108
d) family of three adults and two children, 37.75 lbs: 87
e) family of three adults and three children, 37.75 lbs: 73
f) family of five adults and one child, 68 lbs: 131
g) family of two adults and five children, 50 lbs: 83
h) family of eight, 58.75 lbs: 85
i) family of two adults and six children, 52.33 lbs: 76
j) family of two adults and six children, 58.75 lbs: 85
k) family of eight, 57.33 lbs: 83
l) family of two adults and seven children, 42 lbs: 54
m) family of nine, 105 lbs: 135
n) family of fourteen, 127.75 lbs: 105
Average of 104 persons: 97

DURING THE TRADE DEPRESSION
o) 6 single male workers, each averaging 10.75 lbs: 124
p) 19 single female workers, each averaging 8.8 lbs: 102
q) 35 families, composed of 228 persons, averaging 6.75 lbs
per head: 78
Average of 253 persons: 81
6.16. 1863 – Edward Smith's survey of indoor workers and
their families:[67] (weekly consumption, assuming all Standard
Wheaten bread):
a) at Spitalfields, Bethnal Green, Coventry, and Maccles-
field, silk weavers and throwsters, and their families; averaging 9.5 lbs per head: 110

b) in London, needle-women and their families; averaging
7.75 lbs per head: 90
c) throughout southern England, kid glove stitchers, and
their families; averaging 8.75 lbs per head: 101
d) in Derbyshire, stocking and glove weavers, and their
families; averaging 11.9 lbs per head: 138
e) at Stafford and Northampton, shoemakers and their
families; averaging 11.25 lbs per head: 130
Mean of 6.16:   114

6.17. A summary by Oddy:[68] of surveys conducted after the
end of the century in review (weekly consumption of bread
per head); if Standard Wheaten:

a) c1887 – Board of Trade, 7.5 lbs: 87
b) c1888 – Booth, 6.5 lbs: 75
c) c1891–4 – Economic Club, 7.0 lbs: 81
d) c1894 – Oliver, 5.5 lbs: 64
e) c1899–1901 – Rowntree, 6.3 lbs: 73
f) c1900 – Paton, Dunlop, and Inglis, 4.7 lbs: 54

Mean of 6.17:   72

7. The Middle and Lower Middle Classes

7.1. Bradford, Wiltshire, c 1796. A clerk; family of seven
consuming 60.0 lbs of bread per week;[69] if Standard
Wheaten: 99
7.2. 1824 – estimates of various middle class diets:[70] (bread
consumed per head per week): where adults only, 6.19 lbs
(assumed 'Wheaten' sort):   76
families with children, 4.6 lbs (also assume 'Wheaten' sort):   56
7.3. 1825 – moderate persons in a frugal family, allow 4 lbs
of ('Standard Wheaten') bread each:[71]   46
7.4. 1825 – family of two, occasionally three, with two
maids and one man servant, taken as 5.5 persons, spending
yearly £18 on bread:[72] when the 'Wheaten' sort cost 2.75d
per lb, so 286 lbs each per annum: 67
7.5. 1840 – private family, residing in a fashionable part of
London: a gentleman and wife, six children, ten servants,
totalling eighteen persons, consuming 5100 lbs of bread:[73]
(assume 'Wheaten') per annum: 66
The same family less one male servant consuming 3,668 lbs
of bread (again assume 'Wheaten') per annum ('either the
discharged servant was a trencherman, or else [there was]
some other, hidden, cause, which shows the danger of
averages':[74])   50

Mean: 58

7.6. 1853 – gentleman of Woburn Place, London; household of eight adult persons, consuming nine 4lb 'Wheaten'
loaves per week:[75]   43

7.7. After the century in review: aggregate by Oddy of six
surveys, conducted between c1887 and 1901;[76] the average
servant-keeping family consumed 5 lbs of bread per head per
week; if Wheaten: 61

8. London – Aggregates:[77]

8.1. 1756 – calculation by Maitland that London's total
wheat consumption, including flour used in puddings, pastries, etc, was 10 oz per head per day;[78] assume 'Wheaten'
sort; extracted at about 60%:   77

8.2. 1851 – estimate by Eliza Acton that the average
Londoner consumed 12.5 oz bread daily;[79] if Standard
Wheaten: 63

BROAD SOCIO-OCCUPATIONAL GROUPS

If Colquhoun's analysis of the society of England and Wales in 1803:[80]
is taken to be roughly representative of wheat-eaters in Britain as a
whole, and is crudely disarticulated, the proportions of the broad
groups I have used would be as listed below.

	Number of families '000
Middle and Lower Middle Classes	
Aristocracy:	27
Middle ranks: freeholders (1), merchants (1) and (2), manufacturers, warehousemen, shipbuilders and ship-owners, surveyors and engineers:	91
Clerks, shopmen:	30
Professions:	85
Tailors, shopkeepers, innkeepers, etc:	150
SUB-TOTAL	383
Urban artisans, labourers, and their families	
Artisans:	446
Seamen and soldiers:	155
Some labourers:	50
Lunatics, debtors, pensioners:	35

SUB-TOTAL	686

Rural labourers and their families

Freeholders (2) and farmers	280
Most labourers:	290
Mines, canals:	40
Paupers, cottagers:	260
Vagrants:	74
SUB-TOTAL	944

Social composition:

Middle and Lower Middle Classes	19.0%
Urban artisans, labourers, and families	34.1%
Rural labourers and families	46.9%

If the Baxter/Perkin macro-estimates for England and Wales in 1867:[81] are similarly arranged in a crude way, with an eye also on the occupations section of the 1871 Census, a corresponding result is:

	Number of families '000
Middle and Lower Middle Classes	
Upper Class	30
Middle Class	90
Lower Middle Class	1456
SUB-TOTAL	1576
Urban artisans, labourers, and families	
Higher skilled	841
Lower skilled	1610
Some unskilled	100
Some wageless	300
SUB-TOTAL	2851
Rural labourers and families	
Some unskilled + agricultural	1417
Some wageless	310
SUB-TOTAL	1727

Social composition:

Middle and Lower Middle Class	25.6%
Urban artisans, labourers and families	46.3%
Rural labourers and families	28.1%

Notes

1. Charles Smith pp 18, 140.
2. HoC Sessional Papers vol 25 Cd 3213, 14.6.1774: Appendix H.
3. Eden p 78.
4. cit Tooke Vol I p 214.
5. HoC Sessional Papers vol 131 Cd 4983, 10.2.1800: Appendix 19 p 37.
6. Orbell: thesis p 11.
7. cit Tooke Vol V p 108.
8. PP XXVIII (6239) 323, HMSO 1863, p 215.
9. Fairlie p 102.
10. Charles Smith, Example 11, p 192.
11. Charles Smith, Example 10, p 192.
12. Drummond & Wilbraham p 408.
13. Drummond & Wilbraham p 408.
14. PP XIV (154.1) 5, HoC 21.3.1857.
15. Letherby, cit Drummond & Wilbraham p 425.
16. Bentham cit Drummond & Wilbraham p 435.
17. Drummond & Wilbraham p 392.
18. Drummond & Wilbraham p 436.
19. Home Secretary's Circular of 21.1.1843, cit Drummond & Wilbraham p 438.
20. PP XIV (154.1) 5, HoC 21.3.1857.
21. PP XIV (154.1) 5, HoC 21.3.1857.
22. Porter pp 583–5.
23. Dodd p 145.
24. ibid, Example 3 p 190.
25. ibid, Example 15 p 193.
26. Davies pp 8–13.
27. ibid, Appendix.
28. Eden p 135.
29. ibid p 226.
30. ibid p 242.
31. ibid p 247.
32. ibid p 261.
33. ibid p 280.
34. ibid p 281.
35. PP IX (668) 1, HoC 18.6.1821, p 133 – Orton.
36. PP IX (668) 1, HoC 18.6.1821, p 41 – Harvey.
37. Cobbett cit Drummond & Wilbraham p 389.
38. Burnett: Plenty & Want p 53.
39. PP V (612) 1; HoC 2.8.1833. Queston 5655.
40. Dodd p 142.
41. PP VIII/I (79) 1; HoC 4.3.1836. Question 1422.
42. Burnett: Plenty & Want p 56.
43. Symons: cit Uselding p 509.
44. PP XII (150) 1843, cit Burnett, Plenty & Want p 31.
45. Drummond & Wilbraham p 425, p 390.
46. PP XXVIII (3416) 1; HMSO 1864. Appendix 6.
47. Charles Smith, Example 14 p 193.
48. ibid.

49. Eden p 191.
50. ibid p 197.
51. ibid p 220.
52. ibid p 228.
53. ibid p 302.
54. ibid p 317.
55. Burnett: Plenty & Want p 51.
56. Family Oracle of Health Vol 1, cit Drummond & Wilbraham p 400.
57. Burnett: Plenty & Want p 52.
58. Porter p 583.
59. *Morning Chronicle* 18.8.1841, cit Longmate p 58.
60. Burnett: Plenty & Want p 55.
61. ibid.
62. Thompson & Yeo p 431.
63. Thompson & Yeo, Appendix II.
64. Thompson & Yeo p 263.
65. cited by Barnsby.
66. PP XXV (161) 1; HoC 14.4.1863. From p 346.
67. PP XXVIII (3416) 1; HMSO 1864. p 237.
68. Oddy p 318.
69. ibid p 344.
70. Family Oracle of Health Vol 1, p 90–92.
71. Dr Kitchiner in Family Oracle of Health Vol 18, January 1825. p 218.
72. ibid p 221.
73. Porter p 583.
74. ibid.
75. Letter in *The Times* 28.10.1853.
76. Oddy p 318.
77. See Chapter 5 Section 6.
78. Charles Smith, Example 2 p 190.
79. Acton p 10.
80. cit Perkin pp 20–1.
81. Perkin p 420.

Population of the London 10-mile Radius Zone

Table A7.1 Basis for calculating the population of the London 10-mile radius zone

Census data:	1801	1811	1821
Total population of all the parishes whose churches are situate within 8 miles rectilinear of St Paul's Cathedral:	1,031,500	1,220,200	1,481,500
ADD			
from Middlesex*:	13,784	15,404	18,800
from Essex**:	4,222	5,834	6,477
from Kent***:	14,727	23,265	23,867
from Surrey****:	16,665	20,574	23,756
TOTAL	1,080,898	1,285,277	1,554,400

* Acton, New Brentford, Ealing with Old Brentford, and Enfield.
** St Mary's Woodford, Chingford, Barking Town, Barking Ripple.
*** Woolwich, Plumstead, East Wickham, West Wickham, Elmsted, Bromley.
**** Croydon, Mitcham, Merton, Wimbledon, Richmond, Kew.

Source: Population: Comparative Account of the Population of Great Britain in the Years 1801, 1811, 1821, and 1831 . . . as required by the Population Act of 1830, HoC 19.10.1831.

Annual populations have been estimated assuming a straight trend between census years.

Marginal Products

Batch bread was, of course, only one of the forms of wheat consumption. An amount of marketed wheat was used for products other than food – and of the categories of wheat food, to batch bread should be added: fancy breads, such as cottage loaves and many regional specialities, some containing milk or sprinkled with seeds (all of which were exempt from assize[1]); morning goods such as rolls, crumpets and muffins; sweet pastries and confections, including gingerbread and cakes; biscuits (largely ships' biscuits) and savoury pastries such as used for pies and puddings.

The other forms in which wheat was eaten may be termed 'marginal products', first because their volume, though substantial, was relatively small compared to batch bread and second, because consumption of them seems to have fluctuated inversely to the prices of wheat and of bread proper. Such a pattern was manifest in the 1920s and 1930s: Stone's research shows that *per capita* bread consumption was highly price inelastic (when real income was held constant), while consumption of other wheat products varied considerably.[2]

Stone's figures for 1924 might roughly represent the average.[3] There is difficulty with flour purchased, when some might have been used to make bread and some for 'marginal' products; but supposing a 50/50 split in the use of flour, then bread represented 72 per cent of the estimated quantity of wheat foods purchased for final consumption in the UK, 'marginal' products, 28 per cent. A 1967 study of wheat usage in the UK[4] gives almost identical results: bread represented 73 per cent of volume, and cakes, biscuits, and 'household' uses, 27 per cent. Both studies, of course, indicate a level of bread consumption much lower than that obtaining during the century in review, so that relative proportions may have been far different. On the other hand, given limited access to meats, fresh vegetables, and dairy products before 1870, arguably the consumption of all farinaceous foods was considerably greater. Also, sweet pastries, for instance, were not necessarily luxuries, but valuable sources of supplementary energy (given their sugar content).

The volume of marginal products *c*1800 and *c*1820 might be very roughly estimated by taking two estimates of London's total wheat and flour consumption and deducting calculated bread consumption as in Table A8.1.

Table A8.1 Rough assessment of marginal volume in London

	Wheat/flour available	Bread consumed	Leaves for marginal products
1800	95%Q	60%Q*	35%Q
1820	91%Q	65%Q**	26%Q

* Average of bakers' returns for 1799–1800 and 1800–01[5].
** Approximate average of recorded diets for the period; see cases 6.4, 6.5, 6.7, and 7.5 in Appendix 6.

Since the consumption figure for 1800 excludes home-made bread, the amount left for marginal products would probably be much closer to the 26%Q given for 1820, and since a fraction might be taken off that amount for non-food uses (starch, etc), a round 25%Q might be the best rough figure for London. But given that the metropolitan density of 'quality' bakers (and pastrycook/confectioners) and catering outlets allowed a great variety of, and easiest access to, all sorts of wheat products, the average may be untypical of the country as a whole. Estimates of wheat output made by Lawes and Gilbert, and Caird, are available for the latter part of the period. If the Lawes and Gilbert estimates are adjusted for Britain, by deducting Irish output, then adding wheat imported into Britain from Ireland and foreign sources (using data tabulated by Dr Fairlie), the result is Table A8.2.

To allow for the 'smoothing' effect of storage, the Lawes and Gilbert figures can be grouped into three 6-year periods. In Table A8.3 these figures are compared to calculations of bread consumption.

This shows bread volume as just below 78 per cent of available wheat on average, leaving 22 per cent as an allowance for marginal products.

Caird's figures for 1862–6, if similarly adjusted and compared, give the results in Table A8.4.

Given an average annual bread consumption of some 17.0 million quarters in this period, consumption accounts for 84.6 per cent of Caird's estimate of wheat availability; that leaves a difference of about 15 per cent for marginal products.

If such estimates, albeit very crude, are added to the estimated average *per capita* consumption of batch bread, taking 79%Q as standard for the century in review, they suggest that the usual 'rule-of-thumb' estimate, of one quarter of wheat per head per year may represent a reasonable 'order of magnitude' of all wheat food consumption justifying its use when assessing the 'wheat-eating equivalent population' in Chapter 7.

Table A8.2   Lawes and Gilbert adjusted for Britain
(thousand quarters)

Year	L&G UK wheat output	Irish wheat output	British wheat net	Retained imports	Irish imported into GB	British total
1853	11,796	875	10,921	6,112	74	17,107
1854	10,662	1,119	9,543	4,371	138	14,052
1855	17,851	1,173	16,678	3,407	171	20,256
1856	14,204	1,270	12,934	5,614	197	18,745
1857	14,484	1,615	12,869	4,305	183	17,357
1858	17,594	1,704	15,890	5,677	164	21,731
1859	16,527	1,424	15,103	5,234	154	20,491
1860	13,315	1,237	12,078	7,780	86	19,944
1861	11,229	833	10,396	8,875	110	19,381
1862	12,486	665	11,821	12,149	81	24,051
1863	14,220	810	13,410	7,531	66	21,007
1864	18,204	847	17,357	6,729	36	24,122
1865	16,527	801	15,726	6,030	–	21,756
1866	14,188	780	13,408	6,853	–	20,261
1867	11,633	705	10,928	9,132	–	20,060
1868	9,696	914	8,782	8,518	–	17,300
1869	17,041	769	16,272	10,371	–	26,643
1870	13,668	732	12,936	8,611	–	21,547

Calculated from Fairlie: 1969, pp 114-5.

Table A8.3   Availability and consumption comparison

Period	L&G adjusted averages m qrs	Bread volume average m qrs	Bread volume as % of wheat available
1853–58	18.2	15.1	83.0%
1859–64	21.6	17.1	79.2%
1865–70	21.3	15.3	71.8%
Average	20.3	15.8	77.8%

Table A8.4 Caird's figures, adjusted for Britain (thousand quarters)

Year	Caird total UK supply	Irish wheat output	Part GB supply	Irish imported into GB	Total GB supply
1862	20,905	665	20,240	81	20,231
1863	23,027	810	22,217	66	22,283
1864	21,029	847	20,182	36	20,218
1865	20,250	801	19,449	–	19,449
1866	18,983	780	18,203	–	18,203
AVERAGE					20,095

Calculated from Caird: Our Daily Food, p 18.

Notes

1. For a selection see David pp 197–205.
2. Stone (ed), pp 18–20.
3. Stone (ed), Table 2.
4. E M Greer cit Britton et al, p 439.
5. See Chapter 5 Section 6.

Illustration of the 'Transfer Effect'

The 'transfer effect' cannot be demonstrated exactly, since suitable data do not exist, but the principle can be sketched. Take, for example, estimated W in 1790 – crudely, 5.9m 'wheat-eaters', and the supposition that perhaps one-third or so of them were wheat growers and their families, supplied on or near the farm without reference to the market – say 2.0m so fed. If the net yield of the harvest of that year was 'normal' – that is, exactly equal to demand, then the amount 'freed' to the market would be the equivalent of 3.9m 'wheat diets'. But if there was a glut – say 25 per cent above norm, then a total of about 7.4m 'wheat diets' could be supplied; deduct the 2.0m 'farm supplied' consumers, and 5.4m 'wheat diets' would be available for sale. Whereas, if there was a dearth – say 25 per cent below norm, then a total of some 4.4m 'wheat diets' could be supplied: deduct the 2.0m 'farm supplied' consumers, and only 2.4m 'wheat diets' would be available to the market. In those circumstances, the spread between a glut and a dearth, as felt by the market, being between 5.4m and 2.4m, would be × 2.25. This would be moderated, of course, to the extent that exports of surpluses or imports in years of deficiency, affected the supply; also, there may have been some extra consumption, or reduction in diet, on the farm, though perhaps not too much, given storage on the one hand, and on the other, the operation of the rural Poor Law.

Then take, say, 1842, when W was 14m or so. By then the farming community was smaller in proportion to the total population, many farm workers were supplied in the ordinary way by the market, and indeed may have eaten, but not grown, wheat. Suppose the number of 'farm supplied' consumers was, at most, still no more than 2m. Therefore, if the net yield was normal, 12m 'wheat diets' would have been available to the market. If there was a glut, at 25 per cent above norm, then 15.5m 'wheat diets' could be sold, and if a dearth: 8.5m. Thus the spread now, between 15.5m and 8.5m would be × 1.82, a spread more readily moderated by the integrated market. But leaving moderators out of account, the fundamental difference is between a spread of × 2.25 for 1790, and of × 1.82: a proportionate narrowing of 19 per cent; if the principles of the Bouniatian formula[1] are applied, the price spread would have been narrower still (though the effect cannot be properly calculated, since that formula subsumes 'farm supplied' diets).

Note

1. See Wrigley: P C W Ch 5.

Wheat Prices and the End-price Indicator

The series of annual average wheat prices, compiled officially from 1771[1], is not in itself a reliable surrogate for the price of bread, but it is an indispensible beginning. Whatever defects, at various places and times, may mar the perfection of the data, the information is broadly national, with spans averaged; and it does indicate commercial trends, given that merchants, millers, and bakers, even if they had bought their own supplies of wheat at different prices, were strongly influenced by the spot market when selling. As the wheat market became ever more integrated, the average spot price not only recorded, but dictated, near uniformity.

However, as extant sources long have indicated, and as Taylor, for instance, has observed[2], wheat and bread prices did deviate from year to year and on trend. One generally evident cause is the effect of the bakers' mark-up. Both assized and unassized bakers (unlike commercial millers) preferred, wherever and whenever they could, to add a fixed-sum mark-up to the price of flour, rather than apply a constant percentage. Therefore, when wheat was cheap, the bakers' mark-up would be proportionately large, and when wheat was dear, it would be proportionately small. The following illustration shows the principle.

First I have assumed that the millers' margin was offset by the sale value of bran and pollard (which was the frequent, and often generous, case) so that the cost of grinding and dressing can be subsumed in the price of the wheat itself. Second, I have added known bakers' mark-ups from an assized jurisdiction (using the allowances for Standard Wheaten bread at Oxford 1771–1835), assuming that the last allowance was then sustained, after abolition, by the bakers' collective (a deduction from Thwaites[3]). These mark-ups have then been added to the prevailing national average annual wheat price for each year, to indicate the end-price value (V) of an Imperial quarter of wheat. V has then been divided by the wheat price, to show the changing relationship.

This illustration gives an average relationship of V to wheat of 124 per cent (or mark-up of 24 per cent), but that aggregates a span from 110 per cent when wheat was exceptionally dear (1801) to 137 per cent when wheat was exceptionally cheap (1822, 1851). The complicating

Table A10.1 End-price indicator (*V* related to the national average annual price of wheat)

Year	Wheat d per qr	Allowance d per qr	Total d per qr	Total/Wheat Relationship
1771	583	120	703	121
1772	627	120	747	119
1773	631	120	751	119
1774	651	120	771	118
1775	598	120	718	120
1776	472	120	592	125
1777	563	144	707	126
1778	519	144	663	128
1779	416	144	560	135
1780	441	144	585	133
1781	552	144	696	126
1782	591	144	735	124
1783	651	144	795	122
1784	604	144	748	124
1785	517	144	661	128
1786	480	144	624	130
1787	509	144	653	128
1788	556	144	700	126
1789	633	144	777	123
1790	657	144	801	122
1791	583	144	727	125
1792	516	144	660	128
1793	591	144	735	124
1794	627	144	771	123
1795	902	144	1046	116
1796	943	144	1087	115
1797	645	144	789	122
1798	622	144	766	123
1799	828	144	972	117
1800	1366	144	1510	111
1801	1434	144	1578	110
1802	838	144	982	117
1803	706	144	850	120
1804	747	144	891	119

Table A10.1 continued

Year	Wheat d per qr	Allowance d per qr	Total d per qr	Total/Wheat Relationship
1805	1077	168	1245	116
1806	949	168	1117	118
1807	904	168	1072	119
1808	976	168	1144	117
1809	1168	168	1336	114
1810	1277	168	1445	113
1811	1143	168	1311	115
1812	1518	168	1686	111
1813	1317	168	1485	113
1814	892	200	1092	122
1815	787	200	987	125
1816	942	200	1142	121
1817	1163	200	1363	117
1818	1035	200	1235	119
1819	894	200	1094	122
1820	814	200	1014	125
1821	673	200	873	130
1822	535	200	735	137
1823	640	200	840	131
1824	767	200	967	126
1825	822	170	992	121
1826	704	170	874	124
1827	702	170	872	124
1828	725	170	895	123
1829	795	170	965	121
1830	771	170	941	122
1831	796	170	966	121
1832	704	170	874	124
1833	635	170	805	127
1834	554	170	724	131
1835	472	170	642	136
1836	582	170	752	129
1837	670	170	840	125
1838	775	170	945	122
1839	848	170	1018	120
1840	796	170	966	121

Table A10.1 concluded

Year	Wheat d per qr	Allowance d per qr	Total d per qr	Total/Wheat Relationship
1841	772	170	942	122
1842	687	170	857	125
1843	601	170	771	128
1844	615	170	785	128
1845	610	170	780	128
1846	656	170	826	126
1847	837	170	1007	120
1848	606	170	776	128
1849	531	170	701	132
1850	483	170	653	135
1851	462	170	632	137
1852	489	170	659	135
1853	639	170	809	127
1854	869	170	1039	120
1855	896	170	1066	119
1856	830	170	1000	120
1857	676	170	846	125
1858	530	170	700	132
1859	525	170	695	132
1860	639	170	809	127
1861	664	170	834	126
1862	665	170	835	126
1863	537	170	707	132
1864	482	170	652	135
1865	502	170	672	134
1866	599	170	769	128
1867	773	170	943	122
1868	765	170	935	122
1869	578	170	748	129
1870	563	170	733	130

effects of wartime inflation are partly compensated for by changes in the allowance. That Oxford wheat prices may have varied from the national average is inconsequential to this illustration, which serves only to indicate the effect of mark-up on any wheat price base.

The illustration suggests the rough indicators of end-price relationships shown in Table A10.2.

Table A10.2   Indicator Guide

| When wheat was: | The end-price relationship was: | | |
	Low	High	Mean
500d or less	125	137	133
501–600d	120	137	128
601–700d	119	131	125
701–800d	119	126	122
801–900d	117	125	120
901–1000d	115	121	118
1001–1100d	116	119	118
1101–1200d	114	117	115
1201–1300d	113	113	113
1301–1400d	111	113	112
1401d or more	110	111	110/111

Of course, since these indicators are worked out from the Oxford allowances, somewhat different results would be obtained by using allowances from elsewhere. But the principle, of the end-price declining in relation to rising wheat prices, is common. So the above indicators, together with the national average annual wheat price, can be used as a guide to the sort of end-price to be expected in most parts of the country in any year, with significant deviations calling for some explanation.

Notes

1. Mitchell pp 756–7.
2. Taylor: S O L p xxxix.
3. Thwaites: Assize pp 174, 178.

Sources of Data on Bread Prices

Here I discuss the sources which I have used. The bread price data is considered in three parts. Firstly, relatively well-known published sources; then some special studies undertaken by Gourvish, Neale, and Richardson; and finally primary material.

Bread prices: published records

1. The London series

The best known series of bread prices (used by Silberling and Clapham, for example) is that for London, which was officially compiled in 1903 and republished in 1904.[1] It is included in Mitchell.[2]
Some features of the London series are:
a – it shows the price of bread of best quality
b – it is an amalgam of sources
c – there is a gap: the annual average for 1815 is for the first ten weeks only and there are no figures for 1816, 1817, 1818, or 1819.

To March 1815 the original source is the official record of the assized price of Wheaten bread set for the London 'conurbation' (by virtue of 31 George II c.29, and subsequent acts). These official prices end with the abolition of the Assize of Bread in London. After a gap the series resumes in 1820 using the following sources:

for:	source:
1820	Haydn's Dictionary of Dates
1821–8	PP LIV (1159) 1850: Tables of Population, etc
1849–	Haydn's Dictionary of Dates

The bread prices given in *Haydn's Dictionary of Dates* are unattributed, but my efforts to cross-check them suggest they are quite reliable, whereas the prices given in PP LIV (1159) 1850 cite a price for the month of June only in each year and so may or may not reasonably represent the whole-year price. In both cases it is apparent that the prices cited are for the best quality of Wheaten bread.

The 1903 Report also included series of the contract prices paid for bread by the Royal Hospital, Greenwich (1818–68) and the Bethlem Royal Hospital, London (1834–), which are helpful as guides but of their nature do not necessarily reflect the market. Also, there are retail prices for the months of July to November in a number of years after 1839, paid by the Grey Coat Hospital at Westminster (which prices were discounted on the bill); and two series for 1858–, one of which was compiled from the bread bills and authenticated statements of certain householders, and the other from prices paid by one of the London clubs: both are helpful in confirming that the main series shows the best quality price, but are too particular for general reliability. None of these further sources was integrated into the main series.

2. Edinburgh/Leith

The 1903 Report also included a series of bread prices compiled by Messrs A & R Todd Ltd of Leith and published in the *Year Book of Scottish Bakers*. The series is in two parts. For 1824–56, it shows the means of the highest quarterly prices only. For 1857–, the means of highest and lowest quarterly prices for best bread, and the mean of both, are given. So, although the Edinburgh series is a useful guide, the prices up to 1856 do not, and for 1857 onwards may not, accurately reflect the weighted average price for each year. A further difficulty, noted by the compilers, is that over the whole period, there was in Edinburgh and Leith (as elsewhere) a change from the old quartern loaf (4 lb 5.5 oz) to the 4 lb loaf, but when that change took place is unclear.

3. Other Official Reports

a) Armed Forces 1793–1800: a series of annual average prices for bread purchased in Great Britain for His Majesty's Service.[3] The prices are given by the hundredweight, and indicate that, contrary to what one might expect, the Crown was paying well over the London best bread price.

b) Birmingham Union bread prices, August 1797–February 1800:[4] the actual prices charged for what, from Loveland's evidence appears to have been, a loaf of household quality, by a leading co-operative.

c) Lewes, May 1812–June 1815: the actual prices charged by a self-regulating bakers' collective.[5]

d) Thorpe (Essex), January 1809–October 1812: the actual prices charged by a rural baker influenced by the London market.[6]

e) Bristol, January 1834–February 1836: the actual prices charged by the self-regulating bakers of Bristol.[7]

Bread prices: special studies

a) Glasgow, 1788–1815: the annual average prices charged by Glasgow's bakers, till 1801 under assize, and by self-regulation thereafter, as calculated by Gourvish from the incorporation's record book (which also has prices from 1816 to 1834, summarized by Gourvish in five-yearly averages).[8] As Gourvish found, bread in Glasgow was dearer than in London until 1805: thereafter prices were very close until 1815, after when the Glasgow prices appear cheaper. He suggests that economical substitutes such as oatmeal may have put pressure on the Glasgow bread price from 1805, and that the intranational wheat market was becoming ever more fluent, but notes the difficulties of comparison, especially after 1815, when the London prices do not reflect underselling.

A probable influence was the effect of different mark-ups operating at different times in the two cities.

b) Bath, 1812–1844: annual average prices for best wheat bread, compiled by R S Neale from the *Bath & Cheltenham Gazette* (in his earlier thesis, Neale also gave some prices for wartime, derived from the Poor and Highway Rate Books of Walcot Parish[9]); these are then indexed to the 1838 average of 9.5d per quartern.[10] I have re-expressed the index to show the price of 4 lb of bread in each year.

Neale observes that there is

> some reason to suppose the cheaper brown household loaf was held to be greatly inferior to white bread and that all classes considered it better value to pay an extra 1d or 2d for a quartern of white bread rather than save on an inferior brown bread. In addition, all bread prices moved in the same direction while remaining in a constant relationship with each other. In Bath the difference between the wheaten and standard loaf was always 1d on a quartern. The difference between the wheaten and the household loaf was always 2d.[11]

c) Richardson's Counties. As part of his research into the standard of living of agricultural labourers, T L Richardson has compiled bread price series for six English counties:[12]

Kent, 1790–1840: derived from the Assize of Bread records of Faversham and Queenborough for 1790-1834, and contract prices paid by the Poor Law Unions of Malling, Elham, and West Ashford for 1834–40.

Essex, 1790–1840: series using, for 1790–1834, the provisions accounts of nine parish workhouses (Chigwell, Halstead, Hatfield Broad Oak, Chelmsford, Cranham, Stisted, Braintree, Rivenhall, and St Botolph Colchester) and for 1835-40 the accounts of six Poor Law Unions (Tendring, Billericay, Chelmsford, Dunmow, Braintree, and Saffron Walden).

Lincolnshire, 1793–1802, 1806–33, and 1838–40: uses, for 1793–1812, the provisions accounts of various households and tradespeople, and for 1813–40 the *Stamford Mercury* reports of prices prevailing in the markets of Horncastle, New Bolingbroke, Boston, and Grantham.

Nottinghamshire, 1790, 1793–1802, 1806–33, and 1838–40: uses, for 1790–1827, the household provisions accounts of several families, and for 1836–40 the quarterly contract prices paid by the Poor Law Unions of East Retford, Basford, and Bingham. For other years Richardson has used Lincolnshire prices.

Dorset, 1790–1834: uses, for 1790–1834, the monthly contract prices paid by six parish workshouses (Beaminster, Blandford Forum, Puddletown, Haselbury, Buckland Newton, and Sturminster Newton) and for 1835–40 the quarterly contract prices paid by five Poor Law Unions (Beaminster, Poole, Wareham, Purbeck, Cerne, and Sherborne).

Hampshire, 1790–1840: derived from *The Hampshire Chronicle* reports of bread prices at Winchester, Basingstoke, Petersfield, Newbury (Berks) and Chichester (Sussex).

Richardson's study has exceptional breadth, but because his sources are variously retail and contract, and it is not necessarily clear which type of bread was being used where and when, I have thought it safer to aggregate all six of his counties, and to assume Standard Wheaten bread throughout.

Price information: further sources

The following bread price information has been calculated from primary sources:

1. *London 1829–31, 1839–52*

For simplicity I shall call the extant London series, discussed above, London A, and this series London B. London B is derived from the reports of metropolitan bread prices carried by *The Buckinghamshire Gazette* (which in October 1849 was absorbed into *The Buckinghamshire Chronicle*)[13] presumably for the convenience of the millers and bakers around Aylesbury. For 1829-31, prices are those charged by the full-priced bakers; for 1839-52 they are the mean of ranges of prices charged for Wheaten bread. To 1848, London B can be compared to the less representative '1850 Report' figures that were incorporated in the London A series, to show significant discrepancies in 1842, 1845, and 1847 especially. The 1849–52 figures, compared to the 'Haydn' prices for those years, correspond closely, and give confidence that Haydn was broadly representative to 1870. The two series are compared in Table A11.1.

Table A11.1 London Bread Prices, 1829–52

Year	London A	London B
1829	10.5	10.7
1830	10.5	10.2
1831	10.0	10.5
1839	10.0	10.1
1840	10.0	9.5
1841	9.0	9.4
1842	9.5	8.6
1843	7.5	7.8
1844	8.5	8.4
1845	7.5	8.8
1846	8.5	8.9
1847	11.5	9.9
1848	7.5	7.8
1849	7.0	7.2
1850	6.75	6.8
1851	6.75	6.7
1852	6.75	6.7

2. Oxford 1770–1835

The records of the Assize of Bread for the City of Oxford are complete from 1733 to abolition during 1836;[14] aspects of this assize have been researched and discussed by Thwaites.[15] The assize was set frequently, especially in the early 19th century, when the slightest change in the local wheat price would prompt a minute alteration in the price of bread.

The two clerks of the market, both of whom were MAs, one appointed by the Chancellor and one by the Vice-Chancellor, made the returns, and the assize was set by the Vice-Chancellor.[16] Until 1790 the Oxford assize went by the second-highest wheat price, though the authorities used considerable discretion; it was set by flour on two exceptional occasions in 1801, but otherwise by the average of all wheat sales.[17] The bakers' allowances have been detailed above.[18]

Wheaten bread was sold at Oxford between 1769 and 1774, then Standard Wheaten bread was the best quality permitted. An assize was set for household loaves throughout the period, but prices suggest that the bread quality varied considerably, and so the household series is less reliable.

Until 1813, the local rule was that six bushels of wheat should produce a Sack of flour and therefore 20 peck (or 80 quartern) loaves,[19] a calculation that, for Standard Wheaten bread, squeezed the bakers;[20] the parliamentary allowance, applied from 1813, rectified that anomaly, and it seems that the Oxford trade then prospered. In 1815 there were 23 bakers in the city and its immediate neighbourhood; in 1824 there were 40, and since the clerks were meticulous in their market inspections, respectable bakers could flourish.[21]

3.　Wallingford (Berks) 1801–3, 1808–11

An assize was set regularly at Wallingford, but discontinued at some time before 1835. The surviving records[22] give prices for what was described as 'household' bread, but this almost certainly corresponded to the Standard Wheaten type. The bakers' allowance varied per assize: in the earlier period from 1s 3d to 1s 11.25d per bushel, averaging about 1s 6d.

4.　Aylesbury 1833–6

This short series is derived from weekly reports in The Buckinghamshire Gazette.[23] At some point in this period, the Aylesbury loaf was changed from the old quartern size to 4 lb, but since the term 'quartern' remained in colloquial use, it is difficult to pinpoint the exact moment of change.

5.　Dorchester (Dorset) 1770–82

Dorchester opted to continue the assize in 1758 (by the vote of a public meeting) and an assize book was opened, in which were recorded the three highest prevailing prices of wheat, and the costs of Wheaten and Household flour. Initial zeal evaporated, so that by 1768 only two wheat prices were given, quoted by the load.[24]

Until the summer of 1778 all bread was sold by price-specie, thereafter larger loaves were sold by weight (only the price of a peck was recorded). There is a gap in the record from the end of 1782 to April 1796, and thereafter the assize was set only in months of dearth (no run being long enough for calendar year weighting). The book ends at January 1801. The bakers' allowance varied from assize to assize.

6.   Chichester 1797–1800

The Chichester assize was set by flour. Records survive for the full years 1797–1800.[25] Until September 1796 all loaves were price-specie, then larger loaves were sold by weight. Also in 1796 the assize of Household bread was discontinued: only Wheaten bread was assized thereafter.

7. Rye 1814–30

In the later 18th century records of the Rye assize were made, *inter alia*, in the General Quarter Sessions book:[26] the authorities went by the price of a load of wheat, and allowed 1s 6d per bushel to the bakers. From 15 February 1800, for three months at least, Wheaten bread was prohibited and Standard Wheaten was the best quality permitted. Discontinuities make these records unreliable for weighted year calculations.

From 29 September 1813 to 18 December 1834 the Rye assizes were recorded on printed forms, completed in manuscript, and bound into a proper bread book.[27] Till 1821 the mayor and *jurati* usually went by wheat, thereafter (and briefly in 1817) by flour. All loaves were price-specie to November 1830, after this date larger loaves were sold by weight. From 1813 to 1824 only Wheaten prices are given; thereafter Wheaten and Household. After 1830 assizes were set in December only, and so may not reflect the true prices prevailing during most of each year: presumably, the authorities wished to flex an ancient right for demonstrative rather than practical purposes.

8.   Worcester 1780–86, 1791, 1802–7, 1818–27

Records from September 1779 to June 1818 are found *inter alia* in the Worcester Wheat Books[28] (apparently these were draft calculations, from which fair copies were then made). Though weight-specie larger loaves were introduced in 1782, Worcester reverted to price-specie from

September 1790 to December 1801, and again briefly in 1807. The only type recorded is Standard Wheaten. The baker's allowance was 1s 0d per bushel of wheat until c1801, then it was 1s 6d, though no compensation was allowed for the salt tax.[29] By 1813 the bakers, making a profit of only 2s or 3s a Sack, were hard-pressed: numbers of them failed, and only 14 or 15 were left, averaging 8-10 Sacks weekly each.[30] Apparently, the assize still operated in 1835.[31]

Notes

1. PP LXVIII (321) 1, HoC 6.8.1903; LXXIX (2145) 495, HMSO 1904.
2. Mitchell pp 769–70.
3. HoC Sessional Papers vol 131 Cd 5101, 18.11.1800 – Appendix G.
4. HoC Sessional Papers vol 131 Cd 5056, Privy Council 4.3.1800 – Clifford p 7.
5. PP V (186) 1341, HoC 6.6.1815 – Appendix.
6. PP III/I (259) 417, HoC 3.6.1813 – Patrick.
7. PP VIII/I (189) 225, HoC 15.4.1836 – Qu 5000.
8. Gourvish: Note.
9. R S Neale: Economic Conditions Bristol University M A Dissertation.
10. Neale: Standard of Living.
11. Neale p 166.
12. Richardson: thesis.
13. Microfilm, Aylesbury Reference Library.
14. Oxford University Archives MR 3/5/1 – MR 3/5/6, also UA NEP supra 13; Bodleian MSS Top Oxon d68–70.
15. Thwaites: thesis; Assize; Dearth.
16. PP III/I (82) 401, HoC 12.3.1813 – Stacey.
17. Oxford University Archives MR 3/5/3; Thwaites: Assize p 173.
18. See Appendix 10.
19. Oxford University Archives MR 3/5/5.
20. PP III/I (82) 401, HoC 12.3.1813 – Stacey.
21. PP VI (212) 465, HoC 8.4.1824 – Bayne; Bodleian MS Top Oxon f2 – Clerks of the Market Notebook of Weights and Bread etc.
22. Berks RO: W/RM 1–2.
23. Microfilm: Aylesbury Reference Library.
24. Dorset RO: B2/25/1.
25. West Sussex RO: Chichester G1.
26. East Sussex RO: Rye MS 2/9.
27. East Sussex RO: Rye 5, vols 1–4.
28. Worcs RO: Shelf B.10 – 7 volumes.
29. PP III/I (82) 401, HoC 12.3.1813 – Everet.
30. ibid.
31. PP XXXVII (128) 601, HoC 3.4.1835.

Calculation of Bread Value: 1771–1870

The following provides further information on the calculation of the value of wheat bread described in Chapter 8. The bread value of an Imperial quarter of wheat is referred to as V and the value figures in the British Bread Table[1] are national averages for V. The sources for price data were discussed in Appendix 11: here the actual data are laid out in some detail. The estimates of V are arrived at by multiplying the price of bread by the standard bread yield[2] of a quarter of wheat. For instance, if Wheaten bread in London in 1771 was priced at 6.5d per 4 lbs, and each quarter of wheat typically yielded 426 lbs of bread, then V for London in 1771 must be 6.5 × 426/4, ie 692d.

To arrive at the national average estimates for V listed in the British Bread Table, I have calculated estimates of V in a number of places and attempted to assess the reliability of each, and to allow for the size of the market covered. The assessment is carried out on a decade by decade basis.

Calculation of Bread Value: 1771–80

Table A12.1   Data on bread value, 1771–80

LONDON A. Wheaten.		
Year	Price (d per 4 lb)	V @ 426/4
1771	6.5	692
1772	7.3	777
1773	7.3	777
1774	7.0	746
1775	6.9	735
1776	5.8	618
1777	6.6	703
1778	6.5	692
1779	5.5	586
1780	5.7	607

Table A12.1 concluded

OXFORD. Standard Wheaten.

Year	Price (d per 4 lb)	V @ 449/4
1774*	6.9	775
1775	6.8	764
1776	5.1	573
1777	5.1	573
1778	5.7	640
1779	5.5	618
1780	5.5	618

* 33 weeks only

DORCHESTER. Wheaten.

Year	Price (d per 4 lb)	V @ 426/4
1771	6.1	650
1772	6.1	650
1773	7.2	767
1774	7.7	820
1775	7.8	831
1776	5.8	618
1777	5.8	618
1778	6.5	692
1779	6.3	671
1780	6.3	671

WORCESTER. Standard Wheaten.

Year	Price (d per 4 lb)	V @ 449/4
1780	4.9	550

Assessment

While, taking the decadal averages, the wheat/bread relationships at London, Oxford, and Dorchester were remarkably close, the annual variances in and between each place were wider than the national wheat indicator would suggest. This might be accounted for by:

a) continuing variations in the price of wheat from place to place, before the national market reached full integration. London was more stable, naturally so, since its prices aggregated wheat from many sources, and therefore the London V should be quite representative of the country as a whole.

b) year-end effects (for example at Dorchester in 1777–80) probably give unrepresentatively high and low figures.

c) baker allowances, which varied as at Dorchester, probably exaggerate swings.

I have decided to take London as representative of the mark-ups in every year except 1774 and 1775, when its prices seem to understate the provincial case, as represented by Oxford and Dorchester, and so might be raised slightly.

Table A12.2   National Estimate of V, 1771–80

Year	V
1771	692
1772	777
1773	777
1774	781
1775	765
1776	618
1777	703
1778	692
1779	586
1780	607

Calculation of Bread Value: 1781–90

Table A12.3   Data on bread value, 1781–90

LONDON A. Wheaten.

Year	Price (d per 4 lb)	V @ 426/4
1781	7.0	746
1782	7.0	746
1783	7.0	746
1784	6.9	735
1785	6.1	650
1786	5.5	586
1787	5.7	607
1788	6.4	682
1789	6.0	639
1790	7.0	746

Table A12.3 concluded

OXFORD. Standard Wheaten.

Year	Price (d per 4lb)	V @ 449/4
1781	6.7	752
1782	7.0	786
1783	7.4	831
1784	7.1	797
1785	6.0	674
1786	5.6	629
1787	5.4	606
1788	6.4	719
1789	6.9	775
1790	7.3	820

DORCHESTER. Wheaten.

Year	Price (d per 4 lb)	V @ 426/4
1781	7.5	799
1782	7.6	809

WORCESTER. Standard Wheaten

Year	Price (d per 4 lb)	V @ 449/4
1781	5.9	663
1782	6.8	764
1783	7.3	820
1784	6.7	752
1785	5.9	663
1786	5.4	606

GLASGOW. Wheaten.

Year	Price (d per 4 lb)	V @ 426/4
1788	7.6	809
1789	7.1	756
1790	8.3	884

RICHARDSON'S COUNTIES. Standard Wheaten.

Year	Kent	Essex	Notts	Dorset	Hants	Mean	V @ 449/4
1790	6.2	6.4	7.4	7.4	6.2	6.7	752

Assessment

In the 1780s the bread/wheat relationship in London declined on trend, the well-attested effect of improvements in milling, and especially, of competition from the Albion Mills. London, therefore, is less representative of the country as a whole, where in places (such as Glasgow) the bread/wheat relationship was considerably higher. Probably the Oxford series best represents the country during this decade.

Table A12.4   National Estimate of *V*, 1781–90

Year	V
1781	752
1782	786
1783	831
1784	797
1785	674
1786	629
1787	606
1788	719
1789	775
1790	820

Calculation of Bread Value: 1791–1800

Table A12.5   Data on Bread Value, 1791–1800

LONDON A. Wheaten.

Year	Price (d per 4 lb)	V @ 426/4
1791	6.3	671
1792	5.9	628
1793	6.8	724
1794	7.0	746
1795	9.6	1022
1796	9.7	1033
1797	7.6	809
1798	7.7	820
1799	9.6	1022
1800	15.3	1629

Table A12.5 continued

OXFORD. Standard Wheaten.

Year	Price (d per 4 lb)	V @ 449/4
1791	6.7	752
1792	6.2	696
1793	6.6	741
1794	6.9	775
1795	8.7	977
1796	–	–
1797	8.4	943
1798	8.2	921
1799	10.0	1123
1800	14.8	1662

ARMED FORCES. Wheaten.

Year	Price per cwt	Price per lbd	V @ 426
1793	20s 4d	2.18	929
1794	20s 9d	2.22	946
1795	27s 2d	2.91	1240
1796	31s 10d	3.41	1453
1797	20s 11d	2.24	954
1798	21s 0d	2.25	959
1799	23s 11d	2.56	1091
1800	44s 4d	4.75	2024

BIRMINGHAM UNION. Household.

Year	Price (d per 4 lb)	V @ 484/4
1798	5.7	690
1799	7.0	847

GLASGOW. Wheaten.

Year	Price (d per 4 lb)	V @ 426/4
1791	7.8	831
1792	7.6	809
1793	7.6	809
1794	8.3	884
1795	9.0	959
1796	9.4	1001
1797	8.7	927
1798	8.5	905

Table A12.5 concluded

Year	Price (d per 4 lb)	V @ 426/4
1799	8.1	863
1800	17.7	1885

RICHARDSON'S COUNTIES. Standard Wheaten.

Year	Kent	Essex	Lincs	Notts	Dorset	Hants	Mean	V
1791	5.5	5.5	–	–	7.4	5.5	6.0	674
1792	5.8	5.5	–	–	7.4	5.8	6.1	685
1793	5.8	6.4	8.1	8.1	7.4	5.8	6.9	775
1794	6.9	6.9	8.1	8.1	7.4	6.9	7.4	831
1795	10.1	10.1	11.0	11.0	9.7	11.5	10.6	1190
1796	9.2	9.2	11.0	10.0	8.7	7.4	9.3	1044
1797	7.4	7.4	8.1	8.3	8.5	7.4	7.9	887
1798	6.7	6.7	8.1	8.3	7.4	6.7	7.3	820
1799	11.5	11.5	11.0	9.7	9.7	11.5	10.8	1213
1800	14.5	14.3	15.9	13.8	14.5	14.5	14.6	1640

CHICHESTER. Wheaten

Year	Price (d per 4lb)	V @ 426/4
1797	7.0	746
1798	6.9	735
1799	8.6	916
1800	14.0	1491

WORCESTER. Standard Wheaten.

Year	Price (d per 4 lb)	V @ 449/4
1791	6.6	741

Assessment

The data well reflects the price turbulence of the 1790s, which would exaggerate the 'staggering' effect at year ends (as suggested by the Glasgow series). It shows too the wide variety in bread value, from cheap Birmingham (an example seized upon by Lord Hawkesbury) to the high prices paid by the Crown. The London series shows, in the early years of the decade, the continuing effect of the Albion Mills on flour prices, and then the effect of the Voluntary Agreement (and to some extent of the City Act) on bakers' profits; thus London continued to be unrepresentatively low-priced compared to the country as a whole.

The Richardson series, based on price information from six counties, would seem far more representative, except for 1791 (too low) and 1799 (too high); in these years, the Oxford figures appear to be a better choice.

Table A12.6 National estimate of V, 1791–1800

Year	V
1791	752
1792	685
1793	775
1794	831
1795	1190
1796	1044
1797	887
1798	820
1799	1123
1800	1640

Calculation of Bread Value: 1801–10

Table A12.7 Data on bread value, 1801–10

LONDON A. Wheaten.

Year	Price (d per 4 lb)	V @ 426/4
1801	15.5	1651
1802	9.5	1012
1803	8.7	927
1804	9.7	1033
1805	13.1	1395
1806	11.7	1246
1807	10.8	1150
1808	11.6	1235
1809	13.7	1459
1810	14.7	1566

Table A12.7 continued

OXFORD. Standard Wheaten.

Year	Price (d per 4 lb)	V @ 449/4
1801	14.3	1606
1802	8.7	977
1803	7.5	842
1804	8.3	932
1805	11.5	1291
1806	10.6	1190
1807	9.8	1101
1808	10.5	1179
1809	13.1	1471
1810	14.5	1628

GLASGOW. Wheaten.

Year	Price (d per 4 lb)	V @ 426/4
1801	16.6	1768
1802	14.7	1566
1803	9.0	959
1804	9.2	980
1805	12.9	1374
1806	11.5	1225
1807	11.5	1225
1808	12.0	1278
1809	14.5	1544
1810	14.5	1544

RICHARDSON'S COUNTIES. Standard Wheaten.

Year	Kent	Essex	Lincs	Notts	Dorset	Hants	Mean	V
1801	14.7	15.2	14.7	13.8	15.4	15.4	14.9	1673
1802	8.7	8.7	11.0	11.0	8.5	8.5	9.4	1056
1803	8.7	8.7	–	–	7.4	7.4	8.1	910
1804	9.9	9.7	–	–	8.5	11.0	9.8	1101
1805	12.0	12.9	–	–	11.5	11.0	11.9	1336
1806	10.8	11.5	11.0	12.0	11.5	9.9	11.1	1247
1807	10.4	10.1	11.5	11.5	10.6	9.7	10.6	1190
1808	11.0	11.5	12.9	12.9	9.7	9.7	11.3	1269
1809	13.1	13.8	14.3	14.3	11.5	11.7	13.1	1471
1810	13.8	14.3	13.8	13.8	14.0	13.6	13.9	1561

Table A12.7 concluded

WALLINGFORD. Standard Wheaten.

Year	Price (d per 4 lb)	V @ 449/4
1801	17.4	1954
1802	10.0	1123
1803	8.8	988
1804	–	–
1805	–	–
1806	–	–
1807	–	–
1808	10.4	1168
1809	14.7	1651
1810	16.7	1875

WORCESTER. Standard Wheaten.

Year	Price (d per 4 lb)	V @ 449/4
1802	8.5	955
1803	6.8	764
1804	7.4	831
1805	11.0	1235
1806	10.3	1157
1807	9.2	1033

THORPE (Essex). Standard Wheaten.

Year	Price (d per 4 lb)	V @ 449/4
1809	12.6	1415
1810	13.2	1482

Assessment

Prices became ever more uniform throughout this decade. The years of cheap flour in London came to an end, so that metropolitan figures again become fairly representative of the country as a whole; and Glasgow prices were falling on trend (apart from a freak figure in 1802), so as to reach near parity with London (as Gourvish has observed). However, Worcester shows the effect of a repressively low allowance to the bakers, and every series has some quirk: therefore this decade is perhaps best represented by an average.

Table A12.8 National estimate of V, 1801–10

Year	V
1801	1721
1802	1031
1803	918
1804	1033
1805	1346
1806	1234
1807	1175
1808	1269
1809	1459
1810	1566

Calculation of Bread Value: 1811–20

Table A12.9 Data on bread value, 1811–20

LONDON A. Wheaten.

Year	Price (d per 4 lb)	V @ 426/4
1811	14.0	1491
1812	17.0	1811
1813	15.7	1672
1814	11.4	1214
1815	–	–
1816	–	–
1817	–	–
1818	–	–
1819	–	–
1820	10.1	1076

OXFORD. Standard Wheaten.

Year	Price (d per 4 lb)	V @ 449/4
1811	13.4	1505
1812	16.2	1819
1813	14.4	1617
1814	10.2	1145
1815	8.9	999
1816	10.5	1179

Table A12.9 continued

Year	Price (d per 4 lb)	V @ 449/4
1817	13.7	1539
1818	11.9	1336
1819	10.2	1145
1820	9.3	1044

GLASGOW. Wheaten.

Year	Price (d per 4 lb)	V @ 426/4
1811	12.9	1374
1812	17.0	1811
1813	15.6	1661
1814	11.7	1246
1815	9.7	1033

RICHARDSON'S COUNTIES. Standard Wheaten.

Year	Kent	Essex	Lincs	Notts	Dorset	Hants	Mean	V
1811	13.6	13.6	13.8	13.1	12.7	12.7	13.3	1494
1812	16.6	16.6	16.8	17.9	16.6	15.6	16.7	1875
1813	14.7	14.7	15.0	15.6	15.4	13.8	14.9	1673
1814	10.4	10.4	9.7	9.7	10.6	9.9	10.2	1145
1815	9.9	9.9	9.0	9.0	9.7	8.7	9.4	1056
1816	11.5	11.5	10.6	9.9	10.6	10.6	10.8	1213
1817	15.4	12.9	13.1	13.1	15.4	13.8	14.0	1572
1818	11.5	11.7	11.7	11.3	11.5	10.8	11.4	1280
1819	9.9	10.1	9.9	9.7	9.7	9.4	9.8	1101
1820	10.1	9.9	9.7	9.0	9.7	9.0	9.6	1078

WALLINGFORD. Standard Wheaten.

Year	Price (d per 4 lb)	V @ 449/4
1811	15.7	1763

RYE. Wheaten.

Year	Price (d per 4 lb)	V @ 426/4
1814	9.8	1044
1815	9.0	959
1816	11.1	1182
1817	14.3	1523
1818	12.0	1278

Table A12.9 concluded

Year	Price (d per 4 lb)	V @ 426/4
1819	10.0	1065
1820	9.6	1022

LEWES. Wheaten.

Year	Price (d per 4 lb)	V @ 426/4
1813	15.5	1651
1814	9.9	1054

THORPE (Essex). Standard Wheaten.

Year	Price (d per 4 lb)	V @ 449/4
1811	12.5	1404

BATH. Wheaten.

Year	Price (d per 4 lb)	V @ 426/4
1812	16.6	1768
1813	14.3	1523
1814	11.0	1172
1815	10.1	1076
1816	11.6	1235
1817	15.6	1661
1818	12.0	1278
1819	10.6	1129
1820	10.1	1076

WORCESTER. Standard Wheaten.

Year	Price (d per 4 lb)	V @ 449/4
1818	11.4	1280
1819	10.3	1157
1820	9.0	1011

Assessment

Though prices still were turbulent in the last years of war and first years of peace, there was (allowing for staggered year-ends) close uniformity throughout the country, no doubt owed to the near-complete integration of the wheat and flour markets, but also to the reintroduction of parliamentary allowances in all assized jurisdictions in 1813. Because the London series breaks, I have used the Oxford series to represent the country as a whole, except for 1818–19, when it needs a slight downward adjustment.

Table A12.10 National estimate of V, 1811–20

Year	V
1811	1505
1812	1819
1813	1617
1814	1145
1815	999
1816	1179
1817	1539
1818	1294
1819	1117
1820	1044

Calculation of Bread Value: 1821–30

Table A12.11 Data on bread value, 1821–30

LONDON A/B. Wheaten.

Year	Price (d per 4 lb)	V @ 426/4
1821	9.5	1012
1822	9.5	1012
1823	10.3	1097
1824	10.5	1118
1825	10.5	1118
1826	9.5	1012
1827	9.5	1012
1828	9.5	1012
1829	10.7*	1140
1830	10.2*	1086

* London B. Others London A.
1829: 45 weeks only.

OXFORD. Standard Wheaten.

Year	Price (d per 4 lb)	V @ 449/4
1821	8.9	999
1822	7.5	842
1823	7.9	887
1824	9.0	1011

Table A12.11 continued

Year	Price (d per 4 lb)	V @ 449/4
1825	9.8	1101
1826	8.5	955
1827	8.0	898
1828	8.8	988
1829	9.3	1044
1830	9.1	1022

RICHARDSON'S COUNTIES. Standard Wheaten.

Year	Kent	Essex	Lincs	Notts	Dorset	Hants	Mean	V
1821	9.2	8.7	8.3	8.1	8.5	8.1	8.5	955
1822	6.4	7.8	6.7	6.9	7.6	6.9	7.1	797
1823	6.4	8.1	7.8	7.4	7.6	7.4	7.5	842
1824	8.3	9.2	9.0	9.0	9.7	8.7	9.0	1011
1825	8.3	9.4	9.4	9.0	9.7	9.0	9.1	1022
1826	8.3	8.3	8.3	8.1	7.6	7.8	8.1	910
1827	8.3	7.6	8.1	7.6	7.6	7.6	7.8	876
1828	8.3	8.1	8.5	8.1	8.5	8.7	8.4	943
1829	9.2	8.1	9.2	9.2	9.7	9.4	9.1	1022
1830	8.3	7.8	9.2	9.2	9.7	8.7	8.8	988

BATH. Wheaten.

Year	Price (d per 4 lb)	V @ 426/4
1821	8.9	948
1822	8.5	905
1823	8.5	905
1824	9.6	1022
1825	10.1	1076
1826	8.7	927
1827	8.3	884
1828	9.2	980
1829	10.1	1076
1830	9.2	980

RYE. Wheaten.

Year	Price (d per 4 lb)	V @ 426/4
1821	8.2	873
1822	7.9	841
1823	8.2	873
1824	9.8	1044

Table A12.11 concluded

Year	Price (d per 4 lb)	V @ 449/4
1825	10.4	1108
1826	9.1	969
1827	8.5	905
1828	9.6	1022
1829	10.8	1150
1830	10.0	1065

WORCESTER. Standard Wheaten.

Year	Price (d per 4 lb)	V @ 449/4
1821	8.4	943
1822	8.1	910
1823	8.0	898
1824	9.1	1022
1825	9.9	1112
1826	8.9	999
1827	8.6	966

EDINBURGH. Wheaten.

Year	Price (d per 4 lb)	V @ 426/4
1824	9.8	1044
1825	9.5	1012
1826	9.5	1012
1827	9.0	959
1828	9.3	990
1829	11.3	1203
1830	9.3	990

Assessment

The overall bread/wheat relationship suggests that, either bread was becoming proportionately dearer (which is unlikely, given the opportunities to undersell) or else, that the wheat now sold in open markets was generally of a poorer quality than that used by bakers. However, exceptionally high relationships, especially in 1822, also suggest some significant understatement of wheat prices in the official returns.

The London series for the 1820s is rather crude, and the Edinburgh series, beginning in 1824, is for mean highest prices only. Given the fluency of the wheat market, and the meticulous operation of its assize, the Oxford series probably best represents the country as a whole.

Table A12.12   National estimate of *V*, 1821–30

Year	V
1821	999
1822	842
1823	887
1824	1011
1825	1101
1826	955
1827	898
1828	988
1829	1044
1830	1022

Calculation of Bread Value: 1831–40

Table A12.13   Data on bread value, 1831–40

LONDON A/B. Wheaten.

Year	Price (d per 4 lb)	V @ 426/4
1831	10.5*	986
1832	10.0	1065
1833	8.5	905
1834	8.0	852
1835	7.0	746
1836	8.0	852
1837	8.5	905
1838	10.0	1065
1839	10.1*	1076
1840	9.5*	1012

* London B. Others London A.

OXFORD. Standard Wheaten.

Year	Price (d per 4 lb)	V @ 449/4
1831	9.5	1067
1832	8.3	932
1833	7.7	865
1834	6.9	775
1835	5.9	663

Table A12.13 continued

EDINBURGH. Wheaten.

Year	Price (d per 4 lb)	V @ 426/4
1831	9.3	990
1832	9.3	990
1833	7.9	841
1834	7.3	777
1835	6.3	671
1836	6.1	650
1837	8.1	863
1838	8.8	937
1839	9.4	1001
1840	9.4	1001

RICHARDSON'S COUNTIES. Standard Wheaten.

Year	Kent	Essex	Lincs	Notts	Dorset	Hants	Mean	V
1831	8.5	7.4	9.4	9.4	9.7	9.0	8.9	999
1832	7.8	7.4	8.3	8.3	7.6	8.3	8.0	898
1833	6.9	6.9	7.8	7.8	7.6	7.4	7.4	831
1834	6.7	6.4	–	–	7.6	6.9	6.9	775
1835	5.8	5.1	–	–	6.7	6.0	5.9	663
1836	5.8	6.4	–	–	7.8	6.4	6.6	741
1837	6.9	6.4	–	–	6.7	7.4	6.9	775
1838	7.4	6.9	9.0	9.0	8.1	8.5	8.2	921
1839	7.1	7.1	8.3	8.3	8.7	9.0	8.1	910
1840	7.1	6.9	8.3	8.3	8.5	9.0	8.0	898

BATH. Wheaten.

Year	Price (d per 4 lb)	V @ 426/4
1831	9.2	980
1832	8.3	884
1833	7.3	777
1834	7.3	777
1835	6.5	692
1836	7.3	777
1837	8.3	884
1838	8.7	927
1839	9.2	980
1840	9.2	980

Table A12.13 concluded

BRISTOL. Standard Wheaten.

Year	Price (d per 4 lb)	V @ 449/4
1834	6.2	696
1835	5.1	573

AYLESBURY. Wheaten.

Year	Price (d per 4 lb)	V @ 426/4
1833	7.7	820
1834	6.6	703
1835	6.2	660
1836	7.0	746

Assessment

The London series remains weak, and though there is considerable uniformity between the other series, there are individual quirks. Therefore I shall use an approximation.

Table A12.14   National estimate of V, 1831–40

Year	V
1831	1035
1832	929
1833	838
1834	748
1835	661
1836	757
1837	871
1838	930
1839	1018
1840	955

Calculation of Bread Value: 1841–50

Table A12.15   Data on bread value, 1841–50

LONDON A/B. Wheaten.

Year	Price (d per 4 lb)	V @ 426/4
1841	9.4*	1001
1842	8.6*	916
1843	7.8*	831
1844	8.4*	895
1845	7.5	799
1846	8.9*	948
1847	9.9*	1054
1848	7.8*	831
1849	7.0	746
1850	6.8*	724

* London B. Others London A.

EDINBURGH. Wheaten.

Year	Price (d per 4 lb)	V @ 426/4
1841	8.8	937
1842	8.4	895
1843	6.6	703
1844	6.9	735
1845	6.8	724
1846	8.0	852
1847	8.8	937
1848	7.0	746
1849	6.8	724
1850	6.1	650

BATH. Wheaten.

Year	Price (d per 4 lb)	V @ 426/4
1841	8.7	927
1842	8.3	884
1843	6.9	735
1844	7.3	777

Assessment

The London series (mostly B figures) is now stronger, though it shows a considerably higher bread/wheat relationship than the two provincial series. I have used a series that approximates the average.

Table A12.16 National estimate of V, 1841–50

Year	V
1841	965
1842	893
1843	751
1844	800
1845	763
1846	905
1847	1004
1848	788
1849	733
1850	691

Calculation of Bread Value: 1851–60

Table A12.17 Data on bread value, 1851–60

LONDON A/B. Wheaten.

Year	Price (d per 4 lb)	V @ 426/4
1851	6.8	724
1852	6.7*	714
1853	8.3	884
1854	10.5	1118
1855	10.8	1150
1856	10.8	1150
1857	9.0	959
1858	7.5	799
1859	7.5	799
1860	8.8	937

* London B. Others London A.

EDINBURGH. Wheaten.

Year	Price (d per 4 lb)	V @ 426/4
1851	6.1	650
1852	6.1	650
1853	7.3	777
1854	9.4	1001

Table A12.17 concluded

Year	Price (d per 4 lb)	V @ 426/4
1855	10.3	1097
1856	10.1	1076
1857	8.6	916
1858	6.9	735
1859	6.9	735
1860	7.9	841

Assessment

I shall again use an approximation that roughly averages the two sources.

Table A12.18 National estimate of V, 1851–60

Year	V
1851	688
1852	685
1853	831
1854	1060
1855	1120
1856	1121
1857	940
1858	769
1859	767
1860	895

Calculation of Bread Value: 1861–70

Table A12.19 Data on bread value, 1861–70

LONDON A. Wheaten.

Year	Price (d per 4 lb)	V @ 426/4
1861	9.0	959
1862	8.5	905
1863	7.5	799
1864	7.0	746
1865	7.5	799
1866	8.8	937

Table A12.19 concluded

Year	Price (d per 4 lb)	V @ 426/4
1867	10.3	1097
1868	9.3	990
1869	7.8	831
1870	8.0	852

EDINBURGH. Wheaten.

Year	Price (d per 4 lb)	V @ 426/4
1861	8.3	884
1862	8.3	884
1863	7.4	788
1864	6.9	735
1865	6.8	724
1866	8.1	863
1867	9.4	1001
1868	8.7	927
1869	7.4	788
1870	7.6	809

Assessment

I shall again use a series that roughly averages the two sources.

Table A12.20   National estimate of V, 1861–70

Year	V
1861	923
1862	898
1863	795
1864	742
1865	763
1866	899
1867	1051
1868	956
1869	809
1870	833

Notes

1. See Chapter 8 Section 4.
2. See Appendix 3.

Estimated Other-bread Eating Populations

Table A13.1 Annual estimates of other-bread eating populations

Year	Barley eaters m	Oats' eaters m	Rye eaters m	Total m
1771	0.9	1.7	1.2	3.8
1772	0.9	1.8	1.2	3.9
1773	0.9	1.8	1.1	3.8
1774	0.9	1.8	1.1	3.8
1775	0.9	1.8	1.0	3.7
1776	0.9	1.8	0.9	3.6
1777	0.9	1.9	0.9	3.7
1778	0.9	1.9	0.8	3.6
1779	1.0	1.9	0.8	3.7
1780	1.0	1.9	0.7	3.6
1781	1.0	1.9	0.7	3.6
1782	1.0	1.9	0.8	3.6
1783	1.0	1.9	0.7	3.6
1784	1.0	1.9	0.6	3.5
1785	1.0	2.0	0.6	3.6
1786	1.0	1.9	0.6	3.5
1787	1.0	2.0	0.5	3.5
1788	1.0	2.0	0.5	3.5
1789	1.0	2.0	0.5	3.5
1790	1.1	2.0	0.4	3.5
1791	1.1	2.0	0.4	3.5
1792	1.1	1.9	0.4	3.4
1793	1.1	2.0	0.4	3.5
1794	1.2	1.9	0.3	3.4
1795	1.4	2.1	0.3	3.8
1796	1.4	2.1	0.3	3.8
1797	1.2	2.0	0.2	3.3
1798	1.2	2.0	0.2	3.4
1799	1.2	2.0	0.2	3.4
1800	1.6	2.5	0.2	4.3

Table A13.1 continued

Year	Barley eaters m	Oats' eaters m	Rye eaters m	Total m
1801	1.7	2.5	0.2	4.4
1802	1.3	2.2	0.2	3.7
1803	1.3	2.1	0.2	3.6
1804	1.3	2.1	0.2	3.6
1805	1.5	2.4	0.2	4.1
1806	1.5	2.4	0.2	4.1
1807	1.5	2.3	0.2	4.0
1808	1.4	2.2	0.2	3.8
1809	1.3	2.1	0.2	3.6
1810	1.5	2.4	0.2	4.1
1811	1.6	2.4	0.2	4.2
1812	1.7	2.6	0.2	4.5
1813	1.8	2.6	0.2	4.6
1814	1.7	2.5	0.2	4.4
1815	1.6	2.4	0.2	4.2
1816	1.7	2.6	0.2	4.5
1817	1.9	2.8	0.2	4.9
1818	1.8	2.7	0.2	4.7
1819	1.8	2.6	0.2	4.6
1820	1.8	2.7	0.1	4.6
1821	1.8	2.6	0.1	4.5
1822	1.8	2.5	0.1	4.4
1823	1.7	2.5	0.1	4.3
1824	1.7	2.5	0.1	4.3
1825	1.9	2.6	0.1	4.6
1826	1.9	2.7	0.1	4.7
1827	1.8	2.5	0.1	4.4
1828	1.9	2.5	0.1	4.5
1829	1.9	2.6	0.1	4.6
1830	1.9	2.6	0.1	4.6
1831	1.9	2.6	0.1	4.6
1832	1.8	2.6	0.1	4.5
1833	1.7	2.6	–	4.3
1834	1.6	2.6	–	4.2
1835	1.5	2.6	–	4.1
1836	1.4	2.6	–	4.0
1837	1.3	2.6	–	3.9
1838	1.3	2.8	–	4.1

Table A13.1 concluded

Year	Barley eaters m	Oats' eaters m	Rye eaters m	Total m
1839	1.3	3.2	–	4.5
1840	1.4	3.2	–	4.6
1841	1.1	3.2	–	4.3
1842	1.1	3.2	–	4.3
1843	1.0	3.2	–	4.2
1844	0.9	3.1	–	4.0
1845	0.9	3.2	–	4.1
1846	1.0	3.7	–	4.7
1847	1.0	3.6	–	4.6
1848	0.8	3.2	–	4.0
1849	0.8	3.3	–	4.1
1850	0.8	3.1	–	3.9
1851	0.8	3.2	–	4.0
1852	0.7	3.1	–	3.8
1853	0.7	3.1	–	3.8
1854	0.7	3.2	–	3.9
1855	0.7	3.2	–	3.9
1856	0.7	3.2	–	3.9
1857	0.6	3.2	–	3.8
1858	0.6	3.2	–	3.8
1859	0.5	3.4	–	3.9
1860	0.5	3.4	–	3.9
1861	0.5	3.4	–	3.9
1862	0.4	3.3	–	3.7
1863	0.4	3.4	–	3.8
1864	0.4	3.4	–	3.8
1865	0.4	3.5	–	3.9
1866	0.4	3.5	–	3.9
1867	0.4	3.6	–	4.0
1868	0.4	3.4	–	3.8
1869	0.4	3.4	–	3.8
1870	0.4	3.5	–	3.9

Other Bread: Estimates of Volume and Value

The figures for the volume and value of other-bread consumption are derived in a similar manner to that for wheat. The volume estimates for barley, rye and oats are obtained by multiplying the other-bread eating populations listed in Appendix 13 by the appropriate estimates of *per capita* consumption (see Tables 8.9 and 8.10). The data on value are calculated using information on prices from grain markets, combined with a mark-up to allow for the cost of baking.[1]

Barley Bread: Estimate of Volume and Value

BQ in Table A14.1 represents the amount of barley eaten by the barley-eating equivalent population. The mark-up for the cost of baking is taken as 10s (or 120d) per quarter; this is added to the price of a quarter of barley. Multiplying this total price by the volume estimate gives BQV, the figure for the value of barley bread consumed.

Table A14.1 Volume and value of barley bread

Year	BQ m	Price per qr (d)	+120d	BQV £m
1771	1.1	317	437	2.00
1772	1.1	313	433	1.98
1773	1.1	350	470	2.15
1774	1.1	352	472	2.16
1775	1.1	321	441	2.02
1776	1.1	249	369	1.69
1777	1.1	253	373	1.71
1778	1.1	280	400	1.83
1779	1.2	241	361	1.81
1780	1.2	210	330	1.65
1781	1.0	212	332	1.38
1782	1.0	278	398	1.66
1783	1.0	375	495	2.06
1784	1.0	344	464	1.93
1785	1.0	297	417	1.74

Table A14.1 continued

Year	BQ m	Price per qr (d)	+120d	BQV £m
1786	1.0	301	421	1.75
1787	1.0	280	400	1.67
1788	1.0	272	392	1.63
1789	1.0	282	402	1.68
1790	1.1	315	435	1.99
1791	0.9	322	442	1.66
1792	0.9	–	–	1.75*
1793	0.9	373	493	1.85
1794	1.0	381	501	2.09
1795	1.1	449	569	2.61
1796	1.1	424	544	2.49
1797	1.0	326	446	1.86
1798	1.0	348	468	1.95
1799	1.0	434	554	2.31
1800	1.3	718	838	4.54
1801	1.4	822	942	5.50
1802	1.0	400	520	2.17
1803	1.0	304	424	1.77
1804	1.0	372	492	2.05
1805	1.2	534	654	3.27
1806	1.2	464	584	2.92
1807	1.2	472	592	2.96
1808	1.1	521	641	2.94
1809	1.0	564	684	2.85
1810	1.2	577	697	3.49
1811	1.3	507	627	3.40
1812	1.4	801	921	5.37
1813	1.4	702	822	4.80
1814	1.4	448	568	3.31
1815	1.3	363	483	2.62
1816	1.4	407	527	3.07
1817	1.5	592	712	4.45
1818	1.4	646	766	4.47
1819	1.4	549	669	3.90
1820	1.4	406	526	3.07
1821	1.4	312	432	2.52
1822	1.4	262	382	2.23
1823	1.4	378	498	2.91
1824	1.4	436	556	3.24
1825	1.5	480	600	3.75

Table A14.1 continued

Year	BQ m	Price per qr (d)	+120d	BQV £m
1826	1.5	412	532	3.33
1827	1.4	451	571	3.33
1828	1.5	394	514	3.21
1829	1.5	390	510	3.19
1830	1.5	391	511	3.19
1831	1.5	456	576	3.60
1832	1.4	397	517	3.02
1833	1.4	330	450	2.63
1834	1.3	348	468	2.54
1835	1.2	359	479	2.40
1836	1.1	394	514	2.36
1837	1.0	364	484	2.02
1838	1.0	377	497	2.07
1839	1.0	474	594	2.48
1840	1.1	437	557	2.55
1841	0.9	394	514	1.93
1842	0.9	330	450	1.69
1843	0.8	354	474	1.58
1844	0.7	404	524	1.53
1845	0.7	380	500	1.46
1846	0.8	392	512	1.71
1847	0.8	530	650	2.17
1848	0.6	378	498	1.25
1849	0.6	333	453	1.13
1850	0.6	281	401	1.00
1851	0.6	297	417	1.04
1852	0.6	342	462	1.16
1853	0.6	398	518	1.30
1854	0.6	432	552	1.38
1855	0.6	417	537	1.34
1856	0.6	493	613	1.53
1857	0.5	505	625	1.30
1858	0.5	416	536	1.12
1859	0.4	402	522	0.87
1860	0.4	439	559	0.93
1861	0.4	433	553	0.92
1862	0.3	421	541	0.68
1863	0.3	407	527	0.66
1864	0.3	359	479	0.60
1865	0.3	357	477	0.60

Table A14.1 concluded

Year	BQ m	Price per qr (d)	+120d	BQV £m
1866	0.3	449	569	0.71
1867	0.3	480	600	0.75
1868	0.3	516	636	0.80
1869	0.3	473	593	0.74
1870	0.3	415	535	0.67

* guesstimate

Rye Bread: Estimate of Volume and Value

RQ represents the amount of rye eaten by the rye-eating equivalent population. The estimate of value is RQV.

Table A14.2   Volume and value of rye bread

Year	RQ m	Price per qr (d)	+120d	RQV £m
1771	1.3	424	544	2.95
1772	1.3	453	573	3.10
1773	1.2	412	532	2.66
1774	1.2	424	544	2.72
1775	1.1	406	526	2.41
1776	1.0	332	452	1.88
1777	1.0	346	466	1.94
1778	0.9	350	470	1.76
1779	0.9	288	408	1.53
1780	0.8	274	394	1.31
1781	0.7	332	452	1.32
1782	0.7	356	476	1.39
1783	0.7	441	561	1.64
1784	0.6	398	518	1.30
1785	0.6	346	466	1.17
1786	0.6	336	456	1.14
1787	0.5	342	462	0.96
1788	0.5	342	462	0.96
1789	0.5	369	489	1.02
1790	0.4	420	540	0.90
1791	0.4	391	511	0.85
1792	0.4	358	478	0.80
1793	0.4	434	554	0.92
1794	0.3	449	569	0.71

For 1795 on, *RQV* is subsumed in the final rounding of other-grain consolidated value.

Oat Bread: Estimate of Volume and Value

OQ represents the amount of oats eaten by the oat-eating equivalent population. The price information has been treated in a slightly different way to that for barley and rye. In the case of oats the cost of milling is a significant factor and has been allowed for by adding 50 per cent to the grain-price of oats. A further addition of 5s, or 60d, is then made for the cost of baking (see Chapter 8 Section 3 for further details on this). The price figure is then multiplied by volume *OQ*, to obtain the figures for value listed under *OQV*.

Table A14.3   Volume and value of oat bread

Year	OQ m	Price per qr (d)	+50%, + 60d	OQV £m
1771	2.4	206	369	3.69
1772	2.5	200	360	3.75
1773	2.5	212	378	3.94
1774	2.5	220	390	4.06
1775	2.5	204	366	3.81
1776	2.5	185	338	3.52
1777	2.7	193	350	3.94
1778	2.7	187	341	3.84
1779	2.7	173	320	3.60
1780	2.7	158	297	3.34
1781	2.1	169	314	2.75
1782	2.1	187	341	2.98
1783	2.1	245	428	3.75
1784	2.1	226	399	3.49
1785	2.2	212	378	3.47
1786	2.1	222	393	3.44
1787	2.2	206	369	3.38
1788	2.2	193	350	3.21
1789	2.2	198	357	3.27
1790	2.2	233	410	3.76
1791	1.6	217	386	2.57
1792	1.5	201	362	2.26
1793	1.6	246	429	2.86
1794	1.5	255	443	2.77
1795	1.7	293	500	3.54

Table A14.3 continued

Year	OQ m	Price per qr (d)	+50%, + 60d	OQV £m
1796	1.7	262	453	3.21
1797	1.6	195	353	2.35
1798	1.6	233	410	2.73
1799	1.6	330	505	3.37
1800	2.0	472	768	6.40
1801	2.0	444	726	6.05
1802	1.8	244	426	3.20
1803	1.7	258	447	3.17
1804	1.7	291	497	3.52
1805	1.9	340	570	4.51
1806	1.9	331	557	4.41
1807	1.8	340	570	4.28
1808	1.8	400	660	4.95
1809	1.7	377	626	4.43
1810	1.9	343	575	4.55
1811	1.9	331	557	4.41
1812	2.1	534	861	7.53
1813	2.1	462	753	6.59
1814	2.0	308	522	4.35
1815	1.9	283	485	3.84
1816	2.1	326	549	4.80
1817	2.2	389	644	5.90
1818	2.2	389	644	5.90
1819	2.1	338	567	4.96
1820	2.2	290	495	4.54
1821	2.1	234	411	3.60
1822	2.0	217	386	3.22
1823	2.0	275	473	3.94
1824	2.0	298	507	4.23
1825	2.1	308	522	4.57
1826	2.2	320	540	4.95
1827	2.0	338	567	4.73
1828	2.0	270	465	3.88
1829	2.1	273	470	4.11
1830	2.1	293	500	4.38
1831	2.1	304	516	4.52
1832	2.1	245	428	3.75
1833	2.1	221	392	3.43
1834	2.1	251	437	3.82

Table A14.3 concluded

Year	OQ £m	Price per qr (d)	+50%, + 60d	OQV £m
1835	2.1	264	456	3.99
1836	2.1	277	476	4.17
1837	2.1	277	476	4.17
1838	2.2	269	464	4.25
1839	2.6	311	527	5.71
1840	2.6	308	522	5.66
1841	2.6	269	464	5.03
1842	2.6	231	407	4.41
1843	2.6	220	390	4.23
1844	2.5	247	431	4.49
1845	2.6	270	465	5.04
1846	3.0	284	486	6.08
1847	2.9	344	576	6.96
1848	2.6	246	429	4.65
1849	2.6	210	375	4.06
1850	2.5	197	356	3.71
1851	2.6	223	395	4.28
1852	2.5	229	404	4.21
1853	2.5	252	438	4.56
1854	2.6	335	563	6.10
1855	2.6	329	554	6.00
1856	2.6	302	513	5.56
1857	2.6	300	510	5.53
1858	2.6	294	501	5.43
1859	2.7	278	477	5.37
1860	2.7	293	500	5.63
1861	2.7	285	488	5.49
1862	2.6	271	467	5.06
1863	2.7	254	441	4.96
1864	2.7	241	422	4.75
1865	2.8	262	453	5.29
1866	2.8	295	503	5.87
1867	2.9	312	528	6.38
1868	2.7	337	566	6.37
1869	2.7	312	528	5.94
1870	2.8	274	471	5.50

Notes

1. See Chapter 8 Section 3 for more on the cost of baking.

Bibliography

1. Principal statutes concerning bread

51 Henry III, 1265. Assize of Bread (and Ale).
8 Anne c.18, 1709. Price and Assize of Bread.
31 Geo II c.29, 1757. Price and Assize of Bread.
32 Geo II c.18, 1758. Rewards to Informers.
3 Geo III c.6, 1762. Operation in Scotland.
3 Geo III c.11, 1762. Priced or Sized loaves.
13 Geo III c.62, 1773. Standard Wheaten Bread.
33 Geo III c.37, 1793. Bread from inferior grains.
34 Geo III c.61, 1794. Baking on Sunday.
36 Geo III c.22, 1795. Wheatmeal and Mixed Bread.
37 Geo III c.98, 1797. City Act (London).
38 Geo III c.62, 1798. Salt Duty and Bread.
38 Geo III c.lv, 1798. Revised London returns.
39 & 40 Geo III c.74, 1800. Extension of Assize table.
39 & 40 Geo III c.97, 1800. The London Company.
41 Geo III c.12, 1801. Wholemeal bread.
45 Geo III, c.xxiii, 1805. London Bakers' Allowance.
48 Geo III, c.lxx, 1808. London standards.
50 Geo III c.lxxiii, 1810. Provincial standards.
53 Geo III c.116, 1813. Country Bakers' Act.
55 Geo III, c.xcix, 1815. Repeal of London Assize.
59 Geo III c.cxxvii, 1819. Weight of loaves.
3 Geo IV c.cvi, 1822. Weight of loaves in London.
6 & 7 Will IV c.37, 1836. Repeal of last Assizes.

2. Selected bills

a) House of Commons Sessional Papers, edited by Sheila Lambert.
Vol 2:
1757–8 (8.12/13.3) Cd 2284. Price and Assize of Bread.
Vol 116:
1798 (7.5) Cd 4846. Revised London returns.
b) House of Commons Bills.
1813 (29.4) I (158) 641. Country Bakers Bill.
1813 (3.6) I (265) 653. Revised Country Assize Table.
1814 (28.7) II (345) 1037. Repeal of London Assize.

1815 (30.6) II (421) 841, (449) 859. Repeal of London Assize.
1819 (18.6) I–B (464) 1071. London weight regulations.
1821 (19.4) II (433) 691. London weight regulations.
1822 (12.6) I (184) 701, (334) 719, (384) 737, and (421) 755. London weight regulations.
1824 (14.4) I (238) 269. Country Bakers' Allowance.
1827 (21.5) II (374) 87. London weight regulations.
1835 (24.6) I (188) 249 and (322) 267. Repeal of last Assizes.
1836 (28.6) I (384) 465. Repeal of last Assizes (inc Scotland).
1848 (16.6) VI (411) 255. Weight to be marked on loaves.
1849 (6.7) VI (468) 311. Weight to be marked on loaves.
1853 (21.7) VII (798) 437. Truck Act Amendment.
1854 (21.2) V (21) 423. Truck Act Amendment.
1855 (22.5) VI (145) 283. Truck Act Amendment.
1863 (25.6) I (54) 133. Bakehouses' Regulation.

3. Selected parliamentary reports

a) House of Commons Sessional Papers, edited by Sheila Lambert.
Vol 25:
1767 (16.4) Cd 3064. Assize of Bread.
1772 (21.12) Cd 3144. Assize of Bread.
1774 (14.6) Cd 3213. Proposed Assize of Flour.
Vol 131:
1800 (10.2) Cd 4983. Supply of Bread and Corn (1st Report).
1800 (6.3) Cd 4989. Proceedings on above.
1800 (6.3) Cd 4990. Supply of Bread and Corn (2nd Report).
1800 (9.6) Cd 5056. Birmingham Union (Privy Council).
1800 (25/30.6, 1.7) Cd 5080. The London Company.
1800 (18.11) Cd 5101. Statistics on Corn and Flour Supply.
1800 (19.12) Cd 5120. Purchases for H M Services.
1800 (24.11) Cd 5105. High Price of Provisions (1st Report).
1800 (31.12) Cd 5125. High Price of Provisions (Supplement to above).
1800 (9.12) 5112. High Price of Provisions (2nd Report).
1800 (31.12) Cd 5127. High Price of Provisions (3rd Report).
1800 (17.12) Cd 5116. High Price of Provisions (4th Report).
1800 (18.12) Cd 5117. High Price of Provisions (5th Report).
1800 (31.12) Cd 5126. High Price of Provisions (6th Report).
1800 (22.12) Cd 5122. Lords' reports communicated to the Commons.
b) House of Commons Reports.
1801 (23.2) I/2 Item 12. High Price of Provisions (2nd Report).

1801 (20.3) I/2 Item 13. High Price of Provisions (4th Report).

1801 (2.4) I/2 Item 14. High Price of Provisions (5th Report).

1801 (22.5) I/2 Item 15. High Price of Provisions (6th Report).

1801 (24.6) I/2 Item 16. High Price of Provisions (7th Report).

1804 (27.4) IV/I (74) Item 43. London Bakers' Petition.

1813 (12.3) III/I (82) 401. Country Bakers' Petition.

1813 (3.6) III/I (259) 417. Country Bakers' Petition.

1813–14 (1.7.14) III (290) 131. Weights & Measures.

1815 (22.2) X (109) 481. Price of Bread in London 1758–1814.

1815 (27.2) X (109) 497. Prices of Wheat, Flour, and Bread in London 1804–13.

1815 (1.3) X (130) 499. Average Wheat and Flour Prices, London 1797–1814.

1815 (6.3) X (133) 511. Wheat Returns, 12 Maritime Districts.

1815 (15.3) X (161) 539. Wheat Flour and Bread Prices, London 7.1.1815–11.3.1815.

1815 (17.3) X (166) 541. National Average Wheat Prices.

1815 (20.3) X (169) 543. Wheat and Wheat Flour Imports.

1815 (6.6) V (186) 1341. Assize of Bread in London.

1818 (22.5) IX (345) 227. Regulation of Weight and Quality.

1820 (8.7) II (255) 101. Agricultural Distress.

1821 (17.4) V (426) 1. Regulation of Weight and Quality.

1821 (18.6) IX (668) 1. Depressed State of Agriculture.

1822 (1.4) V (165) 1. Distressed State of Agriculture (1st Report).

1822 (20.5) V (346) 9. Distressed State of Agriculture (2nd Report).

1824 (8.4) VI (212) 465. Country Bakers' Allowance.

1824 (2.3) VII (94) 431. Weights and Measures.

1831–2 (6.8.32) VII (697) 253. Sabbath Observance.

1833 (2.8) V (612) 1. Agriculture.

1834 (7.3) XLIX (92) 321. Price of Bread in London 1780–1815.

1834 (7.7) XVIII (464) 243. Weights and Measures.

1834 (25.7) VII (517) 1. Sale of Corn.

1835 (3.4) XXXVII (128) 601. Where Assize still set.

1836 (4.3) VIII/I (79) 1. State of Agriculture (1st Report).

1836 (15.4) VIII/I (189) 225. State of Agriculture (2nd Report).

1836 (21.7) VIII/II (465) 1. State of Agriculture (3rd Report).

1840 (10.7) V (472) 1. Bonded Corn.

1842 (16.6) XIV (333) 1. Bonded Corn.

1842 (20.7) IX (471) 125. Payment of Wages (Truck).

1845 (HMSO) XV (609). Condition of the Framework Knitters.

1846 (29.1) XLIV (7) 31. Price of Bread in London and around the world cNovember 1845.

1846 (28.7) XIII (530) 425. Railway Labourers.

1847 (28.6) LIX (152) 497. Price of Bread, Flour, and Wheat in London and Paris November to February 1847.

1847 (28.6) LIX (581) 499. Price of Bread, Flour, and Wheat in London and Paris March to June 1847.

1847–8 (29.5.48) LI (362) 367. Health of Bakers.

1857 (21.3) XIV (154/1) 5. Dietaries for Convicts, etc.

1862 (HMSO) XLVII (3080) 1. Journeymen Bakers (1st Report).

1863 (HMSO) XXVIII (6239) 313. Journeymen Bakers (2nd Report).

1863 (14.4) XXV (161) 1. Nourishment of Distressed Operatives (in Lancashire).

1864 (HMSO) XXVIII (3416) 1. 6th Report of Medical Officer of P C 1863, esp App 6: the Food of the Poorer Labouring Classes in England.

1864 (20.5) XLIX (313) 543. Dietaries of County and Borough Prisons.

1864 (20.6) LII (406) 97. Reception and Relief of Casual Poor at Workhouses.

1865 (13.2) XXXII (13) 805. Soldiers' Trades.

1865 (31.3) XLVII (175) 265. Working of Bakehouses Regulation Act of 1863.

1866 (6.7) LXVI (394) 373. Working of Bakehouses Regulation Act of 1863.

1903 (6.8) LXVIII (321) 1. Wholesale and Retail Prices.

1904 (HMSO) LXXIX (2145) 495. Commercial Statistics.

Accounts of the London Company (for the Manufacture of Flour, Meal, and Bread): 1801 V (34) 319; 1801–2 IV (54) 261; 1805 IX (58) 87; 1806 XII (93) 319; 1806–7 IV (141) 81; 1808 VI (144) 161; 1809 IX (100) 223; 1810–11 XI (86) 19.

c) House of Lords Report.

1842. XXVI (006) 1. Sanitary Condition of the Labouring Population.

4. Selected archives

Abingdon Town Council:

Church Records, Box 3, packet 27. Overseers' bread bills.

Berkshire Record Office:

A/AM. Abingdon Assize of Bread, 1797.
W/RM 1–2. Wallingford Bread Book, 1800–3, 1808–12.
B/TU/LON. Pearce typescript, Reading Central Library, Local Studies Collection.

Buckinghamshire Archaeological Society:

Records of Buckinghamshire, Aylesbury (1854–)

Cornwall Record Office:

CF 3069. Map of bakeries, 1798.
DDX 142/2. Camelford Court Books 1768–1887.

Devon Record Office (Exeter):

DQS/L101/2. Bridewell Mill Committee, 1821–2.

West Devon Record Office (Plymouth):

W648. Corn Law Agitation, 1814.
W684. Papers re corn, flour, and bread, 1800–26.

North Devon Record Office (Barnstaple):

3992. Barnstaple Sessions Book Vol 22, 1795–1826.

Dorset Record Office:

D1/LL612. M/s copy of Assize table.
B2/25/1. Dorchester Assize of Bread Book, 1758–1801.
B2/25/2–3. Dorchester: wheat prices 1789–91, 1804–12.

(Hampshire) Portsmouth Record Office:

R1/25. Handbill re Assize of Bread, 1786.

(Hampshire) Southampton Record Office:

Trade directories 1783–1861.

(Hampshire) Winchester Record Office:

W/DI/258. Presentments (Clerk of the Market), 1794.
QI/18. Court Order Book: Bread for Prisoners, 1773.

(Lancashire) Manchester Central Library, Archives (MCL–A):

McLI/12/34/1–48. Papers re suppression of handmills, 1546–1821.

City of London Record Office (CLRO):

Corporation of London:

P.A.R. Books 2 and 4. Miscellaneous Acts, Reports, and Papers, 1702–1817.

MSS 117.4. High Price of Grain and Provisions, 1767.

MSS 171.8. High Price of Provisions 1767–8.

MSS 301.1. Total quantities of wheat sold, and average price, 1767–1802.

MSS 118.1. Price of Corn and Provisions, 1772–3.

MSS 172.11. High Price of Provisions, etc, 1779.

MSS 118.2. High Price of Provisions, etc, 1786–8.

Misc MSS 4–7. Assize of Bread, 1795.

MSS 113.3. High Price of Provisions, 1795, Price of Flour 1796–7, and proposals to erect corn mills 1797–8.

PD 32.8. High Price of Flour, 1796.

70B. Register of Bakers' Certificates, 1797–8.

427D (5 boxes). Bakers' Certificates 1797–1803.

431C (5 vols). Lord Mayor's Assize of Bread Books, 1799–1815.

MSS 119.2. Corn Mills 1797–1803, and High Price of Bread, 1813.

PD 10.188. Notice soliciting information on causes of high prices, 1800.

MSS 94.24. High Price of Provisions, 1800–2.

MSS 282.1. High Price of Bread, 1813–22.

Gaol Cttee Misc Papers No 4, 537C. Cost of making bread at Holloway prison versus cost of buying in, 1861.

(London) Guildhall Library (G).

Corporation of London:

A.8.5, 24/51. Self Denying Ordinance, 1795.

Fo Pam 3426. Transcript of evidence of Mr Luke Ideson, 1796.

Common Council Reports 1810–15, No 13. High Price of Bread, 1814.

Millers:

Fo Pam 894. Representation against Bill to incorporate the London Company, 1800.

Fo Pam 895. Observations on two Bills, 1800.

Master Bakers:

Ms 7798A. Trade Minutes 1783–4, especially against undersellers.
Pam 1093. Masters' and Journeymens' complaint against Sunday baking, 1794.

Worshipful Company of Bakers of London:

Ms 7800. List of assized bakers, c1770.
Ms 7799. Observations of Mr Pelham, c1772.
Fo Pam 5251. Observations on Assize Bill, 1800.
Broadsides 8.12. Statement of grounds for 1804 Bill.
Ms 7801 (2 boxes). Assize papers 1740–1848.
Ms 7798B. Country Bakers' Assize papers (also in Ms 7801 2/2).
Ms 5177. Court Minute Books, vols 10, 11, 12, and 13, 1760–1836.
Pam 16570. Brief history of the Worshipful Company, 1982.

Miscellaneous:

Satires 53C. Rowlandson print, 1813.
A.3.5, no 32. Trial of John Rusby, 1800.

Oxford University Archives:

MR 3/5/1–6. Corn Books of the Clerks of the Market, 1732–1822.

(Oxford) Bodleian Library:

MSS Top Oxon d68–70. Assize of Bread forms, 1821–36.
MS Top Oxon f2. Clerks of the Market: notebook re weights and bread, etc, 1808–28.

Somerset Record Office:

T/PH/hmy 3 (C/2936). Bakers' Petition, 1796.
DD/NE22. Notes on bread, corn, etc, 1813–17.

(East) Sussex Record Office:

Rye 5, vols 1–4. Assize of Bread Book, 1813–34.
Rye MS 2/9. Rye Sessions Book, 1772–1828.
QAV/EW1. Bread Act Record, 1801.

(West) Sussex Record Office:

Add MS 18,338–18,341. Baker's accounts, 1858–63.
Add MS 27,807. Baker's accounts, 1855–65.
City of Chichester: G1. Chichester Assize of Bread Book, 1796–1801.

Worcester Record Office:

Shelf B.10. Worcester Wheat Books, 7 vols, 1779–1828.

Scottish Record Office (West Register House, Edinburgh):

CS 96/3223. Arbroath baker's ledger, 1789–98.
CS 96/3890. Dundee baker's ledger, 1799–1802.
CS 96/3601. Edinburgh baker's account book, 1821–2.
CS 96/3526–7. Glasgow baker's incidents' book, 1810–20.

5. Newspapers

See footnotes for particular issues.

6. Books and pamphlets to 1870

The names of the known or probable authors of works published anonymously are given in square brackets.

Accum, Frederick: *A Treatise on Adulteration of Food, and Culinary Poisons . . . And Methods of Detecting them.* London, 2nd ed, 1820.
Acton, Eliza: *The English Bread Book.* London, 1857. Also 1990 with different pagination.
———: *Modern Cookery for Private Families.* London, 1845. Condensed in: *The Best of Eliza Acton*, London 1968/86.
Anderson, R C: *The Assize of Bread Book 1477–1517.* Southampton 1923.
Anon (A Journeyman Baker): *Observations on the Table of Assize.* Dublin, 1753.
Anon: *Lying Detected.* Bristol, 1758.
Anon: *A Proposal for Supplying London with Bread, at a Uniform Price.* London 1798.
Anon: *Bread Riots at Oxford.* 1867.
Atwood, G: *Review of the Statutes and Ordinances of Assize.* London 1801.
Bacon, Richard Noverre: *The Report on the Agriculture of Norfolk.* London, 1844.
Bain, Donald: *The Egregious and Dangerous Fallacies of the Anti-Corn Law League.* Edinburgh, 1843.
Burke, Edmund: *Thoughts and Details on Scarcity.* London, 1800.

Caird, James: *English Agriculture in 1850–1*. London, 1852.
———: *Our Daily Food*. London, 2nd ed 1868.
Campbell, R: *The London Tradesman*. London 1747/1969.
Capper, Benjamin Pitts: *A Statistical Account of the Population and Cultivation, Produce and Consumption of England and Wales*. London, 1801.
Cobbett, William: *Cottage Economy*. London, new ed 1828/1979.
Colquhoun, Patrick: *A Treatise on the Wealth, Power, and Resources of the British Empire*. London, 1814.
Copley, Esther: *Cottage Comforts*. London, 23rd ed 1858.
Crell, A F and Wallace, W M: *The Family Oracle of Health*. Vols I–XVIII. London 1824–5.
Culverhouse, C: *An Arrangement of the Bread Laws*. Bath, 1813.
Davies, Reverend David: *The Case of Labourers in Husbandry Stated and Considered*. London, 1795.
Defoe, Daniel: *Complete English Tradesman*. Edinburgh, 1726/1839.
———: *A Tour Through the Whole Island of Great Britain*. 4 Vols. London, 1769.
[Dickenson, Alderman]: [untitled] explanation of 31 Geo II c.29 for guidance of magistrates. London, 1759?
Dodd, George: *The Food of London*. London, 1856.
[Dumbell, John]: *A Letter to the Rt Hon Sir William Domville, Bart, the Lord Mayor of London*. London, 1814.
Eden, Sir Frederick Morton: *The State of the Poor*. London, 1797. Abridged and edited by A G L Rogers. London, 1928.
Edlin, A: *A Treatise on the Art of Bread-Making*. London, 1805.
[Egmont, Lord]: *Important Considerations upon (31 Geo II c.29) relating to the Assize of Bread*. London, 1767.
Engels, Frederick: *The Condition of the Working Class in England*. 1844/London 1969.
Girdler, J S: *Observations on the Pernicious Consequences of Forestalling, Regrating, and Ingrossing*. London, 1800.
Grant, Daniel: *Home Politics, or the Growth of Trade Considered in its Relation to Labour, Pauperism, & Emigration*. London, 1870.
Hassall, Arthur Hill: *Food and its Adulterations*. London, 1855.
Heslop, Reverend Luke: *Observations on (31 Geo II c.29) concerning the Assize of Bread*. London, 1799.
Hodson, Reverend Septimus: *An Address to the Different Classes of Persons in Great Britain on the Present Scarcity and High Price of Provisions*. London, 1795.
Jackson, H: *An Essay on Bread*. London, 1758.
Jacob, William: *Tracts Relating to the Corn Trade and Corn Laws*. London, 1828.

King, Gregory: *Natural and Political Observations*. London, 1696/ 1973.

McCulloch, J R: *A Dictionary, Practical, Theoretical, and Historical, of Commerce and Commercial Navigation*. London, 1859 edition.

Malthus, Thomas: *An Essay on the Principle of Population, and A Summary View of the Principle of Population*. London 1798–1830/ 1970.

Marx, Karl: *Capital*, Volume I. London, 1867/1976.

Maton, James: *Tricks of Bakers Unmasked*. London, 1824.

Mill, James: *Selected Economic Writings* (introduced and edited by Donald Winch). 1966.

Mill, John S: *Principles of Political Economy*, Books IV and V. London 1848/1970.

Mountmorres, Viscount: *Impartial Reflections upon the Present Crisis*. London, 1796.

Nield, William: 'Comparative Statement of the Income and Expenditure of certain Families of the Working Classes in Manchester and Dukinfield, in the years 1836 and 1841'. *Journal of the Statistical Society of London*, 1841.

Penkethman, J: *Authentic Accounts of the History and Price of Wheat, Bread, Malt, &c*. London, 1745 edition.

Playfair, Lyon: *On the Food of Man*. Edinburgh, 1865.

Porter, G R: *The Progress of the Nation*. London, 1851 edition.

Pownall, Thomas: *The Measure of Regulating the Assize and of the Due Making of Bread, Explained*. London, 1795.

Read, George: *A Brief History of the Bread Baking Trade*. London, 1848.

Rundell, Maria E: *A New System of Domestic Cookery*. London 1807/ 1859.

[Sanderson, Sir John]: *Observations and Examples to Assist Magistrates in setting the Assize of Bread*. London, 1759.

Silvester, Eusebius: *The Causes of the Present High Price of Corn and Grain*. London, 1758.

Sinclair, Sir John: *Analysis of the Statistical Account of Scotland*. Edinburgh, 1825.

Smith, Adam: *An Inquiry into the Nature and Causes of the Wealth of Nations*. 1775–6. 4th edition, with introduction, notes, and supplemental dissertations by J R McCulloch, Edinburgh, 1853.

Smith, Sir Charles: *Three Tracts on the Corn-Trade and Corn-Laws*. London, 1766.

Smith, Edward: *Practical Dietary*. London, 1864.

————: *The Present State of the Dietary Question.* London, 1864.

(see also post-1871 books)

Thompson, Sir Benjamin (Count Rumford): *An Essay on Food and Particularly on Feeding the Poor.* 1795/ Dublin ed 1847.

Timbs, John (ed): *Lady Bountiful's Legacy to her Family and Friends.* London, 1868.

Tooke, Thomas: *History of Prices* (5 volumes). London 1838–57.

[Turton, Sir Thomas]: *An Address . . . in behalf of the Dealers in Corn.* London, 1800.

Walsh, J H: *A Manual of Domestic Economy.* London, 1857.

Wilson, James: *Influences of the Corn Laws.* London, 1839.

————: *Fluctuations of Currency, Commerce, and Manufactures; referable to the Corn Laws.* London, 1840.

————: Capital, Currency and Banking. London, 1847.

Young, Arthur: *A Six Months' Tour through the North of England* (3 vols). Dublin, 1770.

————: *A Six Weeks' Tour through the Southern Counties of England and Wales.* London, 3rd ed 1772.

————: *Travels in France.* Bury St Edmunds, 1794/London 1889.

7. Books, theses, and articles since 1871

Adam, James S: *A Fell Fine Baker: the Story of United Biscuits.* Private, London, 1974.

Aldcroft, Derek and Freeman Michael (eds): *Transport in the Industrial Revolution.* Manchester U, 1983.

Alexander, David: *Retailing in England during the Industrial Revolution.* London, 1970.

Allen, Robert C, and O Grada, Cormac: 'On the Road Again with Arthur Young: English, Irish, and French Agriculture during the Industrial Revolution'. *Jnl Ec H*, 1988.

Anon: *The Incorporation of Bakers of Glasgow.* Glasgow, 1891/1931.

Appleby, Andrew B: 'Grain Prices and Subsistence Crises in England and France'. *J Ec H*, 1979.

Ashley, Sir William: *The Bread of Our Forefathers.* Oxford, 1928.

Ashton, John: *The History of Bread from Pre-historic to Modern Times.* London, 1904.

Ashton, T S: 'Changes in the Standards of Comfort in 18th-Century England'. *Proc B A*, 1955.

————: The Industrial Revolution, 1760–1830. Oxford, 1948/68.

————: 'The Standard of Life of the Workers in England, 1790–1830'. In A J Taylor (ed), *The Standard of Living in Britain during the Industrial Revolution.*

Bagehot, Walter: *Lombard Street.* London 1873/1931.

————: 'Memoir of the Right Honourable James Wilson'. In Norman St John Stevas (ed), *The Collected Works of Walter Bagehot* Vol III. London 1860/1968.

Bagwell, Philip S: *The Transport Revolution.* London, 1974.

Bairoch, Paul: 'Agriculture and the Industrial Revolution 1700–1914'. In C M Cipolla (ed), *The Fontana Economic History of Europe* III, London, 1973.

Ballard, Adolphus: 'The Assize of Bread at Oxford, 1794–1820'. *J R S S*, 1907.

Banks, Sarah J: 'Open and Close Parishes in Nineteenth Century England'. PhD thesis, U of Reading, 1982.

Barber, William J: *A History of Economic Thought.* London 1967.

Barker, T C, Oddy, D J and Yudkin, John: *The Dietary Surveys of Dr Edward Smith, 1862–3.* London, 1970.

Barnes, Donald G: *A History of the English Corn Laws from 1660 to 1846.* London, 1930.

Barnsby, G J: 'The Standard of Living in the Black Country during the Nineteenth Century'. *Ec H R*, 1971.

Barton, Rita M: *Life in Cornwall in the mid-Nineteenth Century.* Truro, 1971.

————: *Life in Cornwall in the late Nineteenth Century.* Truro, 1972.

Beckaert, Geert: 'Caloric Consumption in Industrializing Belgium'. *J Ec H* 1991.

Beckett, J V: *The Agricultural Revolution.* Oxford, 1990.

Bennett, Richard, and Elton, John: *History of Corn Milling* (4 volumes). London, 1898–1904.

Benney, D E: *An Introduction to Cornish Water-Mills.* Truro, 1972.

Berg, M and Hudson, P: 'Rehabilitating the Industrial Revolution'. *Ec H R* 1992.

Bernstein, George L: *Liberalism and Liberal Politics in Edwardian England.* London, 1986.

Blackman, Janet: 'The Development of the Retail Grocery Trade in the Nineteenth Century'. *Business History*, 1967.

————: 'The Food Supply of an Industrial Town. A Study of Sheffield's Public Markets, 1780-1900'. *Business History*, 1963.

Blandy, John (ed): *The Bakery World.* London, nd.

Bohstedt, John H: 'Riots in England 1790–1810 with special reference to Devonshire'. Ph D thesis, Harvard, 1972.

Braudel, Fernand: *The Structures of Everyday Life.* London 1981/88.

Britton, Denis K, with Cracknell, Basil E, and Stewart, Ian M T: *Cereals in the United Kingdom*. Oxford, 1969.

Burnett, John: 'The Baking Industry in the Nineteenth Century'. *Business History*, 1963.

———: *Plenty and Want*. London 1966/1989.

———: *Destiny Obscure*. London 1982/1984.

Cage, R A: 'The Standard of Living Debate: Glasgow 1800–1850'. *J Ec H*, 1983.

Campbell Bruce M S and Overton, Mark, (eds): *Land, Labour and Livestock*. Manchester, 1991.

Camporesi, Piero: *Bread of Dreams*. Cambridge, 1989.

Cernovodeanu, Paul and Marinescu, Beatrice: 'British Trade in the Danubian Ports of Galatz and Braila between 1837 and 1853'. *Jnl Euro Ec H*, 1979.

Chambers, J D and Mingay, G E: *The Agricultural Revolution, 1750– 1880*. London, 1966.

Chartres, John: 'Introduction'. In Chartres (ed), *Agricultural Markets and Trade*. Cambridge, 1990.

Church, R A: *The Great Victorian Boom, 1850–73* London, 1975.

Clapham, Sir John: *An Economic History of Modern Britain* (3 volumes). Cambridge, 1926–38.

Clark, John M: Strategic Factors in Business Cycles. New York, 1934.

Clarke, Delia and Herbert, Elizabeth: *Food Facts*. London, 1986.

Clay, C G A: *Economic Expansion and Social Change: England 1500– 1700*. 2 vols. Cambridge 1984.

Cole, G D H: *A Century of Co-operation*. Manchester, 1945.

Collins, E J T: 'Dietary Change and Cereal Consumption in Britain in the Nineteenth Century'. *Ag H R*, 1975.

Crafts, N F R: 'English Workers' Real Wages During the Industrial Revolution: Some Remaining Problems'. *J Ec H*, 1985.

———: 'Economic Growth in France and Britain, 1830–1910: A Review of the Evidence'. *J Ec H*, 1984.

———: 'English Economic Growth in the Eighteenth Century: A Re-Examination of Deane and Cole's Estimates'. *Ec H R*, 1976.

———: *British Economic Growth during the Industrial Revolution*. Oxford, 1985.

Cunningham, W: *The Growth of English Industry and Commerce in Modern Times* (2 vols). Cambridge, 1903 ed.

Damon, Albert and McFarland, Ross A: 'The Physique of Bus and Truck Drivers: with a Review of Occupational Anthropology'. *American Journal of Physical Anthropology*, 1955.

Daniere, Andre: 'Feudal Incomes and Demand Elasticity for Bread in late Eighteenth-Century France'. *J Ec H*, 1958.

————: 'Rejoinder to D S Landes', *J Ec H*, 1958.

David, Elizabeth: *English Bread and Yeast Cookery*. London, 1977.

Davies, Jennifer: *The Victorian Kitchen*. London, 1989.

Davies, Norman: *God's Playground* (2 vols). Oxford, 1981.

Drummond, Sir Jack and Wilbraham, Anne: *The Englishman's Food*. London, 1939. Revised by Dorothy Hollingsworth, 1957/1991.

Dyer, Christopher: *Standards of Living in the Later Middle Ages*. Cambridge, 1989.

Elsas, Madeleine (ed): *Iron in the Making: Dowlais Iron Company Letters, 1782–1860*. Cardiff, 1960.

Elster, Jon: *Ulysses and the Sirens, Studies in Rationality and Irrationality*. Cambridge, 1979.

————: *Sour Grapes, Studies in the Subversion of Rationality*. Cambridge, 1983.

Fairlie, Susan: 'The Corn Laws and British Wheat Production, 1829–76'. *Ec H R*, 1969.

————: 'The 19th Century Corn Law Reconsidered'. *Ec H R*, 1965.

Falkner, F and Tanner, J M: *Human Growth* 3. 2nd ed, New York, 1986.

Fay, C R: 'The Miller and Baker: a Note on Commercial Transition, 1770–1837'. *Cam H J*, 1923–5.

————: *The Corn Laws and Social England*. Cambridge, 1932.

Feinstein C H: 'Capital Formation in Great Britain' in *The Cambridge Economic History of Europe*, Vol VII, Part 1. Cambridge, 1978.

————: 'Capital Accumulation and the industrial revolution' in Floud and McCloskey (eds), Vol I.

————: and Pollard, Sidney: *Studies in Capital Formation in the United Kingdom, 1750–1920*. Oxford, 1988.

Fieldhouse, Paul: *Food and Nutrition: Customs and Culture*. London, 1986.

Flinn, M W (ed): *Scottish Population History*. Cambridge, 1977.

————: 'Trends in Real Wages, 1750–1850'. *Ec H R*, 1974.

————: '(Criticism of) The Population History of England, 1541–1871'. *Ec H R*, 1982.

Floud, Roderick and McCloskey, Donald (eds): *The Economic History of Britain since 1700* (2 vols). Cambridge, 1981.

————: Wachter, Kenneth and Gregory, Annabel: *Height, Health, and History*. Cambridge, 1990.

Freeman, Edward A: *Exeter*. London, 1901.

Freeman, M Diane; 'A History of Corn Milling *c* 1750–1914, with special reference to South Central and South Eastern England'. Ph D thesis, U of Reading, 1976.

Freeman, Michael J and Aldcroft, Derek H: *Transport in Victorian Britain*. Manchester U, 1988.

Fussell, G E: 'Population and Wheat Production in the Eighteenth Century', *History Teachers' Miscellany* VII, 1929.

Galpin, W Freeman: *The Grain Supply of England during the Napoleonic Wars*. New York, 1925.

Gatrell, P: *The Tsarist Economy*. London, 1986.

Gayer, Arthur D, Rostow, W W and Schwartz, Anna J, assisted by Frank, I: *The Growth and Fluctuation of the British Economy, 1790–1850* (2 vols). Oxford 1941.

Giffen, Sir Robert: *Economic Inquiries and Studies*. London, 1904.

Gilboy, E W: 'The Cost of Living and Real Wages in Eighteenth-Century England'. In A J Taylor (ed), *The Standard of Living in Britain during the Industrial Revolution*.

Glennie, Paul: 'Continuity and Change in Hertfordshire Agriculture 1550–1700'. *Ag H R* 1988.

Goddard, Nicholas: *Harvests of Change*. London, 1988.

Gourvish, T R: 'A Note on Bread Prices in London and Glasgow, 1788–1815'. *J Ec H*, 1970.

———: 'The Cost of Living in Glasgow in the Early Nineteenth Century'. *Ec H R*, 1972.

———: *Railways and the British Economy, 1830–1914*. London, 1980.

Granger, C W J, and Elliott, C M: 'A Fresh Look at Wheat Prices and Markets in the Eighteenth Century'. *Ec H R*, 1967.

Grantham, George: 'Agricultural Supply during the Industrial Revolution: French Evidence and European Implications'. *J Ec H*, 1989.

Gras, N S B: *The Evolution of the English Corn Market*. Harvard, 1915.

Hammond, J L, and Hammond, Barbara: *The Town Labourer*, 1760–1832. London, 1917/New York 1967.

———: *The Village Labourer*, 1760–1832. London 1911/Gloucester 1987.

Haydn's Dictionary of Dates (ed by Benjamin Vincent). London, 25th edition, 1910.

Herlihy, Patricia: *Odessa, A History, 1794–1914*. London, 1986.

Hilton, Boyd: *Corn, Cash, Commerce*. Oxford, 1977.

———: 'The Political Arts of Lord Liverpool'. *T R H S*, 1988.

Hobsbawm, Eric: 'The British Standard of Living, 1790–1850'. In A J Taylor (ed), *The Standard of Living in Britain in the Industrial Revolution*.

Holderness, B A: 'Prices, Productivity, and Output'. *Ag H of E & W VI*, Cambridge, 1989.

Holyoake, George Jacob: *The Jubilee History of the Leeds Industrial Co-operative Society*. Leeds, 1897.

Hopkins, Eric: *A Social History of the English Working Classes, 1815–1945*. London, 1979.

Horne, Robert Sutherland: 'Britain's First Co-op in Portsmouth?' *Hampshire* (magazine), 1969.

Hueckel, Glenn: 'Relative Prices and Supply Response in English Agriculture during the Napoleonic Wars'. *Ec H R*, 1976.

Hunt, E H: *British Labour History, 1815–1914*. London, 1981.

———: *Regional Wage Variations in Britain, 1850–1914*. Oxford, 1973.

Ignatieff, Michael: *A Just Measure of Pain*. London, 1978/1989.

Jackson, R V: 'Growth and Deceleration in English Agriculture, 1660–1790'. *Ec H R*, 1985.

Jago, William: *Principles of Bread-Making*. *The British Baker and Confectioner*, 1889.

Jasny, N: *Competition among Grains*. Stanford U, 1940.

Jevons, H Stanley: *The Future of Exchange and the Indian Economy*. Oxford, 1922.

Jevons, W Stanley: *Investigations in Currency and Finance*. London 1884 (includes some papers given before 1870).

Johnston, David: *Autobiographical Reminiscences*. Private, Chicago, 1885.

Jones, D J V: 'The Corn Riots in Wales, 1793–1801'. *Welsh History Review*, 1965.

Jones, E L (ed): *Agriculture and Economic Growth in England 1650–1815*. London, 1967.

Jones, E L: *The Development of English Agriculture, 1815–73*. London, 1968.

Kahn, R F: 'The Relation of Home Investment to Unemployment'. *Economic Journal*, 1931.

Kain, Roger J P and Price, Hugh C: *The Tithe Surveys of England and Wales*. Cambridge, 1985.

Kemp, Betty: 'Reflections on the Repeal of the Corn Laws'. *Victorian Studies*, 1962.

Ketteridge, Christopher and Mays, Spike: *Five Miles from Bunkum*. London, 1972.

Kindleberger, Charles P: *Manias, Panics, and Crashes*. London, 1978.

King, Peter: 'Customary Rights and Women's Earnings, the Importance of Gleaning to the Rural Labouring Poor 1750–1850'. *Ec H R*, 1991.

Kirkland, John: *Three Centuries of Prices of Wheat Flour and Bread*. London, 1917.

Kuhlmann, Charles B: *The Development of the Flour-milling Industry in the United States*. New York 1929/1973.

Kussmaul, Ann: *Servants in Husbandry in Early Modern England*. Cambridge, 1981.

———: *A General View of the Rural Economy of England, 1538–1840*. Cambridge, 1990.

Landes, David S: 'The Statistical Study of French Crises'. *J Ec H*, 1950.

———: 'Reply to M. Daniere'. *J Ec H*, 1958.

———: *The Unbound Prometheus*. Cambridge, 1969.

Langton, John and Morris, R J, eds: *Atlas of Industrializing Britain*. London, 1986.

Levy Leboyer, Maurice and Bourgignon, François: *The French Economy in the Nineteenth Century*. Cambridge, 1990.

Lindert, Peter H: 'English Population, Wages, and Prices, 1541–1913'. *Jnl of Interdisciplinary History*, 1985.

——— and Williamson, J G: 'English Workers' Living Standards during the Industrial Revolution: A New Look'. *Ec H R*, 1983.

———: 'English Workers' Real Wages: Reply to Crafts'. *J Ec H*, 1985.

Livi-Bacci, Massimo: *Population and Nutrition*. Cambridge, 1987/1991.

Longhurst, George and Longhurst, G A: *Diary* (ed by B L Pearce). Private, 1964 (Reading Central Library – Local Studies Collection).

Longmate, Norman: *The Breadstealers*. London, 1984.

Macdonald, Stuart: 'Agricultural Response to a Changing Market during the Napoleonic Wars'. *Ec H R*, 1980.

Marshall, J D: *The Old Poor Law, 1795–1834*. London 1968/1985.

Maslow, Abraham H, *Motivation and Personality*. New York, 2nd ed, 1970.

Mayhew, Henry: *London Labour and the London Poor*. Selection by Victor Neuberg: London, 1985.

McCance, R A and Widdowson, E M: *The Composition of Foods*, HMSO 1978.

Mennell, Stephen: *All Manners of Food*. Oxford, 1985/1987.

Messinger, Gary S: *Manchester in the Victorian Age*. Manchester U, 1985.

Minchinton, Walter (ed): *Population and Marketing: Two Studies in the History of the South-West*. Exeter, 1976.

——— ed: *Essays in Agrarian History*. Newton Abbot, 1968.

Mingay, G E (ed): *The Agrarian History of England and Wales*, Vol VI. Cambridge, 1989.

Ministry of Agriculture, Fisheries and Food: *Manual of Nutrition*. 9th ed, London, 1985.

Mitchell, B R: *British Historical Statistics*. Cambridge, 1988.

Mokyr, Joel: 'Is there still Life in the Pessimist Case? Consumption during the Industrial Revolution, 1790–1850'. *J Ec H*, 1988.

Moore, C: *Brief Notes relating to Municipal Oxford 912–1896, affixed to Abstract of Accounts of the City of Oxford, y/e 25.3.1896*, 2nd ed.

Morgan, David Hoseason: *Harvesters and Harvesting, 1840–1900*. London, 1982.

Mui, Hoh-cheung and Mui, Lorna H: *Shops and Shopkeeping*. London, 1989.

Muir, Augustus: *The History of Baker Perkins*. Cambridge, 1968.

Mutch, A: 'The Mechanization of the Harvest in South-West Lancashire, 1850–1914.' *Ag H R*, 1981.

Neale, R S: 'Economic Conditions and Working Class Movements in the City of Bath 1800–50', Bristol University M A Dissertation.

———: 'The Standard of Living, 1780–1844: a Regional and Class Study'. In A J Taylor (ed), *The Standard of living in Britain in the Industrial Revolution*.

Newman, Lucile F (ed): *Hunger in History*. Oxford, 1990.

O'Brien, Patrick K: 'Agriculture and the Home Market for English Industry, 1660–1820'. *E H R*, 1985.

———: 'Agriculture and the Industrial Revolution'. *Ec H R*, 1977.

———, Heath, D, with Keyder, C: 'Agricultural Efficiency in Britain and France, 1815–1914'. *Jnl of Euro Ec History*, 1977.

O Grada, Cormac: *The Great Irish Famine*. London, 1989.

Oddy, D J: 'Working-Class Diets in Late Nineteenth-Century Britain'. *Ec H R*, 1970.

———, and Miller, D (eds): *The Making of the Modern British Diet*. London, 1976.

Offer, Avner: *The First World War: An Agrarian Interpretation*. Oxford, 1989.

Orbell, M John: 'The Corn Milling Industry in the Industrial Revolution, 1750–1830'. Ph D thesis, U of Nottingham, 1977.

———: 'The Corn Milling Industry, 1750–1820', in Feinstein & Pollard, eds.

Outhwaite, R B: 'Dearth and Government Intervention in English Grain Markets, 1590–1700'. *Ec H R*, 1987.

Patterson, A Temple: *Portsmouth: A History*. London, 1976.

———: *A History of Southampton, 1700–1914*, Vol 1. Southampton U, 1966.

Percival, John: *Wheat in Great Britain*. Private, Reading, 1934.

Perkin, Harold: *The Origins of Modern English Society, 1780–1880*. London 1969/1985.

Perren, Richard: 'Markets and Marketing'. *Ag H of E & W VI*, 1989.

——: 'Structural Change and Market Growth in the Food Industry: Flour Milling in Britain, Europe, and America, 1850–1914'. *Ec H R*, 1990.

Perry, R J: 'High Farming in Victorian Britain: Prospect and Retrospect'. *Ag H*, 1981.

Petersen, Christian: 'The Crisis of Free Trade'. B A thesis. Oxford, 1989.

Phelps Brown, E H, and Hopkins, Sheila V: 'Seven Centuries of the Prices of Consumables, Compared with Builders' Wage-rates'. *Economica*, 1956.

Potter, Beatrice (Beatrice Webb): *The Co-operative Movement in Great Britain*. London, 2nd ed, 1891/1987.

Pounds, N J G: *An Historical Geography of Europe, 1500–1840*. Cambridge, 1979.

Presnell, L S (ed): *Studies in the Industrial Revolution*. London, 1960.

Prince, Hugh C: 'The Changing Rural Landscape, 1750–1850'. *Ag H of E & W VI*, 1989.

Quisenberry, K S, and Reitz, L P: 'Turkey Wheat: the Cornerstone of an Empire'. *Ag H*, 1974.

Richardson, Thomas L: 'The Standard of Living Controversy 1790–1840, with Special Reference to Agricultural Labourers in Seven English Counties'. Ph D thesis, U of Hull, 1977.

Robertson, A B: 'The Foundation of the Mark Lane Corn Exchange.' *Guildhall Miscellany*, 1953.

Rodger, Richard: *Housing in Urban Britain, 1780–1914*. Basingstoke, 1989.

Ross, A S C: 'The Assize of Bread'. *Ec H R*, 1956.

Rostow, W W: *British Economy of the Nineteenth Century*. Oxford, 1948.

Rotberg, Robert I, and Rabb, Theodore K (eds): *Hunger and History*. Cambridge, 1983/1985.

——: *Population and Economy*. Cambridge, 1986.

Rude, George E: 'Prices, Wages and Popular Movements in Paris during the French Revolution'. *Ec H R*, 1954.

——: *The Crowd in the French Revolution*. Oxford, 1959.

Salaman, Redcliffe: *The History and Social Influence of the Potato*. Cambridge, 1949/1985.

Schumpeter, Joseph A: *Business Cycles* (2 vols). New York, 1939.

Schwartz, L D: 'The Standard of Living in the Long Run: London 1700–1860'. *Ec H R*, 1985.

——: 'Trends in Real Wage Rates: A Reply to Hunt and Botham'. *Ec H R*, 1990.

Shammas, Carole: 'Food Expenditure and Economic Well-Being in Early Modern England'. *J Ec H*, 1983.

———: 'The Food Budget of English Workers: a Reply to Komlos'. *J Ec H*, 1988.

———: *The Pre-Industrial Consumer in England and America*. Oxford, 1990.

Shaw, Timothy: 'A Blaze for the London Mob'. *Country Life* 29.12.1966.

Sheppard, Ronald, and Newton, Edward: *The Story of Bread*. London, 1957.

Slicher van Bath, B H: *The Agrarian History of Western Europe, 500–1850*. Translated by Olive Ordish. London, 1963.

Smith, Edward: *Foods*. London, 1873. (See also pre–1870 books)

Smout, T C: *A History of the Scottish People, 1560–1830*. London 1969/1972.

———: *A History of the Scottish People, 1830–1950*. London 1986/1987.

———: 'Exploring the Scottish Standard of Living Before 1796'. Paper read at Oxford 23 January 1990.

Snell, K D M: *Annals of the Labouring Poor*. Cambridge 1985/1987.

Southampton Corporation: Southampton Records I. Southampton, 1983.

Stainer, C L (ed): *Studies in Oxford History chiefly in the eighteenth century*. Oxford, 1901.

Steegman, A Theodore: '18thC British Military Stature; Growth Cessation, Selective Recruiting, Secular Trends, Nutrition at Birth, Cold, and Occupation'. *Human Biology*, 1985.

Stern, Walter M: 'The Bread Crisis in Britain, 1795–96'. *Economica*, 1964.

Stevenson, John: *Popular Disturbances in England, 1700–1870*. London, 1979.

Stone, Richard (ed): *Studies in the National Income and Expenditure of the United Kingdom*, I. Cambridge, 1954.

Storck, John, and Teague, Walter D: *Flour for Man's Bread*. U of Minneapolis, 1952.

Szostak, Rick: *The Role of Transportation in the Industrial Revolution, a Comparison of England and France*. Quebec, 1991.

Tann, Jennifer: 'Co-operative Corn Milling: Self-help during the Grain Crises of the Napoleonic Wars'. *Ag H R*, 1980.

———: 'Corn Milling'. *Ag H of E & W VI*. Cambridge, 1989.

Tannahill, Reay: *Food in History*. London 1973/1988.

Taylor, Arthur J: *Laissez-Faire and State Intervention in Nineteenth Century Britain*. London, 1972.

—— (ed): *The Standard of Living in Britain in the Industrial Revolution*. London, 1975.

Thacker, Fred S: *The Thames Highway*. New York, 1968.

Thirsk, J (ed.) *Agrarian History of England and Wales*. Vols IV and V. Cambridge, 1984/5.

Thomas, Brinley: 'Escaping from Constraints, the Industrial Revolution in a Malthusian Context'. *Jnl of Interdisciplinary History*, 1984/5.

Thompson, E P: 'The Moral Economy of the English Crowd in the Eighteenth Century'. *P & P*, 1971.

—— and Yeo, Eileen, (eds): *The Unknown Mayhew*. London 1971/ 1984.

Thompson, F M L: 'The Second Agricultural Revolution, 1815–1880'. *Ec H R*, 1968.

—— (ed): *The Cambridge Social History of Britain, 1750–1950* (3 vols). Cambridge, 1990.

Thrupp, Sylvia: *A Short History of the Worshipful Company of Bakers*. London, 1933.

Thwaites, Wendy: 'The Marketing of Agricultural Produce in Eighteenth Century Oxfordshire'. Ph D thesis. U of Birmingham, 1980.

——: 'Dearth and the Marketing of Agricultural Produce: Oxfordshire *c* 1750–1800'. *Ag H R*, 1985.

——: 'The Assize of Bread in 18th-Century Oxford'. *Oxoniensa*, 1986.

——: 'Women in the Market Place: Oxfordshire *c*1690–1800'. *Midland History*, 1984.

Tucker, R S: 'Real Wages of Artisans in London, 1729–1935'. In A J Taylor (ed), *The Standard of Living in Britain in the Industrial Revolution*.

Tull, Anita: *Food and Nutrition*. Oxford, 1987.

Turnbull, Gerard: 'Canals, Coal, and Regional Growth during the Industrial Revolution'. *Ec H R*, 1987.

Turner, Michael: 'Arable in England and Wales, Estimates from the 1801 Crop Return'. *Jnl of Hist Geog*, 1981.

——: 'Agricultural Productivity in England in the Eighteenth Century, Evidence from Crop Yields'. *Ec H R*, 1982.

——: *Enclosures in Britain, 1750–1830*. London, 1984.

Unwin, George: *The Gilds and Companies of London*. New introduction by William F Kahl. London 1908/1963.

Uselding, Paul: 'Wage and Consumption Levels in England and on the Continent in the 1830s'. *Jnl of Euro Ec H*, 1975.

Vamplew, Wray: 'The Protection of English Cereal Producers: the Corn Laws Reassessed'. *Ec H R*, 1980.

————: 'A Grain of Truth: the Nineteenth-Century Corn Law Averages'. *Ag H R*, 1980.

Vincent, David: *Bread, Knowledge, and Freedom*. London, 1981.

Walter, John and Schofield, Roger: *Famine, Disease, and the Social Order in Early Modern Society*. Cambridge, 1989.

Walton, John K: *Lancashire: A Social History, 1558–1939*. Manchester U, 1987.

Webb, Sidney and Beatrice: 'The Assize of Bread'. *Economic Journal*, 1904.

————: *English Local Government: The Manor and the Borough. Part 1*. London, 1908.

Weir, David R: 'Life Under Pressure: France and England, 1670–1870'. *J Ec H*, 1984.

Wells, Roger: *Wretched Faces*. Gloucester, 1988.

Wentworth, Philip: 'Old Lancashire Sayings, Old Ways of Living, and Old Customs'. *East Lancashire Review*, 1890.

Westworth, O A: 'The Albion Steam Flour Mill'. *Economic History* (suppt to *Economic Journal*), 1930–3.

Willan, Thomas Stuart: *River Navigation in England 1600–1750*. Oxford, 1936.

————: *The Inland Trade*. Manchester, 1976.

Williams, Dale E: 'Morals, Markets and the English Crowd in 1766'. *P & P*, 1984.

Williams, P H: *The Tudor Regime*. Oxford, 1979.

Wood, George H: 'Some Statistics relating to Working Class Progress since 1860'. *J R S S*, 1899.

————: 'The Investigation of Retail Prices'. *J R S S*, 1902.

Woodward, Sir Llewellyn: *The Age of Reform*. Oxford 1938/1962.

Wrigley, E A: 'The Supply of Raw Materials in the Industrial Revolution'. *Ec H R*, 1962.

————: *Continuity, Chance and Change*. Cambridge, 1988.

————: *People, Cities and Wealth*. Oxford, 1987.

Wrigley, E A, and Schofield, R S: *The Population History of England, 1541–1871*. Harvard, 1981.

Young, Sidney: *The Worshipful Company of Bakers of London: A List of the Masters and Wardens*. London, 1912.

Index